D1195709

FIDEL CASTRO

REPÚBLICA DE CUBA

EJÉRCITO REVOLUCIONARIO

COMANDANCIA GENERAL

February 14, 1959

Mr. Jules Dubois:

      I understand that you are writing a book entitled:
FIDEL CASTRO, Rebel, Liberator Or Dictator.

      I do not know what you will write and I do not know
what opinions you will express in the book.

      Every person in the society of free nations--and even
those who are oppressed under the heels of dictators--has a right to
express his or her opinion. Under the tyranny of Fulgencio Batista that
right was denied to the people of Cuba.

      It is the duty of every newspaperman to report the news,
for only with freedom of the press can there be political freedom.

      Should your book contain errors and should your opinions
expressed therein be mistaken or unjust, I shall not hesitate to express
my own opinions about the contents of the book when it is published.

FIDEL CASTRO

FIDEL CASTRO

REBEL—
LIBERATOR OR DICTATOR?

by JULES DUBOIS

the NEW *Bobbs-Merrill* COMPANY, INC.
AN ASSOCIATE OF HOWARD W. SAMS & CO., INC.
Publishers • INDIANAPOLIS • NEW YORK

Copyright © 1959 by Jules Dubois

PRINTED IN THE UNITED STATES OF AMERICA

Library of Congress Catalog Card Number: 59-10236

First Edition

To

Lucille, the most wonderful mother and bravest wife in the world, who, with our children Lucy, Jules, Jr., Victor and Mary, suffered a thousand tortures during my trips to strife-torn Cuba, especially when Dictator Fulgencio Batista cut us off from all communication by telephone or mail.

"Condemn me! It doesn't matter! History will absolve me!"

—FIDEL CASTRO

INTRODUCTION

The Latin-American dictator is an egomaniac, a man of greed and at times a sadist.

He is determined to enrich himself from the income of the national treasury and considers the entire nation is his personal domain.

He crushes everyone who is an obstacle in his path.

He demands nonintervention in his affairs but is always intervening in the internal affairs ,of other nations.

He orders the persecution, torture, assassination and exile of his political, military and commercial obstructionists.

He restricts freedom of assembly for opposition political parties or bans adverse political activity.

He converts the labor bosses into docile political tools of his regime or bars unions.

He professes to be anti-Communist but gives the Communists a free rein to operate so he can undermine and destroy his political and labor opposition.

He always brands his critics and opponents as Communists—in order to ingratiate himself with the State Department and the American public—when an overwhelming majority of them are the contrary.

He acquires a personal fortune by devious means and becomes the owner of steamship lines, air lines, bus lines, newspapers, radio stations, farms, plantations, businesses and industries.

He eradicates the independent press and radio and television by bribery, threat, intimidation, legislation, confiscation, destruction and seldom by purchase.

He denies to the people the right to dissent.

He directs the thought control of the entire population and insists upon the deification of his person and of his relatives.

He has hospitals, plazas, stadiums, ports, towns, cities and even states named after himself, his wife and his relatives.

He has monuments and busts profusely displayed to honor him, his wife and his relatives.

He forbids the citizens to read newspapers or magazines published abroad or to listen to radio broadcasts from abroad.

To him the truth is subversive.

He bans the publication of any news or commentaries that might be critical of him, of his administration or of his relatives, and distorts the local and national news.

He instills fear and total subjugation among his subordinates. He demands blind loyalty and adulation.

He purges the judiciary to destroy the independence of the courts and governs with a servile congress or none at all.

He operates a police state with mail, telephone, telegraph, press, radio and television censorship and limitless spies.

He prepares the machinery for the dynastic succession by his son or by a faithful relative or friend.

He orders the national history rewritten to minimize the achievements of his predecessors and to accentuate the praise for his person and work.

Those presidents who are not dictators and also enrich themselves in a fabulous and scandalous manner, while they do nothing to check poverty and misery, perform a devastating disservice to the forces of freedom. They create an atmosphere that is made to order for ambitious military men who, taking advantage of the moral decomposition of the regime, can perpetrate a successful coup and destroy constitutional government.

A disillusioned people, who have been mesmerized into a state of helplessness, refuse immediately to take up arms in defense of the grafters who have sullied the honor of their nation and who have wrecked their dreams and hopes for peaceful and certain evolution to civic and political maturity.

The newborn dictator, or the veteran who may have returned to power, is thus enabled to consolidate his position because of the inertia of the opposition.

That is what happened in Cuba, and it was not until Fidel Castro came along that the people of that island found the leader they were willing to follow, to fight for their lost liberty.

J. D.

HAVANA, FEBRUARY 1959

6

CHAPTER 1

The clock had just struck midnight at Camp Columbia, the military fortress in the suburbs of Havana, Cuba. A new day and a new year had begun, the year 1959.

General Fulgencio Batista y Zaldivar, dictator of Cuba, entered the door of his sumptuous residence. He had just made a momentous decision that was to change history.

A half hour or so earlier Batista had left his palatial, multimillion-dollar estate at Kuquine, about ten miles away, with nothing more than a casual farewell. Several traveling bags were stowed in the limousine. His second wife, Martha Fernandez de Batista, accompanied him, with three of his children. Two sons had been sent to New York two days earlier.

"Adios!" Batista said to the handful of servants, two butlers, two maids and a librarian, who were present. His face was serious. "We are leaving for a short trip."

"Adios!" they replied almost in unison.

Swiftly the presidential limousine, preceded by three military intelligence staff cars whose occupants carried submachine guns, and followed by five secret service cars filled with men with more submachine guns, sped toward Camp Columbia over the practically deserted highway.

Batista lost no time after he entered his office. He picked up the telephone and called Andres Rivero Aguero, his closest political friend and confidant and the man he had chosen to succeed him as president on February 24, 1959. The conversation lasted many minutes. Batista was brisk and persuasive.

"Come to Camp Columbia immediately," he finally ordered. "Send your family ahead with your luggage."

Aguero's wife and children were quickly dispatched to the Air Force Headquarters building. The children were promptly entranced with the ten-foot-high Christmas tree. Its red, green and white lights and fancy ornaments kept them from noticing the unusual bustle as automobiles continued to stop under the porte-cochere only a few feet from the tree.

On the other side of the room, exiting from the Operations counter, a ramp led down to five transport aircraft almost ready for takeoff. Though their pilots had not yet reported, they were on the way. A casual observer would have thought their mission the pleasant duty of loading and delivering the several thousand New Year's packages stacked and waiting in the Operations corridor. Each corrugated box carried a large imprint which read: A GIFT FROM PRESIDENT FULGENCIO BATISTA AND HIS SEÑORA.

But Batista's main gift to his people was not these packages. The cargo on this night was much more important.

What had immediately preceded this hour of this night of Cuba's history? Let us go back a little.

New Year's Eve in Havana had been warm and cloudless. Stars were twinkling overhead. In the distance could be heard the sporadic staccato of firecrackers, reluctantly ignited by celebrants or more probably by police on orders to simulate enthusiasm. Otherwise there was silence, tense and ominous. Cuba was nearing the dramatic climax of a twenty-five-month-old civil war.

There were isolated parties such as the one on the second floor of the Habana-Hilton, the luxurious hotel built by the Food Catering Workers' Union of Cuba and operated by Conrad Hilton. The ballroom was filled with merrymakers; the men were dressed in black dinner jackets with black ties, and the ladies wore lavish evening gowns and sparkling jewels. Most of them were Cubans who were either pro-Batista or who were indifferent to the tragedy that afflicted their people. They were oblivious to the reality of the situation in their country either because of their partisanship or because of their inclination to believe the government communiqués, which reported army defeats as victories and police killings as accidents or suicides.

There were revelers, also, in the night clubs adjacent to the gambling casinos of the large hotels. They crowded the casinos to try their luck at roulette, chuck-a-luck, blackjack and the dice table. The Tropicana and the Sans Souci had their share of business on the outskirts of the city, for some Cubans and quite a few American tourists had gone there to see in the New Year.

The coolest man in Havana was John Scarne, the card expert who knows every trick in the gambling trade. He walked casually around the tables in the Habana-Hilton casino, performing the chore for which Conrad Hilton had hired him, to detect the sharpies and the cheaters who might try to rob the unsuspecting tourist of more than he wanted to lose. A long Cuban cigar was firmly caught between Scarne's teeth as the short, stocky man made his rounds, occasionally slipping a quarter into a slot machine to break the monotony.

Now just after midnight official cars sped from downtown Havana up Linea—the brilliantly lighted express highway to and from Camp Columbia, connecting with the heart of Havana and the presidential palace. The "clan," summoned by Batista, had begun to gather.

These were the men closest to Batista, those whose tortures of political prisoners, whose summary executions—without trials—of suspects of subversion, whose reprisal killings of innocent civilians, whose direction of the waves of terror, were rewarded by the dictator with promotions and gifts.

There were army officers, naval officers, air force officers and politicians. General Francisco Tabernilla and other officers met in the Army Headquarters building with Major General Eulogio Cantillo, whose command was in Santiago de Cuba, capital of the province of Oriente. Tabernilla was Chief of the Joint General Staff. A tall, robust man, he had reached the retirement age of seventy, but his loyalty to Batista and the latter's need for him kept him on the job.

The situation they had met to discuss was serious. Except for Havana, five of the six provinces of Cuba were aflame. Rebels were overrunning cities and towns, sugar mills and cattle ranches. The sugar crop was seriously threatened. Nineteen of the 31 municipalities in the province of Las Villas had fallen to the rebels. Fourteen in the province of Oriente were in their hands; those not yet occupied were filled with rebel fifth columnists.

The army once so loyal to Batista had lost its will to fight. The military commanders agreed they could not cope with the rebel offensive unless they leveled every city and town in the country, a move which was probably impossible in view of the rebels' own fighter aircraft, which operated from secret bases in the province of Oriente. Some Cuban Air Force pilots had defected, refusing to bomb defenseless cities, while other airmen expressed, in writing, their reluctance to drop 500-pound bombs on open cities, to destroy buildings and homes and kill dozens, if not hundreds, of innocent civilians.

Earlier Tabernilla had reported to Batista that General Cantillo was ready to take over the army, preserving its structure but allowing all the men Batista wished to take with him to leave Cuba. The time to go was now, he added, for Cantillo was afraid he could not prevent a military uprising somewhere, probably in Santiago de Cuba.

The crisis could be overcome by Batista only if he decided to convert Havana into a battlefield. Loyal army troops were defending Santa Clara, the capital of the rich province of Las Villas. Air Force bombers had strafed the city; tanks were firing at the rebels, who advanced steadily from street to street.

Batista had rushed reinforcements to Santa Clara in a desperate attempt to launch a counteroffensive, but the troops, arms and ammunition never got there. The empire of a strong man had collapsed and disintegrated around him.

At two thirty in the morning Batista arrived at the Air Force Headquarters. Waiting for him was General Cantillo. Within the hour the four-engined aircraft which Batista boarded with his wife and others whom he selected taxied down the runway and took off for the Dominican Republic.

Batista had fled from Cuba. The man who drove him out was a tall, vocal, bearded rebel named Fidel Castro.

All this happened only ninety miles from our shores in one of the richest nations in the Americas for its size of 45,000 square

10

miles, including the Isle of Pines. Its soil is blessed with a fertility that enables it to produce 6,000,000 tons of sugar annually, or the equivalent of one ton of sugar for each of the 6,000,000 inhabitants of the land. Its mountains in the eastern end are rich with ores and minerals. Its capital, Havana, has been a favorite port of call for thousands of American tourists.

On the Malecon—the ocean-front drive where the waters of the Gulf of Mexico slap furiously against the sea wall and flow over onto the road, impelled by the winds and the waves—in the wake of the spray stands a monument to the U.S.S. *Maine,* the warship that was blown up in Havana harbor in 1898. That action precipitated our entry into the Spanish-American War and expedited the independence of Cuba from Spain. Not far from the Prado at the eastern end of the Malecon is the presidential palace through whose impressive portals have gone some of the most corrupt politicians in the nation's history.

Readers may find the pages immediately following somewhat confusing. But history has a way of being confusing. Events of the past twenty-some years in Cuba have been especially tangled, not only to observers but to the makers of and the participants in those events. Some of them must be set down so that we may better understand the man named Castro—what he has done, is doing and intends to do.

We begin on August 12, 1933, with one of the worst of the corrupt politicians. He was also a dictator and his name was Gerardo Machado. On that day in August he was finally overthrown, whereupon there followed three weeks of anarchy and chaos. Dozens of men were gunned down in vengeance killings on the streets of Havana and from one end of the country to the other. Hundreds of fires destroyed business establishments and homes. A group of civilians began to meet to discuss ways and means of restoring order and conspired with men in the army to bring it about.

Here enters on history's stage a stockily built former sergeant who was to be a key figure in Cuba's history for twenty-five years, three months and twenty-eight days. He ruled behind the scene or as chief of state for eighteen of those years.

Sergeant Fulgencio Batista was a stenographer at the courts-

11

martial of August 1933. He became well acquainted with many of the opponents of the Machado dictatorship. On September 4, 1933, Batista took over Cuba at the head of a sergeant's revolt, displaced the officers of the army and promoted himself to colonel and head of the army.

That night Batista sent a telegram to one of his sergeant co-conspirators in a provincial capital. "Effective immediately," Batista's telegram read, "you are promoted to the rank of captain. Acknowledge."

"Your telegram is too late," the other ex-sergeant replied. "I already promoted myself to colonel." And a colonel he remained.

During the period when Batista ruled behind the scenes as the strong man, his police and military staff chalked up records of brutality that were only to be surpassed in later years. There was much opposition to Batista's dictatorship. Newspapers were closed, editors were imprisoned, some were tortured; civilians were tortured too, and politicians fled into exile to escape persecution, most of them to Miami.

Batista's one dream was to be popular but he never achieved that goal. To be elected president he first legalized the Communist Party of Cuba in 1938. Two years later he rode into office on the red coattails of the Communists. He rewarded them for their support by naming two of the party leaders as ministers without portfolio in his cabinet. He financed the party purchase of a radio station and helped the party to start a daily newspaper. He also assisted the Communists to gain control of the Cuban Confederation of Workers (CTC).

Batista submitted to pressure by our State Department and our embassy in Havana and held an honest election in 1944. The opposition candidate, Dr. Ramon Grau San Martin, a physician, won by a landslide against Batista's candidate and governed until 1948. Batista lived abroad during the Grau administration, largely because the latter considered it safer for the stability of his administration. Soon after he left office, Batista toured most of Latin America but declined an invitation from Dictator General Rafael Leonidas Trujillo to visit the Dominican Republic.

One of Grau's cabinet ministers was Dr. Carlos Prio Socarras, who in his youth was a fiery revolutionary and who had participated in the overthrow of Machado. The Partido de la Revolucion Cubano (PRC), which Grau headed, was known as the Autentico Party. Prio had designs to be elected president in 1948. As Grau's minister he broke the stranglehold which the Communists had on the labor movement and anti-Reds replaced Lazaro Pena, Secretary General of the CTC, and other Communists who held key posts. Prio was elected in 1948 and succeeded Grau.

Grau gave his former minister one bit of advice when he turned over the presidential sash:

"Don't let Batista back into the country," he warned. "You will regret it."

In 1950 Batista was elected to the senate in mid-term elections, while absent from the country. He had established residence in Daytona Beach, Florida. Shortly thereafter, Prio allowed Batista to return to Havana, even furnishing a military guard to protect his life.

Batista entered the presidential race as one of three candidates. One was Carlos Hevia, once briefly president and former Minister of State in Prio's regime; Hevia was a 1920 graduate of the United States Naval Academy at Annapolis, and an engineer with a reputation for honesty and integrity. The third candidate was Dr. Roberto Agramonte, university professor, and a man of honesty and integrity.

Agramonte was the candidate of the newly born Partido del Pueblo (Ortodoxo), which had been founded by the late Eduardo R. Chibas to fight corruption in government and advocate reform and honest administration. Chibas, depressed over the evident corruption in the Prio administration and in that of Grau before him, committed suicide one Sunday night after he left the CMQ radio station following his regular weekly political talk to the people of Cuba.

One member of Chibas' party was a young lawyer who had recently received his doctorate degree at the University of Havana. He was a candidate for congress from Havana, and his name was Fidel Castro.

Surveys of the voting population of the island on March 1, 1952, indicated that Agramonte was the favored candidate, with

Hevia second and Batista last. The elections were scheduled for June 1, 1952. They were never held.

In the early hours of the morning of March 10, 1952, General Fulgencio Batista entered the sixth gate at Camp Columbia, displaced the army commanders, ejected Carlos Prio as Constitutional President of the Republic and took over the power in Cuba. Within twenty-four hours Batista had control of the entire island. Prio seemed stunned by the coup—although friends had repeatedly warned him it was being plotted. He offered no resistance himself and did not encourage it on the part of his loyal commanders in the provinces, who futilely awaited his orders.

The destruction of constitutional government by Batista and the indifference with which the Cuban people reacted aroused fire in the heart of Fidel Castro. On March 10, 1952, Batista became his enemy, and from that day onward Castro vowed that he would do all within his power—even unto death—to rid Cuba of the man whose arbitrary grab of the presidency disillusioned so many who had believed in Cuba's future. Could this strife-torn island which had seemed to be marching steadily toward institutional stability survive the pitfalls dug for her by corrupt politicians? The idealists and the honest men were utterly discouraged.

Fidel Castro's life has always revolved, from the day of his birth, around the number thirteen. He weighed ten pounds when he was born August 13, 1926, on his father's farm in Biran, a district of the municipality of Mayari on the north coast of the province of Oriente near Nipe Bay.

His father, Angel Castro y Argiz, who was born in Galicia, in northwestern Spain, had lost his first wife, who had given him two children, Lidia and Pedro Emilio. He married Lina Ruz Gonzales, who bore him five children. The first was Angela, the second was Ramon and then came Fidel a year later, followed by Raul and Juana.

Like his sisters and brothers Fidel was baptized by his pious parents as a Roman Catholic. As a chubby, barefoot boy he loved to romp in the fields of Oriente. When he grew older his father used to take him along when he hauled timber from the hills with his tractor, which Fidel loved to ride. The sale of the timber built his father's modest but comfortable fortune.

For Fidel's schooling his parents took him to Santiago de Cuba, the capital of the rich province of Oriente. It was quite a contrast for Fidel, when he left the almost isolated comfort and freedom of the farm for the disciplined confinement of a parochial school. He was registered as a boarding student at the Colegio La Salle, operated by the Christian Brothers, and then was transferred by his parents to the Colegio Dolores, operated by the Jesuits, to complete his grade schooling. Fidel played a bugle in the school band at La Salle and it was there that he first wore a uniform. The outfit was navy blue, and slung over his shoulder was a white Sam Browne belt.

In 1942 his parents sent him to Havana for his high school education, where he was enrolled in the Colegio Belen, also operated by the Jesuits. An outstanding student and athlete, he was graduated four years later in the upper third of his class. He played basketball and pitched on the baseball team and he was pretty fast at track.

The Colegio Belen Year Book in June 1945, when he graduated, had this to say about him:

"1942-1945. Fidel distinguished himself always in all the subjects related to letters. His record was one of excellence, he was a true athlete, always defending with bravery and pride the flag of the school. He has known how to win the admiration and the affection of all. He will make law his career and we do not doubt that he will fill with brilliant pages the book of his life. He has good timber and the actor in him will not be lacking."

In the fall of 1945, after spending the summer months with his family in Oriente, Fidel Castro entered the University of Havana and then began a new and fiery phase of his life. He was a tall young man, nineteen years old, who had passed six feet and was still growing. He began his studies in the Law School and soon became very active in student affairs. This activity was soon to lead him into the vortex of Cuban politics and international intrigue.

There was time, however, for romance. There was a student at the Colegio Immaculada in Havana with whom Fidel fell in love. Unfortunately, the good nuns would not let him inside to woo the girl. Dr. Ernesto Penalver, several years older than Fidel, used to make daily calls at the same door and always managed to gain entrance to visit his fiancée. Upset by the regular rebukes he received, Fidel one day made his concern known to Dr. Penalver.

"Please," he implored Dr. Penalver, "please tell those nuns when you go inside that I am a decent man and that I know how to behave myself and help me to get inside."

Dr. Penalver interceded in his behalf and the lovelorn youth was allowed to call on the student he wished to woo. But she was not the girl he was to marry.

Castro's studies were interrupted in 1947 when he joined an expeditionary force that was training at Cayo Confites, on the coast of Oriente. He knew the hills and valleys of Oriente, having spent his vacationtime hiking there, just as he used to do on weekend trips to the Sierra de los Organos in the province of Pinar del Rio while he was in the Colegio Belen. But he knew nothing about expeditionary forces and was soon to learn how difficult invasion is. The objective of this expeditionary force was to invade the Dominican Republic and to overthrow its dictator, Generalissimo Rafael Leonidas Trujillo.

The operation was financed by a Dominican exile, General Juan Rodriguez, and was led by natives of that island, with volunteers from Cuba, Venezuela and other Caribbean countries recruited. Three thousand men were being trained to sail in surplus landing craft that had been bought in the United States. The Cuban government more than winked its eye at the entire plot. In fact, it seemed to encourage it and even lend financial aid.

The landing craft sailed into the cay, amphibious aircraft began to assemble and D-day was set for some time in the month of August 1947. The Council of Foreign Ministers of the Pan-American Union was meeting at that time in the Quitandinha Hotel in Petropolis, Brazil, forty-five miles north of Rio de Janeiro, the capital. The Dominican delegation denounced the invasion plans at that conference, and there was much commotion over the charges.

16

The invasion expedition set sail from Cayo Confites as planned, but President Ramon Grau San Martin of Cuba ordered it intercepted by frigates of the Cuban navy. Fidel Castro, aboard one of the landing craft, was not going to let himself get caught—a trait that was to be exercised on many occasions—and accordingly jumped overboard with his submachine gun. Despite the drag of the gun, he managed to swim ashore.

He returned to the university and to rabble-rousing student activities, for prominence on the campus is always a stepping-stone to politics in Latin America and Castro had developed an early affinity for politics.

Even on the campus, Castro proved himself an artist at political manipulations. The first to fall under his wangling were the Communists. The Communists supported him for election to the vice presidency of the student government body at the Law School. Once elected, however, Castro began a militant campus campaign against them. The Communists immediately denounced him as a traitor. Upon the resignation of the president, Castro became the head of the student government body.

Castro lived dangerously at the university. He clashed openly with the leaders of the student federation. The fight was so serious and so intense that Castro was several times in danger of being gunned down by rival factions and had to go into hiding until tempers cooled and he could safely roam the campus again.

One of the most controversial episodes of Castro's career was his participation in the "Bogotazo," the riots of April 9, 1948, in Bogota, Colombia, during the Ninth Conference of American States, which was held under the auspices of the Pan-American Union. The United States delegation was headed by General George C. Marshall, Secretary of State. Lieutenant General Matthew B. Ridgway, later to become commander in Korea, was the delegation's military adviser. At that time he was commander of the Caribbean operations, with headquarters in the neighboring Panama Canal Zone.

Diverse elements converged on Bogota with the purpose of disrupting the conference or bringing pressure to bear on particular delegations. The Communists were intent on breaking up the conference. The important elections in Italy were only nine days

17

away. A Communist success in Colombia would have had an effect on the Italian elections and might have given impetus to the campaign of the Reds in that country.

An anti-Colonialism and anti-Imperialist student congress, of which Castro had been invited to be one of the organizers, was scheduled to meet at Bogota at the same time as the Pan-American Conference. Although the students' federations in almost all of the Latin-American countries were the ostensible organizers of this congress, it was also being quietly backed by Senator Diego Luis Molinari, chairman of the Argentine Senate's Foreign Relations Committee, who was there as a delegate to the Pan-American Conference.

Molinari expected the student congress to exert pressure to embarrass the position of the United States regarding European colonies in the Western Hemisphere. Juan Peron, then ruling Argentina, sought to set himself up as the leader of the Latin-American bloc and champion of the liberation of the Americas from European colonial rule. Because of Argentina's claim to the Falkland Islands, its interest in the student congress was made evident by officials of its embassy in Bogota.

Castro planned not only to take part in the student congress at Bogota but also to include in his trip visits to Venezuela and Panama. His plane likewise made a stop in the Dominican Republic, where he narrowly escaped detention. At the airport at Ciudad Trujillo an immigration inspector questioned him: "Aren't you Fidel Castro and weren't you in trouble recently in Cuba?"

"Yes, but I am now out of trouble," Castro answered. He heard the plane's departure being announced and quickly reboarded the aircraft, which left within five minutes.

In Venezuela he called on the university students and became acquainted with former President Romulo Betancourt, who was to head that country's delegation at Bogota.

Castro also visited Panama, talked with the student leaders there and was instrumental in drafting the agenda for the meeting in Bogota after he reached that city.

"We decided to include the question of the independence of Puerto Rico," he told the author. "I was primarily interested in

18

debating the question of the dictatorship in Santo Domingo. While in Panama I met the students there. There was one who had become a martyr with a bullet in his spine because of trouble they had over defense bases with the United States, so we included that in the agenda."

The student congress had not yet begun when the Pan-American Conference got under way. Jorge Elecier Gaitan, popular leader of the Liberal Party, had issued a warning days earlier that the Communists were planning to sabotage the Pan-American Conference. Castro was waiting with a group of students, most of them Colombians and partisans of Gaitan, to interview the Liberal Party leader. The interview was to be held in the offices of the newspaper *El Tiempo* of Bogota. It never was held. The day was April 9, 1948. I was present to observe and report this event and what was to follow in that capital city 8,500 feet above sea level in the central plateau of the Cordillera de los Andes.

Gaitan had visited the Capitolio where the foreign ministers of the twenty-one American republics and their delegates were meeting. He left there shortly after eleven thirty that morning in the company of Roberto Garcia Pena, editor of *El Tiempo*. He was interrupted by well-wishers and partisans as he crossed the Plaza Bolivar on foot to walk the six blocks to the newspaper office. He never reached it.

On Carrera Septima, almost as it intersects with Avenida Jimenez de Quesada, and only a block and a half away from the newspaper office, Gaitan was slain. The news spread like wildfire. A man who was identified as the killer and who had emptied the contents of a revolver into Gaitan at almost point-blank range was beaten to death by an infuriated crowd. His body was stripped of its clothing and only a striped tie was left dangling from his neck.

Fidel Castro, twenty-one years old, felt the indignation of the Colombian crowds around him. There was already an atmosphere of tension because of fratricidal clashes between the members of the Conservative and Liberal parties. Only a spark was needed to ignite a holocaust from one end of Colombia to the other. That spark was the assassination of Gaitan.

Castro followed the students down Carrera Septima toward the presidential palace six blocks away. At the corner of the palace was a police station. The chief of police was a member of the Liberal Party, and the members of his force had been selected for their political loyalty. The President of Colombia, Doctor Mariano Ospina Perez, was a Conservative. The police handed rifles to the advancing mob that was shouting death to almost every Conservative leader. Marching with Castro was another Cuban student, Rafael del Pino, who had been a sergeant in the Army of the United States in World War II.

Castro took his rifle from the police. Repulsed from the vicinity of the palace, the crowd retreated toward the Plaza Bolivar. Other mobs had invaded the Capitolio and destroyed furniture and fixtures, while from Carrera Septima bricks were hurled into the windows of the building and the consequent damage turned much of it into a shambles. Among the rooms to suffer was the press room, where the author, as well as other correspondents, escaped injury.

The manner in which hundreds of natives devoted themselves to the looting of stores appalled Castro; he tried to persuade them to stop, but his efforts were futile. They carried out pianos, electrical appliances, clothing, jewelry and every variety of merchandise. Disorganized mobs carrying rifles roamed the city, overturning streetcars, setting some of them afire, and stealing or burning automobiles. Every vehicle in front of the American embassy offices, including jeeps and pickup trucks, was stolen.

Meanwhile, the Communists were trying to assemble organized bands for directed action. Some Communist students grabbed microphones at radio stations and shouted into them: "People of Colombia! The Leftist Revolution of America has started! Soldiers of Colombia! The Army has joined us! You join us, too! The Leftist Revolution of America is triumphant!"

Within the hour after confirmation of Gaitan's death on the emergency operating table of a hospital, the Communists were in control of the Governor's Palace in the Caribbean port city of Barranquilla, where the giant Magdalena River empties into the sea. The Communist Party flag with its hammer and sickle and red star was flying from the balcony of that palace. Below

20

it was a banner which read: THE REVOLUTION OF RESTORATION HAS BEGUN!

The Colombian students took Castro to the headquarters of the Liberal Party where he talked to some of the leaders, but found no organization for direction of the spontaneous uprising that followed Gaitan's assassination. Del Pino had been arrested in front of the Ministry of War. He managed to talk himself out of custody by convincing his jailers that he was a member of General Marshall's personal bodyguard. His facility with the English language and the fact that he wore khaki slacks and a battle jacket helped his story.

Castro next made his way to the Eleventh Precinct Police Station near the Chapineros district where the police rebels had set up headquarters, but only after he had several close escapes from falling into the hands of the army. Darkness had fallen and martial law had been decreed. He was in a jeep with a police commander and two other Colombians, following another jeep that was occupied by other members of the police force. As they reached the Ministry of War, the front jeep stalled and Castro's jeep had to halt suddenly with a great screeching of tires. Steel helmets bobbed out of the darkness. Finding the police commander in a state of indecision and disinclined to proceed, Castro took the wheel of the jeep, turned around and sped away.

At the Eleventh Precinct Police Station Castro urged some belligerent action. Four hundred policemen, each carrying a rifle, stood in formation in the courtyard. Recalling the theory of Cuban revolutionaries, Castro was determined that the police should break ranks and go into action, for a station full of troops usually meant that sooner or later the whole force would go over to the wrong side. Nobody would pay him heed.

He sat down by himself, hugging his rifle between his long legs and his equally long arms and began to wonder what he was doing in Bogota in the midst of a revolution. He tried to rationalize his participation in the events of the day, arguing with himself and then refuting his arguments. This went on for some time. Finally, he decided he had done the right thing. He went out on several missions with one of the officers, mostly on liaison tasks, and managed to return safely despite the curfew.

As an isolated tank rolled by on its way to the center of the city, some of the police opened fire on it. Bogota was aflame, many of the public buildings and some private ones burning. In spite of the drizzle which had settled over the city since the afternoon, the sky was lighted by the fires, which burned all night.

In the morning Castro and all of Colombia learned via radio that an agreement had been made between President Ospina and the Liberals to end the conflict. With a few students Castro now dug himself in on the hills flanking the city below the 11,000-foot peak of Monserrate, where he remained for twenty-four hours, firing sporadically with the others until he had expended the eleven cartridges that remained for his rifle. It was Fidel Castro's first taste of guerrilla fighting.

When Castro came out of the hills he found himself in a bad position. In a nation-wide broadcast President Ospina had denounced the Cuban students in Bogota as "Communists" and had accused them of playing a leading role in the frustrated uprising. The Pan-American Conference had been disrupted. Although no one knew at that time, it was not to resume until April 14 and then at a school in the Chapineros district which was heavily guarded by a battalion of crack troops.

Castro had no money to pay for his room at the Hotel Claridge, which he had left on the morning of April 9. There was no food available because Bogota was paralyzed by both a strike and fear. At a boardinghouse where some student acquaintances were quartered, he was given a cup of coffee. When the proprietor, a Conservative, voiced his animosity for the Liberals, the rebellious Castro, having left his rifle in the hills, fired away at the man with his tongue. He told the proprietor he believed the Liberals were right, but his contentious attitude resulted only in his being ejected from the boardinghouse.

It was fifteen minutes before the six o'clock curfew; anyone on the streets after that hour was shot on sight by the soldiers, almost all of whom were sharpshooters. At the Hotel Granada (which has since been torn down), Castro met a secretary of the Argentine embassy, who had been active with the student congress preliminary preparations.

"You've got to get me out of here! You must get me out of

here!" Castro said to the secretary. He spoke not only for himself but for Del Pino, who had joined him. The diplomat ignored him and headed for his automobile parked in front of the hotel. The engine was started and the car was about to leave when Castro jumped in and Del Pino followed. The Argentine then decided to drop them at the Cuban embassy.

No sooner were they inside the embassy than Del Pino boasted that he had killed a priest in the April ninth fighting. Thus began the inaccurate story that Castro had killed anywhere from three to six priests in Bogota.

Dr. Guillermo Belt, Cuba's Ambassador to Washington, who was the head of his country's delegation to the conference, was at the embassy when Castro arrived. Also there was Eduardo ("Guayo") Hernandez, Cuban newsreel cameraman. Belt arranged to ship Castro home aboard a cargo plane that had arrived at Bogota a few days earlier to load breeding bulls for transport to Cuba. Instead of the bulls the cargo was Castro and other Cuban students. Guayo Hernandez made newsreel shots of their departure from the Techo airport.

Thus ended the odyssey of Fidel Castro, law student, organizer of an international student conference, newborn guerrilla and rebel, in the Bogotazo.

CHAPTER 2

No priest had been killed in Bogota, and the boast
of Rafael del Pino was nothing more than that, without any basis
in fact. The author had luncheon with the Apostolic Delegate
to Colombia at the Italian embassy a week later, and he reported
that he had not received any word of casualties in the clergy.
His own residence and embassy had been destroyed by fire set
by enraged arsonists. Much damage had been done in churches
where pews had been hurled out onto the streets, and bonfires
were set with some of the debris.

But Del Pino's boast was to give Fidel Castro's enemies a thin
thread on which to hang their accusations that he was a "Communist." The Cuban Ambassador to Bogota submitted a report
to the Ministry of State in Havana in which he recorded the
boast, and this was amplified to place the blame on Castro.

Castro had returned to Havana in time to witness the final
drive in the presidential campaign for the elections of June 1,
1948. Running for the presidency and vice presidency, respectively, were Carlos Prio Socarras and Guillermo Alonso Pujol
for the party in power; Eduardo R. Chibas and Roberto Agramonte for the newly formed Partido del Pueblo Cuban (Ortodoxo); and Ricardo Nunez Portuondo and Gustavo Cuervo Rubio
for the Liberal Party.

Living in comfort from the remains of the estimated forty-

24

million-dollar fortune which he had acquired since 1933 was Fulgencio Batista at Daytona Beach, Florida. He financed his candidacy *in absentia* as senator for the province of Las Villas. The Prio-Alonso Pujol ticket was victorious, and Batista was elected to the senate. Voting for the first time, Castro favored the Chibas-Agramonte ticket.

Now Fidel fell in love with Mirtha Diaz Balart, a student in the Faculty of Philosophy. She was a native of Banes, and on October 12, 1948, they were married in the Roman Catholic church of that city in the province of Oriente, not far from his own birthplace. On their honeymoon in Miami Fidel was forced to pawn his watch and other valuables; his financial difficulties were relieved when he obtained money from home to retrieve his property and complete his honeymoon without preoccupation.

He graduated from the University of Havana in 1950 and became a member of the law firm of Azpiazu, Castro y Rezende. His name on the shingle read DR. FIDEL CASTRO RUZ, and he devoted his time to people of the poorer classes, handling most of these cases without fees. He found time for politics, and in his spare time at home played with his son, Fidel, Jr., who was born September 1, 1949.

Castro was a devoted follower of Eduardo Chibas and, with thousands, if not several millions, of Cubans used to listen to that leader's political reform broadcasts every Sunday night. Chibas had developed a following far greater than he had anticipated. Although his campaign to rid the administration of graft and corruption was like butting his head against the Malecon, Chibas had managed to rally around him most of the younger generation and those older people who yearned for better government and improvement of the lot of the common man.

Chibas ignited flames of hope and passion for the future of Cuba in the heart of Fidel Castro and in others of his generation. He preached sentiments of nationalism, and his left-of-center ideology was absorbed by Castro and his friends.

Despite warnings from Grau, Prio allowed Batista to return home. Batista came back on March 10, 1952, and thus began the bloodiest phase of Cuban history since the War of Independence almost a century earlier.

25

At 2:43 A.M. on March 10 Batista entered Camp Columbia and once again took over the armed forces. When he entered the presidential palace the next day, Prio obtained political asylum in the Mexican Legation. Prio's departure for Mexico with his family a few days later eliminated all possibility of an immediate counterrevolt.

The author interviewed Batista on March 11, 1952, in the palace and talked to dozens on dozens of other Cubans, as well. The man in the street was disillusioned, angered and filled with shame over what had happened. Batista was filled with euphoria. He attributed his coup to what he described as an imperative necessity because of reports, that he claimed to have, of a preventive coup planned by Prio to keep his Autentico Party in office. Five years later in another interview Batista changed his story: he engineered the coup, he said, because Dr. Roberto Agramonte was almost certain to win the presidential election and the triumphant Ortodoxo Party would have "persecuted" many people.

To the average Cuban, the real reason for Batista's maneuver was quite apparent. His fortune had been somewhat depleted in an out-of-court settlement with his first wife when she divorced him. A vain man who could not withstand the resounding defeat that was certain to be administered to him in the presidential election, the only way he could rebuild his fortune and prevent the rout was to take over the government.

Five days after the coup Fidel Castro, who had been on the list of candidates for the Ortodoxo Party for the congress, seethed with anger and shame, as did most Cubans. Prio had not furnished the leadership needed to stop Batista, even though thousands of university students and workers, besides untold thousands of average citizens, were disposed to rally around him to defend constitutional government when they might have been political adversaries. And on March 15, 1952, Castro wrote a letter to Batista.

It was a prophetic letter; in it Castro told Batista that his coup of March 10 was going to produce for Cuba graft and corruption, torture and death for many and a reaction of the people which would eventually overthrow him.

26

Nine days later Castro filed a brief before the Court of Constitutional Guarantees in Havana in which he requested that the assumption of power by Batista be declared unconstitutional. He submitted a slightly varied brief to the Urgency Court in Havana in which he advocated prison terms totaling 100 years against the dictator for violation of six articles of the Code of Social Defense.

His brief to the Urgency Court, which handled all criminal cases, was the only one which any Cuban dared to submit. It said:

"Fidel Castro Ruz, lawyer, with offices in Tejadillo 57, deponeth the following before this Court of Justice:

"The deeds that motivate this brief are well known, but nevertheless I come to make a formal complaint of the same under my absolute responsibility, and to demand *the application of the existing laws,* which, although it may appear absurd in the face of the reigning conditions, is adjusted to juridical standards not abolished by anything nor by anyone, making therefore all the more difficult and overwhelming the duty of the Judges, and the compliance thereof more meritorious and worthy of the fatherland.

"In the early morning of the 10th of March, a senator of the Republic, betraying his own rights and attributions, penetrated the military camp of Columbia prior to concert with a group of officers of the Army.

"Assisted by the night, by surprise and by treachery, they arrested the legitimate chiefs, assuming their command posts, they took the controls, incited the uprising of all the districts and issued a general call to the troops who assembled tumultuously at the parade ground of the camp where they harangued them to turn their arms against the Constitution and the lawfully constituted Government.

"The citizenry, who were completely unaware of the treachery, awoke to the first rumors of what was happening. The violent overpowering of all the radio stations by the rebels prevented the people from getting news and orders for mobilization and resistance.

"Tied by its feet and its hands, the nation contemplated the sweep of the military apparatus which crushed the Constitution, putting lives and farms at the whims of the bayonets.

"The chief of the insurrectionists, assuming the absolute government and arrogating to himself omnipotent powers, ordered the immediate suspension of elections which were scheduled for the first of June.

"The most elemental personal guarantees were suppressed with one sweep.

"All the administrative positions of the State were distributed among the protagonists of the coup just like loot.

"When the congress pretended to meet, answering the ordinary call, it was dissolved by gunfire.

"The total transformation of the republican regime is being carried out at present, and the substitution of the National Constitution, a product of the will of the people, is planned through a juridical farce engendered in the barracks behind the back of popular opinion.

"All these deeds are foreseen and punished in a definite manner in the Code of Social Defense."

Then Castro quoted the articles of the code, which stipulated the following: he who changes in full or part the constitution or the government by use of force will be imprisoned for from six to ten years; he who incites an armed uprising against the constitutional powers of state will be imprisoned for from three to ten years; the penalty will be from five to twenty years if the insurrection is carried out; he who prevents the senate, the congress, the President or the Supreme Court from exercising their constitutional functions will be imprisoned for from six to ten years; he who prevents the holding of elections will be imprisoned for from four to eight years; he who is guilty of sedition will be imprisoned for from three to eight years; he who tries to seduce troops or any other members of the armed forces to commit the crime of sedition will be imprisoned for from two to five years.

"For all those articles and others that would be too numerous to enumerate," Castro continued in the brief, "Señor Fulgencio Batista y Zaldivar has incurred crimes whose punishment make him liable to more than 100 years in jail.

"It does not suffice that the rebels say now so gloatingly that

28

the revolution is source of right if instead of revolution what there is, is 'restoration,' if instead of progress, there is 'retrocession,' instead of justice and order, 'barbarity and brute force.' Ask for the opinion of the illustrious criminal lawyer Jimenez de Asua.

"The action of this court before the deeds related will have a high significance for the people of Cuba. It will show whether it continues functioning with plenitude of powers, whether it is not prevented from doing so by force, whether it also has not been abolished by the coup.

"It would be well that the third power of the State would give signs of life when the other two have been decapitated, provided the judicial power has not been decapitated in the same way.

"To the Urgency Court a citizen is taken when he is accused of sedition or of any other crime of its competence, he is tried and if proven he is condemned. This has been done many times.

"If he refuses to appear he is declared in contempt and the pertinent orders are issued."

After reviewing the competence of the court and citing its legal authority to act in Batista's case, Castro continued:

"If in the face of this series of flagrant crimes and confessions of treachery and sedition he is not tried and punished, how will this court later try any citizen for sedition or contempt against this unlawful regime, product of unpunished treachery? It is understood that it would be absurd, inadmissible, monstrous in the light of the most elemental principles of justice.

"I do not prejudge the thought of the court. I only expound the reasons that support my determination to make this complaint.

"I resort to logic, I pulse the terrible reality, and the logic tells me that if there exist courts in Cuba Batista should be punished, and if Batista is not punished and continues as master of the State, President, Prime Minister, senator, Major General, civil and military chief, executive power and legislative power, owner of lives and farms, then there do not exist courts, they have been suppressed. Terrible reality?

"If that is so, say so as soon as possible, hang up your robe, resign your post: let those who legislate, the very same ones who execute, administer justice, let a corporal sit at once with his

29

bayonet in the august courtroom of the Magistrates. I do not commit any offense upon expounding thus with the greatest sincerity and respect; to keep it quiet is bad, to resign oneself is a tragic, absurd reality, without logic, without norms, without sense and without justice."

The Court of Constitutional Guarantees had already rejected Castro's petition against Batista, and the second brief, of March 24, 1952, was ignored. The Court of Constitutional Guarantees ruled that the "revolution is the source of the law" and therefore, Batista, being in office as a result of the revolution, could not be declared the unconstitutional president of the country.

That might have been the verdict of the court, but to an overwhelming majority of the people of Cuba—and especially to Fidel Castro—Batista was not and never could become their constitutional chief executive.

From that day the determined young lawyer decided there was only one way to settle the issue: revolution. He met with friends in an apartment house at Twenty-fifth and O streets in the Vedado District of Havana to plan a military operation that would not only electrify the people of Cuba but might have an excellent chance of successfully sparking a nation-wide revolt against Batista. Coupled with the military was a political program which Castro and his friends deemed expedient for the island.

The young men—and none had reached thirty—met regularly to discuss the future of Cuba. They contributed their savings or what money they could scrape together to purchase weapons and ammunition. Always present was the memory of Eddy Chibas and the reforms he had advocated.

Chief organizer of the group was Fidel Castro. Second in command was Abel Santamaria. The remainder of the friends gathered by Castro were fervent followers of Chibas. Revolutionary cells were founded in Havana and in Artemisa in the province of Pinar del Rio to the west of the nation's capital. The one resident of Santiago de Cuba chosen to be briefed on the plan was Renato Guitart, a native of Cardenas in the province of Matanzas. It was Guitart who set up Ernesto Tizol, a Cuban who had a prosperous business in Miami, as a chicken farmer at Siboney, on the outskirts of Santiago de Cuba in April 1953. Consign-

30

ments of chicken feed and egg boxes arrived regularly at the farm; inside were weapons and ammunition.

Haydee Santamaria, sister of Abel, joined the residents of the chicken farm and set out to purchase two dozen mattresses for the friends of Fidel who were soon due to arrive. As she gave the order at the store for the mattresses, somebody asked her if the farm were being converted into a barracks, and she replied they planned to take in boarders for a coming carnival celebration. Haydee Santamaria left for Havana to confer with Castro; she returned by train with Melba Hernandez and baggage containing weapons and uniforms.

Fidel Castro traveled to Santiago de Cuba by automobile and stayed at the home of a friend in the center of the city. On July 25 more of the revolutionaries began to gather there. Fidel advised them all that H-hour was set for the next morning, and sent them to the chicken farm at Siboney where Haydee and Melba had prepared cots for them to spend the night. At ten o'clock that night Fidel Castro joined the 170 young men at the farm. Thirty more had halted at Bayamo, ready for action. Castro ordered each one to drink a glass of milk. As they drank he addressed them.

"Colleagues," he began, "you will win tomorrow or be beaten, but no matter what happens this movement will triumph. If you win tomorrow, it will be what Marti aspired to. But if not, the gesture will serve as an example to the people of Cuba. The politicians will be shown by these two hundred young men with such few resources what could have been done with the money which they themselves stole. The people will back us in Oriente and in the entire island; as in '68 and in '95, here in Oriente we give the first cry of liberty or death!"

Some of the men had questions, and Castro listened and replied. Then he asked Abel Santamaria, his top lieutenant, to say a few words.

"It is necessary that we all start off tomorrow with confidence." Haydee's brother spoke in a soft voice. "The triumph will be ours. But if destiny is adverse we must be brave in defeat because what happens there will be known some day; history will record it and our disposition to die for the fatherland will be imitated by

31

all the young men of Cuba. Our example deserves the sacrifice and mitigates the sorrow that we may cause our parents and our other beloved ones. To die for the fatherland is to live!"

Among those who remained awake were Fidel and Raul Castro, Lester Rodriguez, Pedro Miret, Melba and Haydee—names of young people who were to make Cuban history. Under cover of darkness the weapons and munitions were removed from the deep well on the chicken farm. The well itself was discreetly hidden under the boards of an improvised garage. The men assigned the grades of officers to themselves. Those awake softly sang the Cuban national anthem. Castro himself took off for Santiago de Cuba, returning at three o'clock in the morning.

He awakened all of his troops and ordered them to put on their uniforms, which were almost duplicates of the army uniforms, but to leave their civilian clothing beneath the khaki.

"You already know the objective," he told them. "The plan without any doubt is dangerous, and everyone who goes on with me now should do so of his own free will. There is still time to decide to remain behind, and anyway some will have to stay because of the shortage of arms. Those who are determined to go step forward!"

Everybody stepped forward. Then Castro learned that ranks and weapons had been distributed by the men as they saw fit, with everybody wanting to be a noncommissioned officer. After redistributing the arms and selecting the officers, Castro addressed the formation again.

"I tell you," he said, "not to kill unless it is absolutely necessary. We should take the sentry post at Moncada by surprise. This is a suicide action, and for it we need volunteers."

Again everybody stepped forward to volunteer. Castro selected the men to attack the sentry post. They were: Pepe Suarez, Renato Guitart and Jesus Montane. He ordered his brother Raul, then only twenty-two years old, to take the Palace of Justice, which was situated on a hill opposite Moncada and set up a machine gun on the roof. Abel Santamaria was ordered to take the Saturnino Lora Civil Hospital, which was located in front of the main entrance of the fortress.

"I am not going to the hospital," Santamaria protested. "The

32

women and the medico should go to the hospital, but I should fight if there is going to be a fight. Others can take care of the electrical transcriptions and distribute the proclamations."

"You have to go to the Civil Hospital," Fidel replied sternly, "because I order you to do so. You will go because I am the chief and because I have to go at the head of the men. You are my second in command, and I possibly may not come back alive."

"We are not going to do what Marti did," Santamaria replied with insistence. "You have chosen to go to the most dangerous place, to immolate yourself when you are more needed than anyone else."

Castro placed his hands on Santamaria's shoulders. They were big hands. He looked at him with wistful but persuasive eyes.

"I am going to the fort and you are going to the hospital," Castro said, "because you are the soul of this movement and if I die you will replace me."

There was no further argument. Castro ordered the men into the automobiles. There were twenty-six cars waiting. They left in two groups, one of sixteen cars and one of ten. It was not unusual for such caravans to be seen on the road or in the streets of Santiago de Cuba at that hour of the morning of July 26, 1953. The people of the city were ending the annual celebration of their patron saint, and many revelers still thronged the streets.

The Castro caravan crawled up the streets of Santiago de Cuba amid the merrymakers. At the intersection of avenues Trocha and Garzon the caravan separated into three groups, all heading for the sentry gate on the Avenida de las Enfermeras (Avenue of the Nurses). Fidel Castro was in the third group. The first of the vehicles entered the gate as if the occupants were regular passengers to and from the fort.

Another group was preparing to capture a radio station. Electrical transcriptions were ready. One was to be the last broadcast by Eddy Chibas before he committed suicide. The other was a lengthy proclamation outlining the purposes of "The Cuban Revolution." After a review of the political situation of the country, it continued in Fidel Castro's unmistakable language:

"1. Rising from the most genuine sectors of creole values, the Revolution is born in the soul of the Cuban people, with the vanguard of a youth hoping for a new Cuba, clean of past errors and niggardly ambitions. It is the revolution emanating from new men and new procedures, prepared with the patience, bravery and decision of those who dedicate their life to an ideal.

"2. The Revolution declares it is free of all obstacles with foreign nations and free also of influence and of appetites of politicians and other personages. The men who have organized and who represent it pact with the sacred will of the people to conquer the future they serve. The revolution is the decisive struggle of a people against those who have deceived them.

"3. The Revolution declares that it respects the integrity of the free citizens and of the men in uniform who have not betrayed the national heart nor have they scorned their glorious flag nor have they abridged their constitution. It salutes in this hour all the Cubans who are filled with shame, wherever they are, and publicly embraces the decided ones who sincerely gather under its arch of triumph.

"4. The Revolution declares its firm decision to situate Cuba on a plane of welfare and economic prosperity that guarantees its rich subsoil, its geographic position, its diversified agriculture, and its industrialization, which have been exploited by legitimate and spurious governments, by ambitious as well as disinterested culpable persons.

"5. The Revolution declares its love of and confidence in virtue, in the honor and decorum of our men, and expresses its intention to use all those who are of true value in the function of those forces of the spirit in the regal task of the reconstruction of Cuba. Those men exist in all places and institutions of Cuba, from the peasant's shack to the headquarters of the armed forces. This is not a revolution of caste.

"6. The Revolution declares its respect for the workers and students and as masses accredited in the defense of the legitimate rights of the people, the establishment of a total and definitive social justice based on the economic and industrial progress under a synchronized and perfect plan, fruit of laborious and measured study.

"7. The Revolution declares that it recognizes and bases itself on the ideals of Marti, contained in his speeches, on the platform

34

of the Partido Revolucionario Cubano, and on the Manifesto of Montecristi; and it adopts as its own the revolutionary programs of Young Cuba, A. B. C. Radical and the Partido del Pueblo Cubano (Ortodoxo).

"8. The Revolution declares its respect for the free nations of America, sisters who have known how to conquer at the cost of great sacrifices the position of economic freedom and social justic, which is the index of our centuries.

"9. The Revolution declares its absolute and reverent respect for the Constitution which was given to the people in 1940 and restores it as the Official Code. It declares that the only Cuban flag is the tricolor of the lone star and carries it as always, glorious and firm, into the heat of combat and that there is no other hymn than the Cuban national anthem, recognized in the entire world by the vibrant line: 'That to die for the Fatherland is to live!'

"In name of the martyrs.

"In name of the sacred rights of the Fatherland.

"For the honor of the Centenary."

There was no signature other than "The Cuban Revolution," and the proclamation was dated July 26, 1953. The centenary was of the birth of Jose Marti, the apostle of liberty of Cuba.

The group led by Abel Santamaria, which included Dr. Mario Munoz, a medico, Julio Trigo, Melba Hernandez and Santamaria's sister Haydee, entered the hospital. They carried small arms and a package of leaflets containing the proclamation above. Abel Santamaria was in an officer's uniform.

"This is not the army," he said to the policeman who was on duty at the main door. "We are the people who will occupy the hospital. We are not going to harm you; we are only going to disarm you."

The policeman stared at the intruders in amazement.

Santamaria pointed to Munoz. "He is the medico," Santamaria explained, "and they—" pointing to the two women—"are his nurses. We hope there will be no dead or wounded, but if dead and wounded should become inevitable they will attend to them."

As soon as Santamaria and his party entered the hospital they heard the first shots from the fortress.

Everything seemed to be going according to Fidel Castro's carefully worked-out plan except for one automobile. Its driver took the wrong turn on the approach to Moncada and crashed into a curb. The occupants jumped out and made a dash for the sentry post at the nearest gate. Castro stood near the post, shotgun in hand. He covered them as they raced inside, and headed for what they thought was the armory. Their objective was a cache of rifles supposed to have been deposited there. But plans often go awry; the "armory" turned out to be a barbershop. The time was exactly 5:15 A.M.

There was heavy firing, for one of the sentries had alerted the fort, and rifle and machine-gun fire met the attackers. Renato Guitart was among the first to fall. Realizing they had failed in their objective, Castro ordered an immediate withdrawal to Siboney. Part of the insurrectionists headed for the Civil Hospital while others discarded their uniforms and fled into the heart of the city, where they received shelter in the homes of some of the residents.

Two hours after the initial attack firing could still be heard in the vicinity of the fortress. The rumor soon spread throughout Santiago de Cuba that there had been an uprising within the army. This rumor was easily explained by the similarity in the uniforms of Castro's commandos and those of the regular soldiers.

The dozen or more who had fled into the Civil Hospital could see no chance to escape from the building. Quickly Dr. Munoz suggested that they should pretend to be patients. Dr. Mauricio Leon, who was on duty as intern, showed them where the patients' gowns were stored. Dr. Munoz, aided by Melba and Haydee, speedily bandaged legs, arms and eyes to feign injuries. Meanwhile, wails of fright emanated from the children's ward, and Melba and Haydee, still dressed in slacks, went in to console the sick and frightened tots.

The hospital had been quiet for nearly an hour when soldiers rushed inside, carrying their rifles and submachine guns at the ready. They went through the wards but saw only patients and soon withdrew, their profanity ringing through the halls. The soldiers had been gone only a few minutes when a thick-set man of medium height halted them. He wore dark trousers, a checkered shirt and eyeglasses. His dark hair was neatly combed. Melba Hernandez and Haydee Santamaria saw him talking to the officers in command of the troops.

Long would they remember this man, for at once the soldiers raced back into the wards of the hospital, straight to the beds of the fake "patients." The informer had scored.

Abel Santamaria was the first to be caught. His eyes were bandaged. Now the bandages were ripped off. "So you have bad eyes, have you?" one of the soldiers sneered as he pushed him. "Well, we are going to pull them out for you."

Herded together like cattle, the twenty Castro men were taken from the hospital. Now the informer called the attention of the soldiers to Melba and Haydee in the children's ward.

"They are not nurses, nor are they mothers visiting their children," the informer said, pointing to the two women. "They came with them, too, together with that man disguised as a doctor." And the finger pointed to Dr. Munoz.

The entire group was marched out of the hospital toward the Moncada fortress. Dr. Munoz was ordered to go ahead of the others. When he was about twelve paces in front of the rest of the group, he was shot in the back and died on the spot.

Castro and the remnants of his commandos made their way toward Siboney, on the Caribbean coast to the southeast of Santiago de Cuba. The army pursued them; but in a reverse maneuver the rebels managed to penetrate safely into the foothills of the Sierra Maestra.

The army and police had raided homes in Santiago de Cuba and arrested all suspects of the Moncada attack, including some who had had nothing at all to do with it. Monsignor Enrique Perez Serantes, the Archbishop of Santiago de Cuba, conferred with Colonel Alberto del Rio Chaviano, commander of the Regiment Maceo at Moncada. Chaviano promised to spare the lives of the remainder of the survivors of the Moncada attack if they surrendered.

Batista lost no time in reacting to the bold assault on the principal fortress of the province of Oriente. He suspended civil rights immediately, summoned his ministers and enacted a Law of Public Order which made it an offense to print almost any-

37

thing and everything that was displeasing to the government.

Batista dispatched Major General Martin Diaz Tamayo by military transport from Camp Columbia to Santiago de Cuba with orders for Chaviano: ten civilians were to be killed in reprisal for each soldier who fell in the attack. The order was carried out with interest.

Several of Castro's men who were discovered in the hills by Monsignor Perez Serantes surrendered themselves to his custody. He saw them safely to the Moncada fortress. Castro was the main target sought by the army. Their orders were not to take him alive.

An army patrol commanded by Lieutenant Pedro Sarria scoured the hills in search of Castro. The only one in the patrol who knew Castro was Sarria, who had been a student at the University of Havana at the same time as Fidel.

Castro had gone into hiding in a shack at the foothills of the Sierra Maestra near El Caney to the north of Santiago de Cuba. He had a small, starved and practically unarmed squad of three rebels with him, and they had expended all their ammunition. When Sarria's patrol surrounded the thatch-roofed shack, they found Castro and the men lying down, weakened from hunger and thirst.

"Don't tell anybody your name," Sarria whispered to Castro as he simulated a search of his body, "because your life is in danger, and ideas cannot be killed."

Sarria turned to his men and in a severe voice of command ordered them to take the prisoners to the civilian jail, which the Cubans call the "vivac."

"To the Vivac or to Moncada?" one of the soldiers asked in surprise.

"To the Vivac!" Sarria repeated. And Castro, together with his loyal friends, was taken to the jail.

Sarria was severely reprimanded when he returned with his patrol to Moncada.

"Didn't you know what the orders were?" Major Morales demanded. Sarria remained silent and Morales returned to the charge.

"Fidel Castro was not supposed to be brought back alive,"

Morales said, "and if you had to bring him back he should have been brought to Moncada and not taken to the jail."

Not only was Sarria reprimanded but he was retired involuntarily from the army as "unreliable."

At the Municipal Jail in Santiago de Cuba, Castro lost no time in making his position clear to the troops and police who were there.

"I didn't go to Moncada to kill soldiers," he said. "I attacked Moncada because it is the second military fortress of the republic, and those military fortresses sustain the regime. We revolutionaries are not against the army but we are against Batista, who does much damage to the army. Batista harms you, and you have to convince yourself of that. Batista forces you to fight against the people. Batista is the main enemy of the army and of the soldiers."

While Moncada was being attacked, there was a simultaneous assault on the military fortress at Bayamo, to the west of Santiago de Cuba. Thirty men hit the sentry posts at 5:15 A.M., but were repelled by the loyal troops.

Chaviano submitted a certified report of the Moncada attack to the Urgency Court in Santiago de Cuba. The court was composed of three judges and heard all criminal cases. The Moncada attack was listed as "Cause 37." Chaviano's report read in part:

"Armed groups with very, very modern instruments of war, tried to take by assault the Moncada Fort. Within that group of rascals were men who were not natives of the country, for by their type and presence they could have been Mexicans, Guatemalans or Venezuelans. Although many knew that they were coming to this province to start a civil war, others were deceived by being told they were going to take a ride to the fort, but upon seeing that they were going to have to fight against the soldiers of this regiment, some fled and the others tried to do so and were wounded by their leaders because they refused to fight."

Chaviano added that almost all the weapons had, according to the evidence obtained, come from Montreal, Canada. This was an attempt on the part of the government to link Castro's attack with former President Prio, who had conferred in Mon-

39

treal some months earlier with opposition leaders from Havana; they had agreed to try to overthrow Batista.

The report to the court accused the rebels of having fired at will inside the hospital against occupants there, of having knifed three patients in the stomach, of having used dum-dum bullets and of having hurled hand grenades in the attack on Moncada.

One hundred and twenty men and two women were to face trial. The army had decided that terror should rule. The lives of some were snuffed out while they were in prison; among the victims were others who were removed from homes where they had taken refuge in Santiago de Cuba and summarily executed. The slaughter took place for three days. Many of the executed—without trials—were innocent youths of the city.

Castro and the other prisoners were transferred from the Vivac to the Provincial Jail at Boniato. This modern penitentiary is situated in a hollow in the Sierra Maestra and is backed up by the rugged mountain. The military supervisor of Boniato was a young lieutenant, Jesus Yanes Pelletier. He drove the Buick automobile in which Castro and two other prize prisoners, Melba Hernandez and Haydee Santamaria, were taken to Boniato. The guard in the big car included an army captain and his two soldier sons. Lieutenant Yanes was soon to be cashiered from the army because of his suspected friendship for Castro's cause and was to spend considerable time in exile in Miami and New York.

Twenty-six defense lawyers were present in the courthouse at Santiago de Cuba on September 21, 1953, when the trial of the Moncada attackers and others charged with complicity began. A court-appointed lawyer defended those who had confessed their guilt. Fidel Castro elected to act as his own counsel. The judges were Adolfo Nieto Pineiro-Osorio, Juan Francisco Mejias Valdivieso and Ricardo Diaz Oliveira. The government had filed charges against friends and former friends of President Prio, among them Aureliano Sanchez Arango, who was Minister of State (equivalent to our Secretary of State) on March 10, 1952.

The approaches to the courthouse were heavily guarded. Castro's attack on Moncada, although a failure, had served to awaken the spirit of resistance among the people of Oriente. The terror that followed when the army tortured and killed prisoners accelerated the ire against Batista. Only one person in all of Santiago de Cuba had known in advance of Castro's plan to try to capture Moncada. Afterward, the women of that city—mothers and daughters who did not even know the prisoners—visited the jails to take food, cigarettes and other necessities to the men held for trial. They also attended the trial.

There were fears in the city on the eve of the trial that the government might apply the *ley de fuga,* or fugitive law, to many of the prisoners and shoot them before they ever reached the court. Thse fears were dissipated the following morning. The precautions taken by the government converted the approaches to the courthouse into a virtual battlefield. Armored cars closed the access from Avenida Garzon to the central highway where the courthouse was located. Another cordon of armored cars blocked the access to the highway via the Avenida de las Enfermeras, and a third cordon prevented all traffic from circulating from Marti and Sueno streets to the Avenida de los Libertadores.

One thousand soldiers with automatic weapons were stationed along both sides of the road from Boniato prison, a distance of six miles. The prisoners, except Castro, were transported to the courthouse by busses; they were not allowed to open the windows very much.

Castro rode in an army jeep under heavy escort. He wore a dark blue serge suit, which produced much perspiration in the tropical heat, white shirt, a tie with a background of red and black shoes and socks. He had not yet grown even a mustache, much less the famous beard. He was handcuffed securely. Spectators lined the route quietly to watch him ride by. Like the other prisoners he was taken to the basement elevator to be conveyed to the library. The other prisoners were led into the building in twos. They met their lawyers for the first time in the library.

Chaviano ordered Captain Pedro Rodriguez Miranda and Lieutenants Vicente Camps and Luis Figueroa to take personal command of the guards and he banned photographs of the prisoners, although the court had authorized pictures to be taken.

Fidel Castro was the first to be led into the courtroom. His entrance was met with silence, except for some murmuring by

41

the spectators. "That is Fidel," they whispered. "That is he!"
Other prisoners followed. Dr. Roberto Garcia Ibanez, former congressman of the Ortodoxo Party, was the first to be accused in court. He denied the charges that he was the mastermind of the Moncada attack. Dr. Ramiro Arango Ansina followed and denied the accusation that he had served as the bridge between Castro and former President Prio and other signatories of the pact of Montreal.

Then came Castro's turn. He took his oath and swore to tell the truth. He listened to the charges that he had been the material author and leader of the insurrection against the constituted powers of the state. Then the prosecutor, Dr. Mendieta Hechevarria, began his questions.

"Did you participate in the attacks on the forts of Bayamo and Santiago de Cuba the last 26th of July in a physical or intellectual manner?" the prosecutor asked.

"Yes," Castro replied with defiance. He pointed to his friends who were seated on one of the prisoners' benches, "And those young men love as I do the liberty of their Fatherland and fight for it."

The chief justice admonished Castro to limit his answers to the prosecutor's questions. And Mendieta Hechevarria returned to the attack. He warned Castro not to make a political oration in reply to a comprehensive question as to whether he had explained to his followers his entire plan, the political connections therewith "and the criminal act thereof from a legal standpoint."

"I am not interested in making any political oration," Castro answered. "I only want to open the path to the truth. All my companions militate in the Ortodoxo Party, or, better said, almost all my companions. In reality I did not have to convince them. They were pleased to take this road, and I took advantage of the psychological moment in order to tell them of my plan, which they accepted. I am unacquainted with the purpose or thinking of the leaders of the party, but I am convinced that ninety percent of the young men of Cuba think just like those young men who are on the prisoners' benches, and understand that the only possible way to overthrow this regime, which the people detest, is war. Harmony could not be achieved, although

42

that was the wish of all, because the dictator is intransigent."

"Why didn't you use civil means in order to accomplish your purpose?" the prosecutor asked.

"Simply because there is no freedom in Cuba," Castro shot back, "because since the tenth of March nobody can talk. I already said that efforts were made but the government, always intransigent, did not want to give ground. I accused Batista before the tribunals of justice, but the courts did not resolve the case as we expected."

"Where did you get the money to buy arms and with which to organize the uprising?"

"The money was obtained through the generous donation of the men who followed me," Castro said with a note of gratitude in his voice. "I have a list of all their names with the amounts they contributed. The majority of them have died, but I have the facts to prove that they were the persons who put up the money for the revolution. The sum collected reached $16,480 and every cent of it was spent. Just as Jose Marti did not accept money from Manuel Garcia, king of the plantations of Cuba, this revolution will not accept the ill-gotten money of anyone."

Castro then described in detail the weapons that were purchased with the money collected from among his friends. "We had only one machine gun, and we did not have any hand grenades," he said. "If we had tossed any hand grenades then we would have opened an enormous hole in a wall. We had ten thousand cartridges of all calibers and different types of weapons, among them three Winchesters of the time of Buffalo Bill. They were few and mostly deficient weapons.

"Among those of us who are alive and those who are dead, the following persons gave money." Castro read from his list: "Jesus Montane, who is present, gave the sum of $4,000 which he collected as severance pay from General Motors when it liquidated its business in Cuba. Ernesto Tizol, owner of a chicken farm, placed his property at the disposition of the revolution. Oscar Alcade mortgaged his laboratory for the sum of $3,600 and liquidated an accounting office which he owned, thus making another contribution. Renato Guitart gave $1,000. Pedro Marrero sold the dining room set of his house, the refrigerator and

43

the living room set—he didn't sell the bedroom set because I forbade him to do so. Moreover he borrowed $200 from a money-lender to increase his contribution to the cause; and he didn't seem to mind losing his job in the Tropical Brewery, where he earned $250 a month.

"Fernando Chenart pawned his personal belongings, including his camera. He was the photographer who took the picture for the magazine *Bohemia* of the studio of the sculptor Fidalgo when it was raided by the state. His only crime, you remember, was having sculptured a statue of Marti that was called: 'For Cuba that Suffers.' Chenart gave $1,000. Elpido Sosa sold his job as treasurer of an important company. Abel Santamaria mortgaged his automobile, but that was not his only contribution. He gave much more and, if it seemed little, he gave his life. Thus I could go on amplifying the list, but it appears to me that it would be better if I deliver it in writing to this court."

Castro handed over the list. Whereupon the prosecutor asked him if Abel Santamaria had stolen checks from the firm where he had worked in order to augment the funds of the revolution.

"That is a calumny!" Castro replied. "Abel Santamaria was one of the bravest men I knew, and it is painful that an attempt should be made to stain his memory so ignominiously!"

"Why didn't you attack Camp Columbia?" the prosecutor asked. "The bulk of the force of the country was concentrated there and not in Moncada."

"Because we had very poor weapons and munitions," Castro answered. "We had hoped to take Moncada without firing a shot. I had warned my companions not to shed blood except in an emergency. The plan was to attack by surprise. Military psychology says that a soldier only fires in response to the order to fire, and if he doesn't get such an order he will not react. That is why we did not want any shots fired. Moreover, the liberty of Cuba was born in Oriente and if necessary we proposed to retrace the invasion, rising in the mountains. That is why I told my companions to return to Siboney and later to intern themselves in the Sierra Maestra."

Castro repudiated Chaviano's charge that knives had been used by the rebels in the Civil Hospital or anywhere else. He underscored the fact that none of his men was acquainted with the Military Hospital where they were charged with having killed soldiers. He expressed surprise that there were so many of his men killed when some of them didn't even participate in the attack. The men under command of his brother Raul, for instance, had not even wounded a single guard as they took the Palace of Justice, whereas the soldiers had killed revolutionaries in cold blood.

"If you had no contact with political leaders in this movement, then what support were you counting on?" the prosecutor asked.

"If we had been able to make contact with the people," Castro said with full confidence, "they would have responded. There is our ally: the people. Our plan was to take the radio stations as soon as possible and to broadcast simultaneously over all of them the last speech delivered by the dead leader Eduardo R. Chibas. We felt that all the opposition leaders of the republic would then have joined us, and, in that way, we would have overthrown the de facto government, the dictatorship of Batista."

"On what political prestige did you count in order to persuade a people so unbelieving and so deceived as the people of Cuba to rise?"

"On what prestige did the little lawyer Carlos Manuel de Cespedes and the oxcart driver Antonio Maceo count when they rose in the redeeming hinterland?" Castro countered. And he pursued the outline of Chibas' last speech.

"But that leader is dead!" the prosecutor interjected.

"That doesn't matter," Castro replied. "Men do not follow men but ideas, Mr. Prosecutor."

Defense attorneys began to cross-examine Castro. Finally the assistant prosecutor asked if any leader of the Partido Socialista Popular (the name of Cuba's Communist Party) had taken part in the attack; Castro denied that any had. The same lawyer, Luis Perez Rey, asked Castro if his companions had been reading any books.

"They all like books," he answered.

"Was a book by Lenin found on Santamaria?" Perez Rey insisted.

"It is possible," Castro answered, "because we read all types of

45

books. Anyone who was never interested in socialist literature is an ignoramus."

One question was put to Castro by Dr. Ramiro Arango Alsina, who was acting as his own lawyer. "Have I been the intellectual author of this movement?"

"No, you have not been the intellectual author. The only intellectual author of this revolution is Jose Marti."

Several other witnesses were called, among them Andres Garcia Diaz, who confessed that he had participated in the attack on the fort at Bayamo.

"They arrested me in Manzanillo with my brother," he said. "In Veguita they beat us and then they assassinated my brother. I ask the court to record my accusation. I saw them hang him, and although I was wounded I was able to run away. Monsignor Perez Serantes delivered me to the army."

Fidel Castro, exercising his right as counsel, began to interrogate Garcia Diaz.

"Those soldiers whom you say committed the crimes," Castro asked, "and who beat you, did they act on their own or were they obeying orders of the officer on duty?"

"They obeyed orders," Garcia Diaz answered.

Castro was about to ask another question when the court ordered a recess. The trial could not be resumed the next day because most of the army troops had to be transported to Holguin to protect Batista on a visit to that northern city of the province of Oriente. This produced a two-day recess.

When the trial was resumed on September 26, Fidel Castro was not in the courtroom. The chief judge, irritated, asked the officer of the guard for an explanation, and the captain handed him an envelope. He opened it, read it and circulated it among the other judges and the prosecutor.

"The accused, Dr. Fidel Castro Ruz," Judge Nieto announced, "will not be able to be present. I have just received a communication from the prison in which it is certified that he is sick and needs absolute rest."

After conferring with his two colleagues, Judge Nieto addressed the counsel:

"The court considers that should this trial be suspended in-

46

definitely, it would cause inconveniences with the natural damage for the right of defense of the accused who have already appeared. In view of that—" he heaved a sigh and resumed—"in view of that the trial is partially annulled in so far as it relates to the accused, Dr. Castro Ruz."

Judge Nieto dropped the letter onto the bench and rang the bell to open the session. (In Cuban courts a bell similar to that used by schoolteachers, which is rung by the judge, suffices to call the court to order.)

"Mr. President!" a feminine voice electrified the courtroom. "Fidel Castro is not sick!"

The voice was that of Dr. Melba Hernandez, acting as her own defense counsel.

"Mr. President," she continued rapidly, "here I bring a letter from Dr. Fidel Castro, written in his own hand and addressed to this respectable and honorable court."

From her hair she removed an almost minute piece of paper that had been rolled up so it could easily be hidden. The officers of the guard and the soldiers looked at her with death in their eyes. She walked slowly toward the bench, her lithe frame upright. She climbed a step and handed the paper to the chief judge. The three judges leaned over and read it. With Melba Hernandez's success in smuggling out the handwritten paper, Castro had scored another psychological blow.

"As for this letter which has just been delivered to this court," Judge Nieto announced, "it will be considered at the opportune moment."

Like the proceedings of the trial, the brief handed to the court by Melba Hernandez could not be published in the newspapers or broadcast because of the ironclad censorship. It was a scathing denunciation by Castro of Batista's machinations. The text read:

"To the Urgency Court:

"Fidel Castro Ruz, attorney appearing in his own defense in Cause 37 of the present year before said Court respectfully expounds the following:

"1. That efforts are made to impede my presence in the trial, by which the fantastic falsehoods that have been woven around the deeds of the 26th of July would be destroyed, and to prevent the revelation of the horrible crimes that were committed that day against prisoners, which were, I say, the most frightful slaughter ever known in the history of Cuba. Because of that today I have been informed that I will not attend the trial because I am sick, the truth being that I am in perfect health without any physical illness of any kind. Thus they are pretending in that way to abuse the Court in the most shameful manner.

"2. That despite repeated communications from the judicial power and the last one that the Court addressed to the authorities of the prison, demanding the end to our isolation, because it is unlawful and criminal, I am totally incommunicado. During the fifty-seven days in which I have been in this prison I have not been allowed to see the sun, to talk to anyone nor to see my family.

"3. That I have been able to learn with all certainty that my physical elimination is being plotted, under the pretext of escape, poisoning me or some other similar thing and for that purpose they have been elaborating a series of plans and plots that facilitate the consummation of the deeds. I have repeatedly denounced this. The motives are the same as I expounded in number one of this brief.

"Like danger faces the lives of other prisoners, among them two of the girls who are exceptional witnesses of the massacre of the 26th of July.

"4. I request the Court to proceed to order immediately my examination by a distinguished and competent doctor such as the President of the Medical Association of Santiago de Cuba. I propose also that a member of that Court, especially appointed, accompany the political prisoners on the trips that they make from this prison to the Palace of Justice and vice versa. That the details of this brief be communicated to the Local and National Bar Associations, to the Supreme Court of Justice and to as many legal institutions as that Court esteems should know these facts.

"The importance and the category of the trial that is being held imposes exceptional obligations.

"If it is carried out under the conditions which I have de-

48

nounced, it will not be more than a ridiculous and immoral farce with the full repudiation of the nation.

"All of Cuba has its eyes focused on this trial. I hope that this Court will worthily defend the rights of its hierarchy and its honor which is at the same time, in these moments, the honor of the entire judicial power before the History of Cuba.

"The action of the Court up to now and the prestige of its magistrates accredit it as one of the most honorable of the Republic which is why I expound these considerations with blind faith in its virile action.

"For my part, if for my life I have to cede an iota of my right or of my honor, I prefer to lose it a thousand times: 'A just principle from the depth of a cave can do more than an army.' "

(Signed) FIDEL CASTRO RUZ

September 26, 1953
Provincial Jail of Oriente

"P.S. I appoint Dr. Melba Hernandez to present this brief in my name. F.C."

In the sentence quoted in the last paragraph, Fidel Castro revealed that he had studied the life of the liberator of Cuba, Jose Marti, and forecast that three years later he was to translate into action the counsel of the man he always referred to as the Maestro.

Lieutenant Jesus Yanes Pelletier, the military supervisor of the Boniato penitentiary, stated that one of Colonel Chaviano's aides had ordered him to poison Castro's food. For his refusal Yanes was relieved from duty at the prison, and was forced to retire from the army a few weks later.

The court reacted to Castro's letter by directing Dr. Juan Martorell Garcia, penitentiary physician, to supervise the food served to Castro and to examine him regularly.

Political leaders of the Ortodoxo Party and of Prio's party, who were accused of masterminding Castro's attack, were questioned. They all denied the charges.

Next, eight admitted leaders of the Communist Party, also among the accused, were called to the witness stand. They were Lazaro Pena, Joaquin Ordoqui, Bernardo Hernandez, Jose

Cabrejas, Juan Maria Llosa, Rolando Hevia Ruiz, Antonio Perez and Armando Diaz. They denied the charges, testifying that they all happened to be in Santiago de Cuba to celebrate the birthday of the party boss, Blas Roca, their secretary general.

Several other accused, followers of Castro, were called to the stand; they denied their direct or indirect participation in the Moncada attack although they were very much a part of it. This was Castro's strategy so that some of the men could be acquitted and thus spared for underground work. The trial was now recessed again.

When it was resumed on September 28, Jesus Montane, short, strongly built and intellectual-looking, with thick-lensed glasses, was the first person called. He was asked if he had taken part in the organization of the attack.

"I participated in the organization of the movement of the Generation of the Centenary," he admitted, "because I believe that Cuba must be saved from oppression."

"Did you take part in the action of the sentry gate where the soldiers were assassinated by knife?"

"Nobody was assassinated. When we left, the soldiers were alive. If they were killed later, it was because of the great confusion and the firing among themselves. I was captured with three companions at Siboney. When we arrived at the fort, several of the soldiers said: 'This fellow—' and they pointed to me— 'who has the face of a professor, there is no need to talk about him. We are going to kill him but first we are going to squeeze him a little.' Immediately they started to cut off my testicles. To die for Cuba is a satisfaction for us. Luckily an officer arrived at that moment and halted the outrage that was being committed."

"Can you tell us some more about the movement? Did you know it from inside?"

"The direction of the movement was in charge of a group of ten led by Dr. Fidel Castro. They included Abel Santamaria, Boris Luis Colomba, Pedro Miret, Jose Luis Tassende, Ernesto Tizol and Mario Munoz Monroe—he was the medico but he also built the radio transmitter with which we were going to broadcast to all of Cuba once Moncada had surrendered—Raul Martinez Araras, Gerardo Perez Poey, Renato Guitart and I. The

50

military direction of the movement was comprised of Dr. Fidel Castro, Santamaria, Tizol and Martinez Araras."

Ciro Redondo was called to the witness stand. He confessed to all the charges except that any of the attackers had carried knives or daggers. He denounced the fact that one of his companions, Marcos Marti, was killed after he was arrested.

Raul Castro was the next witness.

"I came on my own," he said. "I received instructions to take the Palace of Justice to prevent the army from taking it and to reinforce our position there. We did not encounter any resistance. We arrested the guards and disarmed them. We took nine prisoners, eight of them police or soldiers and one civilian. We did not carry knives or daggers. That was a trick on Chaviano's part in his first statement to arouse the spirit of the soldiers, in order to incite to crime. With that he demonstrated his weakness. He wanted to pit the soldiers against the people."

Haydee Santamaria and Dr. Melba Hernandez followed Raul Castro on the stand. Haydee denounced a series of tortures that she had witnessed in the Moncada jail, denying that either she or Melba had prevented a wounded soldier from being treated at the Civil Hospital.

"When I saw that soldier fall wounded near the entrance of the hospital," she testified, "I said to a doctor: 'He is not one of ours, but he is a man, a human being.' The medico rushed to his side, but it was already too late. The soldier had died."

Melba Hernandez testified that she and Haydee had seen Dr. Munoz killed. She also told the court that Abel Santamaria and twenty-five others had been killed in prison.

Captain Edmundo Tamayo, army medico, testified that, contrary to the report by Chaviano, none of the wounded or dead soldiers had been stabbed. Ballistics experts testified that no grenade impacts had been visible anywhere. Those witnesses gave the lie to Chaviano's report.

It was not until October 6 that Fidel Castro was once again brought into court. But this time court was held in the nurses' lounge of the Civil Hospital for reasons of secrecy and security. Besides the three judges and the heavy armed guard, the only other persons permitted inside the lounge were two prosecutors

51

and six reporters. And because of censorship not a word of the trial could appear in the newspapers.

Castro addressed the court in his own defense for five hours. His summation was an indictment against the government. He included, too, the revolutionary reforms for the Cuba of the future, which were decidedly left of center.

"Never has a lawyer had to exercise his profession under such difficult conditions," Castro began. "Never, against an accused, has there been committed so many overwhelming irregularities. Both lawyer and accused are, in this case, the same person. As a lawyer I have not even been allowed to see the indictment and, as the accused, I have been locked for seventy-six days in a solitary cell, totally and absolutely incommunicado, above all human and lawful prescriptions.

"He who is speaking abhors puerile vanity with all his soul, and it is not in his spirit or in his temperament to affect poses or sensationalisms of any kind. If I have had to assume my own defense before this court, it is for two reasons. One: because I was practically completely deprived of defense otherwise. The other: because only one who has been hurt so deeply and who has seen the Fatherland so forsaken and justice so vilified can speak on an occasion such as this with words that may be blood of the heart and entrails of the truth."

Castro expressed appreciation for the fact that the Havana Bar Association had appointed a defense counsel for him.

"They didn't let him, however, perform his mission," Castro went on. "The doors of the prison were closed to him every time he tried to see me. Only after a month and a half, through the intervention of the court, was he granted ten minutes to interview me and then only in the presence of a sergeant of the military intelligence service. A lawyer should be able to converse with his client privately, a right that is respected everywhere in the world except when it deals with a Cuban prisoner of war in the hands of an implacable despotism that does not recognize lawful or human rules."

That treatment and distortions by the government, with apparent intention to prevent the real truth from becoming known, were what inspired him, Castro told the court, to assume his own defense.

"You have classified this trial publicly as the most transcendental of the republican history, and if you have believed it sincerely," Castro's words rang out in the room, "then you should not have permitted your authority to be soiled with a bale of scorn. The first session of the trial was held September 21. Among a hundred machine guns and bayonets that scandalously invaded the hall of justice, more than one hundred persons sat on the prisoners' bench. A great majority were foreign to the deeds and had been under preventive arrest for many days after suffering every kind of outrage and bad treatment in the prisons of the repressive forces. But the rest of the accused, who were the lesser number, were proudly firm, disposed to confirm with pride their participation in the battle for liberty, to give an example of abnegation without precedent and to liberate from the throes of the jail that group of persons who had with all bad faith been included in the trial. Those who had fought once again returned to the fight. Once again the just cause was on our side; against infamy there was to be fought the terrible combat of the truth. And certainly the regime did not expect the moral catastrophe that approached it.

"How maintain the false accusations? How prevent what really had occurred from becoming known, when such a number of youths were disposed to run all the risks—jail, torture and death, if it were necessary—for denouncing it before this tribunal?"

Castro reviewed the first day of the trial when he was interrogated for two hours and then launched into a counterattack, accusing the government of preferring to blow up the court rather than allow him to exercise his rights as an attorney for his own defense.

"They devised the idea of removing me from the trial," Castro went on, "and they proceeded to do so in military fashion. On Friday night of September 25, on the eve of the third day of the trial, two medicos of the prison came to my cell, visibly ashamed: 'We have come to examine you,' they told me.

" 'And who is so worried about my health?' I asked. Really, as soon as I saw them I understood the purpose. They could not have been better gentlemen, and they told me the truth: That afternoon Colonel Chaviano had come to the prison and had told them that I was 'doing terrible harm to the government at the trial.' Then he had them sign a certificate which stipulated that I was sick and hence could not continue to attend the sessions. The medicos told me, in addition, that they, for their part, were disposed to resign their posts and expose themselves to persecutions; that they would put the matter in my hands for me to decide. It was hard for me to ask those men to immolate themselves without considerations, but neither could I consent, by any concept, to let such plans be carried out. To leave them to their own consciences, I replied only: 'You will know what is your duty; I know well which is mine.'

"After they withdrew they signed the certificate; I know they did it because they believed that it was the only way to save my life, which they saw in great danger. I did not promise to keep silent about our conversation; I am obligated only to the truth. If to tell it in this instance injures the material interests of those good professional men, I leave clean of all doubt their honor, which is worth much more. That same night I wrote a letter for this court, denouncing the plot and requesting the visit of two forensic medicos to certify to my perfect state of health. In that letter also I said that if, to save my life, it were necessary to resort to such an artifice, I preferred to lose it a thousand times. To make it understood that I was resolved to fight alone against such smallness, I added to my brief that thought of the master: 'A just principle from the depth of a cave can do more than an army.' That was the letter which, as the court knows, Dr. Melba Hernandez presented on the third day of the oral trial, September 26. I was able to get it to her despite the implacable vigilance which weighed over me. Because of that letter, naturally, reprisal measures were taken: Dr. Hernandez was placed in solitary confinement, and, as I was already in solitary, they confined me to the most distant place of the prison. From that moment on all the prisoners were searched carefully from head to foot before leaving for the trial.

54

"On the twenty-seventh the forensic medicos came and certified that, in effect, I was perfectly healthy. Despite reiterated orders of the court, however, I was not brought back to any session of the trial. Add to this the fact that every day unknown persons distributed hundreds of apocryphal pamphlets which talked of rescuing me from prison—a stupid trick to eliminate me physically under pretexts of evasion. Those plans failed because of the opportune denunciation of alert friends and the falsity of the medical certificate having been discovered. So there was no other recourse than to prevent my attendance at the trial, which was open and barefaced contempt.

"This was an unusual case, Honorable Judges: a regime that was afraid to present an accused before the courts; a regime of terror and of blood, which was frightened before the moral conviction of a defenseless, unarmed, incommunicado and libeled man. Thus, after having deprived me of all, they deprive me ultimately of the trial where I was the principal accused. Bear in mind that this was done in full exercise of the suspension of guarantees and with the Law of Public Order and Censorship of the Press and Radio functioning in all its vigor. What crimes so horrible had this regime committed that it feared the voice of an accused?

"I must mention the insolent and disrespectful attitude which the military chiefs have maintained toward you. How many times did this court order the inhuman solitary confinement that weighed over me to cease? How many times did you order my most elemental rights to be respected? How many times did you demand that I be presented at the trial? Never were you obeyed. One by one they showed contempt for your orders. Worse yet: in the very presence of the court, in the first and second sessions, I was put beside a pretorian guard to keep me from talking to anybody at all, not even during recess, giving you to understand that, not only in prison but even in the court and in your presence they didn't pay the slightest attention to your dispositions. I planned to present this problem in the following session as a question of elemental honor for the court, but . . . I didn't return any more. And if in exchange for such disrespect they bring us here in order that you send us to jail, in name of a legality they only and they exclusively are violating since March 10, very sad is the role that they wish to impose on you. The Latin maxim, *Cedant arma togae,* has certainly not been fulfilled once in this case. I beg you to bear in mind this circumstance.

"More, all the measures taken were completely useless because my brave companions, with civic action without precedent, fully complied with their duty.

" 'We have come to fight for the liberty of Cuba and we do not regret having done it,' one by one they said when they were called to testify, and immediately, with impressive courage, addressing the court, denounced the horrible crimes that had been committed on the bodies of our brothers. Although absent I was able to follow the trial from my cell in all its details, thanks to the inhabitants of the Boniato prison who, despite all the threats of severe punishment, took advantage of ingenious methods in order to place in my hands all kinds of reports and other information. They avenged in that way the abuses and immoralities of Director Taboada and of Lieutenant Rozabel, who made them work from sunrise to sunset constructing private palaces, and on top of that starved them by embezzling the subsistence funds.

"As the trial progressed the roles were reversed: those who were going to accuse were accused, and the accused were converted into accusers. The revolutionaries were not judged there. There for all time was judged a man named Batista. *Monstrum horrendum!* It doesn't matter that the valiant and worthy young men have been condemned if tomorrow the people will condemn the dictator and his thugs. They were sent to the Isle of Pines in whose circular cell blocks the specter of Castell still lingers and the shout of so many, many of the assassinated has not been extinguished. There they have gone to purge, in bitter confinement, their love for liberty, sequestered from society, torn from their homes and exiled from the Fatherland. Don't you believe, as I said, that under such circumstances it is unpleasant and difficult for this lawyer to fulfill his mission?

"As a result of so many dirty and unlawful machinations by the will of those who rule and the weakness of those who judge, I am here in this little room of the Civil Hospital where I have

56

been brought to be tried in secrecy so that I cannot be heard, so that my voice may be stilled and nobody may know of the things that I am going to say. For what do you want that imposing Palace of Justice, where the magistrates will find, without doubt, many more comforts? It is not convenient, I submit to you, that justice be imparted from the room of a hospital surrounded by sentinels with pointed bayonets because the citizens might think that our justice is sick . . . and jailed.

"I remind you that our procedural laws establish that a trial will be 'oral and public'; however, the people have been completely barred from this session. Only two lawyers and six reporters—in whose newspapers the censorship will not allow a single word to be published—have been admitted. I see that the only public I have in the room and in the halls are nearly one hundred officers and men. Thanks for the serious and amiable attention which they are rendering me! If only I had the entire army in front of me! I know that some day it will burn with desire to wash the terrible stain of shame and of blood that the ambitions of a soulless group has launched over the military uniform. Oh, those who today ride comfortably over their noble warriors . . . as if the people have not unsaddled them long ago!

"Finally, I must say that not even a book on penal law was allowed in my cell in the prison: I can have this minuscule code just lent me by a lawyer, the valiant defender of my companions: Dr. Baudilio Castellanos. Likewise they kept the books of Marti from reaching my hands: it appears that the prison censorship considered them too subversive. Or it is because I said Marti was the intellectual author of the 26th of July?

"It was also forbidden to bring to this trial any work of reference about any other subject. That doesn't matter at all! I bring in my heart the doctrines of the master and in my thought the noble ideas of all the men who have defended the liberty of the people.

"I am only going to ask one thing of the court. I hope you will grant me one thing, in compensation for such excess and abuse as this accused has had to suffer without any protection of the laws: that my right to express myself with full freedom be respected. Without it you will not be able to fill the mere appearances of justice, and this last action would be, more than any other, of ignominy and cowardice.

"I confess that something has deceived me. I thought that the prosecutor would come forward with a terrible accusation, disposed to justify to the end the pretense and the motives for which, in the name of Law and Justice—what Law and what Justice?— I should be condemned to twenty-six years in prison. But no: He has limited himself exclusively to reading Article 148 of the Code of Social Defense by which, more aggravating circumstances, he asks for me the respectable quantity of twenty-six years of imprisonment. Two minutes appear to be very little time to ask and to justify that a man pass to the shadow of more than a quarter of a century. Is the prosecutor by chance disgusted with the court? Because, as I see it, his laconic attitude in this case contrasts with that solemnity with which the magistrates declared with such pride that this was a trial of great importance. I have seen the prosecutors talk ten times as long in a simple case of narcotic drugs to request that a citizen be condemned to six months in prison. The prosecutor has not pronounced a single word to support his petition. I am fair. I understand that it is difficult for a prosecutor who swore to be faithful to the Constitution of the Republic to come here in name of an unconstitutional de facto statutory government of no legality and of less morality, to ask that a young Cuban, lawyer like him, perhaps, as decent as he, be sent for twenty-six years to jail. But the prosecutor is a man of talent and I have seen persons with less talent than his write long treatises in defense of this situation. How, then, believe that he may lack reasons to defend it, even for fifteen minutes, for all the repugnance that this inspires in any decent person? There is no doubt that at the bottom of this is a great conspiracy.

"Señores Magistrates: Why such pressure that I keep silent? Why, inclusive, is every kind of reasoning suspended in order not to present any target against which I can direct the attack of my arguments? Is it that the juridical, moral and political basis for making a serious presentation of the question is entirely lacking? Is it that the truth is so feared? Is it that he wishes that I also speak only two minutes and not touch here the points which have caused certain people to be sleepless since the 26th of July?

"By limiting the prosecution's petition to the simple reading of five lines of an article of the Code of Social Defense, he might have thought that I would limit myself to the same and give turns and more turns around them, like a slave turning a millstone. But I will not in any manner accept that muzzle, because in this trial something more than the simple liberty of an individual is being debated: Fundamental questions of principle are being judged; the right of men to be free is being judged; the very foundation of our existence as a civilized and democratic nation is being debated. When it ends I do not want to have to reprove myself for having discarded principle for a defense without speaking the truth or denouncing crime.

"The famous little article of the prosecutor does not deserve even a minute of reply. I will limit myself, for the moment, to fighting a brief juridical skirmish against him, because I want the field to be clean of dust when the hour arrives to touch the blade against all the lies, falsehoods, hypocrisy, conventionalisms and limitless moral cowardice on which is based that bald comedy which, since the 10th of March and even before the 10th of March, is called in Cuba *justice*.

"It is an elemental principle of penal law that the imputed act has to be exactly the type of crime proscribed by the law. If there is no law exactly applicable to the controverted point, there is no crime.

"The article in question says textually: 'A penalty of from three to ten years will be imposed on the author of an act directed to promote an uprising of armed men against the *constitutional powers of the state*. The penalty will be from five to twenty years' imprisonment if the insurrection is carried into effect.'

"In what country are we living, Mr. Prosecutor? Who has said that we have promoted an uprising against the *constitutional powers of the state?* Two things come to light. In the first place: the dictatorship that oppresses the nation is not a constitutional power, but is unconstitutional; it was engendered against the Constitution, above the Constitution, violating the legitimate Constitution of the Republic. Legitimate constitution is that which emanates directly from the sovereign people. This point I will demonstrate fully further on, in the face of all the stupidities that the cowards and the traitors have invented in order to justify the unjustifiable. In the second place, the article speaks of *powers,* that is to say, plural, not singular, because it is considering the case of a republic ruled by a legislative power, an executive power and a judicial power that balance and check one and another. We have promoted rebellion against a single illegitimate power that has usurped and united into one man the legislative and executive powers of the nation, destroying the entire system that the article of the Code which we are analyzing precisely tried to protect. Of the independence of the judicial power after the 10th of March, I will not even speak because I am not here to joke. For all the efforts to stretch, to shrink or to repair not a single comma of Article 148 is applicable to the acts of the 26th of July. Let us leave it undisturbed, awaiting the opportunity in which it can be applied to those who promoted an uprising against the constitutional powers of the state. Later I will return to the Code in order to refresh the memory of the prosecutor about certain circumstances that lamentably he has forgotten.

"I warn you that I have just started. If in your souls there remains one bit of love for the Fatherland, of love for humanity, of love for justice, listen to me with attention. I know they will compel me to be silent for many years; I know that they will try to hide the truth by all the means possible; I know that against me there will rise the conspiracy of forgetfulness. But my voice will not be drowned because of that. Forces gather in my breast the lonelier I feel, and in my heart is the desire to give all the heat that the cowardly souls deny me.

"I listened to the dictator on Monday, July 27, from a shack in the mountains when we still had eighteen men under arms. Those who have not passed through similar moments will not know the bitterness and indignation of life. At the same time that our hopes so often cherished for the freedom of our people were dashed to the ground, we saw the despot rise more braggart and worse than ever. The flow of lies and calumnies that spewed from his stubborn, odious and repugnant tongue could only be

60

compared with the enormous flow of young, clean blood which the night before was being spilled, with his knowledge, consent, complicity and applause, by the most soulless band of assassins that ever could be conceived. To have believed for one minute what he said is sufficient for a man of conscience to live regretfully and ashamed all his life. He did not even have, in those moments, the hope of recording on his miserable face the truth that stigmatizes him for the remainder of his days and the rest of his time, because around us the ring of more than one thousand men, with weapons of greater reach and power, whose definite order was to return with our corpses, had already closed. Today, the truth begins to be known and I end, with these words which I am pronouncing, the mission that is imposed upon me, completed to the full. I can die calmly and happily.

"It is necessary that I stop to consider a few of the facts. The government said that the attack was carried out with such precision and perfection that the presence of military experts in the elaboration of the plan was evident. Nothing more absurd! The plan was drafted by a group of young men, none of whom had military experience; and I am going to reveal their names, minus two who are neither dead nor prisoners: Abel Santamaria, Jose Luis Tassende, Renato Guitart Rosell, Pedro Miret, Jesus Montane and he who addresses you. Half are dead, and in just tribute to their memory I can say that they were not military experts, but had sufficient patriotism to give, in equality of conditions, a sovereign beating to all the generals of the 10th of March affair together, who are neither soldiers nor patriots.

"It was more difficult to organize, to train and to mobilize men and arms under a repressive regime that spends millions of dollars on espionage, bribery and informers—tasks that those young men and many others realized with seriousness, discretion and truly incredible constancy. More meritorious yet it will always be to give to an ideal all that one has and, moreover, one's life.

"The final mobilization of men who came to this province from the most remote towns of the entire island was carried out with admirable precision and absolute secrecy. It is likewise true that the attack was realized with magnificent co-ordination. It commenced simultaneously at 5:15 A.M., in Bayamo as well as in

Santiago de Cuba, and, one by one, with exactness of minutes and seconds foreseen in advance, the buildings that surrounded the camp started to fall. However, in strictest truth, even when it minimizes our merit, I am going to reveal for the first time another fact that was fatal: Half of the bulk of our forces, and the best armed, because of a lamentable error became lost at the entrance to the city and so was of no use to us at the decisive moment. Abel Santamaria, with twenty-one men, had occupied the Civil Hospital; with him also, to attend to the wounded, went a medico and two ladies. Raul Castro, with ten men, occupied the Palace of Justice; and it fell to me to attack the fort with the other ninety-five men. I arrived with the first group of forty-five, preceded by an advance guard of eight who penetrated gate three. It was here precisely where the fighting started that my automobile encountered a cruising patrol armed with machine guns. The reserve group, which had almost all the long arms, for the small arms were with the advance guard, took the wrong street and became completely lost within a city which they did not know. I must clarify that I do not entertain the least doubt about the valor of those men, who, finding themselves lost, suffered great anguish and desperation. Because of the type of action that developed and the identical color of the uniforms of both fighting parties it was not easy to re-establish contact. Many of them, arrested later, met death with true heroism.

"Everyone had very precise instructions to be, above all, human in the fight. Never was a group of armed men more generous with the adversary. Numerous prisoners were taken from the first moments. There was an instant, at the beginning, in which three of our men, of those who had taken the gate—Ramiro Valdes, Jose Suarez and Jesus Montane—were able to penetrate inside a barracks and hold for a time almost fifty soldiers. These prisoners testified before this court, and all without exception have recognized that they were treated with absolute respect without having to suffer even one unpleasant word. Concerning this aspect I do thank the prosecutor from my heart, for something; that in the trial of my companions, upon delivering his summation, he had the justice to recognize, as an indubitable fact, the very high spirit of gentlemanliness that we maintained in the fight.

"The discipline on the part of the army was bad enough. They conquered in the end because of their number, which gave them a superiority of fifteen to one, and because of the protection which the defenses of the fortress offered them. Our men shot much better and they themselves recognized this. The human bravery was equally high on both sides.

"Considering the causes of the tactical failure, apart from the lamentable error mentioned, I believe that it was an error on our part to divide the unity of commands that we had so carefully trained. Of our best men and boldest chiefs, there were twenty-seven in Bayamo, twenty-one in the Civil Hospital and ten in the Palace of Justice; if another distribution had been made the result could have been different. The clash with the patrol (totally casual, for twenty seconds earlier or twenty seconds later it would not have been at this point), gave time for them to alert the camp; otherwise, it would have fallen into our hands without a shot, for the gate was already in our power. On the other hand, except the .22 caliber rifles which were well supplied, the ammunition on our side was very scarce. If we had had hand grenades, they would not have been able to resist for fifteen minutes.

"When I was convinced that all our efforts to take the fort were already useless, I commenced to withdraw our men in groups of eight or ten. The withdrawal was protected by six snipers who, under command of Pedro Miret and of Fidel Labrador, heroically blocked the route of the army. Our losses in the fight had been insignificant; ninety-five percent of our dead were the product of cruelty and inhumanity when the fighting had ended. The group at the Civil Hospital did not have a single casualty; the rest were surrounded when the troops covered the only exit from the building, and they laid down their arms only when they did not have a single bullet left. With them was Abel Santamaria, the most generous, beloved and intrepid of our young men, whose glorious resistance immortalizes him in the history of Cuba. We will see the fate that befell him and how Batista wished to react to the rebelliousness and heroism of our youth.

"Our plans were to continue the fight in the mountains in case of failure of the attack on the regiment. I was able to gather again, in Siboney, a third of our forces, but we were already forlorn. Some twenty decided to give themselves up; we will see also what happened to them. The rest, eighteen men, with the arms and ammunition they had left, followed me into the mountains. The land was totally unknown to us. For one week we occupied the high part of the Cordillera of Gran Piedra and the army occupied the foothills. We could not descend and they could not decide to go up after us. It was not, then, the weapons but only hunger and thirst that vanquished the last resistance. I had to go on breaking up the men into small groups. Some were able to infiltrate through the army lines; others surrendered to Monsignor Perez Serantes. When only two companions remained with me, Jose Suarez and Oscar Alcalde—all three of us totally exhausted—at dawn on Saturday the first of August a force under command of Lieutenant Sarria surprised us while we were sleeping. The slaughter of prisoners had already ceased because of the tremendous reaction it had provoked in the citizens, and this officer, a man of honor, prevented some killers from assassinating us there in the field with our hands tied.

"My purpose is not to entertain the court with epic narrations. Everything that I have said is necessary for the most exact understanding of what I will say later.

"I wish to record two important things so that our attitude may be serenely judged. First: we could have facilitated the taking of the regiment, simply arresting all the high officers in their quarters, a possibility that we rejected because of the very human consideration of avoiding scenes of tragedy or of fighting in the family quarters. Second: it was agreed not to take any radio station until such time as the camp was secure. This attitude of ours, seldom seen because of its gallantry and grandeur, saved the citizens a river of blood. With only ten men, I could have occupied a radio station and hurled the people into the fight. It was not possible to doubt their spirit: I had the last speech of Eduardo Chibas in C.M.Q., transcribed in his own words; practical poems and war hymns capable of shaking the most indifferent, with more reason when they are listening in the fever of combat, and I did not want to make use of it despite our desperate situation.

"It has been repeated with much emphasis by the government

that the people did not second the movement. Never have I heard such an ingenuous denial and, at the same time, one so full of bad faith. They pretend to show it by the submission and cowardice of the people; there is little left for them to say but that the people support the dictatorship, and they do not know how they offend the brave men of Oriente. Santiago de Cuba believed it was a fight between soldiers and had no knowledge of what had happened until many hours later. Who doubts the bravery, civism and limitless courage of the rebel and patriotic people of Santiago de Cuba? If Moncada had fallen into our hands, even the women of Santiago de Cuba would have taken up arms! Many rifles were loaded for our combatants by the nurses of the Civil Hospital. They also fought. That we will never forget.

"It never was our intention to fight against the soldiers of the regiment, but to take over by surprise the control and the arms, to call the people, to assemble the soldiers later and invite them to abandon the hated flag of tyranny and to embrace that of *liberty;* to defend the great interests of the nation and not the niggardly interests of a little group; to turn and fire against the enemies of the people, and not against the people where their sons and fathers are; to fight beside them, as brothers that they are, and not against them, as the enemies that the dictatorship wants them to be; to go united toward the only beautiful ideal, alone worth offering your life for, which is the grandeur and happiness of the Fatherland. Of those who doubt that many soldiers would have joined us, I ask: 'What Cuban does not love glory? What soul does not light up in a dawn of liberty?'

"The navy did not fight against us and would without doubt have joined us later. It is known that that sector of the armed forces is the least addicted to tyranny and that there exists among their members a very high index of civic conscience. But as for the rest of the national army, would they have fought against the rebellious people? I say no. The soldier is a man of flesh and bone, who thinks, who observes and who feels. He is susceptible to the influence of the opinions, beliefs, sympathies and antipathies of the people. If he is asked his opinion, he will say that he cannot give it; but that does not signify that he lacks opinion. He is affected by exactly the same problems which concern the

65

other citizens: subsistence, rent, the education of his sons, their future, etc. Each family is a point of inevitable contact between him and the people and the present and future situation of the society in which he lives. It is foolish to think that because a soldier receives a wage from the state, very modest, that this resolves his vital preoccupations, his needs, duties and sentiments as a member of a family and of a social group."

Castro then explained why he found it necessary to refer to the soldiery:

"The 10th of March took place in the moment in which the prestige of the civil government had descended to the minimum, a circumstance which Batista and his clique took advantage of. Why didn't they do it after June 1? Simply because, if they had waited for the majority of the nation to express its sentiments at the polls, no conspiracy would have found echo in the troops."

Castro referred briefly to the former regimes and then made this prophetic statement:

"A second affirmation can, therefore, be made: the army never has rebelled against a regime of popular majority. These are historic truths. If Batista is determined to remain in power at all cost, against the absolutely majority will of Cuba, his end will be more tragic than that of Gerardo Machado."

Castro had more to say about the army and some of the former officers. He told the court that he thought Camp Columbia, the military fortress, "should be converted into a school and, instead of soldiers, ten thousand orphan children should be installed there."

Then Castro reviewed some heroic features of the War for Independence—the bravery of the people of the province of Oriente.

"That is how the people fight," he said, "when they want to win their freedom: they throw stones at airplanes and turn tanks upside down!"

And he told the court of his plans after the capture of the Oriente capital.

"Once the city of Santiago de Cuba was in our power, we would have placed the people immediately on war footing. Bayamo was attacked precisely to situate our advanced forces

66

along the Rio Cauto. Do not ever forget that this province, which today has a million and a half inhabitants, is without doubt the most warlike and patriotic of Cuba. It was she that kept the fight for independence burning for thirty years and gave the greatest tribute of blood, sacrifice and heroism. In Oriente the air of that glorious campaign is still breathed. At dawn when the roosters crow like bugles calling reveille and the sun rises radiant over the rugged mountains, it appears that once again we are going to hear the cry of Yara or of Baire. [The cry of Yara on October 10, 1868, was the first shout for independence. The cry of Baire on February 24, 1895, was the declaration that preceded the final drive for liberty from Spain.]

"I said that the second reason on which the possibility of our success was based was one of social order. We had the certainty of counting upon the people. When we speak of the people, we do not understand as such the accommodated ones and the conservatives of the nation, those to whom any regime of oppression, any dictatorship, any despotism comes well; they prostrate themselves before the master of the moment until they smash their faces against the ground. We understand by the people, when we speak of struggle, the great unredeemed mass, to whom all offer and whom all deceive and doublecross; who hope for a better and more dignified and more just Fatherland; who are moved by the ancestral desires of justice, having suffered injustice and scorn generation after generation; who hope for grand and wise transformations in all the orders and are disposed to give to achieve when they believe in something or in someone—above all when they believe sufficiently in themselves, even to the last drop of blood. The first condition of the sincerity and good faith in a plan is to do precisely what nobody does, that is, to speak with complete clarity and without fear. The demagogues and the professional politicians who work the miracle of seeming to be in everything and on the side of all, are necessarily deceiving all in all. The revolutionaries have to proclaim their ideas valiantly, to define their principles and to express their intentions so that nobody is deceived, neither friends nor enemies."

Castro now addressed himself to the people of Cuba rather than to the court. His defense was the presentation and lament for the sorry conditions that confronted many workers. He appealed for their support through the enunciation of a platform that had to sound good to their ears and stimulate their hopes as they read it, even though they were not to have the opportunity of reading it for more than a year and a half because of censorship.

"We call on the people," he continued, "the seven hundred thousand Cubans who are without work but who desire to earn their bread honestly without fear of having to emigrate from their country in search of sustenance; the five hundred thousand camp workers who dwell in miserable shacks, who work four months of the year and are hungry the rest, sharing the misery with their sons, who do not have an inch of land to plant and whose existence should move more to compassion if there were not so many hearts of stone; the four hundred thousand industrial workers and stevedores whose retirement funds, all, have been embezzled, whose conquests are being taken away, whose homes are infernal habitations of the rustlers, whose salaries pass from the hands of the boss to the usurer, whose future is a pay reduction and dismissal, whose life is perennial work and whose rest is the tomb. We call on the one hundred thousand small farmers who live and die working a land that is not theirs, always sadly contemplating it like Moses and the promised land, only to die without possessing it; who have to pay for their parcels like feudal slaves with a part of their products; who cannot love it, nor improve it, nor plant a cedar or an orange tree to beautify it because they do not know the day when a sheriff or a rural guard will come to tell them that they have to go. On the thirty thousand teachers and professors so devoted, sacrificed and necessary to the better destiny of future generations and who are so badly treated and paid; on the twenty thousand small businessmen overwhelmed with debts, ruined by the crisis and harangued by a plague of filibusters and venal officials; on the ten thousand young professionals: medicos, engineers, lawyers, veterinarians, pedagogues, dentists, pharmacists, newspapermen, painters, sculptors, etc., who leave the classrooms with their degrees, desirous of working and full of hope, only to find themselves in a dead end street, all the doors closed, deaf to clamor and supplication.

"These are the people who suffer all the unhappiness and are therefore capable of fighting with all courage! To the people whose roads of anguish are stony with deceit and false promises we were not going to say: 'We are going to give you,' but: 'Here you have it. Fight now with all your forces so that liberty and happiness may be yours!'

"In the documents of this Cause there must be recorded five revolutionary laws that would have been proclaimed immediately after the capture of the Moncada fort and broadcast by radio to the nation. It is possible that Colonel Chaviano has destroyed all of those documents, but if he has destroyed them, I conserve them in my memory.

"The first revolutionary law would have restored sovereignty to the people and proclaimed the Constitution of 1940 as the true supreme law of the state, until such time as the people should decide to modify it or to change it. And to effect its implementation and the exemplary punishment of all who had violated it— organs of popular election to carry it out not existing—the revolutionary movement, as momentous incarnation of that sovereignty and only source of legitimate power, would have assumed all the faculties inherent in it except that of modifying the Constitution: power to legislate, power to execute and power to judge.

"This attitude could not be more correct and devoid of trash and sterile charlatanism: a government acclaimed by the mass of combatants would receive everything necessary in order to effect implementation of the popular will and of true justice. From that moment, the judicial power, which has been placed since the 10th of March against the Constitution and outside the Constitution, would cease, and an immediate and total purge of such power would begin before it would assume anew the powers which the supreme law of the Republic grant it. Without those prior measures, the return to legality, placing its custody in the hands of dishonorable leaders, would be an embezzlement, a deceit and one more treachery.

"The second revolutionary law would grant property, not

69

mortgageable and not transferable, to all planters, subplanters, lessees, partners and squatters who occupy parcels of five or less caballcrias of land [a caballeria is 33⅓ acres], the State indemnifying their former owners on the basis of the rental which they have received for said parcels on an average of ten years.

"The third revolutionary law would grant to workers and employees the right to share in thirty percent of the profits of all the large industrial, commercial and mining companies, including sugar mills. The merely agricultural firms would be excepted in consideration of other laws of agrarian order that would be implemented.

"The fourth revolutionary law would grant to all planters the right to share in fifty-five percent of the cane crop; a minimum quota of forty thousand arrobas [each arroba is twenty-five pounds] would be allotted to small planters who have been established for three years or more.

"The fifth revolutionary law ordered the confiscation of all of the property of all the malfeasants of all the governments—and of their legatees and heirs to property received by will or intestate of ill-gotten origin. To implement this special courts with access to all sources would have full powers to investigate the corporations registered in the country or which operate in it where malfeasant properties may be hidden, and to request of foreign governments the extradition of persons and the attachment of property. Half of the property recovered would be given to the workers' retirement banks and the other half to hospitals, asylums and charitable homes.

"It was declared, moreover, that the Cuban policy in America would be one of close solidarity with the democratic people of the Continent, and that those politically persecuted from bloody tyrannies that oppress the sister nations would find in the Fatherland of Marti, not persecution, hunger and treachery as today, but generous asylum, brotherhood and bread. Cuba should be the bulwark of liberty and not the shameful abode of despotism."

Castro then told the court those laws would be "proclaimed immediately and would be followed, after a minute study, with another series of equally fundamental laws and measures such as agrarian reform, total reform of education and the nationali-

70

zation of the electric trust and the telephone trust; the return to the people of the unlawful excess that they have been charged in their rates and payment to the public treasury of all amounts owing to it."

Castro said all the above was based on two essential articles of the constitution, one of which proscribes land hoarding and the other of which obligates the state to use every means within its reach to provide employment for the citizen.

"The first government of popular election that rises immediately after," Castro continued, "would have to respect them [the laws], not only because they would have a moral obligation to the nation, but because when the people achieve the conquests which they have been hoping for during several generations there is no force in the world capable of taking them away again.

"The problem of the land," he went on, "of industrialization, the problem of housing, the problem of education, the problem of unemployment and the problem of the health of the people—here are the six problems whose solution our efforts would have resolutely begun, together with public liberties and political democracy.

"Perhaps this exposition appears cold and theoretical if one does not know the frightening and tragic situation in which the country is living in respect to those six areas, to say nothing of the most humiliating political oppression."

Castro pointed out that the United Fruit Company and the West Indian Company jointly owned land from the north to the south coasts of Oriente province while 200,000 Cuban families residing there do not own a small plot of land.

And he proceeded to outline his plans for educational reform.

"Our teaching system perfectly complements all the above: In a field where a guajiro [native peasant] is not the owner of the land, why do we want agricultural schools? In a city where there are no industries, why do we want technical schools? All this falls within the same absurd logic: there is neither one thing nor the other. In any small country of Europe there exist more than two hundred technical and industrial arts schools; in Cuba there are no more than six, and the boys graduate with their degrees without having a place to work. They attend the small public schools of the field, barefoot, half-dressed and undernourished—even then, less than half of the children of school age. Many times the teacher has to acquire with his own salary the material necessary for use in class and for the students. Is that the way to build a great country?"

Castro voiced his scorn for the politicians who lived in comfort in mansions on Fifth Avenue in the Miramar residential district of Havana, preaching "absolute freedom of enterprise, guarantees for investment capital and the law of supply and demand."

"A revolutionary government with the backing of the people and the respect of the nation," he insisted, "after cleaning the institutions of venal and corrupt officials, would proceed immediately to industrialize the country. It would mobilize all the inactive capital, which exceeds presently five hundred million dollars, through the Banco Nacional and the Industrial, Agricultural and Development Bank, and submit the large task to study, direction, planning and realization by technicians and men of absolute competence, completely foreign to the maneuvers of politics.

"A revolutionary government, after placing over their parcels as owners the one hundred thousand farmers who today pay rent, would proceed to end definitely the land problem. How? First it would establish, as the constitution orders, a maximum holding for each type of agricultural enterprise, acquiring the excess through expropriation, claiming the usurped lands for the State, filling in mangrove and other swamplands, planting enormous areas and reserving zones for reforestation. Second, such a government would distribute the remaining land among the farming families with preference to the most numerous; it would encourage agricultural co-operatives for the common use of costly equipment, cold storage plants and a single professional technical direction in cultivation and breeding; and would facilitate, finally, distribution of resources, equipment, protection and useful knowledge to the farmers."

As Castro continued to discuss the housing and the educational problems, the judges listened attentively and the prosecutor entered no objections. All were enraptured by the tall crusader who faced them, who addressed them with a missionary zeal, who had already accepted the fact that he would be condemned. It was a most unusual defense by the accused at any trial, but Cuba was living under most unusual circumstances.

Here was a young man who had just passed his twenty-seventh birthday, who, together with most of his companions, had been only seven years old when Batista first became the strong man of Cuba, defiantly telling a court of justice—sitting in secrecy in a nurses' room in a hospital in the city of Santiago de Cuba because the government feared the impact of a public trial of the accused—what he considered should be the political, social and military blueprint for the future of Cuba.

"Only inspired by such elevated purposes," Castro resumed after lashing at the politicians and the system of bribery, corruption and graft which they employed, "is it possible to conceive the heroism of those who fell in Santiago de Cuba. The scarce material means on which we had to count prevented certain success. The soldiers were told that Prio had given us a million dollars; they tried to thrust aside the most serious fact of all: that our movement had no relation whatsoever with the past, that it was a new Cuban generation with its own ideas which had risen against the tyranny, of young men who were only children when Batista committed his first crimes in the year 1934. The lie could not be more absurd. If with less than twenty thousand dollars we armed a hundred sixty-five men and attacked a regiment and a squadron, with a million dollars we could have armed eight thousand men, attacked fifty regiments and fifty squadrons! Let it be known that for every one who came to fight, twenty perfectly trained men didn't come because there were no arms. Those men paraded through the streets of Havana with the student demonstration on the Centenary of Marti, filling six blocks in compact mass. Two hundred more who would have been able to come or twenty hand grenades in our possession and perhaps we would have saved this honorable court so much bother."

Castro returned to the subject of the contributions made by his friends and companions to the cause and then lashed out at Batista once more.

"The tyrant Batista was never a man of scruples who hesitated to tell the people the most fantastic lies," Castro told the court.

73

"When he wanted to justify the traitorous coup of March 10, he invented a supposed military coup that was to have erupted in the month of April which 'he wished to avoid so that the Republic would not be bathed in blood,' a ridiculous fable that nobody believed. When he himself wanted to bathe the republic in blood and to drown in terror, torture and crime the just rebellion of young men who did not want to be his slaves, he then invented more fantastic lies yet. How little respect he has for a people when he tries to deceive it so miserably! The same day I was captured, I publicly assumed the responsibility for the armed movement of the 26th of July; if only one of the things which the dictator had said against our combatants in his speech of July 27 had been true, it would have sufficed to wrest from me all moral force in this trial. But why were all the laws of proceeding violated and contempt scandalously shown for all the orders of the Court? Why did they do things never seen in any public trial in order to prevent, at all cost, my appearance? I, on the other hand, did the unusual by being present, by denouncing the maneuvers that were being realized to prevent it. I wanted to confront them, person to person and face to face. They did not want such a confrontation. Who had the truth and who did not have it?"

Castro discussed the brutality of the Spanish generals against the Cuban patriots during the War of Independence, which served to increase the ranks of the insurrectionists. Then he returned again to Batista.

"The treachery of December 1933 [when Batista ousted the provisional president] was insufficient, as were the crimes of March of 1935 [when political prisoners were tortured and killed and many Cubans were forced to flee into exile], and the forty million dollars of fortune that crowned his first phase. The treachery of March of 1952, the crimes of July of 1953 and the millions of dollars which Batista will now acquire were also necessary for him.

"Dante divided his inferno into nine circles: he placed the criminals in the seventh, the thieves in the eighth and the traitors in the ninth. The devils will have a hard time finding an adequate site to place the soul of this man—if this man should have a soul! He who encouraged the atrocious acts of Santiago de Cuba does not even have entrails.

74

"I know many details of the manner in which those crimes were carried out. The details were given to me by some officers who, full of shame, told me about the scenes they had witnessed.

"When the fighting ended, the troops were launched like wild animals over the city of Santiago de Cuba to satiate their initial anger against the defenseless population. In the street and very far from the place where the fighting had taken place they killed an innocent child, who was playing near the door of his house, with a bullet through his chest. And when his father rushed to pick him up, they killed *him* with a bullet through his head.

"A child named Cala, who was returning to his house with a loaf of bread in his hands, was shot down without a word. It would be interminable to refer to the crimes and outrages committed against the civilian population. And if they acted in this manner against those who had not participated in the action, you can imagine the horrible luck that befell the participating prisoners or those who they thought had participated. Just as in this trial many persons were involved who had nothing to do with the deeds, they also killed many of the prisoners who had nothing to do with the attack. These are not included in the figures of the victims that have been given, which refer exclusively to our men. Some day the total number of those immolated *will* become known.

"The first prisoner murdered was our medico, Dr. Mario Munoz, who carried no arms, wore no uniform and was dressed in a doctor's cloak. He was a generous and competent man who would have treated a wounded adversary with the same devotion as a friend. On the road from the Civil Hospital to the fort they shot him in the back and left him lying there face downward in a pool of blood. But the mass slaughter of prisoners did not begin until after three o'clock in the afternoon. They waited for orders until that hour. General Martin Diaz Tamayo arrived from Havana then and brought concrete instructions given him during a meeting Batista held with the Chief of the Army, the Chief of the Military Intelligence Service and other officers. Batista told him:

" 'It was a shame and a dishonor for the army to have had three times the casualties of the attackers in battle. Ten prisoners must be killed for every dead soldier.' That was the order!

"In every human group there are men of low instincts, born criminals, beasts, carriers of all the ancestral atavisms superimposed on the human form, monsters more or less restrained by discipline and social habit, who if they were given water to drink in a river would not stop until they had drunk it dry! All those men needed was precisely that order. The best of Cuba died in their hands: the bravest, the most honest, the most idealistic. The tyrant called them mercenaries, but they died like heroes at the hands of men who collected a salary from the republic, and by the arms which had been delivered for defense. Defense! Instead the soldiers serve the interests of a band and murder the best citizens.

"In the midst of tortures our comrades were told their lives would be spared if—betraying their ideological position—they would falsely declare that Prio had given the money. When they indignantly rejected the proposition, the soldiers continued torturing them horribly. They shattered their testicles and yanked out their eyes, but no one gave in. Nor was a lament or a supplication heard. Even when they had been deprived of their virile organs they continued being a thousand times more men than all their executioners together. Photographs do not lie and those cadavers appear destroyed. They experimented in other ways: they couldn't break the bravery of the men so they probed the bravery of the women.

"With a bleeding human eye in his hands a sergeant went with several others to the cell where Melba Hernandez and Haydee Santamaria were held. Addressing the latter, showing her the eye, he said: 'This was your brother's, and if you do not tell us what he refused to tell us we will yank out the other eye.'

"She, who loved her valiant brother above everything, replied full of dignity: 'If you yanked out one eye and he did not tell you anything, much less will I tell you.'

"Later they returned and burned her arms with hot irons, trying to force her to talk, until finally, full of spite, they told Haydee: 'You don't have a sweetheart any more because we have killed him, too.'

"And she, imperturbable, replied once again: 'He is not dead, for to die for the Fatherland is to live.'

76

"Never had there been placed on so high a pedestal of heroism and dignity the name of Cuban womanhood.

"These monsters didn't even respect the wounded in different hospitals in the city. They went looking for them like vultures following their prey. In the Centro Gallego they broke into the operating room at the very instant that two seriously wounded men were receiving blood transfusions. They yanked them from the tables and dragged them to the lower floor where they left their dead bodies.

"They couldn't do the same in the Colonia Espanola where Gustavo Arcos and Jose Ponce were hospitalized because Dr. Posada valiantly prevented it, telling them they would have to take those two patients over his dead body.

"Air and camphor were injected into the veins of Pedro Miret, Abelardo Crespo and Fidel Labrador to try to kill them in the Military Hospital. They owe their lives to Captain Tamayo, army medico and a true soldier of honor, who at pistol point took them away from the executioners and transfererd them to the Civil Hospital. Those five young men were the only wounded who survived.

"Before dawn groups of men—already deformed by torture—were removed from the camp, their hands tied and their mouths taped. They were taken in automobiles to Siboney, La Maya, Songa and other places to be killed in solitary fields. Later these deeds were recorded as deaths in combat with the army. This they did during several days and very few prisoners of all those who were arrested survived. Many were forced to dig their own graves. One of the young men, when he realized the purpose of the operation, wheeled around and hit one of the assassins on the face with the pick. Others were buried alive with their hands tied behind their backs. Many solitary places serve as the cemetery for those brave men. On the rifle range alone there are five buried. Some day they will be disinterred and carried on the shoulders of the people to a monument next to the tomb of Marti which the free Fatherland will have to erect to the 'Martyrs of the Centenary.'

"The last young man who was murdered in the zone of Santiago de Cuba was Marcos Marti. He had been arrested in a cave near Siboney on Thursday the thirtieth, together with our companion Ciro Redondo. While they were taking Marti on foot up the highway, they shot him in the back and then pumped several rounds into him as he lay on the ground to finish him. When Ciro Redondo was brought to camp and Major Perez Chaumont saw him he exclaimed: 'And this fellow? Why did you bring him to me?'

"The court can hear the narrative of this incident from the lips of the young man who survived, thanks to what Perez Chaumont called: 'a stupidity of the soldiers.'

"The order was general throughout the province. Ten days after the twenty-sixth, a newspaper of this city published the news that on the highway from Manzanillo to Bayamo the bodies of two young men had been found hanged. Later it was learned that these were the cadavers of Hugo Camejo and Pedro Velez. Something extraordinary also occurred there. There were really three victims! The soldiers had taken the three out of the fort at Manzanillo at two o'clock in the morning. At a certain point on the highway they forced them out of the automobiles and beat them until they became unconscious, strangling them with a rope. But when they had already been left for dead, Andres Garcia regained consciousness and sought refuge in the house of a peasant. Thanks to him, the court could be informed of the crime with full details. This young man was the only survivor of all the prisoners that were taken in the zone of Bayamo.

"Near the Rio Cauto at a place known as Barrancas you will find at the bottom of a blind well the bodies of Raul de Aguiar, Armando del Valle and Andres Valdes, murdered at midnight on the Alto Cedro-Palma Soriano road by Sergeant Montes de Oca, officer of the guard of the Miranda fort, Corporal Maceo and the lieutenant in chief of Alto Cedro where they were arrested."

Castro told the court of an incident in a bus that picked up passengers at the Boniato prison to take them to Santiago de Cuba. A sergeant named Eulalio Gonzalez, stationed at Moncada, boarded the bus and recognized the mother of Haydee Santamaria, dressed in mourning because of the murder of her son. Gonzalez boasted in a loud voice that he had yanked out both eyes of Abel Santamaria, while the mother wept softly as she had to listen to his bragging.

"Oh, Cuba is not Cuba and those responsible for those deeds will have to suffer the terrible reckoning!" Castro exclaimed. "They are soulless men who rudely insulted the people when they removed their hats as the cadavers of revolutionaries passed by en route to the cemetery."

Castro reiterated to the court his belief that the government feared that he would cross-examine the witnesses and bring out all of the above facts and so prohibited him from continuing at the public trial.

"Señores Magistrates," he asked, "where are our companions who were arrested the twenty-sixth, twenty-seventh, twenty-eighth and twenty-ninth of July? It is known there were more than 60 in the zone of Santiago de Cuba. Only three of them and two girls have appeared. The rest of our prisoners were arrested later. Where are our wounded companions? Only five have appeared. The rest were also murdered. The figures are irrefutable. On the other hand, twenty soldiers who were our prisoners have appeared as witnesses; according to their own testimony they did not even receive a word of offense from us. Twenty wounded soldiers paraded by you, many of them wounded in street fighting, and none was killed. If the army had nineteen dead and thirty wounded, how is it possible that we have eighty dead and five wounded? Who ever saw a battle of twenty-one dead and not a single man wounded, according to the illustrious Perez Chaumont?"

To reinforce his argument that the wounded generally outnumber the dead in battles, Castro cited the figures of the invading columns during the War of Independence that marched from Oriente province to Havana. He excoriated Batista and his army for having killed defenseless prisoners. He reviewed history and his own futile efforts to persuade the courts in Havana to declare Batista's government unconstitutional and force him out of office without firing a shot. He read the laws to support his arguments and reiterated that Batista should have been sentenced to 100 years' imprisonment.

Castro was nearing the end of his protracted speech. He reminded the court that "the right of rebellion against despotism has been recognized since the most ancient times up to the present by men of all doctrines, of all ideas and all beliefs." And he cited authorities from ancient China to ancient India, Greece and Republican Rome: John Salisbury; St. Thomas Aquinas; Martin Luther; Juan de Mariana, the Spanish Jesuit of the epoch of Philip II; the French writer François Hotman; the Scotch reformers John Knox and John Poynet; John Altusio, German jurist of the seventeenth century: John Milton; John Locke; Jean Jacques Rousseau and his *Social Contract;* Thomas Paine and our own Declaration of Independence.

Castro then made this legal argument:

"Cuba is suffering a cruel and ignominious despotism, and you cannot ignore the principle that resistance against despotism is legitimate. It is a universally recognized principle, and our Constitution of 1940 consecrated it expressly in the second paragraph of Article 40: 'Adequate resistance for the protection of the individual rights previously guaranteed is legitimate.' "

The Cubans so fervently believe in that principle that at the Bogota Conference in 1948 they tried tenaciously to have it written into the Charter of the Organization of American States. Their delegation, headed by Dr. Guillermo Belt, who was then Ambassador in Washington, introduced the article at a meeting of the political committee. It was referred to a subcommittee and was debated and defeated. The Cubans reintroduced it at a meeting of the full committee. Again it was debated, and again it was defeated. Finally, the Cubans reintroduced it from the floor at the final plenary session of the entire conference, which was held in the Elliptical Salon of the Capitolio, and carried on a floor fight to urge its adoption. The resolution was defeated by a tie vote of 10 to 10 with one abstention.

"I think I have sufficiently justified my point of view," Castro said as he approached the end of his defense. "There are more reasons which assist us than the prosecutor showed in order to ask that I be condemned to twenty-six years of prison. They all concern the men who fight for the liberty and happiness of a people, none which oppress and mercilessly vilify and loot; that is

80

why I have had to bring forward many and he could advance only one. How can the presence of Batista in power, to which position he arrived against the will of the people, violating by treachery and by force the laws of the republic, be justified? How can a regime of blood, oppression and ignominy be classified as legitimate? How can the high treason of a court whose mission was to defend our Constitution be considered juridically valid? What right does it have to send to prison citizens who came to give their blood and their life for the decorum of the country? That is monstrous before the eyes of the nation and the principles of true justice!

"But there is another reason that assists us, which is more powerful than all the others: we are Cubans. To be Cuban implies a duty, and not to fulfill it is crime and treason. We live proud of the history of our country; we learned it in school and we have been raised listening to talk of liberty, justice and rights. We were taught to venerate from an early day the glorious example of our heroes and of our martyrs. Cespedes, Agramonte, Maceo, Gomez and Marti were the first names that were engraved in our brain. We were taught that Titan had said that you cannot beg for liberty but that it is conquered at the point of a machete.

"We were taught that for the education of the citizens in the free country, the Apostle [Marti] wrote in his *Book of Gold*: 'A man who conforms to obey unjust laws and allows the country where he was born to be stepped on, where the men mistreat him, is not an honest man. . . . In the world there has to be a certain amount of decorum as there has to be a certain amount of light. When there are many men without decorum, there are always others who have inside of them the decorum of many men. Those are the ones who rebel with terrible force against those who steal the liberty from the people, which is to steal from them the men of decorum. They are joined by thousands of men, by an entire people, by human dignity.'

"We were taught that the 10th of October and the 24th of February are glorious holidays of national rejoicing because they mark the days on which Cubans rebelled against the yoke of infamous tyranny [Spain]. We were taught to love and to defend the beautiful flag of the lone star and to sing every afternoon a hymn whose verses say that to live in chains is to live in opprobrium, subjected to affronts, and that to die for one's country is to live. All that we learned, and we have not forgotten it although today in our country the leaders are assassinating and imprisoning men for practicing the ideas which they were taught from the cradle. We were born in a free country willed to us by our fathers. The island will first sink into the sea before we will consent to be slaves of anyone!

"It appears that the Apostle was going to die in the year of his centenary, that his memory would have been extinguished forever, such was the affront! But he lives, he has not died, his people are rebellious, his people are worthy, his people are loyal to his memory. There are Cubans who have fallen defending his doctrines; there are young men who in magnificent retribution came to die next to his tomb, to give their blood and their life so that he can go on living in the soul of the country. Cuba, what would happen to you if you had let your Apostle die!

"I end my defense, but I will not do it as the lawyers always do, asking for the liberty of the defendant; I cannot ask that when my companions are already suffering ignominious imprisonment on the Isle of Pines. Send me to join them to share their fate. It is inconceivable that honest men are dead or jailed in a Republic where the President is not a criminal and a thief.

"To the Señores Magistrates, my sincere gratitude for having permitted me to express myself freely, without niggardly coercions; I do not hold you any rancor. I recognize that in certain aspects you have been human and I know that the President of this court, a man of clean life, could not dissimulate his repugnance for the reigning state of things that compels him to dictate an unjust sentence. There remains one more serious problem yet for the court: there are the accusations initiated for seventy murders, that is to say, the greatest massacre which we have known. The guilty continue at liberty with a weapon in hand that is a perennial threat to the life of the citizens. If over them there does not fall the weight of the law, because of cowardice or because of prohibition, and all the judges do not resign in full, I

82

pity your honors and I regret the unprecedented blotch that will fall upon the judicial power.

"As for me, I know that the jail will be hard, as it never has been for anyone, pregnant with threats, with ugly and cowardly ferociousness, but I do not fear it as I do not fear the fury of the miserable tyrant who tore away the life of seventy of my brothers.

"CONDEMN ME! IT DOESN'T MATTER! HISTORY WILL ABSOLVE ME!"

The judges convicted him and sentenced him to fifteen years' confinement in the penitentiary on the Isle of Pines.

Fidel Castro had failed in the attack on Moncada. The 26th of July, 1953, not only proved to be a heroic failure but gave birth to the name of a movement that was to make history.

CHAPTER 3

Fidel Castro was escorted from the hospital "court-room" to the Boniato prison under heavy guard. Then he was flown to the Isle of Pines with the other prisoners who had already been sentenced, including his brother Raul, who was given thirteen years, two less than the leader. The military aircraft took off from the airport at Santiago de Cuba and landed at Nuevo Gerona on the island shaped like a blown-up boomerang and swept by the breezes of the Caribbean Sea.

So in the month of October 1953 he began his confinement in the island's most modern military prison. Never one to remain idle and never discarding his plans, Castro inspired a fervent loyalty in his friends. Throughout their incarceration at Boniato they had maintained closely knit discipline. They sang revolutionary songs and talked and planned for the future. The same *esprit de corps* continued on the Isle of Pines.

Fidel Castro organized a school there. He named it the Abel Santamaria Academy in honor of his comrade who was tortured and killed in the Moncada prison. He taught his fellow prisoners history and philosophy. Later he was isolated from the group because he was considered, by the government, a dangerous influence. The Cuban Bar Association objected to this treatment but to no avail.

Castro spent his time reading assiduously; his favorite books were the works and life of Jose Marti and every volume he could possibly get on the War of Independence. Even in the confines of the prison, Fidel's influence on the Cuban political scene became felt.

Meanwhile, in Mexico City, the Inter American Press Association held its annual convention and adopted a resolution that authorized its president to cable Batista, requesting the abolition of censorship. The report of the Committee on Freedom of the Press, which I had to present in my capacity as its chairman, denounced the persecution and torture of Mario Kuchilan, columnist for the newspaper *Prensa Libre,* and the arbitrary application of censorship in Cuba. Kuchilan, a critic of the Batista regime, was arrested one night, mercilessly beaten, and his feet burned with cigarette butts. He was left half-dead on the shoulder of a lane of a little-traveled road.

Two weeks after that meeting in Mexico City Batista lifted censorship and before the end of January he abolished the ominous Law of Public Order. The pressure of continental public opinion was responsible for this.

For the first time newspapers and magazines of Cuba were able to print some of the details of the Moncada attack, together with photographs. But not many of the Cuban newspapers entertained a disposition to criticize the atrocities committed, largely because they depended on official subsidies, which they considered normal recompense for giving more prominence to news about the government.

Batista began to prepare the way for his "election" as constitutional president, with balloting scheduled for November 1, 1954. Former President Ramon Grau San Martin decided to oppose him and toured the provinces, reaching Santiago de Cuba at the start of the campaign early in 1954. A large crowd turned out for his rally but instead of cheering him the crowd shouted "Viva Fidel Castro! Viva Fidel Castro!" They clamored for his freedom.

The young lawyer had become a hero, for the people had lost faith in the old-line politicians like Grau and Prio. The latter was announcing from Miami that Batista would be overthrown. Arms cache after arms cache would be discovered by the police in Havana, thanks to the dictator's espionage system in the Florida city. The spies had penetrated Prio's household.

The first anniversary of the Moncada attack produced a crisis in Batista's cabinet. Minister of the Interior Ramon Hermida made a secret trip to the Isle of Pines and visited the prison, where he held a secret conference with Castro. Hermida's under-secretary, Rafael Diaz Balart, who was Castro's brother-in-law but an ardent Batistiano—as the dictator's followers were called—wrote an open letter to his chief (Hermida), widely published in the newspapers, in which he censured him for conferring with the "promoter of the criminal attack against the army" at Moncada. The letter produced the resignation of both Hermida and Diaz Balart.

As the presidential campaign progressed there was pressure for the granting of a general amnesty by Batista. Such an amnesty was almost set for October 1954 when Batista reneged. On the eve of the "election" Grau withdrew from the race with a denunciation that it was rigged. Batista went to the polls unopposed and was formally inaugurated on February 24, 1955, for a four-year term.

The talk urging amnesty continued after Batista's inauguration. In his cell Castro wrote a letter to a friend, Luis Conte Aguero, a newspaper columnist, in the middle of March, 1955. He rejected amnesty based on any condition that required promises by him to Batista. Castro wrote:

"My very dear friend:

"To be imprisoned is to be condemned to compulsory silence: to listen to and to read what is talked and written about, without being able to give an opinion; to suffer the attacks of the cowards who take advantage of the circumstances to attack the helpless and to make demands which, if we were not helpless, would receive our immediate reply.

"We know that we must suffer all this stoically, serenely and courageously, as part of the bitter sacrifices that all idealism demands. But there are times when all obstacles must be overcome, because the wounds to our dignity make it impossible to keep silent.

"I am not writing these lines in search of applause, which so

86

frequently is given to the superficial appearance of merit or to a theatrical gesture, while it is denied to those who do their duty simply and naturally. I write with a clear conscience in the light of the consideration, loyalty and respect I owe to the people. And when I address the people of Cuba regarding my opinion (which I should not silence for any reason of convenience) on a problem that affects us and that occupies a great deal of public attention—namely, the political amnesty—I want to do it through you as a brother, rather than a friend, and through your civic *Tribuna Libre,* requesting you at the same time to make my words available to all equally worthy organs of the radio and printed press.

"The interest that an enormous part of the citizens have shown in favor of our freedom originates in an innate sense of justice in the masses and in a deep human feeling emanating from the people, to which one is not and cannot be indifferent.

"Regarding this feeling, which already has become unavoidable, an orgy of demagoguery, hypocrisy, opportunism and bad faith has arisen. What we political prisoners think of all this is probably the question that thousands of citizens and probably not a few members of the regime are asking. The interest in this question increases when, as in this case, prisoners from Moncada are involved. Since they are excluded from the benefit of any amnesty, they are the object of all kinds of persecution and the key to the whole problem. I wonder if we are the most hated or the most feared!

"Some spokesmen have already said that even the Moncada prisoners will be included. We cannot be mentioned without the qualification of 'even,' or 'included' or 'excluded.' They doubt, they hesitate, they know for sure that if a survey were made, 99 percent of the people would request it, because it is not easy to deceive the people nor to hide the truth from them; but they are not sure of what the one percent wearing a uniform think, because they fear displeasing them and they are right when they fear it. Because they have been selfishly poisoning the hearts of the military against us, by denying facts, by clamping censorship during 90 days and a law of public order to prevent the truth of what happened from coming out! Because they do not want known whose conduct was human and who tried to prevent the acts which will be related someday by a horror-stricken historian!

"How strange has been the conduct of the regime toward us! They call us assassins in public and gentlemen in private. They fight us rancorously in public and come to meet us and know us in private. One day an army colonel with his full staff gives us a cigar, offers me a book and everybody is very courteous. Another day three cabinet ministers, smiling, affable and respectful, appear. One of them says: "Don't worry, this will pass over; I planted many bombs and I used to organize ambushes in the Country Club against Machado. I, too, was once a political prisoner."

"The usurper holds a press conference in Santiago de Cuba and declares public opinion is not in our favor. A few days later an unheard-of act takes place, namely, the people of Oriente, acting as one man at the meeting of a party to which we do not belong—which according to reporters was the biggest mobilization of the campaign—incessantly shout our name and demand our freedom. What a formidable answer from a bizarre and loyal people, who were well aware of the history of Moncada!

"It is now proper that we too answer civically the moral demand made upon us by the regime in declaring that there will be an amnesty if the prisoners and the exiled will show the right attitude and make a tacit or express agreement to respect the government.

"Once upon a time the Pharisees asked Christ whether or not they should pay tribute to Caesar. Their idea was that his answer should be displeasing either to Caesar or to the people. The Pharisees of every epoch know that trick. And so today an attempt is made to discredit us before the people or to find the pretext for leaving us in prison.

"I am not in the least interested in making the regime think that they should grant us this amnesty, for I am not worrying about it at all. What I am interested in is showing up the falsity of their demands, the insincerity of their words, the despicable and cowardly maneuver being carried out against the men who are in prison because they combated the regime.

"They have said that they are generous because they are

88

strong, but I say that they are vengeful because they are weak. They have said that they harbor no hate and yet they have talked more hate toward us than ever has been done against any group of Cubans.

" 'There will be an amnesty when there is peace.' With what moral backing can men make such a statement, when during the last three years they have been proclaiming that they made a military coup in order to bring peace to the Republic? Then, there is no peace; *ergo,* the coup did not bring peace; therefore, the government acknowledges its lie after three years of dictatorship; and it at last confesses that Cuba has had no peace from the very day they seized power.

" 'The best proof that there is no dictatorship is that there are no political prisoners.' This is what they said for many months, but today the prisons are full, and 'exile' is a common word. Therefore, they cannot say that we are living in a democratic and constitutional regime. Their own words condemn them.

"If an amnesty is to be granted, the adversaries of the regime must change their attitude. That is to say, a crime is committed against the rights of the people: we are converted into hostages, we are treated just as the people of the occupied countries were treated by the Nazis. This is why we are hostages of the dictatorship rather than political prisoners.

"In order to gain an amnesty, a prior agreement must be made to respect the regime. The cynics who suggest such a thing assume that after twenty months of imprisonment and exile the people of this island have lost their integrity under the excessive rigor imposed upon us.

"Comfortably entrenched in their juicy official positions, where they would like to live forever, they are so base as to talk in those terms to those who, a thousand times more honorable than they, are buried in the cells of the penitentiary. The writer has now been sixteen months isolated in a cell, but feels exceptionally strong, strong enough to reply with dignity.

"Our imprisonment is unjust; I do not see why those who assault army headquarters to depose the legal Constitution which was given by the people can be considered to be in the right, while those who would like to hold it up to respect are not. Nor why those who deprived the people of their sovereignty and freedom can be in the right, while those who have struggled to return it to the people are not; nor why the regime should have the right to govern the Republic against the will of the people, while we, through loyalty to its principles, languish in prison.

"Let the lives of those in power be examined, and it will be found that they are filled with shady activities, fraud and ill-gotten fortunes. Let them be compared with those who have died in Santiago de Cuba or are here in prison, unstained by dishonor. Our personal freedom is an inalienable right as citizens born in a country which does not acknowledge lords of any kind.

"We can be deprived of those rights and of everything else by force, but nobody will ever succeed in getting us to accept enjoyment of those rights through an unworthy agreement. Thus, we shall not yield one atom of our honor in exchange for our freedom.

"They are the one who should undertake to respect the laws of the Republic, for they shamefully violated them on March 10; they are the ones who should respect the sovereignty and the will of the people, for they scandalously made a mock of them on November 1; they are the ones who should propitiate an atmosphere of calm and peaceful coexistence in the country, for they have maintained unrest and anxiety in it for the last three years. The responsibility falls upon them. Without a tenth of March, a twenty-sixth of July would not have been necessary, and there would be no Cuban suffering political imprisonment.

"We are not professional agitators nor blind supporters of violence—if the better land which we hope for can be attained with the weapons of reason and intelligence. No people would follow a group of adventurers trying to sink the country in a civil war if injustice did not predominate there or if peaceful and legal means were open to the citizens to settle a civic conflict of ideas.

"We believe like Marti that 'He who starts a war that can be avoided is a criminal, and so is he who fails to start a war that is inevitable.'

"The Cuban nation will never see us starting a civil war that can be avoided, but I also repeat that whenever the shameful

90

circumstances following the cowardly coup of the tenth of March arise in Cuba, it would be a crime to fail to start an unavoidable rebellion.

"If we are to believe that a change of circumstances and atmosphere, comprising positive constitutional guarantees, were to demand a change of attitude in our struggle, we would make that change exclusively as a sign of respect to the interests and wishes of the nation, but never as a cowardly and shameful agreement with the government. And if that agreement is demanded of us in order to gain our freedom, we say point-blank: no.

"No, we are not tired. After twenty months we are as firm and unmoved as on the first day. We do not want an amnesty at the price of dishonor. We will not undergo the 'Caudinus gallows' of ignoble oppressors. We will suffer a thousand years of imprisonment rather than humiliation! A thousand years of imprisonment rather than sacrificing our dignity! We proclaim it without fear or hate.

"If what Cuba needs now are Cubans willing to sacrifice themselves to save the country from shame, we offer ourselves with pleasure. We are young and we have no illegitimate ambitions. Let the politicians fear us then, politicians who in different ways, more or less disguised, rush toward the carnival of personal appetites, forgetful of the great injustices which harm the nation.

"And far less than amnesty, we will not even demand that the prison system, through which the regime has shown us all its hate and fury, be improved. As Antonio Maceo said once: 'The only thing we would accept willingly from our enemies is the bloody scaffold that our other comrades in arms, more fortunate than we, have faced with their heads high and the peace of mind of those who died on the altar of the just and holy cause of freedom.'

"In the face of today's shameful tolerance, seventy-seven years after his heroic protest, the Bronze Titan will see in us his spiritual children."

Political and civic leaders were not satisfied with the situation, for Batista's "election" had not settled anything except his desire to remain in office. Under pressure for a peaceful solution to a latent crisis, Batista agreed to what was called a "Civic Dialogue." Selected by all quarters to head a group of representative citizens who would strive for political peace was Colonel Cosme de la Torriente, veteran of the War of Independence and former president of the League of Nations.

Formula after peace formula was presented to Batista; each one narrowed down to the need for him to agree to call new and free elections. And each time he found ways and means to reject the formula. Pressure built up, however, for the granting of amnesty and on May 2, 1955, the house of representatives passed an amnesty bill. The senate passed it the next day but Batista did not sign it until noon of Friday the thirteenth. Again Fidel Castro's life was revolving around the figure 13. He had been born on the thirteenth, he attacked Moncada on a day of double 13 and the amnesty was signed on the thirteenth.

It was expected that he and the other prisoners would be released immediately but they were confronted with judicial red tape. Meanwhile, the Hotel Isla de Pinos was filled with relatives and friends of the prisoners, as well as newsmen. Other relatives who could not obtain hotel rooms were kindly taken in by residents of Nuevo Gerona, the capital of the island.

Castro was notified of the amnesty by officers of the prison guard and by his confessor, the Reverend Father Hilario Chaurondo. He prepared for his return to freedom. On the morning of May 15 there was much activity at the prison. Bags were packed, and unwanted books and magazines were left behind for other prisoners. The reporters, who had been waiting for more than a week, were tipped off at their hotel by an opposition congressman, Conrado Rodriguez, who had visited the prison; the story of the release, he said, would break at any moment. They sped to the prison to await it on the spot.

At the prison Major Juan M. Capote, the commander, ordered them to remain at a distance from the gate. Among the first group of relatives to arrive was Lidia Castro, sister of Fidel and Raul. At 11:30 A.M., the ten first liberated came down the stairs of the commander's headquarters. They were all veterans of the attack on Moncada—Eduardo Rodriguez Aleman, Jesus Suarez Blanco, Jesus Montane, Ernesto Tizol, Gustavo Arcos,

92

Pedro Miret, Oscar Alcalde, Fidel Labrador, Ciro Redondo and Abelardo Arias.

The crowd was generally restrained by the troops of the prison guard, but one six-year-old boy broke through the lines. He rushed into the arms of his father, Jesus Montane, leaving his paternal grandmother horrified that some ill fate might befall him at the hands of the soldiers, but he was not molested. There was no sign of Mirtha Diaz Balart de Castro and Fidel, Jr. She had not come to welcome her husband as he left the prison gates.

Soon Fidel Castro walked down the steps, followed by his brother Raul. Melba Hernandez and Haydee Santamaria, who had been freed some time before, were there with Castro's sister. Lidia burst into tears as she saw Fidel and Raul.

As Fidel walked toward them and stopped, he looked at Haydee. She lowered her head with emotion and burst into tears. Not a word was spoken. The tears expressed with salty eloquence the feeling of a heroine who had lost her brother and her sweetheart for a cause.

Reporters and photographers surrounded Castro. There were motion picture, television and still cameramen. Near by stood Lieutenant Roger Perez Diaz, one of the prison-guard officers.

"I want you all to listen to me," Castro said, addressing the reporters. "I want you to know that we men of the Moncada attack are very grateful to Lieutenant Perez Diaz. He is a fine and gentlemanly officer. We have had the best of treatment from him."

He turned to Perez Diaz. "I want you, Lieutenant," he said, "and all the members of the army to know that we are not enemies of the armed forces but only adversaries. Because of the circumstances that exist in the country we were guided when we went to Moncada only by the objective to fight against the regime."

Castro and Perez Diaz locked themselves in an embrace of friendship.

"I don't want to harm you by this demonstration," Castro said, "which is an honor to both of us. I would like the newspapermen to report this objectively."

"I accept any responsibility," Perez Diaz replied. "That is

93

why I am here. I hope these things bring better days to Cuba."

Castro and the others rode away toward Nuevo Gerona and entered the Hotel Isla del Pinos. The entire population of Nueva Gerona turned out to welcome him, and crowds milled in the vicinity of the hotel for the rest of the day.

At eight o'clock that night he boarded the ferry *El Piñero* for the voyage down the Rio Las Casas to the sea. Nobody aboard tried to sleep. Tears of joy were still flowing from the eyes of beloved ones who had made the journey to the island to return home with the liberated prisoners. The ferry reached the port of Batabano in the gulf of the same name just before dawn. The passengers disembarked to board the northward-bound train for Havana. The train left Batabano at 7:45 A.M. Fidel was dressed in a *guayabera,* the comfortable Cuban shirt which hangs outside of the trousers.

A crowd gathered early at the station in Havana the next morning. The entire national committee of the Ortodoxo Party was there, headed by its president, Raul Chibas, brother of the late Eddy Chibas. All the officers and most of the members of the University of Havana Students' Federation were there. The crowd was noisy and militant but the noise subsided reverentially when the mother of Abel Santamaria walked onto the platform dressed in her mourning black.

The train arrived at 7:45 A.M., but Castro was not allowed to disembark. Instead the crowd broke into the coach. His big frame was pushed through a window, and he was grabbed by eager hands and carried on the shoulders of his admirers. A group of mothers, who had lost their sons after the Moncada attack, stood on the platform dressed in their mourning, holding a Cuban flag. They sang the Cuban national anthem as Castro emerged from the window.

The hero was carried on the shoulders of the university students to his sisters' apartment on 23rd Street in the Vedado District. With him went Haydee and Melba and Tizol, Miret, Benitez and Montane. The house was mobbed with newspapermen, photographers, relatives, friends and well-wishers. The apartment was too small for so many, and the crowd overflowed onto the sidewalk below. Fidel's *guayabera* was smudged with lip-

94

stick. His shoelaces were untied. His sister Lidia wiped the sweat from his face while his sister Emma brought him a glass of water.

An old lady dressed in black reached Castro. She had lost a son at Moncada.

"I don't know where they buried my son," she said. "I would like to find him, if only his bones are left. Help me, Fidel."

He hugged the lady tightly and both he and the bereaved mother cried. He was unashamed of his tears.

"We will look for him, *viejita*," he said. "We will look for him together." The *viejita* (little old lady), still crying, walked away after thanking Castro.

Castro had already become a legend in Cuba, and his views were sought by those who saw in him some hope for regeneration in the country.

"I do not have any intention of creating a new political party," he told Enrique Delahoza, editor of the section "In Cuba" of the popular weekly magazine *Bohemia*. "We are not abandoning our plans of co-operating for unity in the Partido Ortodoxo. We consider the designation of Dr. Raul Chibas as leader a wise choice even though it cannot be said that he has had long political experience. We are of the opinion that all the moral and healthy forces of the country should unite under the same flag and under the same slogan."

Castro was told that a petard had exploded the night before in Havana. He had a ready comment on that and for the first time, though indirectly, referred to Senator Rolando Masferrer, chairman of the armed services committee, who was to figure largely in the drama of Cuba in the near future.

"These bombs that explode every now and then," Fidel said, "are very suspicious when nobody arrests the authors of the explosions. I seriously think that they are placed by *tanquista* [army tank groups] and gangster elements desirous of maintaining a state of unrest that allows them to commit excesses. Terroristic tactics are negative and counterproductive. Nobody who is halfway sensible can think that because they place a petard in front of the door of any building the government is going to fall."

A few days after his return to Havana, which he had not seen since July of 1953, Castro appraised the political situation that confronted the country.

"I see," he said, "that there is almost unanimous sentiment for general elections and the demand is such that everyone agrees with this political equation: Political amnesty, plus a regime of positive guarantees plus immediate general elections, is equal to the peace which the Cuban people hope for so much."

But Fulgencio Batista had no intention of accepting such a logical equation, and the first person to realize that was Castro. Minister of Communications Ramon Vasconcelos barred him from the air waves. Although radio stations would invite him to speak, the government would ban him. Wherever he went he was followed by crowds of admirers, but Batista saw to it that he was also harassed by some of his own trusted hirelings.

Castro had left prison determined to overthrow Batista unless the dictator gracefully exited through honest general elections. During the months on the Isle of Pines he outlined in his own mind preliminary plans to invade Cuba from Mexico and arouse the youth of the country to take up arms to oust the dictator. He never doubted that he would succeed.

Batista's obvious persecution of Castro clipped the wings of the young man who had so eloquently denounced his enemy in the hospital room in Santiago de Cuba before three judges of the republic. Early in July 1955 he decided to leave Cuba for Mexico to prepare for his invasion.

There had been no reconciliation with his wife, but he was allowed to see his son Fidel, Jr. His sisters and some friends saw him off at the airport as he boarded the plane to Mexico City. Already waiting for him there was his brother Raul.

Raul Castro was the first to reach Mexico in exile after the release of the prisoners from the Isle of Pines. He was met by other exiles of the 26th of July Movement who had moved to Mexico from Guatemala. They introduced him to a young Argentine doctor, Ernesto Guevara. The Argentine was immediately nicknamed "Che," a form of familar prefix used in that country when addressing a man.

Guevara was the son of an architect and builder in Buenos Aires, Ernesto Guevara Lynch, whose forebears emigrated to

96

California from Argentina before the gold rush to escape the dictatorship of Juan Manuel Rosas. After the overthrow of Rosas they returned to Argentina and lived in Rosario. The son, Ernesto, Jr., was afflicted with asthma at an early age, and the family moved to Buenos Aires. I came to know the father of Che very well in the Argentine capital. He told me the story of his son's escapades and participation in two conspiracies against dictator Juan Peron. He insisted his son was a leftist but not a Communist. He had left Argentina during the Peron dictatorship to conduct research in tropical disease allergies. He practically hitchhiked his way to Guatemala which he reached in 1954 at the height of revolutionary activity against the pro-Communist government of Jacobo Arbenz.

Guevara was offered a job in the Arbenz government provided he became a member of the Communist Party. He refused, although he was in need of an income. Four days before the overthrow of Arbenz in June 1954 he offered his services to the government and was assigned to the army. Guevara claims that he offered to fight for the Arbenz government because he did not believe it was a tool of Moscow; he also was of the opinion that our State Department had been intervening against Arbenz and in behalf of Colonel Carlos Castillo Armas, the leader of the Army of Liberation.

Guevara obtained refuge in the Argentine embassy after the fall of the pro-Communist government. From there he made his way to Mexico where he was to meet Fidel Castro.

Mirtha Diaz Balart divorced Fidel Castro shortly after his arrival in Mexico. By the time Fidel had reached the 7,500-foot-high Aztec capital a bond of friendship had been established between Raul Castro and Guevara. They were joined by Jesus Montane, the third of the Moncada attackers to reach Mexico. Fidel discussed plans to return to Cuba with an invasion force, and Guevara promptly volunteered to go along as a fighter, not as a medico. More exiles began to arrive to join Fidel, among them Rafael del Pino, who had been with Castro in the Bogotazo. At the same time the number of Batista's spies in Mexico City increased.

But in the presence of Cubans Castro made no secret of his

97

plans. On the contrary, he was boldly outspoken about them. The Mexican authorities, pressured by the Cuban government, also kept close watch on Castro and his friends. Fidel began to plan to mobilize men and to purchase arms. His men would need intensive training. After much investigation he learned of the presence in Mexico City of a former colonel of the Spanish army and air force, who had had considerable experience in guerrilla warfare and had written textbooks on the subject. The man, Colonel Alberto Bayo, was an anti-Communist, anti-Franco fighter for freedom who preferred to live in exile rather than under dictatorship in his homeland.

Bayo was born in Camaguey of Spanish parents in 1892, his mother having also been born in Cuba. After Cuba gained its independence from Spain, his parents took him to the mother country and in 1912 he entered the Infantry Academy of Madrid, graduating as a second lieutenant. In 1916 he entered the Military Aviation School and was graduated as a military aviator. After that he studied aerial gunnery, bombardment and observation in the Alcazares Flying School. He was assigned to Africa as a captain of the Spanish Foreign Legion and organizer of guerrilla warfare operations. When the Spanish Civil War erupted, Bayo was aide-de-camp to General Batet, military commander of Barcelona, who later was executed by the Franco forces. From there Bayo was transferred to the War Ministry as aide to the minister. In July 1937 he commanded the republican troops in an amphibious expedition to secure the Balearic Islands. After that operation he spent the remainder of the civil war in southern Spain as commander of an air combat wing. He lost his right eye during the war. In 1939 he crossed the frontier into France and into exile. He returned to Cuba where he lived until 1942 and then proceeded to Mexico to become an instructor in the Military Air Academy at Guadalajara. Then he opened a furniture factory in Mexico City.

Fidel Castro first met Bayo at the end of 1955 when a friend brought him to the colonel's home at Avenida Country Club 67, Colonia Churubusco. What Castro saw was a stocky man with a square-jawed face. He wore a neatly trimmed Van Dyke beard.

They sat and talked casually for some time. Then Castro asked, "Could you please get me a glass of water?"

98

On his way back to the room with the glass, Bayo was intercepted by Castro who had taken pains to make certain the friend would not be listening.

"Tomorrow at four o'clock I will come to see you alone," Castro told Bayo. At the time Bayo did not know the purpose of Castro's intended visit. The next day Castro returned to Bayo's home.

"I am a Cuban lawyer," he told Bayo without wasting any time. "I want to fight with weapons in my hands against Batista. Though I am only twenty-nine years old, I know that you were in Africa and fought in guerrilla warfare against the Moors for eleven years and that you have written several textbooks on the subject. I also know you were the chief in the organization of the guerrillas in the Spanish Civil War. And you were born in Cuba. Please help me train my men."

"How many men do you have?" Bayo asked.

"Nobody yet," Castro replied with perfect frankness. "But I am going to the United States to get men and money, and I would like to know if you could be the instructor for my men."

"I will do it," Bayo replied, "but I'm afraid I don't have much faith in your possible success in such an undertaking. A young man only twenty-nine?"

"I will be successful," Castro insisted.

Castro obtained a visa from the American Embassy in Mexico City and flew to Miami in October 1955. There he conferred with exiles and with Juan Manuel Marquez, former city councilman of Marianao, a borough of Havana, who resided now in Miami. He appointed Marquez to head the underground organization of the 26th of July Movement in Miami, conferred with other exiles, collected money and proceeded to Key West and to Tampa for the same purpose. He also went on to New York.

When he returned to Mexico City and conferred again with Colonel Bayo, his pockets bulged with voluntary contributions obtained from Cuban exiles in the cities he had visited in the United States.

"I now have the money and the men," Castro told Colonel Bayo. "When can you start to train my recruits?"

"How many hours daily of training do you want?" Bayo asked.

"I want you to devote the entire day, every day of the week," Castro replied, "and I want you to come to Cuba with me."

"But what about my furniture factory in Calle Canaria 73, Colonia Portales?" Bayo protested. "I can't give that up."

"What do you want a furniture factory for?" Castro asked. "We will go to Cuba, you will come with us and we will win in three or four months."

Bayo looked at the determined young man. He must have said to himself something like: "This boy is so simpatico, so attractive, so intelligent, so convincing and so determined that I will help him."

"All right," Bayo assured Castro. "I will sell my factory and help you and I will not collect one penny of salary."

Bayo sold the factory to his manager who agreed to pay for it at the rate of 1,000 pesos [$80.00] per month. Incidentally, the manager soon sold it to someone else and Bayo never got paid.

Castro's money-raising campaign in the United States invited the enmity not only of Batista but of certain politicians, and sniping articles began to appear in newspapers and magazines. The clippings which he received from Havana irritated him and he lost little time in replying. On Christmas Day of 1955 he wrote an article which he entitled: "Against Everybody!" It was lengthy, frank and vitriolic.

"The wolf pack has come upon me," he began. "It is not Batista who is being attacked; it is I, absent abroad. That is the result of the money-grabbing political opposition, scared by the increasing strength of the revolutionary movement that threatens to oust them all from public life.

" 'Fidel, do not serve Batista!'

" 'Reply to Fidel!'

" 'Fidel is not the owner of the Country!' etc.

"A few paragraphs pointed toward the embezzlers who met in the Flagler Theater [in Miami] made the worms turn.

"The members of the regime also attack me in packs. Their daily libelous insults against me take up tons of paper. On the other hand, they shut down the only daily paper in which I used to write because they could not resist the well-reasoned and proved truth coming from those who collaborated there.

100

"Four years ago nobody bothered me. I passed unnoticed by the all-powerful lords who discussed the fate of the country. To-day, strangely, everybody is plotting against me. Why? the people will ask, What wrong has he done? Did he give up? Did he abandon his ideals? Did he change his line? Did he sell out for a position or for money? Did he betray his principles? No, far from that!

"The astonishing thing is that the mean, cowardly plot of the embezzlers and the spokesmen of the regime against a fighter who has stood up for four years without rest against the tyranny (sixteen months of silent and arduous work prior to that 26th of July, two years in prison and six months in exile) is due precisely to the contrary, namely: it is due to my having kept a firm line of conduct since March 10, when so many have changed their attitude, just as one changes one's shirt; it is due to everybody's knowing that my rebellious attitude cannot be bought for any money or position and to awareness of my loyalty to an ideal, free from all duplicity and hesitation—loyalty to the truth which I preach and practice and to a task which, although hard and thorny, I am performing successfully over and above a multitude of obstacles and powerful interests.

"The spokesmen of the Dictatorship, who insult me with so much hate and fury, would not even mention my name if I were one more of that timid kind who can look with indifference upon the crime that is being committed against Cuba. If I were a mercenary or a bootlicker, the libelous headlines they publish against me would be devoted to praising me.

"If upon leaving prison I had chosen to run for any electoral position, using my imprisonment and sacrifices as a political banner, the timid politicians who work at their profession for bread-and-water fees would have said that I was an excellent citizen, a great patriot, a sensible and civic man. That is because shamelessness is the fashion.

"If upon undertaking once more the road of sacrifice and risk, by leaving the country where the Dictatorship stupidly closed all the doors to a civic protest, I had knocked at the doors of the embezzlers to scrounge a part of the gold that they stole from the Republic to use it for the revolution, I would have instantly

101

had at my disposal hundreds of thousands of pesos, and no embezzler would have made common cause with the spokesman of the tyranny against me.

"But I did everything to the contrary.

"I gave up immediately any electoral ambition; I gave up the presidency of the Municipal Assembly of Havana, which the Ortodoxo Party offered me, which was indeed a high stepping-stone to a nomination for the second position in the Republic. I also gave up an appointment in the Executive Council that they offered me simultaneously in the same party. I gave up a salary of five hundred dollars a month that an insurance company offered me, because I do not trade on my prestige, because it is not mine but that of a cause. I gave up the salary that an important newspaper in the Capital offered me to become a co-worker of theirs, and I engaged in writing for Luis Orlando's newspaper, which could not pay anybody a single cent. I gave up everything that could mean personal calm and safety. I gave up silence, which is a comfortable refuge against defamation or danger for the timid. I denounced crimes, unmasked assassins and put the dots on the *i*'s over everything that happened in Moncada.

"I left Cuba without a cent, determined to do what others had not been able to do with millions of pesos. And far from knocking on the doors of those who had enriched themselves, I appealed to the people, visited emigrants, issued a manifesto to the country asking for help. I engaged in begging for the Fatherland, to scrape together cent by cent the necessary funds for conquering freedom.

"How comfortable and how simple, how free from sacrifice and sweat, from hard work and fatigue, it would have been to follow the easy way! The way that others, less convinced of the purity of the cause and the greatness of its people, would have adopted: to request help from those who have a lot of money because they have stolen it, to ask for a small part of their fortune in exchange for a promise of protection and respect. It would have been easy to get in good with the big shots having the money; I could have used political finagling! But no, I did all

102

to the contrary! How strange this mania to do just the opposite of what everybody has always done up to now!

"At Palm Garden, New York, I said publicly: 'The Cuban people want something more than a mere change of command. Cuba earnestly desires a radical change in every field of its public and social life. The people must be given something more than liberty and democracy in abstract terms. Decent living must be made available to every Cuban; the state cannot ignore the fate of any of its citizens who were born and grew up in the country. There is no greater tragedy than that of the man capable and willing to work, suffering hunger together with his family for lack of work. The state is unavoidably bound to provide him with it or to support him until he finds it. None of the armchair formulas being discussed today include a consideration of this situation, as though the grave problem of Cuba comprised only how to satisfy the ambition of a few politicians who have been ousted from power or who long to get there.'

"I said publicly in the Flagler: 'We will join our co-nationals bound together behind an ideal of complete dignity for the people of Cuba, of justice for the hungry and forgotten men, and of punishment for those many responsible. . . . Money stolen from the Republic is of no use to the Revolution. Revolutions are carried out on a basis of morals. A movement having to assault banks or take money from thieves is not a revolution. Belligerence cannot be granted to thieves who pretend to ingratiate themselves with the people by giving 10 percent of what they steal. We will knock at their doors after the revolution is won. . . . The embezzlers have no public opinion behind them. The embezzlers cannot be enemies of the Dictatorship because the Dictatorship is protecting their ill-gotten gains. The embezzlers prefer the tyranny to the Revolution. That is why the embezzlers want the Society of Friends of the Republic to make an agreement with the regime as the sole means of their political survival.'

"These words become truer than ever, because right now the embezzlers and the tyranny are about to make, not a gentlemen's agreement as they would like to call it in this era of shamelessness, but a bandits' agreement, the first clause of which will be to forget all of the crimes and all of the thefts and to respect all of the privileges and confirm all of the injustices.

"I was impugned in a recent article in *Bohemia* entitled 'Fidel Is Not the Whole Country' as follows: 'Nobody can really say that Fidel has taken public funds. It is also fair to state that there has been no opportunity to test his probity, because he never was a minister and never had a chance to grab at an appetizing and provoking heap of taxes, nor the impunity of taking money without leaving fingerprints. Possibly the only big money Fidel has ever had the chance to handle in his life is the money that the Cuban emigrants are now placing in his hands . . .'

"To that I can simply reply that I have handled money previously. It was not so much as what, maybe, Justo Luis del Pozo handed over to the Organizing Committee of the Autenticos Party to carry out the reorganization in connection with the electoral farce of November 1, thanks to which Batista now says that his government is constitutional and legitimate. But I handled nearly twenty thousand pesos that modest young fellows like Fernando Chenard saved by dint of a thousand sacrifices, including his selling all of his photographic equipment, with which he earned his living, or Pedro Marrero, who mortgaged his salary for several months and whom we had to forbid selling the furniture from his home, or Elpidio Sosa, who sold his job for three hundred dollars.

"How different from those fellows who on November 1, as the article in question says, as a token of civic example 'gambled their economic future in order to go to the polls by mortgaging up to their bones'! Those whose names I mention are now dead: those who 'mortgaged up to their bones' are now collecting from the Republic five thousand pesos per month in the senate.

"I handled nearly twenty thousand pesos. Yet how many times were we lacking in milk for my son! How many times did the hard-hearted electric company cut off my electricity! I still keep the miserable court papers by which the landowners dispossess tenants from the houses. I had no personal income, but practically lived on the charity of my friends. I know what it is to see a son suffering from hunger while having, in my pockets, money belonging to the cause.

104

"I never have believed that the country belongs to me. Martí said: 'The country belongs to no one, and if it did, it would be to who serves it most unselfishly, and then only in spirit.' Those who evidently have believed that the country was theirs are the embezzlers, who exploited it when they were in power as if it were private property.

"It is as unfair to say that one can be honest only when one does not handle public funds—as though our unfortunate people were incapable of producing a single honest man!—as it is to make the absurd and inconceivable statement that those who surrounded me 'were not humble emigrants, but rather happy owners of Miami real estate.' I would like to know which of those suffering Cubans who were present at our meetings and form part of the Revolutionary Clubs of Bridgeport, Union City, New York, Miami, Tampa and Key West, which of these humble co-nationals of ours—who are earning a hard living away from their homes—is a happy owner of real estate. If anyone owns a private home it would be an exception, and certainly the product of the money of honest work and not of stealing from the Republic. I saw how they lived in cramped apartments where no children are allowed, where women who are working ten hours in a factory have to wash and cook; where life is hard, tiresome and sad, and yet one hears only the exclamation: 'I would prefer to work in Cuba with only half of what I am earning here!'"

"Previously there were little more than one hundred exiles. Many were well off; their children appeared in the papers often; they longed for their friends and their homes in the native land. But nobody remembered the poor children of the emigrants, who in the northern United States had to live in a climate often many degrees below zero, who had no school where they could learn their mother tongue, nor doctors who could understand the language of their fathers. To say that they are happy real estate owners shows the resentment of the politicians against the Cuban emigrants, because those tens of thousands of families away from Cuba constitute a live and grievous accusation against the bad governments that the Republic has had to tolerate. The politicians used to say that the Cuban problem will be solved when the exiles can return to Cuba.

"We say that the problem of Cuba will be solved when the emigrants can go back.

"Likewise, when it is said capriciously in that same article in *Bohemia* that 'I recommended that my friends vote for Grau because I was thinking of the prompt freedom by means of his justice,' an evident lack of seriousness and capacity is shown which could disqualify anybody saying so from entering into discussions of public affairs or from rendering public service. I never made such a recommendation, because I do not become involved in such contradictions of principles. I would give up public life if they would show me the copy of *Bohemia* in which that statement appears.

"I could hardly have been aspiring to freedom by way of that undignified cause when, at the time of the most heated public discussion of whether amnesty should or should not include the men who attacked the Moncada—and they were speaking of the prerequisites of its granting—I wrote a letter in *Bohemia* saying: 'If an agreement is demanded of us in order to gain our freedom, we say point-blank: no. No, we are not tired. After twenty months, we are firm and unmoved as on the first day. We do not want an amnesty at the price of dishonor. We will not undergo the "Caudinus gallows" of ignoble oppressors. We will suffer a thousand years of imprisonment rather than humiliation! A thousand years of imprisonment rather than sacrificing our dignity!'

"Only a lowdown person, lacking themes for an argument, or a coward convinced that I am engaged in a cause, above personal grievances, which prevents me from calling him to account, would dare to say so irresponsibly that I had attacked 'colleagues and men who were also pure idealists in their own way.' I would have no need to resort to lies in order to combat an adversary, because I have a reservoir more than enough from which to draw facts and reasons.

"It is possible that if the writer of that article believes what he says, he would not have the courage to say it, because I never saw him writing an article against the gangsterism that was in full swing at the time.

"My enemies are so unfounded in their attacks upon me, that they resort to digging up the old calumnies from the govern-

106

mental sewers, as good allies of the tyranny against the revolution.

"Every time that my opponents tried the vile trick of involving me in acts of the kind, I stood up resolutely against their slander, I appealed to the courts, and well-reputed judges like Hevia or Riera Medina (there are few like them) can attest to my innocence. Thousands of students who are today professional men saw my actions in the university for five years. I have always counted on their support (because I have always fought with the weapon of public denouncement by resorting to the masses); it was with their co-operation that I organized great meetings and protests against the existing corruption. These men can be witnesses to my conduct. There they saw me, from the beginning, without experience but full of youthful rebellion, take a stand against the power of Mario Salabarria (I refrain from personal attacks, because he is in prison and it is not right to judge a person who cannot defend himself). It would be proper to ask a prior question, namely, why is Mario Salabarria in prison and not those who assassinated eighty prisoners in Moncada? I will only say by way of information that at that time, in the first years of Grau's government, Salabarria was in charge of all the police forces of repression, no less than those of today, and he was the master of Havana.

"In an era of unprecedented corruption, when many youthful leaders had access to dozens of government positions and so many were corrupted, to have led student protests against that regime for several years, without ever having appeared on a government payroll, is worthy of some merit.

"It is unheard-of, cynical and shameless that the sponsors, protectors and subsidizers of that gangsterism should now use this kind of argument to combat me. Could they be any more barefaced? To mention gangsterism in the humble home of the Great Pretender is like talking about the rope in the home of the person hanged. The members of the regime are in the same situation. They shipped Policarpo Soler off to Spain loaded with money and, on the other hand, murdered 'El Colorado' on Durege Street. It should be mentioned with respect for the latter, that by dying in active opposition to the tyranny, he vindicated himself after his errors.

"Strange things took place before the tenth of March! Very

strange things, if it is remembered that those who bombed the 'Ingelmo' shoe store and the killers of Cossio del Pino have never appeared.

"Since they are forcing me to do so, will it be necessary for me to again publish the statement I filed with the Court of Accounts on March 4, 1952, which was published in *Alerta* on the following day, naming and denouncing one by one the persons occupying the 2,120 positions that the groups had in the Ministries? Who ever dared to file such a statement? It certainly was not Batista, who lived at his Kuquine farm thoroughly protected by Carlos Prio and who had permission to go around armed and with a personal guard. I walked the streets of Havana alone and unarmed.

"Suffice it now to quote a paragraph with which I opened the statement which was a premonition: 'I appeal to the Court of Accounts patriotically to ask the miracle that may save the nation from the constitutional disaster that threatens it.' The miracle did not occur, and one week later the disaster of March 10 was a reality. Gangsterism was a pretext, but the man who invoked it had been one of the mainsprings of it when he encouraged the organization of the University goons through Jaime Marine.

"The evil that germinated in the Autentico Party had its roots in the resentment and hate that Batista sowed during eleven years of abuse and injustice. Those who witnessed the murder of their colleagues wanted to avenge it, and the regime that was not capable of doing justice allowed such vengeances. The blame cannot be placed upon the young men who, influenced by natural anxiety and the legend of the heroic era, longed for a revolution that at that time could not have been carried out. Many of those who, victims of deceit, died as gangsters might have been heroes today.

"The revolution that has not been achieved at the time when it can be achieved will be carried out so that the mistake is not repeated, and there will be justice instead of vengeance. When justice is done, nobody will have the right to pretend to be a wandering avenger and the full weight of the law will fall upon him. Only the people, constituting sovereign power, has a right to punish or pardon. There never has been justice in Cuba; to

108

send a poor person to jail for stealing a chicken, while the big-time embezzlers in power enjoy immunity, is simply an unjustifiable crime. When did we ever hear of our judges of correction courts sentencing a powerful person? When did an owner of a sugar mill ever go to jail? When has a rural guard ever been arrested? Can it be that they are pure? Can they be saints, or is it that in our social order justice is a vile lie applied when it suits certain interests?

"The fear of justice is what has put the embezzlers and the tyranny into agreement.

"The embezzlers, bewildered at the shouts of *Revolution!* that thunder with increasing force, like bells calling the evil to final judgment, have listened to the prudent words of Ichaso in his column of *Bohemia* dated December 4, 1955: 'Fidel Castro becomes a competitor too dangerous for certain heads of the opposition, who during three and a half years have not succeeded in taking the right attitude toward the Cuban situation. They know it only too well. They now feel that they have been displaced by the volume of the 26th of July Revolutionary Movement in the battle against the 10th of March. The logical reaction of the politicians in the light of this evident fact should be to take a resolute stand of political action in the face of the revolutionary action of Fidelismo.'

"The embezzlers have hearkened to the cordial appeal made to them by the Batistiano Havana alderman Pedro Aloma Kessel in a government paper dated December 14: 'All of us without exception are deeply interested in stopping Fidel Castro's insurrectional plans. If we sleep at the rudder and continue stubbornly, closing all political solutions, we shall be opening the revolutionary road to Fidel Castro. I would like to see who, either from opposition or from the government, are going to save us if Fidelismo wins out in Cuba.'

"They know that I left Cuba without a cent; they know that I have not knocked at the doors of the embezzlers and yet they fear that we shall start a revolution. In other words, they acknowledge that we can get the backing of the people.

"The nation is at the point of witnessing the great betrayal of the politicians. We know that for us, who maintain a dignified position, the struggle will be hard. But we are not frightened by the number of enemies before us. We shall defend our ideals in the face of all. To be young is to feel within oneself the strength of one's own destiny, to be able to think of it against outside resistance and to sustain it against the interests.

"The political business of opposition is fully discredited and decadent. First they demanded a neutral government and immediate general elections. Then they stopped at demanding only general elections in 1956. They are no longer talking about a particular year. They will end up by taking off their last fig leaf and accepting any arrangement with the Dictatorship. They will not discuss a question of principles, but only details of time so as to plunder the budget of the unfortunate Republic.

"But the real piece of business will not be so easy as they think! The people are alert! The peasants are tired of speeches and promises of land reform. They know that they cannot expect anything from the politicians. A million and a half Cubans who are unemployed because of the incapacity, avarice and lack of foresight on the part of all the bad governments we have had know that nothing can be expected of the politicians.

"Thousands of sick persons without beds or medicines know that they cannot expect anything from the politicians, who seek their votes in exchange for a little favor and whose business thrives on the always large number of needy people whose sanction can be bought for little.

"The hundreds of thousands of families living in huts, open sheds, empty lots and tenements, or paying exorbitant rentals; laborers who earn wages of hunger, whose children have neither clothes nor shoes for school; citizens who pay for electric current at a price higher than in any other country in the world, or who requested telephone service ten years ago still to no avail; and finally, all those who have had to suffer or do suffer those horrors of a miserable existence know that they have nothing to expect from the politicians.

"The people know that with hundreds of millions exported by the foreign trusts, plus the hundreds of millions that the embezzlers have stolen, plus the graft that thousands of parasites have taken without rendering service or producing anything for the

110

community, plus the losses of all kinds caused by gambling, vice, black market, etc., Cuba would be one of the most prosperous and richest countries of America, without emigrants, without unemployed, without starving people, without unbedded sick people, without illiterate people and without beggars. . . .

"From political parties or from organizations headed by protected friends (male and female) for the purpose of appointing congressmen, senators and mayors, the people can expect nothing. From the REVOLUTION, which is an organization of combatants, united in a great patriotic ideal, they expect everything and they will get it!"

As in his eloquent argument before the court at Santiago de Cuba, Castro reiterated his plan for the new Cuba, free from graft and corruption and replete with social reforms. He was bitter against the large American corporations who ship most of their profits abroad. What he probably did not recall, though, was the fact that the Prio regime had enacted a law which required all companies to pay dividends that fluctuated anywhere from 35 to 100 percent and therefore left no reserves for reinvestment. Some of the companies might have been pleased with such a law, but others, like Sears, Roebuck and Company, would have preferred to see it stricken from the statute books to enable them to reinvest their profits in Cuba, help finance factories to manufacture some of the products they sell and to build more stores.

Castro found an outlet for his written thoughts in the magazine *Bohemia,* whose editor and publisher, Miguel Angel Quevedo, defied possible reprisals by the government. After Batista's coup of March 10, 1952, Quevedo published an editorial in which he censured the overthrow of constitutional government and warned Batista that his regime would produce only persecution, death and sorrow for the people of Cuba.

Back in Mexico City, Bayo began a search for a suitable place to train Castro's men. Preliminary instruction was to take place in the Aztec capital. Castro rented ten houses and billeted eighty "students" in them. Bayo went from house to house in different sectors of the city under the guise of an English teacher (he speaks the language very well), and began to cram into the men selected for the expeditionary force all the instruction they would receive in a three-year course at a military academy—within the short space of three months. It was grueling work for the young men and more grueling for the sixty-four-year-old soldier-professor.

Bayo's instruction included operations in light campaign, fortifications, armament, mortars, organization of aviation, use of aviation against guerrillas, the way to fight airplanes from the ground, observation against aircraft, vulnerability of formations, manufacture of chemical bombs, dynamite bombs, combination of time bombs with explosives, grenades, anti-tank mines, anti-personnel mines, topography, map and sketch work—preparing maps and sketches on scales of from 1:500,000 down to 1:10,000—campaign sketches, general staff organization, cover for air attacks, trenches and foxholes against air attacks, infantry tactics, closed ranks exercises, the tactics of "minuet"—to retreat when the enemy advances and to advance when the enemy retreats, to attack at night from all sides and withdraw before daybreak but not to lose contact with the enemy and not to fire at him at all during daylight.

This instruction got under way early in 1956. To find a place for field training, Bayo undertook to reconnoiter the not too proximate vicinity of Mexico City with Ciro Redondo, who also had rejoined Fidel. Bayo found a large rancho owned by a Mexican named Rivera at a place called Chalco in the state of Mexico, twenty-five miles away on the Popocatepetl-Sleeping Lady volcano road that leads to Cuautla. Rivera had been a fighter with Pancho Villa, and General Pershing's troops had, presumably, executed him in the Chihuahua cemetery. But he rose as if from the dead and crawled his way to a native shack where he was given help and lived to own a rancho grande.

Bayo liked the looks of Chalco. It was six miles long by ten miles wide and buried itself inside the mountains. It was protected by towers and a ten-foot-high wall. Fidel Castro had given him a ceiling of 3,000 pesos ($240.00) a month for rental for a training ground. That was too low a rent for Rivera, so Bayo proposed its purchase. Rivera asked 300,000 pesos for it, but

112

there was not that much money available. Bayo countered with an offer to buy it at that price, provided Rivera would let him have the property on a six-month trial basis. Rivera agreed and accepted 100 pesos a month rental on the trial basis. After the provisional deal was closed, Bayo told Rivera that he was going to put eighty men to work on the property for cattle-ranching purposes. Rivera made no objection.

Bayo moved Castro and his students to Chalco and started them on their field training. They were given target practice with rifle, machine gun and pistol, exercises in medical aid to the wounded, administering first aid and the carrying of litter patients. They were taken on forced marches with Bayo and Castro at the head of the column—five hours the first day, then seven hours, then nine hours, then eleven, twelve, thirteen, fourteen and fifteen hours a day, marching into the mountains and up the hills, cutting trails, taking cover, simulating ambush attacks and withdrawals. They marched with full packs, crawling along the ground with rifle and machine-gun fire overhead, and they camped in the mountains for several days at a time.

CHAPTER 4

Castro had now been out of Cuba for six months. The progress he had made in the planning and organization of his invasion-revolution was already truly remarkable. In the midst of all that activity he never took his eye off political developments within Cuba. And he had become thoroughly disillusioned with the vacillations and compromising attitude of the leaders of his own Ortodoxo Party.

On March 19, 1956, he decided that the moment had arrived to divorce himself entirely from the veteran politicians and to pursue his revolutionary plans without the apparent support of the party to which he had belonged. At the same time he decided he would not obligate himself either to the Ortodoxo Party or to any other political party.

Castro wrote of his disillusionment and made absolutely no effort to hide the fact that he was embittered by the lack of forthrightness within the Ortodoxo Party, whose national executive committee had virtually pulled the supporting rug from under his feet. He announced the formal and definitive organization of the 26th of July Movement as an independent revolutionary organization that would fight to overthrow Batista, punish grafters, embezzlers and murderers and reform Cuba. Never once did he doubt he would be triumphant. He emphasized this confidence at all times in every one of his written communications as well as in his oral conversations.

"The names of those who impede the task of liberating their country should be recorded in the same place of infamy and shame as the names of those who oppress it," he wrote. "In Cuba there are, unfortunately, a great number who have up till now done absolutely nothing to redeem it from tyranny while, at the same time, they have interfered as much as possible.

"Those of us who have not rested one minute in doing our rough and hard task for years know it quite well.

"When we left the prison ten months ago, we understood quite clearly that the rights of the people would never be restored if a decision were not reached to conquer those rights with their very blood. So we engaged in creating a strong revolutionary organization and preparing it with the necessary elements to fight the final battle with the regime. That was not the hardest part for us who have made this our lifework.

"The struggle that has become more arduous and fatiguing has been against the bad faith of the politicians, the intrigues of incapable persons, the envy of the mediocre, the cowardice of the interests and that kind of low and cowardly plotting which always arises against any group of men who attempt to do something great and worthy where they live.

"The military coup that plunged the country into despair and chaos was an easy task. It took the people and the government by surprise. It was conceived secretly by a handful of amoral persons, who moved around freely and perpetrated their criminal plans while the nation, confident and innocent, slept. In a few hours Cuba, normally a democratic country, became, in the eyes of the world, one more link in the group of Latin-American nations enchained by tyranny. The task of restoring its international prestige, of recovering the liberty which had been snatched from its people and of returning to a new era of true justice and redemption for those suffering most from hunger and exploitation is, on the other hand, by a bitter paradox, incomparably harder and more exacting.

"We have been fighting for four years to rebuild what was destroyed in a single night. We are fighting against a regime that is alert and fearful of the inevitable attack. We are fighting against political gangs that apparently—contrary to the situation—

115

are not interested in a radical change in the life of the country; rather they want to push it further back to the deadly and sterile policy whereby legislative offices are fabulously remunerated and high political offices, with the fortunes attached thereto, can be assured for a lifetime and, if possible, be made hereditary. We are fighting against the intrigues and maneuvering of men who speak in the name of the people but do not have their backing; and against the false prophets who preach wickedly against the revolution in the name of peace, while forgetting that in the homes hunger, fear and mourning stalk and there has been no peace in the last four years. We are fighting those who shout anathema against our uncompromising stand, offer the poison of their electoral compromise as a cure-all and, at the same time, take good care to hide their complex maneuvering and mediations, which during the fifty-four years of our republican life have not only failed to cure the evils at their roots, but have produced the horrifying misery of the peasantry and the industrial poverty of our cities. The result of their machinations has been that hundreds of thousands of our families, descendants of our liberators, are without a piece of land and more than a million persons are without employment. To our disgrace some forty-five percent of our population are illiterate. Compare all this with the fortunes, the properties, the palaces and the personal progress attained by hundreds of politicians throughout our republican existence. Money stolen, invested in Cuba, in the United States and all over the world. And all of this has become so natural—by putting aside the most elemental justice—and moral concepts have become so contradictory and paradoxical that the Society of Friends of the Republic, for example, recently made dramatic declarations against the common amnesty, based on the danger to the community if crimes were allowed with impunity! At the same time, they sat in solemn discussions with Anselmo Alliegro, Santiago Rey, Justo Luis del Pozo and other government figures on whose shoulders, as representatives of the present and past situations, involving blood and thefts, there rests more blame than all that could be put upon all the occupants of the prisons of the Isle of Pines together.

"But I do not conform to the political fatalism under which we

116

have lived up to the present; I want my country to have a better destiny, a more decent public life. I wish a higher moral level for all, because I believe that the nation does not exist for the exclusive benefit and privilege of a few, but belongs to all. I say that each and every one of its present six million inhabitants, and of the millions that will populate it in the future, is entitled to a decorous life, to justice, work and well-being. With incomparable disinterest hundreds of men of our generation are now fighting for that ideal, without shrinking from any risk or sacrifice, without hesitating to give up the best years of life and youth. Yet our opponents attempt to show us, in the eyes of the public, as being little more than outcasts of society, or capricious advocates of a line of action not considered as honorable, loyal and patriotic.

"This article, therefore, is not exclusively a reply to the last one published against us in the magazine *Bohemia* by one who, forgetting the many ties of comradeship in the struggle—as though it were convenient to deny them in moments of adversity—described the opinion of the official leaders of the mediators' group of the Ortodoxo Party. It is also a reply to all those who attack us in either good or bad faith; it is a reply to the politicians who disown us either because it suits them or through cowardice; it is the reply on behalf of our entire Movement, to many merely blind and to all those puny coxcombs who have no faith in their country.

"First, to clear up concepts and to put things in their place, I repeat here what I said in the message to the congress of militant Ortodoxo members, on August 16, 1955: 'The 26th of July Revolutionary Movement does not constitute a tendency within the party: it is the revolutionary apparatus of Chibasism [the followers of Eduardo R. Chibas] which is rooted in the masses and from which it arose to fight against the dictatorship when the Ortodoxo Party lay impotent and divided into a thousand pieces. We have never given up those ideas of ours and we have remained faithful to the purest principles of the Great Combatant, whose fall we commemorate today.'

"That message proclaiming the revolutionary line was unanimously approved by five hundred representatives of the Ortodoxo Party from all parts of the island, who stood up to applaud it for a full minute. Many of the official leaders were present and none

117

of them spoke up against it. From that moment the revolutionary thesis was the thesis of the members of the party, who had expressed their sentiments unequivocally, but from that minute the members and the leaders started to follow different directions.

"When did the militants of the party annul that agreement? It could not have been at the provincial mass meetings where the unanimous shout was 'Revolution! Revolution! Revolution!' And who but us sustained the revolutionary thesis? And what group could carry it into effect but the revolutionary apparatus, that group of followers of Eduardo Chibas—that is to say, the 26th of July Movement?

"Seven months have elapsed since then. What have the official leaders done from that day but defend the thesis of dialogue and mediation? What have we done? Defended the revolutionary thesis and given ourselves to the task of carrying it out effectively. What was the result of the former? Seven months hopelessly lost. What was the result of the latter? Seven months of fruitful efforts and a powerful revolutionary organization that will soon be ready to go into combat.

"I am speaking about facts, not about fancies; in words well founded and proved, not on sophisms. We could prove that the enormous majority of the members of the party—the best of them— follow the line, and yet we do not go about proclaiming it every day, nor talking in the name of the Ortodoxo Party as others do, whose backing is, at this juncture, very questionable.

"A lot of water has run under the bridge since the last reorganization of the party five years ago, and who says that leaders are eternal, or that situations do not change, and even more in a convulsion which changes everything with dazzling speed? Things change so much that somebody like Guillermo de Zendegui, a product of that reorganization, is now comfortably installed in the government!

"On the other hand, it is not yet known in what part of Oriente Raul de Aguiar and Victor Escalona, delegates from the glorious municipal assembly of Havana, are buried, after their assassination by the regime. It would have been well to inquire about that among the governmental commissioners present at the affable

118

meetings of the Civic Dialogue, where electoral offices were re-membered—but not the dead.

"It is timely to point out that an examination of my record in the past, where I was seen by all fighting incessantly, does not show me to be appearing in any office nor as taking part either before or after March 10 in those disgraceful discussions that did such harm to the faith of the party masses. Newspapers are full of those quarrels, and yet my name appears in none. I devoted my time and my energies entirely to organizing the struggle against the dictatorship, without any backing from the exalted leaders. The unpardonable thing is that history repeats itself and that at a moment when the Civic Dialogue breaks up and the facts show how right we were—when it was to be expected that the party machinery would back the Movement—we have received from it the most unjustifiable aggression, using as a low-down pretext an incident for which we are not in the least responsible.

"They have chosen to quote that ridiculous episode as a heroic triumph—but not against Batista, rather against the Movement that is in the vanguard of the struggle against the regime. Besides being false, a plain lie, the supposed victory will be a Pyrrhic one! It is the height of infamy that now they are trying to absolve me from all blame and to put the full weight of the intrigue on the shoulders of my self-denying colleagues who are the national leaders of our Movement. They do this to our Movement, which in Cuba is waging the stiffest and most risk-laden fight, without ever appearing in any newspaper, because they know how to suffer in silence, have no longing for publicity and do not practice the disgraceful exhibitionism indulged in by those who under the hood of patriotism are even now campaigning for aldermen, congressmen and senators. The names of those leaders of our Movement do not appear publicly today, but later they will appear in history. The envious detract from them now, but if any of them fall in battle, those same ones who slander them would not hesitate to invoke their names in political speeches as martyrs even while asking for the vote of the audience.

"I do not want to sharpen my pen so as to permit my calm indictment to be called a merciless attack, as was done to my previous article. But I will not stop before clearing up the points of principle, in order to demonstrate who have interpreted best the ideals of the founder of the Ortodoxo Party.

"Let us make a brief journey into the history of the Party subsequent to March 10. As the result of the Montreal meeting, it was divided into three groups. The interminable clashes between Agramonte and Ochoa became a schism at the time when Pardo Llada made a motion at the 'Artistica Gallega' assembly in favor of reaching an understanding with the other parties for the insurrection against the regime. The group in favor of maintaining a line of political independence declared, through a dramatic speech by Professor Bisbe, that there was no reason for a discussion because the question of principle was involved; therefore, they left the meeting completely. From there on three tendencies arose: the Montrealists, the independents, and the electoralists. The independent group threw Pardo Llada out because he sat down in Montreal with Tony Varona, Hevia and other *auténticos,* and because they alleged that he had violated the line of independence. The Montrealist group, in turn, qualified the position of the independent group as static and inoperative. Both of them threw the electoralist group out, alleging that it had chosen to follow the election legislation of the dictatorship. The party members fell into a state of complete despair and disorder. Many sincere Ortodoxo members signed up with Aureliano Sanchez Arango's 'Triple A,' considering that any road was good for ousting the regime; others could not overcome the scruples of their conscience, which had been awakened by the denouncements of the line of Chibas independence; and still others, although certainly the fewest, drifted into the electionist group.

"The Ortodoxo members who sympathized with the Montreal group were not satisfied, owing to their doubts about its ideological position; the followers of the independent group, in turn, were irked by the lack of action. It was then, in the midst of that chaos, that there arose in the ranks of the party a Movement that was capable of satisfying the true aspirations of the people, owing to its projection; a Movement which, without violating the Chibas line of independence, resolutely assumed revolutionary action against the regime; a Movement which could not create qualms

120

of conscience in anyone wishing to do his duty in a totally clean way: that was the 26th of July Movement.

"The question to be asked is not whether we were successful that first time; neither was Chibas successful in 1948, albeit it was a moral victory. The question to be asked is what could be done with a group without a party name, without resources of any kind, but possessed with everything that could be expected of decent and dignified men. The question to be asked is whether success would not have been possible if we could have counted on the backing of the party.

"I am one of those who firmly believe that Batista would not be in power today if in the moment of the military coup the Ortodoxo Party—with its fine moral principles and the immense influence of Chibas among the people, its fine reputation even among the Armed Forces, since the propaganda spread against the party that was thrown out of power could not be directed against them—had stood up resolutely against the regime through revolutionary action.

"As a means of calculating the possibilities of collecting funds for the struggle, it is enough to remember the public collection of one cent per person to free Millo Ochoa, which in twenty-four hours amounted to seven thousand pesos! Men and women on the street would say: 'If it were for the Revolution, I would give ten dollars instead of one cent.'

"Three years have passed since then and only the Movement has maintained its posture and its principles. The independent group which excommunicated those who attended the Montreal meeting because they sat down there with the representatives of other parties, we now see on the Pier of Light, seated with the leaders of the parties they had previously rejected. It is curious that those who rejected an understanding with the other parties for a revolutionary action join, now, with the same parties to beg for general elections; and more curious yet that all those who excommunicated the registration group because they accepted a law of the regime, meet now with the delegates of the dictatorship to implore an electoral agreement.

"And what infamy! There, in that same meeting, in the presence of the adulators of the dictator, the delegate of the Ortodoxo mediation faction declared that 'the line of Fidel Castro does not have the support of the Executive Committee.' Our line was, however, the line unanimously approved in the Congress of Ortodoxo Militants on August 16, 1955. Today they renege and disavow my name. They did not renege, though, when, on my leaving the two years of honorable imprisonment which I suffered, they needed a statement of my adhesion to strengthen the weakened prestige of the official leadership. Then my modest apartment was constantly honored with the visits of those same leaders. Today, when to support the worthy line of him who has honestly fulfilled his duty may be dangerous, it is logical that they intone a *mea culpa* before the demanding delegates of the tyranny.

"It is true that later that delegate defended us; he defended us in his way. He said our attitude was justified because the regime had shut off every opportunity for us to act in Cuba. And I ask the group in whose name the delegate spoke: if our line was justified because the regime closed to us every possibility of acting in Cuba, is not the adoption of that line by a party from which victory was snatched eighty days before elections and which for four years has been unable to act in Cuba more than justified?

"The mediation has turned out to be a complete failure. We were resolutely opposed to it because we discovered from the first instance a maneuver of the regime whose only purpose since the 10th of March has been to perpetuate itself indefinitely in power. Behind the formula of the Constitutional Assembly is the intention to re-elect Batista until the end of his term. But in the first place the dictatorship proposed to gain time, and that it has fully achieved, thanks to the prodigious ingenuity of Don Cosme de la Torriente, whom first they insulted, later praised and now insult again. Batista received him in the palace in the most critical days of his government when the country was in convulsion because of the heroic student rebellion and the formidable movement of the sugar workers in demand of the differential which had not been given to them. Batista needed a pause: he summoned Don Cosme again fifteen days later. In the first interview he gave the impression that he would grant everything; in the second, he showed more reserve, and gained in this way almost three months until the 10th of March, when from Camp Columbia, in the midst of

122

the full Civic Dialogue, he effected another coup against the expectant opposition delegates.

"If they did not believe in the results of the dialogue what did they expect to accomplish by attending the talks? Was it necessary to show up the regime before the people? Do the people need to be shown that this regime is an atrocity and a shame for Cuba? For that was it worth while to lose so many months that could have been dedicated to another type of struggle? Or did somebody by chance sincerely believe in finding a solution through that course? Can one be so ingenuous? Is it not sufficient to observe how the principal chiefs and officials of the regime openly enrich themselves and buy farms, residential districts and businesses of every kind in the country, in view of the nation, showing the intention to remain in power for many years? Do not the statue of Batista at Camp Columbia and the modern arms of all types that he is constantly acquiring say anything?

"It is really dishonest to go and sit down there with the delegates of the government when it is not yet known where many men whom the regime has assassinated have been buried; when not one of those who have killed more than a hundred compatriots has been punished. And the dead: will they be forgotten? And the ill-gotten fortunes: will they be reclaimed? And the treachery of March 10: will it remain without punishment so that it can be repeated? And the ruin of the Republic, the frightful hunger of hundreds of families: will that remain without hope of real and true solution? It is not our fault if the country has been conducted toward an abyss from which there is no other saving formula than revolution. We do not love force. We do not love violence. Because we detest violence we are not disposed to go on supporting the violence which for four years has been exercised on the nation.

"Now the fight is of the people. And in order to help the people in its heroic fight to regain the freedoms and rights that were snatched from them, the 26th of July Movement has been organized and strengthened.

"The 26th of July against the 10th of March!

"For the Chibas masses the 26th of July Movement is not different from the Ortodoxo Party: it is the Ortodoxo without a

123

leadership of landholders of the type of Fico Fernandez Casas, without sugar barons of the type of Gerardo Vazquez; without stock-market speculators, without magnates of industry and commerce, without lawyers for big interests, without provincial *caciques,* without small-time politicians of any kind. The best of the Ortodoxo is fighting this beautiful fight together with us. To Eduardo Chibas we offer thus the only homage worthy of his life and his holocaust: the liberty of his people, which those who never have done anything other than shed crocodile tears over his grave will never be able to offer.

"The 26th of July Movement is the revolutionary organization of the humble, for the humble and by the humble.

"The 26th of July Movement is the hope of redemption for the Cuban working class, who will never get anything from the political cliques; it is the hope of land for the peasants who live like pariahs in the country that their grandfathers liberated; it is the hope of return for the emigrants who had to leave because they could not live or work in it; it is the hope of bread for the hungry and justice for the forgotten.

"The 26th of July Movement makes its own the cause of all those who have fallen in this hard fight since March 10, 1952, and calmly proclaims before the nation, before their wives, their sons, their fathers and their brothers that the Revolution will never compromise with their killers.

"The 26th of July Movement is the warm invitation to close ranks, extended with open arms to all revolutionaries of Cuba, without niggardly partisan differences, whatever may have been the previous differences.

"The 26th of July Movement is the sound and just future of the country, the honor pawned before the people, the promise that will be fulfilled."

There were other dramatic events that were to have a bearing on Castro's plans and future operations. On April 4, 1956, a military conspiracy to overthrow Batista was discovered. Behind the conspiracy was a civilian group known as "Montecristi," and the military leaders were two young army officers, Colonel Ramon Barquin, Cuba's representative on the Inter American Defense

124

Board, and Lieutenant Colonel Enrique C. Borbonnet, the tank commander at Camp Columbia. When it was decided to postpone H-hour for three days, somebody talked inadvertently and Barquin, Borbonnet and other officers were arrested, tried, convicted and sentenced to six years and more in the military prison on the Isle of Pines. Dr. Jose Miro Cardona, dean of the Havana Bar Association, defended Barquin at the court-martial.

The Barquin conspiracy was planned to end Batista's rule and prevent the blood bath that was certain to follow in Cuba. If it had succeeded, Justo Carrillo, who had been President of the Industrial, Agricultural and Development Bank (Banfaic) under Prio, and whose honesty and integrity were universally recognized, would have become president of a provisional government. The conspiracy had absolutely no link with Prio.

Twenty-five days later a group of men trying to emulate Castro at Moncada attempted to capture the Goicuria army fort at Matanzas. It was a Sunday afternoon, April 29, 1956. Ten of the men were captured and killed inside the fort following their successful penetration of the gate by truck. An eleventh body was mysteriously added to the list of casualties.

I interviewed Batista at the palace a few days later, and he blamed everything that had happened at Goicuria on Prio. He also made some unkind remarks about Trujillo. He revealed that Trujillo's ambassador in Havana had made an offer to Senator Rolando Masferrer, attempting to enlist the senator's aid in a plot to oust Batista. Masferrer recorded the conversation on a portable tape recorder and then called on Batista. He played back the conversation for his chief. Not many days passed before the ambassador, Fernando Llaverias, was removed from his post in Havana.

After the general amnesty of May 1955, Prio had been allowed to return to Cuba and was living on his La Chata estate when the Goicuria attack took place. In my interview Batista had given me no indication of his plans, but the following day Prio was summarily exiled to the United States. He landed in Miami without baggage and wearing a *guayabera*. Prio lived in exile for the remainder of Batista's tenure.

The Cuban embassy in Mexico City and the Batista govern-

125

ment in Havana denounced Castro's conspiratorial activities to the Mexican police. As a result the first of a series of detentions was made by the federal authorities, who arrested Castro for questioning.

One of the detentions occurred in June 1956. A police car was pursuing some thieves on a highway outside Mexico City. Castro, Calixto Morales and Captain Alberto Bayo, Jr.—aviator son of the instructor—were traveling on a lateral road, returning to Chalco. The thieves' car reached the lateral road at a place known as Tepito. Castro's car was halted by the police, who thought it to be the thieves'. The police opened fire; Castro and his companions, not knowing the reason for the attack, found themselves caught in a virtual ambush. They were surrounded by police and arrested. The police searched Castro's car and found it full of weapons. After the police had questioned Castro and his party, they proceeded to Chalco and raided the place, arresting Castro's men who were there and confiscating all the arms and ammunition that had been stored at that rancho grande. Castro and twenty-three of his companions spent twenty-three days in the Mexican immigration jail for that incident.

Before they were released, the authorities told Castro that he and his men would have to disperse or seek refuge in Latin-American embassies, or they would be shipped back to Cuba.

"That is wonderful!" Castro exclaimed. "Ship us back to Cuba. That is exactly where we want to go!"

The Mexican authorities then reversed themselves and ordered Castro and his men to report daily to the immigration office. Castro told them it would be impossible for him to report daily and they modified the order, directing him to report once a week.

One of the immigration officers ventured the news that they would be shipped back to Cuba anyway.

"Viva Cuba!" Castro led his men in shouting.

"Ship us back!" Castro challenged. "Let Batista execute us. It doesn't matter!"

The authorities released Castro and his men. Some of them left for Tampico and others for the vicinity of Tuxpan in the state of Vera Cruz.

Their training had been completed. Colonel Bayo had rated

them and at the head of the class was Ernesto Guevara, the Argentine medico. Castro was not rated, Bayo explained, because he was not present for the entire course of field training, having had to spend much of his time commuting between Chalco and Mexico City.

"Why did you rate Guevara No. 1 in the class?" Castro asked Bayo.

"Because he was the best student," the Spanish veteran answered. "He is the best."

"I would have so rated him, too," Castro commented.

Batista's feud with Trujillo was anything but silent by this time, having been aggravated after an exiled Dominican labor leader was murdered in Havana. It was theorized that Trujillo agents had committed the crime. Batista's police and writers flailed Fidel Castro in print and accused him of accepting aid from Trujillo for his planned expedition.

Castro was quick to react to those charges. He denounced any alliance with Trujillo while voicing his intention to support any future movement to overthrow the Dominican dictator. On August 26, 1956, he wrote to Miguel Angel Quevedo, editor of *Bohemia:*

"Dear friend:

"I must write you this letter. Neither my heart pierced with bitterness nor my hands weary with so much strife, so much writing against the infamy and evil and even the repugnance which causes me sometimes to take up my pen against the lowest and most vulgar traps set against me—all this, I say, will not stop me from doing my duty with the same faith as on the first day four and a half years ago, and I will never end until I fulfill my promise or die.

"The barrage of slander hurled against us by the dictatorship is now beyond all limits. Hardly five weeks ago I had to send your magazine an article, because of the report of Señor Luis Dam. As a result of our arrest in Mexico, his report reflects, among other things, the accusation that I was a member of the Mexican-Soviet Institute and an active member of the Communist Party. Weeks later, in spite of the unassailable conduct of all my co-workers in Mexico—who have never been seen in a bar or a cabaret and whose high standard of morality and discipline is known by all, including the Mexican police themselves—a writer paid by the embassy was low enough to state that on several occasions he had had to defend Cubans against charges of 'having created public scandal by excessive drinking,' and so on.

"I open *Bohemia* magazine of August 19, at the section 'En Cuba,' and read a summary of the denouncements made by Salas Canizares, where he is barefaced enough to cynically and shamelessly link my name—which is the name of a tireless fighter against the tyranny that is oppressing our people—with that of the despicable tyrant who has been oppressing the people of Santo Domingo during the last twenty-five years.

"Since the chief of police takes it upon himself to pass political judgment and write whatever he wants about the reputation of the opponents of the dictatorship—in reports to the courts which are published everywhere in the national and foreign press—and since these evil, criminal and cowardly denouncements are taken as a basis by the spokesmen of the regime for repeating with Goebbels-like emphasis the guttersniping attacks of the government, I consider it my duty to defend my prestige and also pass judgment upon my opponents as I see fit. And this in spite of the fact that I do not have at my disposal all of the means of publicity of the Republic that they do, which they use to combat ceaselessly any exiled adversary, who is persecuted with unequal fury even beyond the borders of his own country.

"I have the right to defend myself, because one does not devote one's life to a cause, sacrificing everything which others cherish and care for—namely, peaceful living, a career, a home, the family, youth and existence itself—just so that a handful of evildoers, who enjoy power through blood and fire against the people, for the exclusive benefit of their personal fortunes, can with impunity throw mud, slander and shame against such sacrifice, self-denial and disinterest, a thousand times proven to be at the service of a holy ideal.

"It becomes repugnant to have to reply to such an accusation, but if the feeling is not stifled, the spokesmen of the dictatorship will get away with their infamy. Somebody must step up and tell them a few truths.

128

"There can be no understanding between Trujillo and ourselves, just as there can never be any between Batista and us. The moral and ideological abyss separating us from Batista also separates us from Trujillo. What difference is there between the two dictators? Trujillo has been oppressing the Dominicans for twenty-five years; Batista, in two stages, has been going now for more than fifteen years and is on the way to copying his Dominican colleague. There is a dictator in Cuba just as there is in Santo Domingo; a regime sustained by force in Cuba as in Santo Domingo. Elections are filthy farces, without any guarantees for the adversaries of the regime, in Cuba as in Santo Domingo. There is a rapacious, ambitious and vile gang enjoying all the offices of the state, provinces and municipalities, nourishing themselves to the full in Cuba as in Santo Domingo.

"The overlord hires and fires officers and governs from his private farm and seats a servant of his own in the presidential chair in Cuba as in Santo Domingo. Terror and repression prevail, homes are broken into at midnight, men are arrested, tortured and disappear without leaving any traces in Cuba as in Santo Domingo. Moncada and Goicuria massacres are perpetrated in Cuba as in Santo Domingo. Civic parades are prohibited, the press is censored, newspapermen are beaten up and newspapers are closed down in Cuba as in Santo Domingo. Poor and defenseless peasants are lashed with machete blows, laborers are terrified and beaten with rifle butts and the most elemental rights are denied to the humble in Cuba as in Santo Domingo. Trujillo's bloodhounds kidnap and murder the opponents in exile—Jesus Galindez, Mauricio Baez, Andres Requena. Batista's bloodhounds persecute and also prepare the assassination of his opponents who are in exile. On this very day the Mexican paper *Ultimas Noticias* publishes on page 5, column 1, the following:

" 'The Chief of the Cuban Bureau of Investigations, Colonel Orlando Piedra, and the Chief of the Bureau of Subversive Activities, Captain Juan Castellanos, have just arrived in Mexico to investigate privately the activities of Cuban refugees who are involved in the plot against General Batista.

" 'The presence of these Antillean policemen has sown alarm among the Cuban residents in our country, who fear that they will be the object of retaliation on the part of the traveling agents of General Batista's government.

" 'Colonel Picdra and Captain Castellanos have come to our country accompanied by various agents who, as simple "tourists," will investigate the activities of the Cubans who are against the present policies of the Cuban government now in power.'

"What difference is there between these two tyrannies? Both the Cuban and the Dominican peoples want to rid themselves of Batista and Trujillo. Cuba and Santo Domingo will be happy the day each of these tyrants is deposed.

"Trujillo's government was the first one to recognize with delight the coup of the 10th of March. When Batista was in the opposition, he repeatedly criticized the Autentico governments for the generous help offered to Dominican revolutionaries. Neither Batista nor Trujillo can wish to see a democratic regime in their respective countries. The most that Trujillo can hope to see is the installation of a military dictatorship or a maffia of gangsters.

"The revolution directed by the 26th of July Movement would give its backing to a democratic Dominican movement. Now that our Movement is the vanguard of the revolutionary struggle, the only thing that can suit the tyrant Trujillo is that Batista remain in power.

"No matter how great may be his personal grudge, no dictator can afford to act against his own interests. Are not Batista's relations with Perez Jimenez—a dictator just like Trujillo—magnificent? Was it not in Venezuela that Santiago Rey proposed the re-election of Batista? Why did not Batista denounce Trujillo at Panama? Or did he not embrace cordially the brother of the jackal? On the other hand, why did the democratic President Jose Figueres refuse even to speak to the Cuban dictator? What explanation can the regime give for these contradictions?

"If Batista's dictatorship felt itself strong against us, if it were not sure that the clash is inevitable and decisive, it would not have used the low-down trick of suggesting an agreement between Trujillo and us. The use of such methods implies the kind of irresponsibility which has no limits.

"What is intended is to create a state of confusion so that when the fighting breaks out we can be accused of heading a Trujillist

130

revolution, and so Batista can bridle the people and throw his soldiers against us under the guise of defending the national sovereignty rather than fighting against the revolution which actually has the support of many military men. This maneuver must be brought clearly into the light.

"If it was true that an insurrectional agreement exists between Trujillo, Prio and us, that would imply an open and barefaced intervention of a foreign tyrant in the internal politics of our country. Then what is Cuba waiting for to reply in a worthy manner to such an aggression? The government cannot make an official charge like that and at the same time remain indifferent. Therefore, the time has come to unmask this infamous maneuver. Either the government must deny the existence of an insurrectional pact between the 26th of July Movement and Trujillo, or the government must declare war on Trujillo in defense of the national honor and sovereignty. The regime is bound to support or deny the charge.

"If at any time the sovereignty and dignity of our country are attacked, the men of the 26th of July Movement would fight as comrades of the soldiers of our army. What cannot be allowed is this kind of game with the international prestige and honor of the country, by sticking the term 'Trujillist' on anyone opposing a regime no more enviable than Trujillo's.

"If certain gangsters such as Policarpo Soler, who left Cuba through Rancho Boyeros airport with Batista's help, are now in cahoots with the Dominican despot, it is not fair to involve in this game men who have given more than enough proof of their idealism, honesty and love of Cuba.

"It is a positive fact that ambitious officers of the 10th of March coup have been in contact with Trujillo. Pelayo Cuervo denounced it courageously and ended up in the Castillo del Principe. The regime has not said a word regarding this, but has only accused all of its opponents of being Trujillists, whereas the truth is that Trujillism was born in the ranks of the regime. I am sure that the charge is also false and slanderous insofar as Prio is concerned.

"If I have defended the thesis of uniting all revolutionary forces—a concept which does not include gangsters—it is precisely because I believe that we Cubans can attain our freedom alone without the need of any help that could stain our cause. And this attitude has been mortal for the tyranny and has upset its leaders. I declared it in the face of the criticisms of our detractors, because I am a revolutionary who thinks only of what suits our country; I am not a candidate for electoral office, calculating with demagoguery the number of votes I can get in an election.

"The four and a half years that I have been engaged in this struggle, for which I have sacrificed all in spite of constant persecutions and slander, half of which time I have been imprisoned at home and abroad, in solitary confinement for long months, constantly exposed to the murderous bullets of my opponents, without a moment of rest or a moment of hesitation, without any more riches than the clothes I wear—these are the evident proofs of my disinterest and loyalty to Cuba. I have the honor of having been the target of the roughest, most continuous and most infamous attacks of the tyrant. I have withstood and will continue to withstand them to the end.

"Mr. Salas Canizares cannot assail the honesty of my firm democratic convictions, nor my unbending loyalty to the cause of the Dominican people. Juan Rodriguez, Juan Bosch and all the Dominican leaders in exile can attest to my struggle in the university in favor of Dominican democracy, to the three months I lived under disguise on a sandy islet, waiting for the signal to move and to the times I declared myself to be ready to go into the fight against Trujillo. They can speak for me. Therefore, they have to know who their real friends are and they have reasons to be better informed than anyone else regarding the carryings-on of the dictator who oppresses their country.

"The stand I took when I was a student is the stand I take today and it will always be my stand regarding Trujillo.

"I am one of those who believe that in a revolution principles are more important than guns. We went into the fight at Moncada with .22 caliber rifles. We have never had the number of arms that the enemy has; what counts, as Marti said, is the number of stars on your forehead.

"We would not exchange a single principle of ours for the arms of all the dictators in the world. This attitude of the men willing

to fight and die against forces having incomparably superior resources, without accepting outside help, is the most worthy reply
we can give to the spokesmen of the tyranny.

"On the other hand, Batista will not give up the tanks, guns and
airplanes that the United States is sending him, all of which will
not serve to defend democracy, but will be used only to massacre
our helpless people.

"In Cuba the habit of speaking the truth is being lost. The
campaign of slander will earn its reply on a day not far off, in the
fulfilment of the promises we have made that in 1956 we will be
free or will be martyrs.

"I hereby calmly ratify this statement with full understanding of
what it implies four and a half months from December 31. No
reverses will stop us from fulfilling our undertaking. No other
terms can be used in speaking to a people who have become
skeptical from so much deceit and betrayal. When that hour
comes, Cuba will know that those of us who are giving our blood
and our lives are her most loyal sons and that the weapons we will
use to gain our freedom were not paid for by Trujillo, but by the
people, cent by cent and dollar by dollar. If we fail, as Marti
told that illustrious Dominican Federico Hernandez Carvajal, we
will fall also for the liberty of the Dominican people.

"Requesting you to publish these lines in your impartial and
fair-minded magazine, I remain,

"Yours very truly,
"FIDEL CASTRO"

Castro was very anxious to talk with Prio, who was in Miami,
and a meeting was arranged by Teresa Cassuso, who had been
fired from her job in the Cuban embassy in Mexico because of her
friendship for the rebel cause. Prio could not leave the United
States because of pending indictments, and Castro could not obtain a visa to enter. Mexican friends suggested that they try to
meet at McAllen, Texas, across the frontier from Reynoso,
Mexico, with only the Rio Grande separating both cities. Prio
agreed to make the journey from Miami and Castro from Mexico
City. It was the month of September 1956.

With Juan Manuel Marquez, whom he had chosen to be his

133

second in command, Montane and Montane's second wife, Dr. Melba Hernandez, Castro traveled from Mexico City to Reynoso by automobile. The chauffeur was Rafael del Pino, also Castro's bodyguard. At Reynoso, Castro was taken in hand by some laborers, who gave him clothing similar to theirs; he mingled with the workers as one of them. The plan for the wetback crossing of the river had been meticulously prepared. With the other laborers, Castro went for a swim under the hot noon sun. On the United States side friendly Mexican laborers were waiting for him, with a change of clothing and an automobile. He was quickly driven to the Hotel Casa de Palmas in McAllen where Prio had already checked in.

The conference with Prio lasted until nightfall when Mexican oil-worker friends guided Castro across the bridge where their friends were waiting for him. He rejoined Marquez and Jesus Montane and his wife.

It was the first time that Castro and Prio had met each other. Castro needed financial help for the purchase of the yacht, arms, ammunition and equipment. Prio promised to help him. Castro returned to Mexico City and began to speed up his plans to return to Cuba. Prio's friends claim the former president made a financial contribution to the cause that enabled Castro to purchase the invasion yacht, while some of Castro's friends credit the money for the expenses of the yacht *Gramma* to a Cuban named Rafael Bilbao of Mayari, province of Oriente.

Trujillo lost little time in reacting to Castro's letter after it was published by Quevedo in the month of September. He ordered his diplomatic corps to contact several exiles friendly to Prio and to offer to train an expeditionary force of Cubans in the Dominican Republic. The arrangements for this training were made by Eufemio Fernandez, among others, and recruitment of volunteers began in Havana, Miami and Tampa. Castro had not yet learned of this latest maneuver, which was used to justify the accusations by Batista—which Castro had challenged in his letter—that Trujillo was sponsoring a revolution against him.

Upon Teresa Cassuso's offer of help, Castro told her he would like to store a few things in her house in the Lomas de Chapultepec in Mexico City. The few things turned out to be an arsenal.

134

Rafael del Pino helped to store the arms in closets and other available space. Some weapons were stored in Pedro Miret's house next door. The weapons were a new consignment, recent purchases to replace those lost in the raid at Chalco.

During the month of November 1956 the Mexican police raided Teresa Cassuso's home to capture the entire arsenal. The tip to the police—an investigation by the 26th of July Movement showed—was furnished by an informer who furnished the Cuban embassy in Mexico City with a blueprint of the home and the storage of the arms.

"I don't want a penny in advance," the informer told the embassy attaché with whom he spoke. "But when the arms are captured I want $15,000."

The deal was made and the information was transmitted by the embassy to Havana and by Colonel Orlando Piedra, chief of the Cuban detective bureau, to the Mexican police. The Movement had its own spies in the embassy in Mexico City. The finger of accusation pointed to Rafael del Pino as the informer, although there was no definitive proof. Del Pino had hurriedly left the camp early in November with some money and a gun which did not belong to him. Raul Castro and Faustino Perez had chased him for twenty-five miles, but his one-hour head start had been too much. At a meeting of the members of the expeditionary force called by Castro, it was agreed that an investigation should be undertaken of Del Pino's loyalty and activity. It was fifteen days after Del Pino's escape that Teresa Cassuso's home was raided. For storing the arms in her house, Teresa spent more than twenty days in jail.

The raid was another serious blow to Castro. Once again work began to replace the lost weapons, while preparations to buy the invasion yacht continued.

Meanwhile, more dramatic events had been happening in Havana. At 4:30 A.M. of October 27, 1956, the day before the Inter American Press Association was to convene in Havana for its annual convention, Colonel Antonio Blanco Rico, Batista's military intelligence chief, was killed by submachine-gun fire as he was about to leave the Montmartre night club with some friends.

Two days later Colonel Rafael Salas Canizares, who was

Batista's chief of police, broke into the embassy of Haiti with the purpose of arresting some political refugees who were there and who, according to official reports, were suspected of complicity in the Blanco Rico shooting. His violation of the sanctity of political asylum was met with gunfire, and Salas died before he could reach the hospital. A brother, who had accompanied him on the raid, broke into the embassy with a squad of police and machine-gunned to death ten young Cubans.

The attack on Blanco Rico undoubtedly was perpetrated in order to call the attention of the editors, who had gathered in Havana from all over the continent, to the situation existing in the country. The attack on the Haitian embassy compounded the gravity of events.

A Cuban editor asked to appear before the Committee on Freedom of the Press of the Inter American Press Association, which was holding hearings to prepare its annual report to submit to the convention. He was Luis Orlando Rodriguez, whose political newspaper, *La Calle,* had been closed by Batista as "incendiary" in the month of June 1955. Fidel Castro had been a contributor to the paper. All efforts by Rodriguez to obtain the return, at least, of his printing plant, so that he could lease it to someone else, had failed. Batista promised the Inter American Press Association he would return the plant but that never happened. Rodriguez thus decided to join Castro's cause.

Castro's first plan was to buy a surplus United States Navy crash boat. A down payment of $5,000 was made for one by a Cuban, but the deal fell through when the Cuban embassy in Washington was consulted for approval of the sale. It was then that Batista received confirmation of invasion plans.

Castro made a trip to the coast of the Gulf of Mexico and spotted the *Gramma* undergoing repairs in the Tuxpan River. That, he decided, was the yacht he wanted. He contacted Mexican friends again and told them about this boat on the banks of the Rio Tuxpan. Tracing its ownership, they found it was registered in the name of Erickson, an American who lived in Mexico City. Erickson had already offered the yacht to a Mexican physician, Dr. Mario del Rio, who planned to pay $15,000 for it in installments. Castro's friends offered the entire sum in cash.

136

The Ericksons owned a house on the Rio Tuxpan at Santiago de la Pena, which they also wanted to sell, because they wished to return to the United States to live. A Mexican friend, Antonio del Conde, whose livelihood was the sale of arms, acted as the buyer. He bought the yacht in his name, paying $15,000 cash, and made a down payment of $3,000 on the house, obtaining a mortgage for the balance of the $23,000 purchase price.

The *Gramma* had two Gray marine engines and a fuel capacity of nearly 1,000 gallons. But the yacht needed repairs which there was not enough time to make because of increasing pressure from the Mexican authorities. Castro and others of the men were arrested on several occasions and held for questioning. Influential Mexicans managed to obtain their release, but all of them were required to report daily to the Ministry of Interior and sign a register there.

Though the *Gramma* could comfortably hold eight men, Castro planned to carry eighty-two beside the captain and the crew. The clutch of the engines was bad. Leaks in the hull were repaired, but there was no time to fix the clutch. Batista's spies were closing in on them. Castro sent his men ahead by automobile to the Erickson house on the banks of the Rio Tuxpan, where they assembled in small groups. The weapons and ammunition had been stored in the house for loading aboard the yacht.

Castro was concerned about the *Gramma* and its ability to reach the coast of Oriente, the part of Cuba farthest from Mexico. The yacht normally cruised at 1,800 revolutions; now as soon as the engines reached 1,500 revolutions the clutch would slip. This lost valuable time. Instead of the usual 1,000 gallons of fuel, Castro loaded the vessel with another 2,000 gallons for the voyage.

Castro's men carried out secret loading operations near the river town of Tuxpan. Under cover of darkness arms, ammunition and men went on board the 58-foot yacht in that river in the state of Vera Cruz.

En route to Tuxpan by car, Castro had some unfinished business. He took a small pad from his pocket and wrote his last will and testament. He was concerned about his son, Fidel, Jr. He willed the custody of Fidelito to Mrs. Orquidea Pino, a Cuban

137

who was childless and in whose home he had lived. He gave this piece of paper to one of his escorts who was returning to the capital to deliver to Señora Pino.

At 11 P.M. of November 24 they crossed the other bank of the river, with nine men being ferried across in each rowboat.

Castro had not attempted to keep his invasion plans a secret. On November 15, 1956, he had boldly announced that he would land soon in Cuba to overthrow Batista before the end of that year or die as a martyr in the effort.

Colonel Bayo had remonstrated with him for making the announcement. "Don't you know," he asked Castro, "that a cardinal military principle is to keep your intentions secret from your enemy?"

"You taught me that," Castro assured his instructor, "but in this case I want everyone in Cuba to know I am coming. I want them to have faith in the 26th of July Movement. It is a peculiarity all my own although I know that militarily it might be harmful. It is psychological warfare."

On November 25 Castro's expedition sailed down the Rio Tuxpan into the Gulf of Mexico and headed eastward for Oriente province and his war against Batista. Aboard the yacht were his brother Raul and the Argentine medico, Ernesto Guevara, both of whom were to become controversial figures during and after the civil war.

The yacht was crowded with well-trained young men under an inspired and zealous leader. Now as it sailed out into the gulf between Vera Cruz and Tuxpan, and the weak lights of Tuxpan faded into oblivion, the 82 expeditionaries broke into song. The song was the Cuban national anthem.

The next day and for days to come many were seasick as the yacht bucked a norther with winds close to forty knots an hour. The yacht began to ship water, and the pump failed to work. The men had to bail out the water. Hunger and thirst set in, but the captain, Lieutenant Eloy Troque, a cashiered naval officer, cheered them with assurances that they were headed straight for Cuba. Fidel Castro became impatient. His plans were going awry because of delay caused by the rough seas. It was November 30, and there was to be an uprising in Santiago de Cuba to cover his landing at Niquero to the west.

Crescencio Perez was a man respected and beloved by the farmers of the Sierra Maestra. Perez, who knew every trail and every hiding place in the region, was supposed to meet the expedition with trucks and more than 100 men. Castro planned to proceed to Manzanillo to attack simultaneously with the uprising in Santiago.

By radio Castro heard that the attack had taken place in Santiago. The maritime police headquarters had been stormed and burned; 10 political prisoners and 57 common criminals had broken out of the Boniato prison. There was fighting in the streets of Santiago. On the promenade of the cathedral troops fired on rebel snipers and pursued others down the streets. A dynamite warehouse in Holguin was broken open. The reports emphasized the fact that the attackers wore black and red 26th of July armbands.

"I wish I could fly!" Castro complained, but he took the disappointment with a stoicism and confidence that inspired his men.

The radio soon reported that there were 4 dead and 14 wounded in Santiago and Holguin, according to an official announcement. An unofficial figure for Santiago alone gave 20 dead and more than 200 wounded. Batista promptly suspended civil rights in four provinces, excluding Havana and Matanzas. This indicated that he feared uprisings in Pinar del Rio, Oriente, Camaguey and Las Villas. Batista sent Colonel Pedro Barreras, tank commander at Camp Columbia, to Oriente to command field operations.

Before dawn of December 2, Lieutenant Troque fell overboard.

"He must be saved!" Castro ordered. At first Troque could not be found in the darkness. Someone found a lantern and held it out over the water.

"Here! Here! Here!" Troque's voice shouted from out of the dark. He was located and pulled aboard, but more than an hour was lost in the rescue operation.

The *Gramma* neared the shore between Niquero and Cabo Cruz. Now the rowboat was lowered but sank under the excessive weight. The men were bogged down in the loam but finally managed to make their way into the mangrove swamp. When they emerged from the swamp onto firm ground, some of the men knelt down to kiss the soil of Cuba.

Because the yacht had grounded on a loamy cay, the expedition had to leave radio transmitters, ammunition, food and medicines on board. The 82 men landed safely, without a single casualty. Word of the successful landing, however, soon reached the army because by dusk of that day, December 2, 1956, high government sources leaked out the news that Fidel Castro had landed. They added quickly that he and 42 of his men, including Juan Manuel Marquez, his second in command, had been killed when they were bombed and strafed on the beach by aircraft!

The exact location of the landing was at Belic, a small fishing village east of Niquero. One news service reported that Castro had been killed but credited only "reliable sources." By midnight it became apparent that the report was incorrect although no responsible official in the government would deny it. On the contrary, they were anxious to establish preliminary confusion and doubt as to Castro's success.

The next day there was some hedging on the part of the government, but the confusion was not dissipated until Herbert L. Matthews of the *New York Times* interviewed Castro in the Sierra Maestra on February 17, 1957, and published his story ten days later.

When Castro and his men reached some native huts, a peasant stared at them in fright.

"I am Fidel Castro," said the leader, placing his big hand on the man's shoulder. "My companions and I have come to liberate Cuba. Nobody has anything to fear from us because we have come to help the farmer. We are going to give you land on which to work, markets for your products, schools for your sons, sanitary housing for your family. We need something to eat, but we are going to pay you for it."

"Come this way, but be careful with that shotgun," the astonished farmer said. "A shot might go off by mistake. Let us go and kill a pig. I have some *boniato* already on the fire."

As they rested and fancied devouring the roast pig, their comfort was interrupted by a burst of machine-gun fire in the jungle behind them. Castro ordered a hurried withdrawal from the scene. They fled to a presumably safe area but found eight of their men missing, whereupon Castro sent a rescue patrol out after them.

140

Fidel Castro was an unhappy man, for all his plans had mis-fired. With the planned co-ordinated attack by his invaders on Manzanillo and the uprising in Santiago, an island-wide campaign of agitation and sabotage was supposed to begin, to be followed by a revolutionary general strike that would topple Batista. Instead, here he was on the night of December 2, two days behind his planned schedule, far from Manzanillo, encamped in a jungle without food and with a shortage of water.

He ate his first breakfast since his return to Cuba during the next morning when, marching eastward toward the Sierra Maestra, his force came to a native shack. They were served yucca with honey; to hungry, disappointed, fervent idealists with a mission to liberate Cuba it was like a banquet. Loyal aircraft approached on reconnaissance and the men hid under trees until they passed, but the day was a gloomy one. They saw no sign of any natives, they had no guides, they had no food and they had no water; only a good sense of direction guided them eastward.

On the afternoon of the third as they approached a shack, the occupants fled in fright into the jungle at sight of the uniformed and armed men. Castro sent one of his men to trail them. They found some food and water, ate and drank and left a five-peso Cuban bill. [The Cuban peso is on a par with the dollar.] That night they slept in the woods near a trail.

Suddenly the scout who had gone after the fleeing natives returned with a shout. "I found the eight men we lost in the mangrove swamp on the day we landed!"

He went on to explain. "I lost the trail last night when I followed the natives. I walked awhile until I found a light in a house and I asked the farmers there to orient me. They invited me to stay there overnight, but when I saw the man leave, I didn't know what to think. Soon he returned with one of our men, and then all eight of them were there."

The reunion was joyful but not uproarious because of the situation which confronted the expedition. Castro ordered marches during the night and rest during the day, for government aircraft were almost always overhead. On several occasions they observed the aircraft strafing the jungle area and mangrove swamps a considerable distance away. These were a new type of rebels, the natives soon learned. When they asked the natives for food and received some, they paid for it. The farmers, all peasants, were astounded at such treatment. Castro had landed with Cuban pesos in his pocket and intentions of paying for everything he would need until he could get more money.

On December 5—Castro was still dead, according to some, though Batista in Havana gave an interview in which he said he did not believe Castro had even landed in Cuba but was still in Mexico—the rebels camped in an abandoned cane field flanked by jungle. They did not have a radio set with them and therefore were unable to keep abreast of news that might be broadcast about them; neither Castro nor the others were aware that he was believed dead. But the confusion over the story of his death, the failure to attack Manzanillo, the routing of the attackers at Santiago all served to put the brakes on the members of the 26th of July Movement elsewhere in the country who were to have gone into action.

Then Castro's scouts returned with a report on the enemy.

"On the highway to Pilon," they informed him, "a few miles away, there is an army detachment and we are surrounded. We are going to have to break through that encirclement to reach the mountains."

Castro rationed out some of the food that had been purchased from the natives. The ration was half a sausage and a cracker for each man. Here in Alegria del Pio, Castro was to suffer his first military reverse and lose some of his best men and closest friends.

With his tired and hungry men, Castro was seated in the woods. Most of the men had their boots off easing their sore feet. Che Guevara was applying first aid to the worst cases. Castro had ordered the men to be ready to march at four o'clock in the afternoon, but suddenly rifle fire began to come from all directions, and bullets whistled over their heads. Batista's air force made its appearance to bomb and strafe the very area where they were. Castro ordered a strategic retreat back to the cane field. But fragmentation bombs dropped by the aircraft set fire to the cane field, and Castro ordered the men to split up into groups to facilitate their withdrawal and make their way east to the Sierra Maestra.

Raul Castro took off with a patrol that included Ciro Redondo,

Efigenio Almejeiras, Rene Rodriguez and several others. Juan Manuel Marquez left with 13 men, but they became lost and ventured too close to the coast. They were surrounded by the army. Exhausted, starved and their throats parched from thirst, Marquez and his men agreed to surrender. The army commander had assured them they would not be killed. As soon as their weapons were handed over, they were shot.

Fidel Castro with another group hid in a cane field while aircraft strafed the vicinity. None of the men with him was hit. Again without food and water, on the sixth of December and for five successive days, Castro and his men lived on sugar cane. They nourished themselves each morning by sucking the raw cane dry.

"The day when the revolution is triumphant," Castro said to Faustino Perez and Universo Sanchez, the only two survivors of his group, "we will have to erect a monument to our savior sugar cane."

Following Castro's rout at Alegria del Pio, a move was started in Havana to effect a truce in the fighting and stay the army from pursuing the rebels. It was initiated by Ernesto Stock, a member of the Ortodoxo Party who now owns the small Hotel Siboney on the Prado. Stock tried assiduously to involve me in the truce. He asked me to attend a meeting Sunday, December 9, at the office of Miguel Angel Quevedo, editor and publisher of *Bohemia,* together with himself and Manuel Brana, editor of the newspaper *Excelsior.* The talk narrowed down to Stock's proposal that I offer my good offices as Latin-American correspondent of the *Chicago Tribune* and Chairman of the Committee on Freedom of the Press of the Inter American Press Association to the government to bring about a truce between the army and the rebels, to prevent the possible annihilation of the remainder of Castro's force. I rejected the request, pointing out that I could in no way become associated with such a move because I was a foreigner and could not involve either my newspaper or the Inter American Press Association. Quevedo and Brana understood my position. Stock insisted, but I remained firm in my refusal. I suggested that the Cubans act on their own to stop the annihilation of Castro, if that were the objective. Such an effort was made through pressure of public opinion.

For eight days Raul Castro, Ciro Redondo, Efigenio Almejeiras, Rene Rodriguez, also the only survivors of their group,
were without food and water. They, too, lived off sugar cane,
sucking the juice of the raw cane every morning. Every night
they heard the drone of the army aircraft engines and knew they
were surrounded by troops. On the eighth day they headed east
in obedience to Fidel's orders. When they reached a cave in the
foothills of the Sierra Maestra, a *campesino* fed them yucca, rice
and beans and gave them water. Later they were fed codfish and
sugar cane.

Then for four days they marched through sugar cane fields.
They reached a dairy, where Rene Rodriguez just had to have his
milk and coffee. The milk gave him the colic because he had not
had food for days. The *campesinos* were friendly. Raul Castro
told them he was a Mexican newspaperman and showed them a
card with another name.

The next day in one of the sugar cane fields Raul Castro's party
stumbled into Fidel, Perez and Sanchez. Despite the disastrous
defeat, the fatigue, hunger and disillusionment, Castro never lost
his optimism or his qualities of leadership.

"The days of the dictatorship are numbered!" he assured the
six men with him. Rene Rodriguez looked at him with astonishment.

"This man is crazy," Rodriguez said to himself.

"I was very mad at Fidel," Rodriguez relates, "because after all
we had just been through, with many of our men lost, Fidel stands
there telling us with complete confidence that the days of the
dictatorship are numbered, and we were only eight men!"

In all, 22 men had survived but only 12 were to remain in the
mountains. The other 10 were captured in the cities and imprisoned on the Isle of Pines. Camilo Cienfuegos, Che Guevara,
Calixto Morales and Calixto Garcia caught up with Fidel and
Raul Castro, Faustino Perez, Universo Sanchez, Efigenio Almejeiras, Ciro Redondo, Juan Almeida and Rene Rodriguez. When
they reached the foothills before their ascent to the peaks, Castro
had to feign that he was a regular army colonel to escape detection. His ruse was successful.

When Castro reached the Pico Turquino, the 7,000-foot sum-
mit of Cuba in the Sierra Maestra, neither he nor any of his men

had more than eight or ten cartridges left for their weapons.

The ascent was made possible by a chain of native guides organized by Crescencio Perez. By Christmas Eve Castro reached his destination. There he holed up with his men to plan for the acceleration of the organization of the underground throughout the country and the tactics of agitation and sabotage. On the way up hundreds of friendly natives had offered to enlist in his cause, but he had to turn them down because he had no weapons, much less any ammunition for them.

"When we arrived at the Sierra Maestra," Castro relates, "we executed a ranch foreman who had accused tenant farmers and peasants of being pro-rebel, and who had increased the holdings of his landlord from 10 acres to 400 acres by taking the land of those he denounced. So we tried him and executed him and won the affection of the peasants."

Thus Castro was to become the Robin Hood of the Sierra Maestra and was to pursue later the same policy of taking from the rich to give to the poor.

Early in January he sent Faustino Perez—who resembles an inoffensive bookworm although he had finished a medical course at the University of Havana in 1952 (where he refused to accept his degree because Batista had wrecked constitutional government)—to Santiago de Cuba with instructions to arrange for an American newspaperman to climb the Sierra Maestra to interview him. Perez went on to Havana, arranged for Herbert Matthews to get the interview and personally escorted him to Castro's hide-out.

While Castro was holed up in the Pico Turquino and while many people in Cuba and elsewhere ridiculed his brazen effort to overthrow Batista, one man in Havana was predicting he would succeed. This was Father Armando Llorente, who had been Castro's Spanish and public-speaking teacher at the Colegio Belen and also his spiritual adviser. Today Father Llorente is director of the Catholic University Group, an organization of university students.

"Fidel Castro is a man of destiny," Father Llorente would tell anyone who cared to listen to him. "Behind him is the hand of God. He has a mission to fulfill and he will fulfill it against all obstacles."

He recalled that Fidel was the head of the explorers' club at the Colegio Belen. "He demonstrated then that he can rise to greatness in the face of adversity," Father Llorente would say. "One day we were on a hike in the Sierra de los Organos in the province of Pinar del Rio. A heavy rainstorm had swollen the rivers there while we were hiking, among them the Taco-Taco which we had to cross. Fidel reconnoitered the inundated area. When he returned he told us that three hundred feet away where the water had risen several feet, we might be able to cross. He took the rope that we had brought along and gripped it in his teeth. He jumped into the swirling water, which was filled with boulders and timber. As the current dragged him more than sixty feet, we held on to the other end of the rope. He got across to the other bank with the rope in his teeth, and using it as an anchor he helped all of us across."

Father Llorente also recalled another hiking trip, much more important. It was into the Sierra Maestra, which experience was to serve Castro in good stead.

"Fidel is going to do a lot of good for the poor people and the humble," Father Llorente preached to all who would listen to him, and many did. "He was always a man who preferred to cultivate friendships among the humble. His special friends at school were the porters, cooks and workmen there."

To his brother Ramon, who was taking care of the family sugar plantation, which his father had developed long before his death in 1956, Castro gave the mission to funnel supplies to him in the Sierra Maestra. Ramon, perhaps half an inch taller than Fidel, devoutly religious and in love with the farm, developed into a masterful organizer and quartermaster. He mobilized a rebel pipeline from the cities to the mountaintops to get arms, ammunition, medicines, supplies and men to his brothers. He kept an inventory of everything that went up; what could not be bought or obtained through donations by friends of the cause he devised ways and means to manufacture, either the identical product or a synthetic one that would serve the same purpose.

Fidel Castro was safely protected in the Sierra Maestra. Each day that passed in which Batista failed to rout him not only meant a day of defeat for the dictator but signified his certain and ultimate downfall.

146

But in the Dominican Republic an expeditionary force of 120 Cubans was being trained by officers of Trujillo's army and air force. Some of the Cubans had been recruited in Havana by friends of Prio. Others recruited in Miami had only to go to the Miami International Airport and claim their tickets for the flight to Ciudad Trujillo. At the Dominican capital they were met and transported to a camp outside of the city where they were given intensive military training.

Trujillo's powerful radio stations of the La Voz Dominicana network, owned by his brother Lieutenant General J. Arismendi Trujillo, had been beaming their harangues against President Paul Magloire of Haiti across the frontier. Magloire decreed himself dictator and was overthrown by a general strike coupled with a military conspiracy. With Magloire out of the way the Trujillo radio began to beam its signals to Cuba with blistering attacks on Batista. This was in December 1956. In its commentaries La Voz Dominicana demanded that the people of Cuba rise in a general strike just as the people of Haiti had and overthrow Batista. I heard the broadcasts while in Port-au-Prince, Haiti.

The Cuban people as a whole entertain a profound hatred for Trujillo and would never respond to any appeal on his part, or on the part of those who may act for him, to launch a general strike to overthrow anybody. Thus his campaign furnished an inadvertent assist to Batista, but it also served to alert Batista against possible air attack and invasion from Santo Domingo.

It was reported—although definitive confirmation of this could never be obtained—that Trujillo wanted Gerald Lester Murphy, an American pilot from Eugene, Oregon, to bomb Havana; when Murphy refused he was fed to the sharks in the Caribbean Sea. Murphy was said also to have been the pilot who had flown Dr. Jesus de Galindez, the Basque instructor at Columbia University in New York, to the Dominican Republic on the night of March 12, 1956. Galindez has never been heard from since and his Doctorate of Philosophy thesis, *The Era of Trujillo,* has never been published in the English language. It was published in Spanish in Santiago, Chile.

The Trujillo plan, according to trainees of the expeditionary

147

force, called for the support of the 120 Cubans with a battalion of 700 Dominicans who would be used to consolidate the capture of Camp Columbia, the army headquarters and stronghold in Havana. They would be dressed in uniforms of the Cuban Army and appear to be Cubans. Once assured of consolidation, they would immediately be evacuated home.

Why would Trujillo undertake such a dangerous operation? He was afraid of Fidel Castro, who had been a member of the ill-fated Cayo Confites expedition of 1947 and who had minced no words in his recent letter. Once victorious over Batista, Castro, he knew, would turn his eyes toward Santo Domingo and strive to help rid that nation of the Trujillo dynasty. Batista had refused the olive branch of friendship several times from Trujillo. The Dominican dictator has a long memory, which is always reinforced by plans for revenge with a capital *R*.

Trujillo now sent emissaries to confer with Prio in Miami. They carried an invitation from the Dominican dictator for Prio to confer with him aboard his yacht in New York harbor. Trujillo at that time had ordered the Dominican press and radio to conduct a vitriolic campaign against Batista and the attacks appeared almost daily. Prio accepted the invitation and flew from Miami to New York for the meeting.

Among those present during the interview was Eufemio Fernandez. Trujillo offered Prio everything he needed, men, arms, ammunition, supplies and subsequent support in exchange for certain conditions. But these conditions were such that Prio felt he could in no circumstances accept and the conversations came to an end.

Early in January 1957 Trujillo effected a double-cross of convenience and, through emissaries, indicated to Batista he was ready to make peace. La Voz Dominicana ceased its fiery broadcasts against Batista. The training of the 120 men came to a halt, and they were ejected from the camp. Some of the Cubans were imprisoned in the Ozama Fortress in Ciudad Trujillo. Others were allowed to live in the capital until they were returned to Miami. On January 12, 1957, Batista sent a special mission to the Dominican Republic to represent him at a cattle show. Three days later he suspended all civil rights throughout the country

148

and imposed press and radio censorship. The sugar crop, said Batista, had to be protected, and the only way it could be done was through a suspension of civil rights and, especially, the establishment of censorship for a period of forty-five days.

One of his strictest orders to the censors was to ban any criticism of Trujillo or of other dictators. But when the dictator of Venezuela, General Marcos Perez Jimenez, was overthrown on January 23, 1957, several radio news announcers could not refrain from emphasizing the word "dictator" every time they read reports from Caracas.

Batista had secured his eastern air and sea flank through his peace pact with Trujillo. And Trujillo had secured his western air and sea flank through the consequent period of instability that followed the overthrow of Magloire in Haiti and the settlement of his quarrel with Batista.

But Batista had by no means secured the stability of his own government within the confines of the island of Cuba, for below the Pico Turquino in the Sierra Maestra was Fidel Castro, hidden in the jungle with 11 other men who had survived from the group of 82 who had sailed from Mexico in the last days of November of the previous year.

The government had posted notices all over Oriente offering a reward for the head of Fidel Castro and for lesser services by informers. The notices read:

"To All Who May Be Concerned

"By this means it is announced that any person who furnishes information leading to the success of an operation against any rebel nucleus commanded by Fidel Castro, Raul Castro, Crescencio Perez, Guillermo Gonzalez or any other leader will be rewarded in accordance with the importance of the information, with the understanding that it never will be less than $5,000.

"This reward will vary from $5,000 to $100,000, the highest amount, that is, $100,000, being payable for the head of Fidel Castro.

"Note: The name of the informer will never be revealed."

CHAPTER 5

Terror struck again in Oriente soon afterward. Young men were forcibly removed from their homes and from the arms of their mothers by police officers and army officers; their mutilated and bullet-riddled bodies were found the following day in fields, with their vital parts severed and stuffed into their mouths or in their shirt pockets. In this condition the body of William Soler, a fifteen-year-old student, was returned to his home. Two nights earlier a soldier had forced him from the arms of his tearfully pleading mother. His offense: he was sympathetic to the Castro cause.

The terror in the Holguin sector was worse. On Christmas Eve 26 young men were forcibly removed from their homes by troops under the command of Colonel Fermin Cowley. The next day their corpses, bullet-riddled or strangled, were found on the outskirts of the city. That macabre Christmas present from the Batista forces so horrified the people—for word of the massacre leaked out despite the censorship in Oriente—that even the Cuban Press Bloc, whose president was a close friend and associate of Batista, met to adopt a resolution and urge the end of terror and civil strife. No attention was paid to this appeal or to others that were to follow by all civic, religious and professional institutions for months to come.

Early in 1957 Castro's sister Lidia, carrying written authoriza-

150

tion from Mirtha Diaz Balart, who was remarried to the son of Emilio Nunez Portuondo, Cuba's ambassador to the United Nations, took Fidelito to Mexico City to reside with Señora Pino away from the vortex of the civil war that his father was leading.

One day as Fidelito was being taken for a ride near the Chapultepec woods, the automobile in which he was riding with his Aunt Lidia had to halt at a stop sign which, coincidentally, was at the intersection of Marti and Revolucion in Tacubaya. Two *pistoleros* alighted from an automobile next to them and at gun point demanded Fidelito. They sped off to the Cuban embassy, which was not very far away, and deposited the boy there.

The kidnaping of Fidel, Jr., became a scandal in Mexico and Cuba. Lidia denounced the deed to the Mexican police and the federal authorities began an investigation. While the probe was on, Fidelito was surreptitiously whisked out of Mexico aboard an airplanc to Miami, where he was reclaimed by his mother and flown back to Havana.

On March 6, 1957, I interviewed Batista at the palace. I went there to try to obtain assurances from him that he would not reimpose censorship, for, responding to pressure by the Inter American Press Association, he had lifted it in Havana, although the civil rights were suspended for another forty-five days.

At that interview Batista said to me, "Fidel Castro is a Communist."

"Is that so? Do you have proof?" I asked.

"Yes," Batista replied. "We have proof that he killed six priests in Bogota during the Bogotazo."

"Pardon me, Mr. President," I interjected. "I was in Bogota at that time and no priest was killed."

"Oh, but we have proof," Batista insisted. "We have a report from our ambassador there at that time."

"Perhaps you do," I countered, "but I can assure you the report is not correct. However, if you think you have proof and you care to furnish it to me, I shall be glad to publish it."

Batista promised to send it to me at my hotel. He sent an aide over that night with a folder, which contained a spurious manifesto attributed to Castro and an equally spurious varitype publication also attributed to him. There was no proof furnished to

151

substantiate the statement that Castro had killed six priests.

Batista also insisted that Herbert Matthews never saw Castro. As soon as Matthews' series was published, the Batista government rushed into print to deny that the newspaperman had ever seen Castro. I assured Batista that I knew Matthews well and that he does not invent interviews. Even the publication of a photo of Matthews interviewing Castro failed to convince Batista, for he wanted his wish to be the father to his thought.

Four days later, on March 10, in a speech at Camp Columbia, Batista publicly lashed out at Castro, denouncing him as a Communist and as a tool of Moscow. He might have persuaded American Ambassador Arthur Gardner to believe this but not an overwhelming majority of the Cuban people, including the Roman Catholic Church.

On March 13, just a few minutes before three o'clock, a truck painted with the sign FAST DELIVERY came to a halt at the Calle Colon entrance of the presidential palace. An army telegraph operator on the second floor saw some armed men emerge from it. He ran to give the alarm, but the men had already penetrated the palace, where, their guns blazing away, they rushed to the second-floor office of Batista. Suffering from a headache, he had left the office by a secret exit for his third-floor apartment.

Simultaneous with the attack on the palace Jose Antonio Echevarria, president of the Students' Federation, broke into the CMQ radio station on 23rd Street and broadcast a harangue urging the people to rise.

"The tyrant is dead!" he shouted into the microphone. Batista was supposed to be dead at that moment, but he had escaped. The palace attackers had missed him although not by much. But in this case the old adage that a miss is as good as a mile proved true. Reinforcements were rushed to the palace and loyal troops inside reacted after the initial shock. Before the firing ceased there were 25 attackers dead and several wounded.

Echevarria raced out of the CMQ building and headed for the university near by in his automobile. The police cornered him, ordered him out of his car and shot him on the corner as he alighted.

The palace attack was organized and led by members of the

152

Directorio Revolucionario, the militant rebel organization of university alumni and students. The group disowned any connection with Prio; Echevarria was fulfilling a secret pact that he had signed with Castro on behalf of the University Students' Federation when he visited him in Mexico.

Batista's police raided the university—which had been closed since November 30, 1956, when the students went on a strike in sympathy for Castro—and confiscated a stock of arms that had been stored there.

Batista did not reimpose censorship in Havana, and the news of the palace attack was reported with an abundance of gory photographs of dead and wounded. Downtown Havana had been a battlefield for two hours. I had watched the operation from behind a thick column on a street corner that furnished an excellent view of the palace.

The palace attack had not been co-ordinated with the Castro underground movement, for the rebel chief was opposed to Batista's assassination. Castro preferred to get his hands on him and try him. He criticized the palace attack from the Sierra Maestra.

When the police searched the pockets of Jose Antonio Echevarria after they took his body away, they found, besides the inflammatory manifesto which he had read over the radio, a piece of paper on which was written: "Pelayo Cuervo—President."

Pelayo Cuervo was president of the Ortodoxo Party. He was a distinguished former opposition senator. He was an honest, respected and courageous lawyer. Using his rights as a citizen, he had single-handedly filed a brief against former President Grau, accusing him of having stolen $172,000,000 from the national treasury while he was in office. This case became known as the famous Cause 82 and was still awaiting a decision by the courts. Pelayo Cuervo did not permit it to die or be shelved by the courts. Cuervo lived in a modest second-story apartment in the Miramar district of Havana. I was to visit it two days later under tragic circumstances.

Recovering from the shock of the attack and from the realization that his security at the palace had been shattered, Batista ordered troops and police throughout the country to unleash another wave of terror against members of the opposition. No investigation of the attack had as yet been conducted. Conclusions were drawn in official quarters that Prio was behind it because several of the participants had once belonged to his party but this was contradicted by the government's attempt to blame Pelayo Cuervo.

Members of the palace staff reported that Señora Batista was furious when she was told of the paper found in Echevarria's pocket. "Pelayo Cuervo is to blame! Pelayo Cuervo is to blame!" she was reported to have shouted.

Batista summoned Colonel Mariano Faget, then deputy chief of detectives, who showed him the paper removed from Echevarria's pocket with the penciled name "Pelayo Cuervo" and the penciled word "President." Colonel Orlando Piedra, chief of detectives, followed on the heels of Faget. Both interviews were short. The two detective chiefs returned to their headquarters at the east side of the bridge over the Almendares River, conferred together and issued orders.

Two automobiles left the detective headquarters. In one, a black Cadillac, there were Santiago Linares Rosales at the wheel and four detectives as passengers. In another, a green Studebaker, there were Toribio Arocha Boizan at the wheel and three detectives. Their first stop was at the home of Pelayo Cuervo. His wife, agitated over their visit, informed them that he was not at home and that she did not know where he might be. She became even more alarmed when the detectives left hurriedly and did not search the house. The police spies had since submitted a report: Pelayo Cuervo had been seen entering the home of a friend, Ignacio Aguirre Oteiza, at 3206 Avenida 47 in the La Sierra district. He had sought refuge there reluctantly but at the insistence of friends because no one who dissented from Batista was safe.

At ten o'clock at night the two automobiles came to a halt in front of the Aguirre Oteiza residence. Five of the detectives surrounded the block with submachine guns in their hands. The others knocked on the door and asked for Pelayo Cuervo. They were told he was not there but they did not accept the answer and entered the house. Two of them found the bedroom where Pelayo

154

Cuervo sat reading, ordered him to accompany them and left the house with him. He was placed in one of the automobiles.

"To the beach at Marianao!" The drivers were ordered to step on it. They sped away but as they neared the Coney Island playground in Marianao the orders were countermanded.

"To the lagoon!" The cars sped toward the Country Club. Sergeant Rafael Gutierrez ordered Linares to halt the automobile near the lagoon.

Gutierrez ordered Cuervo to alight. Cuervo stood by the sidewalk near a tree. The night was dark. Sergeant Gutierrez was face to face with him, in his hand a machine pistol.

"Now are you going to tell me where the weapons are stored?" he asked Pelayo Cuervo.

"I don't know anything about any weapons," the distinguished lawyer replied.

Sergeant Gutierrez did not wait for another word, but fired at Cuervo, who fell to the ground in a pool of blood. Gutierrez continued to pump lead into the mortally wounded man.

Gutierrez ordered one of his men to bend the license plates of the cars and daub them with mud so their numbers could not be recognized. He issued a warning to the other eight men in the party. "I will shoot anyone who says anything about this outside of our headquarters!"

Though residents of the exclusive Country Club area had heard some bursts that sounded like machine-gun fire, it was not until two thirty in the morning that someone ventured to investigate. Pelayo Cuervo's bullet-riddled, lifeless body was found not far from the lagoon where it had been left.

The murder of Cuervo shocked the people of Havana. There was no statement from the palace or from any government official condemning it. Sergio Carbo, courageous editor and publisher of the newspaper *Prensa Libre,* published a page-one editorial under his signature in which, while criticizing the assault on the palace and the attempt to kill Batista, he expressed horror over the wave of terror that the government had launched in reprisal, and condemned the murder of such a highly respected national figure as Pelayo Cuervo.

On the morning of March 14, hours after the attack on the

palace and the reprisal murder of Pelayo Cuervo, American Ambassador Arthur Gardner entered the still bullet-marked palace with officers of the economic staff of the embassy, to be present at Batista's signing of a new contract with the Cuban Telephone Company. The effort of Gardner to help Batista convey an impression both at home and abroad that things were normal in Cuba at that moment neither ingratiated him and the State Department with the people of the country nor enhanced the popularity of the Cuban Telephone Company, a subsidiary of International Telephone and Telegraph Company.

Meanwhile, Armando Hart, leader of the Castro underground in Havana, made an electrifying escape from custody while awaiting trial in the Urgency Court in the capital. The underground had paved the way for the dramatic get-away. Now from various hideouts he masterminded sabotage and other subversive operations. Batista's police and army filled the jails of the country beyond capacity. The torture and killing of prisoners continued without surcease. Fingernails were extracted, vital organs were shattered, faces were disfigured, ribs and bones were broken, backs were left with welts and many were the prisoners who never emerged from the jails alive.

I had asked Batista in my interview of March 6: "Why don't you expedite a general election, coupled with a general amnesty, so that you can leave quickly and peace can be restored in Cuba?"

"I have my pride," he replied. "I will not leave a minute before February 24, 1959, when my term is to expire!"

The one dream Batista always entertained was to enjoy popularity with the people of Cuba. The one person the people of Cuba never could stomach was Batista. He has dotted the environs of Havana with public works which will be visible evidence of his late administration for years to come—and enriched himself and his cronies in the process—and he improved roads and highways in the immediate vicinity of the capital and pushed through the building of the tunnel under the harbor of Havana. But he could in no way endear himself to a people who detested him for his brutality and for the corruption and graft of which he, his relatives and friends were part and parcel.

The gambling casinos were thriving, tourists were pouring into

156

Havana and Varadero and the Isle of Pines, but Cuba was bathed in blood, blood that Batista had caused to flow when he destroyed constitutional government on March 10, 1952. Señora Batista was receiving fifty percent of the profits of the slot machines in the gambling casinos that Batista had allowed to be opened throughout the country. Army and police officers and some naval officers were also profiting from this system of official corruption. Batista was receiving his take through intermediaries, and some of the money was being used to buy off army officers and politicians.

The army of Cuba was under command of one family, whose head was the man closest to Batista, General Francisco Tabernilla Dolz. One son, Carlos, was commander of the air force. Another son, Francisco, Jr., was commander of the tank group. His brother-in-law, at this time Brigadier General Alberto del Rio Chaviano, was commander of Moncada and the Theater of Operations in the province of Oriente. Through a Cuban commercial cargo airline that was allowed to operate into the military air base at Camp Columbia, durable consumer goods such as refrigerators, washing machines, television sets and other large household appliances were flown in from Miami, cleared without payment of customs duty and carted away to the warehouses and stores of a man reputed to be in partnership with the Tabernilla family.

All those operations were only too well known by the people of the island, all the graft and corruption and the system of buying off—or at least attempting to buy off—disaffected armed forces officers, newspaper editors and publishers of Cuba and others. They were sick of it, and they were aroused because their fathers, their sons, their brothers, their uncles and aunts, their sisters, their cousins and their friends were being arrested, tortured and killed daily—because they did not like Batista, or they wished to take up arms to overthrow him, or they carried a 26th of July bond which showed that they had contributed perhaps a dollar to the cause, or they wore ties or dresses containing the colors red and black.

The police broke into an apartment at Humboldt 37 in the Vedado district of Havana, where four members of the Directorio Revolucionario were hiding, and shot and killed them. They were Fructuoso Rodriguez, who had succeeded Jose Antonio Echevar-

157

ria as president of the University Students' Federation, Joe West-brook, Jose Machado and Juan Pedro Carbo. Westbrook's mother took up the fight after her son fell. She went into exile in the United States, where she pounded on doors and wrote letters and made speeches on behalf of the revolutionary cause.

Daily more names were added to the list of thousands of Cuban women, unsung heroines in the fight against tyranny. On the night of March 13, for example. Señora Enrique Menocal, despite an eight-month pregnancy, accompanied by Señora Aurorita Botifoll Powell, transported Fructuoso Rodriguez and Juan Nuiry, who were still bleeding from wounds suffered in the day's fighting, in her automobile to a home where they could receive medical atten-tion. Nuiry had accompanied Jose Antonio Echevarria to the CMQ radio station and escaped after being wounded by the police. Nuiry was another student leader. After his recovery he went into exile in the United States.

The same night Señora Felipe Pazos, wife of the former presi-dent of the Banco Nacional, also picked up wounded from hide-outs and transported them in her automobile to a place where they could receive medical attention.

Both Señora Menocal and Señora Pazos would frequently drive from Havana along the central highway as far eastward as Holguin to deliver a precious cargo of bullets for relay to Castro. This was a cause in which Castro inspired faith and confidence in the women. It was in response to the pact which he had signed with Jose Antonio Echevarria in Mexico City, for the rebellious Direc-torio Revolucionario to act at a given time, that the women once again showed their valor as they risked their own lives to save others.

Almost at the same time every possible bullet and weapon that could be obtained was caressingly collected by women under-ground workers. In Santiago de Cuba, society women would call at homes of friends, ostensibly to pay a social call, and leave a gift of a large can of crackers. The can would be filled with .45 caliber bullets and, if luck were at hand, also with a .45 caliber pistol. That same day or the next the cargo of crackers would make its way to the Sierra Maestra, but this time they would be-come firecrackers.

Besides Matthews' rediscovery of and interview with Castro,

158

Fidel received another psychological boost when shortly thereafter three young sons of American personnel at the Guantanamo Bay naval base climbed the Sierra Maestra to join the tiny forces of the rebel chief. When Matthews interviewed him, Castro had only eleven other men there.

The three youths were Charles Ryan, 20, of Monson, Massachusetts; Victor J. Buehlman, 17, of Coronado, California; and Michael L. Garvey, of Watertown, Massachusetts. They spent several months in the rugged mountains and participated in some action before Castro ordered Buehlman and Garvey to return to Guantanamo. They were taken from the Sierra Maestra by Bob Taber and Wendell Hoffman of the Columbia Broadcasting System, who had been filming the Castro campaign. Ryan remained for a few more months and was promoted to the rank of lieutenant. Castro then sent him back, too, suggesting that he could do more for the rebel cause in the United States in propaganda work.

The news that three youths from the Guantanamo Bay naval base in Cuba had joined Castro awakened the imagination and desire for adventure of many another young American throughout the United States. Volunteer after volunteer tried to establish contact with the rebels. Many wrote letters to me, and I always replied that Castro did not need manpower since there were several million Cubans ready to fight under him if they could get their hands on the guns and the bullets that he needed.

Before the three young men from Guantanamo Bay joined Castro, some arms and ammunition had disappeared from the naval base. Among the stolen weapons were two 81-millimeter mortars. These were taken, apparently, by members of the 26th of July Movement cells on the base and were transported westward for use by the Castro forces, desperately in need of guns of any kind.

Special investigators were flown down from Washington by the Navy Department to probe the case.

And in the meantime another expedition was being trained in the vicinity of Miami and again the instructor was Colonel Alberto Bayo. But this time the expedition was being financed and outfitted by Prio.

"I was not tied down to one group or to one party in this fight for Cuban liberation from dictatorship," Bayo explained to me. "I was friendly with Castro, friendly with Prio and friendly with Aureliano Sanchez Arango's Triple A group that had become antagonistic to Prio. I was also friendly with the Directorio Revolucionario. I maintained contacts with all."

Bayo moved to New York after Castro's landing in Cuba, to help in the propaganda work in his behalf. Batista began to label him as a Communist and linked Raul Castro and Che Guevara also with Moscow—all of this branding being designed to ingratiate himself with the State Department and American public opinion. Batista's tirade against Castro on March 10, in which he denounced the rebel chief as a Kremlin agent, had boomeranged, so for a time he carefully avoided repeating those charges against him.

Prio asked Bayo to move to Miami to train an expedition to be led by Calixto Sanchez White, who had been the leader of the Airport Workers' Union. Sanchez had been forced into exile when it was discovered he was smuggling weapons into Cuba by air freight, especially in the interior of refrigerators. As he controlled the cargo at the Jose Marti airport at Rancho Boyeros, Sanchez had managed to get away with this smuggling for a long time before the intelligence service caught up with him.

It was reported that Sanchez had planned to take over the airport simultaneously with the attack on the palace on March 13, and that his failure to do so had preyed on his mind. He wished to revindicate himself, and this expedition which was to sail on the yacht *Corinthia* from the Miami River was the way he hoped to clear his name.

Bayo was furnished a bodyguard in Miami by his rebel friends, but to proceed with the training of the new expedition he had to give the guard the slip.

"One day I told them," he relates, "that I would have to move elsewhere because I had a mission to perform which I could not tell them about. My bodyguard told me that I could not do it because they were responsible for protecting my life and I had to tell them where I was going. I refused, and I eluded them."

Bayo trained Calixto Sanchez, and a cadre he had asked the latter to select, in the art of guerrilla warfare. He impressed on

160

them the fact that they should accept the surrender of prisoners one by one, searching each prisoner, never accepting them as a group and trusting no one.

In mid-May of 1957 the *Corinthia* sailed out of the Miami River. Twenty-seven men and a heavy cargo of arms and ammunition were aboard to land in the northeastern sector of the province of Oriente to try to open a second front against Batista in the Sierra Cristal. Most of the men with Sanchez had been trained in the Dominican Republic the previous year. The landing was made successfully, and the force led by Sanchez marched into the hills toward the planned bivouac area.

"They didn't pay attention to my recommendations," Bayo narrates. "And while they were marching some of Batista's soldiers, dressed as *guajiros,* arrived by truck at the place where the members of the expedition were resting and bathing in a river. The supposed *guajiros* approached them, shouting: 'Viva Fidel Castro! Viva Fidel Castro!' Then more than a dozen of them surrounded Calixto Sanchez and his men. Whereupon they announced:

" 'You are surrounded by 3,500 soldiers. There is no possible escape for you. Surrender and we will guarantee you will not be killed.' Our men were so foolish that, ignoring my recommendations, they surrendered. Seventeen of them were vilely assassinated by Colonel Fermin Cowley's men."

Ten of the expeditionaries successfully escaped and made their way into the hills from where they entered the cities to work in the Organizacion Autentico underground.

None of the members of the ill-fated *Corinthia* force carried any identification papers. Bayo had made certain that the security would be perfect, and it was so perfect that they were able to set sail from Miami without detection. Nevertheless, Batista's spies in Miami were quick to obtain a list of their names; concurrently with the announcement that the men had been killed in combat, the names were released to the press in Havana.

Bayo was invited by Marisol Alba to move into her luxurious house on an island on Venetian causeway at Miami Beach, where he lived until the time when he, too, began to suspect her.

Several months later, in the lobby of the Hotel Mayflower in

161

Washington, Jose Lopez Vilaboy, who was president of the Cubana Airline, which owned the Havana airport, and a business associate of Batista's, told me with tears streaming down his face that—when news reached Havana that Sanchez had been captured with the members of his expedition—he had begged Batista to issue an order to save Sanchez' life.

"Batista finally agreed," Lopez Vilaboy told me, "and he telephoned to Holguin to issue the order. But when he hung up the phone, he told me that it was too late. Sanchez White had already been killed."

Lopez Vilaboy had made the point in an attempt to illustrate that Batista had a soft spot in his heart.

Volunteers trekked to the Sierra Maestra early in the month of March, and soon Castro had a force of several hundred men. He led them down the mountain to attack an army post at Ubero where 60 soldiers were stationed. He left eight men as a rear guard and attacked with 120 men. The soldiers were caught by surprise, 15 were killed, 15 were taken prisoners and the remainder escaped.

That attack, made May 28, 1957, let the people of Cuba know that Castro's guerrillas could come out of their hideouts at night, hit the enemy and get away successfully. More volunteers began to make their way up the mountains to join his army. Parents would find their sons missing from home and learn days or weeks later that they were with Castro.

When Batista's loyal troops repelled the attack on the palace he had won a battle, but when his detectives killed Pelayo Cuervo he had lost the war. His downfall, sooner or later, was inevitable. And the murder of Pelayo Cuervo was not to be the last act to arouse the indignation of the people against Batista.

Cuervo's son, Pelayo, Jr., petitioned the courts to investigate the murder of his father. But he made absolutely no progress in this way and, irritated over the impossibility of obtaining justice, he began the trek from Havana to the Sierra Maestra to join Fidel Castro. Behind him went Raul Chibas and Roberto Agramonte, Jr. The police had raided the Agramonte home and, fearing for the life of the senior Agramonte, the Ortodoxo Party leaders recommended he go into exile. Agramonte left for Miami to live

162

out the remainder of the war abroad. Another man who journeyed to the Sierra Maestra was Felipe Pazos, whose oldest son Javier had already joined the rebel forces and whose youngest son, Felipe, Jr., had been cast for the role of the boy in the motion picture production of Ernest Hemingway's *The Old Man and the Sea*.

In the month of May the heart of Havana was paralyzed and blacked out for fifty-four hours by a dynamite explosion that blew up a gas and electric main in the old sector of the city. The saboteurs had dug a tunnel from a tenement building under the street to the conduit. All business, telephone communications and other transactions were at a standstill until the repair work could be completed. It was the biggest psychological blow by the Castro forces yet scored in Havana.

I interviewed Armando Hart in one of his hide-outs to which I was escorted by a member of the Havana underground, Jose Llanusa. My rendezvous with Llanusa was at the Vedado Tennis Club, of which he was a member; he was also a popular youth leader as a star on the club's basketball team. Llanusa drove me by a circuitous route to a house in one of the outlying districts. Hart told me that the sabotage operation in the heart of Havana had cost the rebels only $600. Hart's wife, Haydee Santamaria, who had only recently left the Sierra Maestra where she had been fighting with Castro, came to fetch him to transfer to another hiding place for both of them for that night. He was the most hunted man in Havana at the time.

In June 1957 I flew to Santiago de Cuba. Among those who met me at the airport was an old friend, Jose M. ("Pepin") Bosch, president and general manager of the famous Bacardi company.

"It is fortunate you came tonight," Pepin said, "because this morning a couple of the Fidelistas killed a soldier who was riding in a bus. Your arrival might prevent the police and army from snatching four boys from their homes and killing them in reprisal."

Pepin proved to be right; no boys were killed that night and the only victim was the proprietor of a tavern on the outskirts of the city, who was a follower of Prio.

The following night a representative group of citizens of Santiago honored me with a banquet at the Country Club. Besides

163

Pepin Bosch there were Dr. Manuel Urrutia, who was still a judge; Daniel Bacardi, the president of the Chamber of Commerce; the president of the University of Oriente; the Reverend Father Chabebe, head of the Catholic Youth Movement; Fernando Ojeda, a leading coffee exporter; the presidents of the Rotary Club, Lions Club, medical association, bar association, civic institutions and other groups. We were the only persons in the club. Santiago had not held any fiestas or celebrations, except those imposed by officialdom, since July 26, 1953. The table was oblong; at the end was an empty chair with a full place setting and a placard that had been carefully and intentionally placed there for my benefit. It read: "Reserved." The toastmaster, Fernando Ojeda, arose and addressed me.

"One of our compatriots had planned to attend this dinner in your honor tonight," he said, "but he sent his regrets that he could not make it. We can understand that and we accept his excuses because he is engaged in an important mission for Cuba. His name is Fidel Castro."

I asked Father Chabebe if he considered Fidel Castro a Communist, and he replied with a definite negative.

"Castro requested chaplains for his rebel army," Father Chabebe told me. "The first chaplain, Father Guillermo Sardinas, reached Castro's headquarters last Thursday, and I sent forty boys up into the hills to join Castro the same day. Last week I sent a gross of blessed medals up there."

It was Saturday night and couriers had already reported back from the Sierra Maestra that Father Sardinas had reached Castro. Father Sardinas had turned over his parish in Nueva Gerona on the Isle of Pines to an assistant and had obtained permission of the Archbishop's Palace in Havana to join the rebel forces. This was in contrast to the army of Batista, which had no chaplain corps and no chaplains.

I found the greatest respect and affection in Santiago de Cuba on the part of all the people to whom I talked (and this includes the members of the Rotary Club at whose weekly luncheon I was guest of honor) for American Consul General Oscar H. Guerra and Vice Consul William Patterson.

Both were heroes to the people, for they had virtually saved the

164

lives of several youths of the city when they happened to appear on the scene while the police were beating up the boys prior to confinement in jail or worse.

The State Department had decided to end the diplomatic career of Arthur Gardner, which he began in 1953 as a political appointee. Batista dispatched his American public relations adviser, Edmund Chester, to Washington to visit the State Department and petition for the continuation of his close friend Gardner as envoy. But Gardner's successor, Earl E. T. Smith, a New York and West Palm Beach broker, was already chosen.

In the last weeks of his service in Havana, Gardner was furnished a special bodyguard by Batista because of the fabricated report that the rebel underground planned to kill him because of his friendship with Batista. Gardner's last act almost on the eve of his departure was to lay the cornerstone for an annex to the American embassy chancery at the rear of the present building on the Malecon; there were neither architectural plans nor a congressional appropriation for such an addition.

The ceremony, held with all due pomp, was attended by Minister of State Gonzalo Guell and other members of Batista's cabinet. A speaker's stand was erected between the Eighth Precinct Police Station on the Malecon and the rear of the embassy chancery. The stand was adorned with flags and the flags were flanked by a Cuban soldier and a United States marine. Speeches were made by Gardner and Guell.

Gardner announced that an eight-story annex would be built there for offices and apartments of embassy personnel, with the first two floors assigned to offices and the rest for residences.

The Cuban government had made available a parcel of land for the purpose but the remainder of the property required was under private litigation with little chance that the case would be settled for years. Taking new facts into consideration, certainly most of those present, including the foreign minister and other cabinet ministers, well knew there would be no construction. But the entire farce was devised to convey the impression to the Cuban people and the army that Batista's government enjoyed the full support of the United States.

The magazine *Bohemia* said farewell to Gardner in a critical

165

editorial on June 14, 1957. It commented that he acted "more like a businessman than an ambassador and that he has made notorious mistakes." The editorial expressed the hope that his successor would not make the same mistakes, but the hope proved to be a vain one.

Castro conferred lengthily with Chibas and Pazos. The presence of these two men was a stimulus for his political mind. It gave him an opportunity to discuss with older men the problems of Cuba and to plan for the future, although his plans were made long ago.

In the month of June the civic institutions comprising forty-five representative organizations of the country issued a strong statement on the situation, which indicated a yearning to reach a compromise to end the civil war.

"We will know how to fulfill our duty if the situation should become worse," the statement read. "If the government demonstrates good faith by deeds, then the insurrectionists should accept a truce."

Castro conferred with Chibas and Pazos and drafted a manifesto from the Sierra. The document emphasized Castro's reverence for civilian, constitutional government. Signed on July 12, 1957, it was the first comprehensive political pronouncement made by Castro to the Cuban people since he climbed the mountain. Also, it will be noted, it contained a request that the United States cease shipping arms to Batista. The manifesto read:

"From the Sierra Maestra, where a sense of duty has united us, we issue this call to our compatriots.

"The hour has arrived in which the nation can save itself from tyranny, through the intelligence, the bravery and the civic action of its sons, through the efforts of all those who have begun to feel deeply the destiny of this land where we have the right to live in peace and in freedom.

"Is the Cuban nation incapable of fulfilling its high destiny or does the blame for impotence and lack of vision fall on its public leaders? Is it that the Fatherland cannot be offered in its most difficult hour the sacrifice of all personal aspirations, just though they may be, of all the subaltern passions, the personal or group rivalries, in spite of whatever niggardly or small sentiment that

166

has prevented placing on the alert as one man this formidable, awakened and heroic people that the Cubans are? Or is it that the vain wish of a public aspirant is worth more than all the blood it has cost this republic?

"Our greatest weakness has been disunity, and the tyranny, conscious of it, has promoted it by all means and in all its aspects. Offering half solutions, tempting ambitions at some times, and at others the good faith or ingenuity of their adversaries, the tyrannical leaders divided all the parties into antagonistic fractions, divided the political opposition along dissimilar lines and, when the revolutionary current was stronger and more threatening, they attempted to pit the politicians against the revolutionaries, with the idea of beating the revolution first and laughing at the parties later.

"It is a secret to nobody that if the dictatorship managed to defeat the rebel bulwark of the Sierra Maestra and to crush the clandestine movement, once free of the revolutionary danger, there would be not even the remotest possibilities of honest elections in the midst of the general bitterness and skepticism.

"Their intentions were evident, perhaps too soon, when by using the senatorial minority, which had been approved with scorn for the Constitution and laughter at the obligations contracted with the very delegates from the opposition, they tried anew to effect a split and prepared the road for the electoral race.

"That the Interparliamentary Commission failed is recognized by the party that proposed it in the Congress. The seven opposition organizations that participated in it and today denounce it as a bloody joke affirm that categorically. All the civic institutions affirm it. And, above all, the facts affirm it. It was doomed to fail because they wanted to ignore the drive acquired by two forces that have made their appearance in Cuban public life: the new revolutionary generation and the civic institutions, much more powerful than many think. The interparliamentary maneuver thus could only prosper on the basis of the extermination of the rebels. The fighters of the Sierra were not offered anything in that niggardly solution other than jail, exile or death. Never would they agree to discuss those conditions.

"To unite is the only patriotic thing in this hour. To unite in what they have in common all political, revolutionary and social sectors that combat the dictatorship. And what do all the opposition political parties, the revolutionary sectors and the civic institutions have in common? The desire to put an end to the regime of force, the violations of individual rights, the infamous crimes, and to seek the peace that we desire by the only road possible, which is the democratic and constitutional transition of the country.

"Is it that we rebels of the Sierra Maestra do not want free elections, a democratic regime, a constitutional government?

"It is because they deprived us of those rights that we have fought since the 10th of March. It is because we want them more than anyone else that we are here. To prove it, there are our fighters dead in the Sierra and our companions assassinated on the streets or locked up in the dungeons of the prisons: fighting for the beautiful ideal of a Free Cuba, democratic and just. What we do not do is to commune with the lie, the farce and the compromise.

"We want elections; but with one condition: truly free, democratic, impartial elections.

"But can there be free, democratic, impartial elections with all the repressive apparatus of the state hanging like a sword over the heads of the oppositionists? Is it that the present government machine after so many jokes on the people can offer confidence to anyone in free, democratic, impartial elections?

"Is it not an anomaly, a deceit, to the people who see what is happening here every day to state that there can be free, democratic, impartial elections under the tyranny, the anti-democracy and the partiality?

"Of what value is the direct and free vote, the immediate count and other fictitious concessions if on the day of the elections nobody is allowed to vote and the ballot boxes are stuffed at bayonet point? Did the Committee on Suffrage and Public Liberties do any good in preventing the closing of radio stations and the mysterious deaths that continue to occur?

"Have the demands of public opinion, the exhortations to peace, the cries of the mothers done any good up to now?

168

"They want to put an end to the rebellion with more blood, to the terrorism with more terror, to the desire for liberty with more oppression.

"The elections should be presided over by a provisional, neutral, government with the support of all, which replaces the dictatorship in order to propitiate peace and to lead the country to democratic and constitutional normality.

"This should be the slogan of a great civilian revolutionary front that comprises all the political parties of the opposition, all the civic institutions and all the revolutionary forces.

"In consequence, we propose to all the opposition political parties, all the civic institutions and all the revolutionary sectors the following:

"1. Formation of a Civilian Revolutionary Front with a common strategy of struggle.

"2. To select as of now a figure to preside over the provisional government, whose election will be made by the civic institutions to ensure the disinterest and impartiality of opposition leaders.

"3. To declare to the country that owing to the gravity of events there is no possible solution other than the resignation of the dictator and the delivery of the power to the figure who counts on the confidence and the majority support of the nation, expressed through its representative organizations.

"4. To declare that the Civilian Revolutionary Front does not invoke nor does it accept mediation or intervention of any kind from another nation in the internal affairs of Cuba. That, on the other hand, it supports the denunciations of the violation of human rights that Cuban emigrants have made before the international organizations and asks the government of the United States, as long as the present regime of terror and dictatorship exists, to suspend all shipments of arms to Cuba.

"5. To declare that the Civilian Revolutionary Front, by republican and independent tradition, will not accept any type of military junta provisionally to govern the republic.

"6. To declare that the Civilian Revolutionary Front plans to divorce the army from politics and to guarantee the nonpolitical status, exempt from reprisal, of the armed forces. That the army has nothing to fear from the Cuban people, but it is the corrupt clique who should fear the people it sends to death in a fratricidal struggle.

"7. To declare under formal promise that the provisional government will hold general elections for all offices of the state, the provinces and the municipalities at the end of one year under the norms of the Constitution of 1940 and the Electoral Code of 1943 and will deliver the power immediately to the candidates elected.

"8. To declare that the provisional government will have to adjust its mission to the following program:

"A. Immediate freedom for all political, civil and military prisoners.

"B. Absolute guarantee of freedom of information, of the spoken and written press and of all the individual and political rights guaranteed by the Constitution.

"C. Designation of provisional mayors in all the municipalities prior to consultation with the civic institutions of the locality.

"D. Suppression of peculation in all its forms and adoption of measures that tend to increase the efficiency of all organisms of the state.

"E. Establishment of Civil Service.

"F. Democratization of labor policy, promoting free elections in all unions and federations of industries.

"G. Immediate start of an intensive campaign against illiteracy and for civic education, exalting the duties and rights which the citizen has in relation to society and the Fatherland.

"H. Establishment of the foundations for an agrarian reform that tends to the distribution of barren lands and to convert into proprietors all the lessee-planters, partners and squatters who possess small parcels of land, be it property of the state or of private persons, with prior indemnification to the former owners.

"I. Adoption of a sound financial policy that safeguards the stability of our money and tends to use the credit of the nation in productive works.

"J. Acceleration of the process of industrialization and the creation of new jobs.

170

"In two points of this document there must be made special insistence:

"First: The need that the person called to preside over the provisional government of the republic be named now in order to demonstrate before the world that the Cuban people are capable of uniting behind a password of liberty and to support the person who, meeting conditions of impartiality, integrity, capacity and decency, can incarnate that password. There is an abundance of men in Cuba capable of presiding over the republic!

"Second: That that person be designated by the joint body of civic institutions because those organizations are nonpolitical. Such support would free the provisional president of every partisan compromise, would allow and lead to absolutely free and impartial elections.

"To integrate this front it is not necessary that the political parties and the civic institutions declare themselves insurrectional and come to the Sierra Maestra. It is enough that they deny all support to the electoral compromise of the regime and declare before the country, before the armed forces and before international public opinion that, after five years of useless effort, of continuous deceits and of rivers of blood, in Cuba there is no other escape than the resignation of Batista, who already has ruled the destinies of the country in two stages for sixteen years, and Cuba is not disposed to fall into the situation of Nicaragua or of Santo Domingo.

"It is not necessary to come to the Sierra to talk. We can be represented in Havana, in Mexico or wherever it may be necessary.

"It is not necessary to decree the revolution: organize the front that we propose and the downfall of the regime will come by itself, perhaps without the shedding of another drop of blood. One must be blind not to see that the dictatorship is in its last days, and that this is the minute in which all Cubans should put forth the best of their intelligence and their effort.

"Can there be another solution in the midst of civil war with a government that is incapable of guaranteeing human life, which

171

does not control even the action of its own repressive forces and whose continued tricks and games have made the slightest public confidence impossible?

"Nobody is deceived about the government propaganda concerning the situation in the Sierra. The Sierra Maestra is already an indestructible bulwark of liberty that has lighted a fire in the hearts of our compatriots, and here we will know how to honor the faith and the confidence of our people.

"Our call could be ignored, but the fight will not halt because of it and nobody will be able to prevent the victory of the people although it will be much more costly and bloody. We hope, however, that our appeal will be heard and that a true solution halts the flow of Cuban blood and brings us an era of peace and liberty."

Slightly more than a week after that manifesto was issued, American Ambassador Earl E. T. Smith arrived to assume his post. He was well received and made a good impression among the Cubans, because of his cautious and moderate statements at his first press conference in the embassy. His initial mission was to remove the stigma of Gardner's excessive partisanship toward Batista. He succeeded forthwith because of a combination of circumstances that played into his hands and made him a hero to the Cuban people overnight.

With Batista's consent, he flew to Santiago de Cuba to get the feel of the situation there. The day before, July 30, Frank Pais, national leader of the Castro underground and a brilliant school teacher, had been shot down in cold blood by Colonel Salas Canizares, police chief, as he was about to change his hideout from one house to another.

The previous month I was unable to see Pais because he was changing hide-outs so frequently that it was dangerous both to him and to me to insist on it. Instead I was able to see his deputy, "Deborah," organizer of the women's underground. "Deborah" was the code name for Vilma Espin, daughter of the attorney for the Bacardi Company in Santiago. She, too, was hunted by the police but her hide-out that day was much safer than that of Pais.

172

On June 30 Pais' younger brother, Josue, had been killed when his car, filled with 26th of July resistance members, was intercepted by a police car. The killing of Pais and of the owner of the house where he had been hiding added to the indignation of the people of Santiago. Castro learned of the killing in a radio news broadcast and sent orders to Santiago that Pais should be buried with full honors as a colonel of the rebel army, a rank higher than Castro's.

Smith reached Santiago at noon July 31. Pais' funeral was scheduled for three o'clock. A group of women, dressed in mourning, gathered for a demonstration for Smith's benefit as he rode to call on the mayor. The women carried a banner which read: STOP KILLING OUR SONS! The police turned fire hoses on the women to disperse them, and Salas Canizares pushed a few around roughly. Smith was horrified by the brutality and it shocked his wife, who was also in the automobile.

When Smith returned to the Rancho Club, he consulted two members of his staff, John Topping, political officer, and Richard Cushing, public affairs officer, about a statement that they recommended he issue. The statement was drafted and redrafted and issued to waiting newspapermen. In it Smith criticized the employment of police brutality in any form.

Smith's statement hit the headlines in Havana and was broadcast over the radio. The population of Santiago de Cuba closed up shop for the funeral of Frank Pais. A spontaneous general strike had begun. Smith returned to Havana that night just as Batista again established censorship of the press and radio and suspended all civil rights.

The general strike began to mushroom throughout the country. There had been neither prior planning nor prior organization for it. It was a spontaneous expression of repudiation of daily brutality, tortures, killings and a protest against corrupt government and equally corrupt labor leaders who had become multimillionaires within a few years, notably Eusebio Mujal, secretary general of the CTC.

The general strike was doomed to fail because of Batista's ironclad censorship, which for four days hid from the workers of Havana the news that Santiago was closed up tight, and that the same thing had happened in other cities of Oriente, as well as in other provinces.

Official reaction against Smith was whipped up. There was a resolution introduced into the senate to declare him *persona non grata,* and Batista senators made strong speeches on the floor. The pro-Batista newspapers lambasted Smith in page-one editorials and told him to go home. There was official and semi-official protests that Smith was intervening in the internal affairs of Cuba. Secretary of State John Foster Dulles, asked for a comment at his news conference, backed up Smith for having made a "humane" statement. The Dulles statement was never published in the Cuban press and of course Batista did not allow it to be broadcast. The statement was such a bombshell that if it had been published or broadcast some of Batista's own supposedly loyal friends might have asked the army chiefs to depose him.

Though the general strike was doomed to fail, it was unfortunate for the rebel cause that it had been launched just at that time. For a conspiracy was under way which had wide ramifications in the armed forces, especially in the navy. The blow was to have been struck August 20 but was postponed because of the need to forge other links in the chain.

I was back in Havana again ten days later to interview Raul Chibas, who had come down from the Sierra Maestra with Roberto Agramonte, Jr., and Pelayo Cuervo, Jr., on special missions for Fidel Castro. Up to then they had been successful in escaping Batista's dragnet, having made the trip from the Sierra Maestra to the capital overland in the remarkable time of forty-one hours. By circuitous routes to avoid detection I was taken to the home of Chibas' brother-in-law in a new residential development and was ushered into an air-conditioned bedroom where Chibas and young Agramonte sat. My interview with them confirmed my estimate that Castro would ultimately rout Batista. The conversation with Chibas could be summed up as follows:

1. Castro wanted them to get to the United States to tell the Castro story to the American people, and Chibas had been commissioned to supervise the collection of money for the cause.

174

2. Castro was in need of arms to equip volunteers who wished to join his force.

3. Castro had ordered a government spy executed. The spy had infiltrated into his force and then disappeared to act as an observer-guide for Batista's air force. When he returned the spy was tried by a summary court and shot.

4. Cuban air force planes had been carrying on indiscriminate bombing of the Sierra Maestra but had yet to hit a rebel target.

5. The morale of the Castro force was superb.

6. Castro enjoyed the voluntary support of natives in the Sierra Maestra.

7. Whenever Batista's troops reached the trails leading up to the mountains toward Castro's hideouts and encountered natives, the soldiers begged them not to reveal to their officers the location of the rebels. This created the belief that most of Batista's troops did not want to fight.

8. Raul Castro, brother of Fidel, had never been wounded in any battle as the government communiqués claimed.

9. Castro had a television set in his headquarters. There was a trap door in the roof which permitted the antenna to be lowered when the set was not in use or whenever there was danger of air attack.

10. Two clergymen were at Castro's headquarters, both of them Cubans. One was a Roman Catholic priest and the other a Baptist minister.

11. Castro insists that an interim government must replace Batista and preside over free and honest presidential elections. He does not want the presidency for himself. He insists the provisional president should be chosen by the leaders of the civil and political groups of the opposition.

12. Castro will not lay down his arms if Batista holds an election. He contends that no election under Batista can be honest and free.

On the night of September 2, 1957, I again interviewed Batista; I was accompanied by Guillermo Martinez Marquez, editor of the newspaper *El Pais,* and president of the Inter American Press Association. Batista objected to a reference I had made to a previous interview in which he had given his word of honor he would never reimpose censorship. He claimed that what he had meant at the time was that he would not reimpose censorship as long as that particular period of suspension of guarantees was in effect. After an hour and a half there was absolutely no reason for optimism: Batista had made it clear that he was not going to abolish censorship.

The palace reporters interviewed us after we left Batista's office. Martinez Marquez told them he was optimistic that Batista would lift censorship, while I expressed pessimism. Martinez Marquez told the reporters not to use my dissenting statement.

Two days later Batista celebrated the twenty-fourth anniversary of his meteoric rise from sergeant to colonel and to ruler of Cuba. That night there was a fete at navy headquarters overlooking the Malecon. At dawn of September 5, 1957, the naval station at Cayo Loco (Crazy Key) in Cienfuegos was captured by a group of cashiered naval officers, 26th of July Movement militia and Carlos Prio's Organization Autentico. There was supposed to have been a simultaneous uprising in Havana where two naval frigates which were in the harbor were to stand out to sea and bombard Camp Columbia out of the reach of the artillery at the military headquarters. Batista's air force was to have been immobilized and there was to have been defection at the San Antonio de los Banos air base to the west.

The two frigate captains changed their minds at the eleventh hour, notifying Lieutenant Juan M. Castineiras, who had been cashiered from the navy by Batista for sympathy to Castro, of the need to postpone H-hour. Castineiras was the naval liaison contact man in the underground; he had planned the revolt along with Lieutenant Jose San Roman Toledo, another cashiered naval officer. San Roman had already left for Cienfuegos and the order countermanding H-hour failed to reach him.

The rebels took over Cienfuegos with little difficulty. They distributed weapons to civilians, who swarmed to Cayo Loco to get them. Again Batista's ironclad censorship saved him. When I returned to Havana at five o'clock that afternoon, hardly anybody knew that there was a revolt in Cienfuegos. Batista dispatched the Third Mobile Force from Santa Clara, capital of Las Villas province, to Cienfuegos to counterattack. At the same

176

time he ordered the air force to strafe the city. Colonel Carlos Tabernilla dispatched the aircraft and for four hours Cienfuegos was strafed with .50 caliber fire from the loyal aircraft. One naval PBY in the hands of the rebels was shot down in the bay off Cienfuegos.

Almost all of the 60,000 inhabitants of the city were sympathetic toward the revolt. The forces that rose against Batista were mainly sergeants of the navy (equivalent to our petty officers) and sergeants of the police force. There were some junior officers of the navy in the grades of lieutenant and lieutenant junior grade involved and a lieutenant commander.

The rebels held Cienfuegos throughout Thursday, September 5, despite government announcements to the contrary. Central Park was the scene of the heaviest fighting within the city. Rebels occupied the municipal palace, the police headquarters and the Colegio San Lorenzo School of Arts and Crafts. The school, which was the latest redoubt, was reduced by a frontal attack by tanks and infantry of the reinforcements that arrived from Santa Clara. At two o'clock in the morning of September 6 all resistance had ceased there, and at eight o'clock in the morning the last four rebels holding out in police headquarters were killed. The Colegio San Lorenzo was pockmarked with shell holes. The city hall was peppered with evidence of shell fire.

I tried to ascertain in Cienfuegos the exact number of casualties but it was impossible. There was no official record because many rebels fled seaward aboard two boats when San Roman realized that Havana had not responded to the rising and the cause was lost. But San Roman remained at Cayo Loco, ready to return the station to the government in order to try to save the men who had rallied to the Castro cause.

To command the maritime police of Cienfuegos Batista assigned a man who had earned the reputation of being one of his most trusted men and a killer. He was Captain Alejandro Garcia Olayon. He had been indicted the previous year for having murdered a naval officer, but when Batista suspended civil rights shortly thereafter the case was transferred from the civilian courts to military justice and quashed.

A common grave was dug by a bulldozer in the cemetery, and

177

I saw fifty-two bodies dumped into it. Officials said they were bodies of men killed in battle; among them were sailors.

Nineteen prisoners, including Lieutenant San Roman, who had surrendered Cayo Loco, were taken to the Cienfuegos airport for flight by military aircraft to Havana and imprisonment in La Cabana Fortress. The prisoners were severely beaten by their soldier escorts. They were repeatedly struck with rifle butts and knocked down as often as they tried to rise. The same treatment was accorded the captured officers.

Cienfuegos was under martial law. Nobody ventured out at night. Troops conducted searches from house to house in an effort to recover some 2,000 weapons which the rebels had distributed to the civilian population.

Although the revolt was crushed, the flame of insurrection continued to burn in Cienfuegos and elsewhere. The men who had fled seaward by boats reached the Sierra del Escambray, a mountain range to the east of Cienfuegos. There they began to organize themselves for what was ultimately to become an active and effective Second National Front of Escambray, in which William Alexander Morgan, a twenty-nine-year old former paratrooper from Toledo, Ohio, was later to play an important role.

In Havana San Roman was mercilessly beaten; he was taken to the home of a high-ranking naval officer in the swank Biltmore residential district for questioning. While being questioned, according to testimony rendered before Judge Francisco Alabau Trelles in the criminal court of Havana, San Roman was shot in the back and killed by Lieutenant Julio Laurent, chief of the Naval Intelligence Service. The news of the death of San Roman was not published at that time because of censorship, and the government made no announcement of it.

Manuel Antonio de Varona, head of Prio's Organizacion Autentico, was arrested and accused of complicity in the naval revolt. He was confronted by the two frigate captains now under arrest, who testified that Varona had conferred with them in the apartment of an American friend about the feasibility of revolting against Batista. Members of the diplomatic corps interceded in behalf of Varona, and he was first granted asylum in the Chilean embassy and then given a safe conduct to leave the country. Within days he was in Miami to set up headquarters to continue conspiratorial operations against Batista.

Varona talked very freely in Miami, especially in the presence of Marisol Alba, a former Cuban television star, who was very friendly with Prio. Soon Batista had all the details of the ramifications of the Cienfuegos naval uprising and there was a complete shake-up in the motorized division of the police force in Havana which, Varona had reported, was involved in the conspiracy. Varona and Prio were suspicious of the leaks that were torpedoing almost every plan of theirs and the former president arranged for the theft of the brief case of Eduardo Hernandez, Consul General of Cuba in Miami.

Three Cubans accosted Hernandez at the Miami International Airport as he was about to depart for Havana. One of them tripped him as he walked toward the gate. The brief case fell from his hands, and two of the men fled from the terminal with it and made their getaway. The contents of the brief case included reports from Marisol Alba and other Cubans resident in Miami who were in Batista's pay as spies operating under the direction of Consul Hernandez. There were copies of letters written to Prio, Varona and others which were handed by courier from Havana ostensibly to reliable sympathizers of the anti-Batista cause in Miami for final delivery. There was also a notebook listing the names of the spies and their code names.

After the contents of the case were duly absorbed and recorded and photocopies were made of all pertinent documents, the brief case was left in the office of Ralph Renick, news director of Station WTVJ, Miami, for return to its owner.

Marisol Alba and others were tried before rebel drumhead courts-martial in Miami, convicted and sentenced to death upon return to Cuba, on the grounds that their espionage work for Batista caused the death of many of their countrymen. Some of the other suspects were brutally beaten by irate Cubans.

The day of the Cienfuegos naval revolt I finished writing a comprehensive special report for the Executive Committee on Censorship of the Inter American Press Association in Cuba. I dispatched it to the headquarters of the association in New York where that committee met on September 12. I reviewed in the

179

report the entire political and military background of Cuba from March 10, 1952, to September 5, 1957, to enable the committee members better to appreciate the situation and to debate my recommendation.

The conclusions in my report were that Batista never again could govern Cuba with freedom of the press as virtually the entire country was opposed to him and considered his government unconstitutional. I did not review the subsidies which most of the newspapers and some of the editors were receiving from the Batista government because I did not have in hand at the time the required documentary proof to substantiate such statements. There was only one recommendation: "that the government of Fulgencio Batista be declared not democratic because, in accordance with the Charter of the Inter American Press, it does not respect or cause to be respected freedom of the press."

The Executive Committee met, debated my report and modified the recommendation to refer it to the membership at the annual convention to be held in Washington the next month. The body of the report, however, was circulated to the members for their background and information. This gratuitous service on my part and on the part of the I.A.P.A. furnished the editors and publishers of the United States and Latin America with the background of the Cuban tragedy. Those who may have read the report, and the annual and semiannual reports that followed, need not have been surprised at recent events in that country.

The resolution was unanimously adopted as part of a general denunciation recommended by the Committee on Freedom of the Press, that included the Dominican Republic, Venezuela, Paraguay and Bolivia. (The situation of the press in Bolivia improved in 1958, and that country was removed from the list, together with Venezuela, which had recovered its freedom.) Several Cuban editors tried to pressure me behind the scenes to exclude their government from the denunciation. I put a quick halt to that lobbying by threatening to read a list of subsidies which each of them was getting from Batista if they insisted.

Two incidents in the month of November 1957 failed to enhance the popularity of the United States government—much less the Pentagon—in the minds of the Cuban people who were suf-

180

fering from the Batista brutality. Early that month Major General Truman H. Landon flew into Havana from his air command in the Panama Canal Zone to bestow the Legion of Merit on Colonel Carlos Tabernilla, head of Batista's air force. Tabernilla had earned the hatred of many Cubans for directing the air attack on Cienfuegos two months earlier. This award by our air force apparently was not previously co-ordinated with the State Department.

On the night of November 21 Batista received the members of the Inter American Defense Board. Havana was the last port of call on a flight to Peru and Panama. General Lemuel C. Shepherd, chairman, spoke for himself and the officers of the other American republics who accompanied him. But he was speaking in the uniform of a four-star general of the United States Marine Corps. He replied to Batista's champagne toast, assuring co-operation in continental defense, with these words:

"I wish to thank you on behalf of my colleagues because those words come not only from a great general but also from a great president."

Batista was swift to take advantage of those words of praise. He ordered his press office to send the text verbatim, with photographs, to the newspapers with instructions to play the story prominently. They did just that on page one, with the full blessing of the censors. The violent public reaction was clandestine because of the censorship.

CHAPTER 6

The rebel underground stepped up its sabotage and terroristic activities throughout the country, including Havana. Homemade bombs, such as Colonel Bayo had taught them to manufacture, would explode intermittently at different points in the capital and people would be driven from motion picture theaters and other places of amusement. Fire bombs also were employed, and show windows of stores suffered from the impact of petards. Rebel bands in the Sierra Maestra harassed army outposts and even ventured into towns to capture arms.

Busses both in cities and on the highways, trucks carrying freight and merchandise, passenger and freight trains, railroad and highway bridges, public buildings and homes and businesses of Batistianos were blown up or burned as part of the agitation and terror designed to maintain a constant state of alarm. A sixteen-year-old girl who had gone to the Tropicana Night Club for a New Year's party with her parents had her arm shattered when a bomb exploded near their table.

Rebel terror was answered by the government with tenfold reprisals. Bodies of boys and men were found hanging from trees or lampposts or lying lifeless in automobiles with grenades on their persons, to convey the impression that they had been caught in terrorist acts.

The jails were filled with sympathizers of the 26th of July

Movement, but hardly a Communist was included among those detained. The Communists, however, did not intend to be denied a place on the victory bandwagon.

The incessant atrocities and brutality by Batista's repressive forces had got so far out of hand that the Cuban Medical Association found it necessary to register a most energetic protest. The action was precipitated by a letter from the president of the Medical Association of Sancti Spiritus, province of Las Villas, who on October 25, 1957, wrote:

Dr. Raul de Velasco Guzman
President of the National Medical Association
Havana

"Distinguished fellow practitioner:

"Complying with the resolution of the governing body of the Medical Association adopted at a special meeting held last night, I have the honor to enclose a certified copy of the minutes of said meeting.

"To further explain said minutes, I will mention the facts as they occurred:

"A young man wounded in the back by firearms, showing paralysis and symptoms of traumatic shock, was carried to the office of Dr. Jorge Ruiz Ramirez at noon. Dr. Ruiz Ramirez at the time was in the town of Taguasco and, owing to the extreme urgency of the case, decided to take the young man by taxicab to a clinic in Sancti Spiritus; but before arriving there, they were intercepted by forces of the army, who took them to the rural guard headquarters of this city.

"Several witnesses saw them at said rural guard headquarters at 12:30 P.M. At 3:00 o'clock in the afternoon the relatives who visited the clinics and the hospitals of the city were alarmed at not finding the young man nor Dr. Ruiz Ramirez, and for this reason members of this Medical Association investigated where they could be found, going to different hospitals, police and the rural guard headquarters, but did not find them there. Army and police officers denied having them in their custody.

"In those hours of uncertainty we were visited by Dr. Julio

Oyarzabal Girbau, who informed us that Lieutenant Mirabal, chief of the army headquarters in Cabaiguan, had ordered him, at 5:00 o'clock that afternoon, to examine three corpses that were lying in the cemetery of Zaza del Medio, and that after great difficulties, owing to the amount of blood covering the corpses and rough treatment of same, he had been able to identify one as being that of Dr. Jorge Ruiz Ramirez.

"Dr. Oyarzabal Girbau claimed the corpse of his dead companion so as to give it proper attention, and same was delivered to him by Lieutenant Mirabal after expressing himself in an insulting way with regard to the corpses.

"Dr. Gregorio Martin Leal, who was allowed to read the reports in the army headquarters at Zaza del Medio, tells us that in said reports it was recorded that Dr. Ruiz Ramirez, the chauffeur and the wounded man were killed in combat in the zone of Jiquima de Pelaez, in the municipality of Cabaiguan, all of which is absolutely false in the light of what has been set forth above, and even more so by the fact that the doctor, who was vilely murdered, was politically affiliated with the government.

"Since it is impossible for me to relate the details by telephone, I am sending this report to the National Medical College by messenger.

"Yours very truly
"Dr. Francisco O. Delgado B.
"President"

NATIONAL MEDICAL COLLEGE

Member of the Pan-American Medical Confederation and
of the World Medical Association
Executive Committee

Havana, October 28, 1957

To the Chief Justice of the Supreme Court
City

"Mr. Chief Justice:

"In compliance with the resolutions of the Executive Committee of the National Medical College, we have the honor to ad-

184

dress you in order to denounce before the honorable court, with all proper intents and purposes, certain deeds of the gravest and most criminal nature that have been occurring in the national territory with alarming continuity in relation to the exercise of the medical profession.

"These deeds culminated on the 24th inst. in the death of Dr. Jorge Ruiz Ramirez, who, according to information which deserves our entire credit, was requested in his office in the town of Taguasco to attend a young man named Palermo who had been shot in the spine.

"Because of the critical condition of the man, Dr. Ruiz Ramirez decided to take him to a clinic in Sancti Spiritus, advising the young man's relatives of his decision.

"The vehicle was intercepted by members of the army, who took them to Jiquima de Pelaez, killing the doctor, the wounded man and the chauffeur of the taxicab.

"Our unfortunate fellow practitioner, who was killed by army forces while doing his duty, which he considered obligatory for reasons of morality, mercy and the provisions of the penal laws, showed bruises caused by the butt of a rifle on his forehead and several gunshot wounds spread over the thorax and abdomen.

"The triple murder that we are denouncing before the high court, Mr. Justice, has deeply moved the population of Sancti Spiritus; and to the grief of the medical class of Cuba caused by the death of a fellow professional there must be added the justifiable alarm due to the threat involved for all medical men, and especially for those who practice in the cities of the interior of the Republic, in the face of the outrages committed by the public forces.

"The penal law protects human life without distinction of race, sex, age, social standing or political affiliation. Article 164 provides sanction for 'those who do not respect the inviolability of the ambulances, hospitals, concentration camps for the wounded, the sick or prisoner' and for 'those who deny the necessary help to the wounded, the sick, the hospitalized or prisoner' and for 'those who in any way attack ships, railways or airplanes engaged in the service of hospitalizing or transporting the wounded, the shipwrecked person or prisoner' as well as 'those who prevent

185

charitable institutions from exercising the duties of their office.'

"The Code of Medical Ethics in Time of War provides that a medical doctor must do his duty at all times and under any circumstances in which his services are requested, without making any distinctions among his patients, save those which are required under the emergency of a case.

"These high moral principles, which are complied with voluntarily by the medical men of Cuba at all times, have been converted by legislation into a penal obligation which under Article 407(A) of the Code of Social Defense provides sanctions for: 'any medical doctor not serving as a paid employee or public officer who may be required by any private party to render any help connected with his profession in a case of emergency and of grave danger for the health or life of a citizen and who should abstain from so serving without justified cause.'

"Upon referring to the principles of ethics and the provisions of the Code of Social Defense relating to the medical profession, we are trying to establish what the duties of a doctor are, while asseverating before you that on more than one occasion doctors have suffered violent interference in the exercise of their profession, hospital premises have been assaulted and the wounded have been removed and subsequently have been found dead.

"These acts have given rise to public protests from municipal medical colleges and from this Executive Committee. What could have been isolated and independent incidents at any particular moment have become an inhuman system with the medical class, and now the medical class contemplates with terror and indignation the indescribable acts we now denounce before you, which show to what extent barbarity has taken hold of our country.

"On this very day we have confronted a new and tragic act, for Dr. Antonio Pulido Humaran was taken from his home in the early morning hours of the twenty-sixth by persons armed with machine guns, and his relatives received no other news of him except the discovery on the next day in the Havana Morgue of his corpse, showing signs of having been brutally beaten to death, as can be proved by the results of the autopsy.

"On the face of this danger, doctors find themselves unprotected in the exercise of their profession, to the extent that they must either deny their professional services or risk losing their lives in giving them, a fact whose seriousness cannot escape you, Mr. Chief Justice.

"The facts which we put before you, in your high authority, have caused the resolution of the Executive Committee of the National Medical College, with which we are complying by presenting the situation to you for proper action, to which effect we attach the following documents:

"1. Certification of minutes number 2 of the Board of Government of the Municipal Medical College of Sancti Spiritus, dated October 24, 1957.

"2. Certification of particulars in minutes number 12 of the Board of Directors of the Municipal Medical College of Santiago de Cuba, dated April 25, 1956.

"3. Photostat copy of the statements of the Board of Directors of the Municipal Medical College of Santiago de Cuba, regarding acts recorded in minutes number 12, of April 25, 1956.

"4. Official copy of public statement of the Executive Committee of the National Medical College, of April 25, 1956, supporting the protest of the Medical College of Santiago de Cuba and calling for guarantees protecting the exercise of the medical profession.

"Your very truly,
"Executive Committee of the National Medical Association"

The above letter was signed by Dr. Raul de Velasco and 26 other doctors representing the national and provincial associations.

The denunciation had no effect. No action was taken to attempt to arrest or punish the culprits.

A move to unite all political and revolutionary groups in the fight against Batista was undertaken in Miami in the month of October 1957. Cuban exiles flocked to Washington to be present when the Inter American Press Association held its annual convention there that month. They distributed inflammatory leaflets against Batista and picketed in front of the Mayflower Hotel with placards to invite attention to conditions in Cuba.

187

The editors and publishers unanimously adopted a resolution submitted by the Committee on Freedom of the Press which labeled the Batista government, together with the governments of the Dominican Republic, Paraguay, Venezuela and Bolivia as not democratic because they did not respect or cause to be respected freedom of the press. Not a single Cuban editor—not even the editor of Batista's own newspaper *Pueblo*—dared rise to vote against the resolution although the latter spoke passionately against it.

Cuban exiles drafted a "Document of Unity of Cuban Opposition to the Batista Dictatorship," which was signed November 1 in Miami Beach at the home of Dr. Lincoln Rodon, former speaker of the house of representatives, by representatives of seven groups. Among them were former Presidents Carlos Prio and Carlos Hevia, together with Dr. Manuel Antonio de Varona, former president of the senate, Dr. Roberto Agramonte, former presidential candidate, and three signatories of the 26th of July Movement. I witnessed the ceremony at Dr. Rodon's invitation.

The document reviewed the situation of Cuba and then went on to say:

"In view of the above, the political parties, the revolutionary organizations and the Federation of University Students, united on free soil belonging to this great democracy that is the United States of America, agree to the following:

"First: Increase the fight against the regime of terror of Batista until a democratic form of government is restored to the island.

"Second: Constitute the Council of Cuban Liberation to unite the civic and material forces of the Cuban people and organize the transition between the dictatorship and a constitutional and democratic government.

"Third: Underline that a constitutional, legal, and democratic government is sought in which the people of Cuba will be able to express their wishes and declare that the existing tyranny has not been able and will never be able to offer anything but anarchy, repression, terror and plunder.

"Fourth: Declare that owing to the dangerous situation existing in the nation, there is no other solution but to bring about the end of the present government and to constitute a provisional

188

government which will preside over the process of reconstruction and summon a general election which will be celebrated as soon as possible, so that the Cuban people can freely elect its candidates, and offer this democratic government a solid backing so that its stability and impartiality will be assured. This provisional government shall in no case exceed the term of eighteen months, at the end of which the new government elected by the people shall take over.

"Fifth: Agree that the provisional president shall not be permitted to become a candidate for any position to be filled by the elections presided over by the provisional government. Agree also, that the ministers, governors and mayors must give up their offices six months before the elections to be able to participate as candidates for the presidency or for any other elective position.

"Sixth: Agree to the minimum program to be undertaken by the provisional government in its work to restore order and democracy under the compliance of the 1940 Constitution. This program should be inspired by the following objectives:

"A. Immediate liberty of all political prisoners, civilians and military.

"B. Restoration of civil liberties.

"C. Establishment of systems of control and punishment to end graft.

"D. Enactment of a Civil Service Act.

"E. Creation of a higher standard of education, scientific research, technical education and the conservation of our natural resources.

"F. Betterment of governmental agencies and institutions violated and plundered by the dictatorship.

"G. Preservation of the monetary stability and work to channel credit in a manner productive to the country.

"H. Establishment of regulations covering agrarian reform.

"I. The organization of free elections in the trade unions, in whose operation the dictatorship has intervened.

"J. Creation of new sources of employment and higher standard of living for farmers and workers through the establishment of new industries and the development of agriculture and mining.

"Seventh: Declare that the Council of Cuban Liberation backs up all the charges of violation of human rights committed by Batista made by Cubans to the United Nations and other international organizations; request that, until peace is obtained in Cuba, all the shipments of arms given to the Cuban government for hemispheric defense be suspended by the government of the United States, as the dictatorship is using such equipment against the Cuban people and not for continental defense. And request from the United States and the Organization of American States the recognition of this Council of Cuban Liberation, in view of the civil war existing on the island.

"Eighth: Invite all the Cuban civic, professional, religious and cultural institutions and the trade unions and financial institutions and organizations to back up these ideals integrating this movement against Batista.

"Ninth: Reiterate our firm decision to separate the armed forces from the political battles and guarantee the proper organization of same, and we appeal to them requesting that they also unite with us and support the common objective of obtaining freedom from the tyranny which has caused Cuba so much bloodshed, so that the present climate of hate and death strangling the Republic ceases, never to return.

"Tenth: Maintain after the success of the revolutionary goal the necessary integration to bring about the task of furnishing our country with the freedom it needs and consolidate a democratic regime for our nation."

There were apparently some secret agreements added.

It took eighteen days for a copy of the document, listing all signatories, to reach Castro's mountain headquarters in the Sierra Maestra from Miami. Castro was busy in battle at the time. A courier left Miami the night of November 1 with a copy of the document. A draft had already been sent to the national committee of the 26th of July Movement, and, aware of the delicacy of the unity question and the attitude of that group, I asked Dr. Felipe Pazos, former president of the Banco Nacional, Dr. Lucas Moran, an attorney of Santiago de Cuba, and Lester Rodriguez, one of the Movement leaders, if they had received authority to sign. They replied in the affirmative. Perhaps the authority had come from the national committee in Havana, but it apparently did not originate with Castro.

He made that clear in a lengthy letter which he addressed to all the signatories except the members of his own party. He rejected the unity pact in blunt and unmistakable language. He did not intend to obligate himself to anyone or to consider himself or his movement so obligated. The letter was brought to Miami from the Sierra Maestra by Dr. Antonio Buch, medico of Santiago de Cuba. With it Buch brought an invitation to me from Castro, hand-written by Armando Hart, husband of Haydee Santamaria, to visit his headquarters.

Word of Castro's denunciation of the Council of Liberation leaked out in Miami, and sponsors of the unity movement pleaded with Castro's representatives in the city at the time, who included Raul Chibas, Luis Buch, Angel Maria Santos Buch and Mario Llerena not to publicize the letter. They were ready and willing to cede every point made by Castro and felt publication of the news would be harmful to the campaign against Batista.

On December 31, 1957, Raul Chibas, who had escorted Dr. Manuel Urrutia Lleo to my office, personally handed to me the following text of Castro's letter in the Spanish language:

To the Directors of the Partido Revolucionario Cubano
Partido del Pueblo Cubano
Organizacion Autentica
Federacion Estudiantil Universitaria
Directorio Revolucionario
Directorio Obrero Revolucionario

"My moral, patriotic and even historical duty obliges me to address to you this letter, based on facts and circumstances that have moved us profoundly during these last weeks, which, by the way, have been the most strenuous and busy ones since we arrived in Cuba. It was precisely on Wednesday, November 20, the day on which our forces sustained three battles in the space of only six hours (and this will give an idea of the sacrifices and efforts made by our men here without the slightest aid from other organizations), when the surprising news was received in our operations zone, together with the document containing the public

191

and private bases of the unity agreement, which is said to have been subscribed in Miami by the 26th of July Movement and those organizations to which I now address myself.

"The arrival of those papers, as though it were another stroke of the irony of fate, at the time when what we need is arms, coincided with the heaviest offensive that the tyranny has launched against us.

"Communications are difficult in the conditions under which we are fighting. In spite of everything, it has been necessary to get the leaders of our organization together in the midst of a campaign, so as to attend to this matter, in which not only the prestige of but also the historical reason for the 26th of July Movement is at stake.

"For those who are fighting against an army incomparable in number and in arms, without any support during a whole year other than the dignity with which we are fighting for a cause which we love sincerely and the conviction that it is worth while to die for it, bitterly forgotten by fellow countrymen who, in spite of having all the ways and means, have systematically (not to say criminally) denied us their help; and for those who have seen so closely the daily sacrifices in their highest form and have so often felt the grief of seeing their closest comrades fall in battle—when nobody knows which of those who fight beside us will fall in new and inevitable disasters without even seeing the day of victory which he is fighting for so earnestly and without any other ambition or consolation than the hope that his sacrifice will not be in vain: for *all* those, it must be understood that the news of a broad and intentionally publicized agreement, which binds the future conduct of the Movement without even having had the consideration—not to say the elementary obligation—of consulting the opinion of the directors and the fighters, must be felt by us to be extremely wounding and the cause of indignation.

"Improper procedure always has the very worst consequences, and this is something that should be taken into account by those who consider themselves capable of such an arduous undertaking as the ousting of a tyranny and, what is even more difficult, to gain the recognition of the country after a revolutionary process.

"The 26th of July Movement did not designate or authorize

192

any delegation to discuss these negotiations. However, there would not be any objection to designating one after the matter had been previously discussed and if care had been taken to give very concrete instructions to the representatives—in view of the fact that something so serious in relation to the present and future activities of our organization is involved.

"On the contrary the news that we had regarding the contacts with certain of those sectors were limited to a report from Señor Lester Rodriguez, delegate for War Affairs abroad, with powers limited to these matters exclusively, to the following effect:

" 'With respect to Prio and the *Directorio,* I held several interviews with them so as to co-ordinate military plans exclusively, until a provisional government could be formed, which would be guaranteed and respected by the three sectors. Logically, my proposal was that the letter from the Sierra, the letter in which it was explained that that government should be formed in accordance with the will of the civic forces of the country, be accepted. This brought the first difficulty. When the commotion of the general strike was produced, we held an emergency meeting. I proposed that all resources immediately at hand be used and that we attempt to decide the problem of Cuba once and for all.

" 'Prio replied that he did not have sufficient resources to attain victory and that it would be madness to accept my demand. I replied that when he should consider that he had everything ready for sailing, he should notify me, so that then we could talk about any possible agreements, but that in the meantime he should do me the favor of letting me and what I represent within the 26th of July Movement work with entire independence.

" 'In other words, no obligations exist with those people and I do not believe that in the future it is recommendable to have any, since just at the time when Cuba most needed it, they denied having the material, which has recently been captured from them, and which amounts to so much that it causes indignation. . . .'

"This report, which is self-explanatory, confirms our suspicion that we rebels could not expect any help from outside.

"If the organizations which you represent had deemed it proper

193

to discuss the bases for joint action with some members of our Movement, such bases (so much more so, because they altered fundamentally the demands made by us in the Sierra Maestra manifesto) could not be published under any circumstances as an agreement reached without the knowledge and approval of the national leaders of the Movement. Acting in any other way is making agreements for publicity and invoking fraudulently the name of our organization.

"The astounding fact is clear that when the national leaders operating from here in Cuba, had received the news, and were ready to refuse the public and private points proposed as a basis for the agreement, they learned from clandestine sources and from the foreign press that the points had been published as an agreement which had been reached. Thus they found themselves confronted by an accomplished fact, in the opinion of the country and the people abroad, with the alternative of having either to deny it—with the corresponding consequence of harmfulness that such denial would imply—or of accepting it without having even expressed their opinions. And, as it is logical to suppose, when the points reached us in the Sierra Maestra, the document had already been published several days previously.

"In this juncture, the national leaders, before proceeding to deny said agreements publicly, placed before you the necessity of having the junta discuss a series of points which would cover the demands of the Sierra Maestra manifesto, while at the same time a meeting was called in rebel territory to weigh the thought of all of its members and adopt a unanimous agreement thereon, as set forth in this document.

"Naturally, any agreement for joint action would have to be favorably accepted by national and foreign public opinion; among other reasons, because the real situation of the political and revolutionary forces opposing Batista is not known abroad, and also because in Cuba the word 'unity' became very important at the time when the correlation of forces was very different from what it is today; and finally, because it is always positive to join the efforts of the most enthusiastic as well as of the most timid persons. . . .

"But the important thing for the revolution is not unity it-

194

self, but rather the bases of such unity, the form in which it is carried out and the patriotic intentions which inspire it.

"To agree upon such unity without even having discussed the bases, to undersign it with persons who are not empowered to do so, and to give it publicity without any more ado from a comfortable city abroad—thereby placing the Movement in the situation of having to confront the deception of public opinion through a fraudulent agreement—is a trap of the worst sort, in which an organization which is truly revolutionary cannot be caught, since it would be deceiving the country and the world.

"And that is possible only because while the directors of the other organizations signing that agreement are abroad, carrying out an imaginary revolution, the directors of the 26th of July Movement are in Cuba, doing the real thing.

"These lines, however, would be unnecessary; they would not have been written no matter how bitter and humiliating the procedure whereby the Movement would be bound to such agreement, since discrepancies in matter of form should never prevail over essentials in view of the positive value of unity, we would have accepted it in spite of everything, because of the usefulness of certain projects conceived by the junta and because of the help which we really need being offered to us—if we were not simply in disagreement with certain essential points of the bases.

"No matter how desperate our situation may be, no matter how many thousands of soldiers the dictatorship may mobilize against us in its effort to annihilate us, we would never accept the sacrifice of certain cardinal points of our way of conceiving the Cuban revolution, and even more so because a burden never humiliates more than when the circumstances are pressing.

"These principles are included in the Sierra Maestra manifesto.

"To leave out, in a document covering joint action, the express point of refusing any kind of foreign interference in the international affairs of Cuba is evidence of a lack of patriotic feelings and a self-evident act of cowardice.

"To declare that we are against intervention is asking not only that the revolution be allowed as a favor since it would be against the interest of our national sovereignty—more, against the principle that affects all the peoples of America—but it is also asking that no intervention be made in favor of the dictatorship by sending them the planes, bombs, tanks and modern arms with which it is sustained in power. No one has suffered in his own flesh as we and, above all, the peasantry of the Sierra. Finally, because successfully avoiding intervention is in itself the ousting of the tyranny, are we going to be so cowardly as not even to demand that no intervention favorable to Batista be made? Or so insincere as to ask in an underhand fashion that others solve our problems? Or so mediocre as not to dare to speak out clearly in this respect? How, then, can we call ourselves revolutionaries and sign a document of unity which pretends to be of historic value?

"In the document of unity our declaration of refusing any kind of military junta to govern the Republic provisionally has been eliminated.

"The most disastrous thing that could happen to our nation at this time is the replacement of Batista by a military junta, because it would be accompanied by the illusion that Cuba's problem would be solved merely by the absence of the dictator. Some civilians of the worst species, including accomplices of the 10th of March movement, today estranged from them, possibly because of their greater ambitions, are thinking of those solutions which could be looked upon favorably only by the enemies of the progress of the country.

"If experience has shown in America that all military juntas drift once more toward autocracy; if the worst of the evils which have lashed this continent is the spreading of the roots of military castes in countries which have fought fewer wars than Switzerland and have more generals than Prussia; if one of the most legitimate aspirations of our people in this crucial hour, in which its democratic and republican fate will be saved or will be lost for many years, is to keep—as the most precious legacy of its liberators—the civil tradition which was initiated in the same wars of emancipation and would be broken on the very day that a military junta should preside over the Republic (something that was never attempted by the most glorious generals of our independence in war or in peace), how can we renounce everything

196

by eliminating such an important declaration of principles for fear of wounding susceptibilities, more imaginary than real, among the honest military men who could support us? Can it be that the people do not understand that a timely definition could prevent the danger of a military junta which would serve no other purpose than to perpetuate the civil war? Then, let us not hesitate to declare that if a military junta substitutes for Batista, the 26th of July Movement will continue its campaign of liberation. It is preferable to fight more today than to fall into new and unfathomable abysses tomorrow. No military junta, no puppet government serving as a toy for the military! Civilians must govern decently and honestly! The soldiers to their barracks and everyone to do his duty!

"Or is it that we are waiting for the generals of the 10th of March, to whom Batista would relinquish power with great pleasure when he considers it no longer sustainable, as the most practical means of guaranteeing his exit with the least harm to his interests and those of his gang? How long will the lack of foresight, the absence of elevated ideas, or the lack of a true will to fight continue to blind Cuban politicians?

"If you have no faith in the people nor in their great reserves of energy and will to fight, then you have no right to touch their fate or to twist it, or to change its course in the most heroic and promising moments of their republican life. Neither the procedure of evil politics, nor childish ambitions, nor the desire for personal aggrandizement, nor prior plans for dividing the spoils can be allowed to contaminate the revolutionary process, because in Cuba men are dying for something better. Let the politicians become revolutionaries if they want, but let them not try to convert the revolution into bastard politics, because the bloodshed and the sacrifices of our people are too great at this time to permit such disastrous future frustration.

"Aside from these two fundamental principles which have been omitted in the document of unity, we are in total disagreement with other aspects of same.

"Even if we are to accept paragraph (B) of secret point number 2, relative to the power of the Liberation Committee, which reads as follows: 'To appoint the President of the Republic who

197

shall take office as such in the provisional government,' we cannot accept paragraph (C) of said point, which includes among other powers the following: 'To approve or disapprove as a whole the Cabinet appointed by the President of the Republic, as well as the changes therein in cases of partial or total crisis.'

"How can it be conceived that the power of the President to appoint and substitute his collaborators be subject to the approval or disapproval of a body foreign to the powers of the state? Is it not clear that once said committee has been formed by different party representatives and therefore of different interests, the appointment of the members of the Cabinet could be converted into a distribution of positions as sole means of reaching an agreement in each case? Is it possible to accept a basis which implies the establishment of two executives within the state? The only guarantee which all sectors of the country should demand from the provisional government is that its mission be adjusted to a given minimum program and absolute impartiality as a moderate power in the transitional stage toward the complete constitutional normality of the country.

"To pretend to interfere in the appointment of each member implies the ambition to control the public administration as a means of putting it at the service of political interests. This is explicable only in parties or organizations bereft of public backing. It can survive only under the provisions of traditional politics, and it is opposed to the high revolutionary and political goals which the 26th of July Movement pursues for the Republic.

"The mere presence of secret agreements which do not involve questions of organizing for a fight, or plans of action, but rather questions of interest to the nation regarding the structure of the future government, and which, therefore, should be publicly proclaimed, is in itself unacceptable. Marti said that in the revolution the methods are secret, but the objectives must always be public.

"Another point which is equally unacceptable to the 26th of July Movement is the secret agreement number 8, which reads textually: 'The revolutionary forces will be incorporated into the regular armed forces of the Republic, with their arms.'

"In the first place, what is understood by 'revolutionary forces'?

Can a police, navy or army badge be given to anyone coming in at the last moment with a weapon in his hands? Can uniforms be given and authority be granted as agents of the government to those who have their weapons hidden while they wait to bring them out on the day of victory, and remain with their arms crossed while a handful of compatriots fight against all the forces of the tyranny? Are we going to allow the very germs of gangsterism and anarchy which were the shame of the Republic not so long ago to enter into a revolutionary document?

"Experience in the territory held by our forces has shown us that the maintenance of public order is a vital question to the country. There are facts to prove that as soon as the existing order is abolished, a series of difficulties will be unloosed and that delinquency will prevail if it is not checked in time. The timely application of severe measures, with the full backing of the public, put an end to the outbreak of banditry. Neighbors, previously accustomed to seeing the authorities act as enemies of the people, hospitably protected prosecuted citizens or those fleeing from justice. Today, when they see our soldiers acting as defenders of their interests, there is complete order, and their best protectors are the citizens themselves.

"Anarchy is the worst enemy of the revolutionary process. It is a fundamental requirement that it be combated from now. If there are any who do not understand this, it is because they are not worried about the destiny of the revolution; and it is logical that those who have not suffered sacrifices for it should not be interested in it. The country should know that justice will be done, but within the strictest order, and that crime will be punished wherever it be committed.

"The 26th of July Movement claims the function of keeping the public order, and reorganizing the armed forces of the Republic for the following reasons:

"1. Because it is the only organization which has organized and disciplined militias in the whole country, and has an army in active service with twenty victories over the enemy.

"2. Because our combatants have shown a chivalrous spirit, free from all hate of the military, invariably respect the lives of prisoners, cure their wounded in combat, never torture an adversary even knowing that he possesses important information, and have maintained this attitude in war with unprecedented equanimity.

"3. Because the armed forces must be inculcated with the spirit of justice and chivalry which the 26th of July Movement has sown in their own soldiers.

"4. Because the calmness with which we have acted in this struggle is the best guarantee that the honorable military have nothing to fear from the revolution nor will they have to pay a price for the faults of those who with their crimes and their acts have covered the military uniform with opprobrium.

"There are still some aspects which are difficult to understand in the document of unity. How can an agreement be reached without first having defined the strategy of battle? Are the 'autenticos' thinking about a 'putsch' in the capital? Will they continue storing arms and more arms, which sooner or later will fall into the hands of the police before they can be delivered to those who are fighting? Have they finally accepted the project of a general strike sustained by the 26th of July Movement?

"Moreover, to our way of thinking, there has been an unfortunate underestimation of the importance of the fighting in Oriente from a military viewpoint. At this time the war in the Sierra Maestra is not guerrilla warfare, but a war of fighting by columns. Our forces, inferior in number and equipment, take advantage of the terrain to the maximum, as well as maintaining a permanent watch over the enemy and great speed in our movements. It is hardly necessary to mention that a question of morale is of singular importance in this struggle. The results have been astounding and some day will be known in full detail.

"The entire population is in rebellion. If we had arms, our detachments would not have to patrol any zone. The peasantry would not allow a single enemy to pass through. The defeats of the tyranny, which insists obstinately on sending numerous forces, would be disastrous. Too much cannot be said about how valor has been awakened in these people. The dictatorship carries out barbarous reprisals. The mass assassinations of the peasantry are no less than the killings made by the Nazis in any European country. Any defeat the enemy suffers is avenged on the helpless populace. The reports from army headquarters announcing casualties among the rebels are always preceded by some massacre. This has led the people to a state of total rebellion. The most grievous thing, which makes one's heart bleed, is to think that no one has sent to these people a single rifle, and that while the peasantry here see their houses burned and their families assassinated and beg desperately for rifles, there are arms hidden in Cuba which are not being used and are waiting for the police to pick them up or for the tyranny to fall, or for the rebels to be exterminated. . . .

"The attitude of many compatriots could not be any more ignoble. But there is still time to rectify it and to help those who are fighting. From our own personal point of view, this matters very little to us. Let no one think that personal interest or pride prompts these words. Our fate is sealed and no uncertainty assails us: we either die here to the last rebel and an entire young generation will perish in the cities, or we will try all the most incredible hardships.

"For us there is no longer any defeat possible. The year of sacrifices and heroisms which our men have survived can never be obliterated; our victories stand and cannot be easily overlooked either. Our men, firmer than ever, will fight to the last drop of blood.

"The defeat will be for those who have denied us their help; for those who, having obligated themselves to us at the beginning, left us alone; for those who, lacking faith in dignity and idealism, wasted their time and their prestige in shameful dealings with the despotism of Trujillo; for those who, having arms, hid them in cowardice at the time of battle. They are the deceived, not we.

"There is one thing that we can say in all certainty: if we had seen other Cubans fighting for liberty, pursued and almost exterminated; if we had seen them resisting from day to day without giving up or diminishing their faith in the struggle, we would not have hesitated one minute in joining them and, if it were necessary, dying with them. Because we are Cubans, and Cubans do not stand by passively even when there is fighting for liberation in any other country of America. Is it said that Dominicans join together on an island to liberate their people? For each Dominican ten Cubans arrive. Do Somoza's bloodhounds invade Costa

Rica? There rush the Cubans to fight. How, then, is it that when the heaviest battle for liberty is being fought in their own country, there are Cubans in exile, expelled by the tyranny, who deny their help to the Cubans who are fighting?

"Or is it that in offering help they demand the lion's share of the rewards? Must we offer the Republic as the spoils of war to gain their aid? Must we forgo our ideals and convert this war into a new art of killing fellow men to gain their help, or shed blood uselessly without offering to the Fatherland the benefit of so much sacrifice?

"The leadership of the struggle against the tyranny is and will continue to be in Cuba, in the hands of the revolutionary combatants. Those who wish now or in the future to be considered as revolutionary leaders should be in this country, confronting directly the responsibilities, risks and sacrifices that Cuba now demands.

"Exiles should co-operate in the struggle, but it is absurd for them to try to tell us from abroad what peak we should take, what sugar cane field we should burn, what sabotage we should perform, or at what moment and in what circumstance and form we should unloose the general strike. In addition to being absurd, it is ridiculous. Help us from abroad, by collecting money among the exiles and Cuban emigrants, by campaigning for the cause of Cuba in the press and in the public opinion. Denounce the crimes that we are suffering here, but do not pretend to direct from Miami the revolution that is being waged in all of the cities and country places of the island through fighting, agitating, sabotaging and striking and thousands of other forms of revolutionary action, which have been the war strategy of the 26th of July Movement.

"The national heads of the Movement are disposed, and have made it clear several times, to talk in Cuba with the directors of any oppositionist organization so as to co-ordinate specific plans and produce concrete deeds which may be considered useful for deposing the tyranny.

"The general strike will be carried out through the effective co-ordination of the efforts of the Civic Resistance Movement, the National Labor Front and any other group outside partisan politics and in close contact with the 26th of July Movement, which, up to the present, is the only opposition organization fighting in this country.

"The 26th of July Movement's Labor Section is organizing strike committees in every work and industrial center, in conjunction with the oppositionist elements of all action groups which are willing to strike and offer moral guarantees that they will do so.

"The organization of those strike committees will be carried out by the National Labor Front, which is the only representative of the proletariat that the 26th of July Movement recognizes as legitimate.

"The deposing of the dictator means implicitly the suppression of the spurious Congress and the removal of the management of the Cuban Confederation of Labor and of all mayors, governors and other officers who directly or indirectly have supported him in order to attain public office in the so called elections of November 1, 1954, or in the military coup of March 10, 1952. It also implies the immediate freedom of political, civil and military prisoners, as well as the indictment of all having complicity in crime, abuse and tyranny itself.

"The new government will be guided by the Constitution of 1940 and will guarantee all rights recognized therein, and will be completely impartial to partisan politics.

"The Executive Board will assume the legislative powers that the Constitution confers upon the Congress of the Republic and its prime duty will be to lead the country to general elections under the Electoral Code of 1943 and the Constitution of 1940, as well as to develop the minimum ten-point program set forth in the manifesto of the Sierra Maestra.

"The present Supreme Court will be dissolved because it has shown itself powerless to solve the lawless situation created by the *coup d'état,* but some of its present members shall be subsequently eligible for appointment, provided that they have defended the principles of the Constitution or have maintained a firm attitude against the crime, the arbitrary action and the abuse of the tyrannical government of these last years.

"The President of the Republic will decide how the new Su-

203

preme Court will be established, which will, in turn, proceed to reorganize all the courts and autonomous institutions, and will relieve of their functions all persons who it may consider to have acted in evident complicity with the tyranny, and may also indict them when proper.

"The appointment of the new officers will be made according to the provisions of the law in each case.

"Political parties will have one and one right only during the provisional government, namely: freedom to defend their program before the people, to mobilize and organize the citizens within the broad framework of our Constitution and to participate in the general elections to be held.

"In the manifesto of the Sierra Maestra it was pointed out that the person to be appointed to preside over the Republic should be selected by the joint committees of civic institutions.

"In view of the fact that five months have passed without this requirement having been fulfilled, and that it is more urgent now than ever to let the country know the answer to the question as to who will succeed the dictator as President, and that it is not possible to wait one day more without satisfying the national curiosity, the 26th of July Movement now answers it by proposing to the people—as the only formula which will guarantee the legality and the institution of the aforementioned bases of unity and of the provisional government itself—the name of the distinguished magistrate of the Court of Appeals of Oriente, Dr. Manuel Urrutia Lleo. It is not we who propose him, but his own conduct, and we hope that he will not refuse to render this service to the Republic.

"The self-evident reasons which pointed out Dr. Urrutia as the future provisional President are the following:

"1. He is the member of the judiciary who exalted the name of the Constitution when he declared on the bench of the court that tried the *Gramma* expeditionaries that it was not a crime to organize armed forces against the regime, but rather something perfectly legal under the spirit and the letter of the Constitution and the laws. This is something, coming from a magistrate, which is unprecedented in the history of our struggles for freedom.

204

"2. His life, dedicated to the strict administration of justice, is proof that he has sufficient knowledge and character to serve fairly all legitimate interests when the tyranny has been deposed by the action of the people.

"3. No one could be more impartial to party politics than Dr. Manuel Urrutia Lleo, because he does not belong to any political group, precisely owing to his judiciary functions, and there is no other citizen of his prestige who, independent of any military activity, has identified himself so much with the revolutionary cause.

"Moreover, by virtue of his being a magistrate, that is the formula closest to the Constitution.

"If our conditions are denied, conditions which are free from party interest and coming from an organization second to none in sacrifices, which was not even consulted when its name was included in a manifesto of unity which it did not underwrite, we will continue the fight alone as at present, without any more arms than those we can take from the enemy in each combat, without any more help than that of the people who suffer, and without any other support than that of our own ideals.

"Finally, it has been the 26th of July Movement that has been, and still is, carrying out combat actions in the entire country; it is only the 26th of July Movement's men of action who are doing the sabotage, meting out justice to the criminals, burning cane fields and performing other revolutionary acts; it is only the 26th of July Movement that has been able to organize the workers in the entire nation toward a revolution; it is only the 26th of July Movement that can undertake today the strategy of the strike committees; and the 26th of July Movement is the only group that has co-operated in the organization of the Civic Resistance Movement now holding together the civic groups of practically every locality in Cuba.

"It is possible that some may consider this pronouncement arrogant; but the fact is that only the 26th of July Movement has declared that it does not desire to participate in the provisional government and that it places its entire moral and material support at the disposal of the citizen most suitable to preside over the necessary provisional government.

"Let it be understood that we have renounced the taking of any office in the government; but let it also be known that the 26th of July Movement will never fail to guide and direct the people from the underground, from the Sierra Maestra or from the very graves of our dead. And we will not fail in that duty because it is not we, but an entire generation that is morally bound before the people of Cuba to provide substantial solutions to its grave problems.

"And we will know how to conquer and to die. The struggle will never be harder than when we were only twelve men, when we did not have behind us a people organized and with experience in war in the Sierra Maestra, when we did not have, as we have today, a powerful and disciplined organization all over the country, or when we did not have the formidable support of the masses, as evidenced in the burial of our unforgettable Frank Pais.

"To die with dignity does not require company."
For the National Leadership of the 26th of July Movement,

FIDEL CASTRO

Sierra Maestra, December 14, 1957.

Castro thus had delivered to Batista on a silver platter the best New Year's gift any person in the dictator's position could ever hope for. Batista was so elated over the news that for the first time in months the name of Castro was permitted by censors to be used in newspaper headlines and to be broadcast over the radio as excerpts of the letter were reported.

Castro's letter contained some good points, but taken in its full context it was to prolong the blood bath even as it was to ensure his eventual total victory. It also contained some contradictions when compared with the manifesto of the Sierra Maestra five months earlier. It demonstrated an impatience on Castro's part over the reluctance of the civic institutions to name a provisional president as he had requested in the July manifesto.

The Council of Liberation had decided on its choice for provisional president and the man selected was Felipe Pazos, but the 26th of July Movement insisted on the election of Urrutia. The council held out for Pazos and a stalemate had resulted.

Castro's letter did not go unanswered. He was politely reminded by Dr. Manuel Antonio de Varona and Dr. Enrique Cotubanaba Henriquez, Prio's brother-in-law, that he had overlooked the fact that the yacht in which his expedition had sailed from Mexico was furnished by the former President.

Castro was right in his forecast in the July manifesto when he said that if the civic institutions did not rally around his call and choose a provisional president, the struggle would be prolonged and cost more blood. The cream of the youth of Cuba continued to die in their heroic struggle to recover the freedom which they were taught to revere.

Castro issued an order to burn the sugar cane fields in order to hurt the country's rich income which was helping to prolong Batista's tenure. One of the first fields to be burned was the plantation owned by his family—at his orders. His scorched-earth policy was destined to produce only one effect: to antagonize many Cubans against him and to cripple the economy in such a manner that it would take years to recover and would present for any provisional government a most serious and dangerous problem. After several plantations were burned, Castro revoked the order.

CHAPTER 7

Cuban exiles in the United States, Mexico, Costa Rica and other countries of Latin America worked feverishly to buy arms and ammunition for Castro and other rebel groups. Every conceivable law of neutrality was violated by them. At times as fast as they bought arms in the United States they were captured by customs officials, who trailed them from New York and other cities to a hoped-for embarkation port in Florida.

The Cubans knew they were violating the laws of the United States, but many hotheads felt that our federal authorities should have winked at those infractions because the arms and ammunition and the expeditionary forces were destined to liberate their country from dictatorship, which the American people abhorred. It took them considerable time to understand that our country is a nation of laws, but once they did, they accepted their risks, and their jail terms when caught, with better grace.

Despite the vigilance by the Cuban navy and air force and by the federal authorities of the United States and Mexico, arms shipments had been reaching Cuba since 1953 when Candido de la Torre, who was a member of Prio's party, sailed from Vera Cruz with eight tons of arms and ammunition for the "Triple A" revolutionary organization headed by Aureliano Sanchez Arango. That cargo was landed at Cayo Sal (Salt Key) off the north coast of Las Villas province. It was delivered to a rebel group directed

208

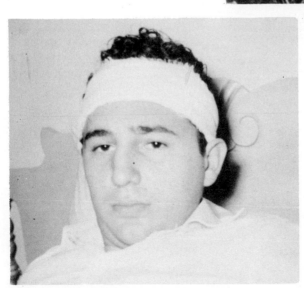

Wistful-eyed Fidel Castro at the age
of three, photographed in his home at
Biran, Mayari, Province of Oriente.

Fidel Castro recovering from headwound received during student riots in Havana in 1948.

Fidel Castro addressing a student meeting on the campus of the University of Havana in 1946.

Fidel Castro after his capture following his unsuccessful attack on the Moncada Fortress on July 26, 1953. He is shown being questioned by Colonel Alberto del Rio Chaviano, commander of Moncada, in Santiago de Cuba.

Fidel Castro leaving the Isle of Pines Military Prison May 15, 1955, having grown a mustache while there. Behind him, smiling at his immediate left is younger brother Raul.

Fidel Castro and other freed political prisoners aboard the ferry for the trip from the Isle of Pines to the mainland.

Fidel Castro being carried out of the railroad train that returned him to Havana after his imprisonment in the Isle of Pines. He is holding one end of a Cuban flag in his right hand.

Fidel Castro at a meeting in the Independent Order of Odd Fellows Lodge Hall in Miami in 1955 with money contributed by Cubans resident there for his revolution. Picture in background is of Jose Marti, Father of Cuba's independence.

Fidel Castro in Palm Garden, New York City, receiving contributions of Cubans in October 1955 for his revolution against Batista.

Fidel Castro strolling through Central Park in New York City in 1955.

The Rancho Santa Rosa in Chalco, Mexico, where Castro and his men trained for the revolution in Cuba, as it was being raided by the Mexican police in June, 1956.

Fidel Castro (marked with x) and other Cuban exiles, after their arrest in Mexico raid in June, 1956. This photo was taken by the Federal Security Police of Mexico. The lady is Mrs. Hilda Gedea Guevara, Peruvian wife of the Argentine hero of the Cuban revolution, Ernesto ("Che") Guevara.

American Ambassador Arthur Gardner, left, hugging General Francisco Tabernilla, Chief of Staff of Batista's army with Rear-Admiral Julio Rodriguez Calderon, Chief of Staff of the Cuban Navy, looking on.

General Alberto Bayo shown with one of his students Major Pedro Miret, trained by him in Mexico together with Castro.

Fidel Castro shown in the Sierra Maestra, from left to right, with Armando Hart, Celia Sanchez, his faithful secretary and the first of the woman fighters, Raul Castro and Javier Pazos. A day after this photo was taken at Castro's headquarters Hart and Pazos were captured by the army near Santiago de Cuba.

Fidel Castro's mother lights a candle for him and her son Raul and their troops while her daughter looks on.

Fidel Castro marching on a hilltop in the Sierra Maestra. He is wearing a 26th of July shoulder patch and a 26th of July armband. In his hand is the telescopic rifle which he had all through the civil war.

A todo el que pueda interesar

Por este medio se hace saber que toda persona que facilite una información que conduzca al éxito de una operación contra cualquier nucleo rebelde comandado por Fidel Castro, Raúl Castro, Crescencio Pérez, Guillermo González o cualquier otro cabecilla será gratificado de acuerdo con la importancia de la información, bien entendido que nunca será menor de **$5,000**.

Esta gratificación oscilará de **$5,000** hasta **$100,000** correspondiendo esta última cantidad o sea $100,000 por la Cabeza de Fidel Castro.

Nota: El nombre del informante no será nunca revelado.

Reward offered for the capture of Fidel Castro and Raul Castro together with Crescencio Perez and Guillermo Gonzalez, their chief guides. The sum offered for all but Fidel is $5,000 and his head, the poster says, is worth $100,000.

Above: Fidel Castro in conference with Raul Chibas, left, and Felipe Pazos in the Sierra Maestra. Crouching behind them is Dr. Julio Martinez Paez, who was chief surgeon at Castro's headquarters.

Below: A moment of relaxation for Fidel Castro in the Sierra Maestra, reading "Kaputt" by Curzio Malaparte. His comment on the book: "It is too effectivist."

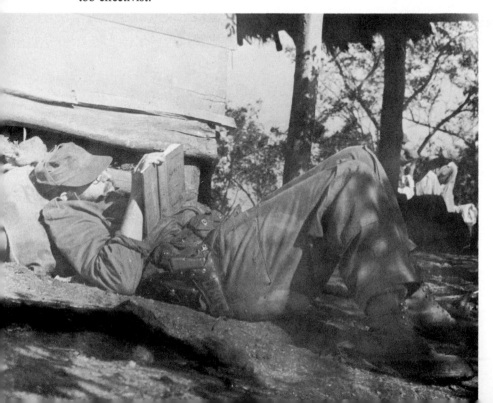

Above: Women of Santiago de Cuba demonstrating for the benefit of American Ambassador Earl E. T. Smith. The poster reads: "STOP THE ASSASSINATIONS OF OUR SONS. CUBAN MOTHERS."

Below: Police dispersing defiant women with hose in demonstration in Santiago de Cuba.

Above: Women of Santiago de Cuba embrace and cheer American Ambassador Earl E. T. Smith during his visit to that city. At the extreme left is John Topping, Political Officer of the embassy. With his back to the camera is Oscar H. Guerra, then Consul General in Santiago.

Below: Fidel Castro meets his son Fidelito for the first time since 1954 on the highway at El Cotorro, on the outskirts of Havana on January 9, 1959 as he neared the capital on his victory march. Standing beside him with a campaign hat and beard is Major Camilo Cienfuegos, now Chief of the Rebel Army.

Above: Fidel Castro addressing the nation from a speaker's stand at Camp Columbia (now Liberty City) on the night of his triumphal entry into Havana. Note the dove on his shoulder and two doves on the railing. Major Camilo Cienfuegos looks intently at him.

Below: The author interviewing Batista, March 6, 1957.

Victory smiles of Fidel Castro and Miguel Angel Quevedo, when the rebel chief visited the office of the Editor and Publisher of *Bohemia*.

Castro with Provisional President Manuel Urrutia.

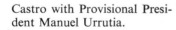

Above: Fidel Castro, conqueror of Cuba, riding in his victory parade into Havana.

Below: Rebel sabotage of a Guantanamo railroad train.

A freight train burned by rebels in Oriente province.

A sugar cane freight train derailed by rebels in Oriente province.

by Menelao Mora Morales at Caibarien, a port of Los Villas, transported to Havana in coke sacks and stored in the home of Francisco Cairol, where some of the weapons later were found by Batista's police.

De la Torre returned to Mexico and deposited another cargo of 200 rifles, some machine guns and 100,000 rounds of ammunition at the port of La Colonna in the province of Pinar del Rio. He sailed back to Mexico again and in 1954 landed an expedition of fourteen men in Pinar del Rio with a cargo of arms and ammunition. Among the men were rebels from the 26th of July Movement and the "Triple A" organization.

Three more successful expeditions followed from Mexico in 1955. The first made a rendezvous with a yacht from Costa Rica at Boca Iglesias in the Yucatan Channel. Aureliano Sanchez Arango was on the yacht from Mexico and Eufemio Fernandez had come from Costa Rica. They were taken to Cuba by De la Torre and landed with their cargo. At the end of that year De la Torre carried men of the 26th of July Movement, headed by Lester Rodriguez, from Mexico to Pinar del Rio with another shipment of arms.

Rodriguez returned with De la Torre to Mexico and sailed anew with him, this time to Oriente province. Aboard the yacht was Frank Pais. They landed their cargo of arms and ammunition and stored them safely. Part of this shipment of arms was used by the attackers on the Goicuria fort at Matanzas, the uprising in Santiago and the attack on the palace.

De la Torre prepared another expedition for August, 1957. He was living at Marisol Alba's house in Miami Beach with Colonel Bayo and the latter's aviator son, Alberto, Jr. Prio bought the ninety-eight-foot yacht *Blue Chip,* and De la Torre sailed from Florida with both Bayos aboard. To escape detection, the husky colonel hid inside a refrigerator until they were well at sea.

Bayo was wanted by the federal authorities in Mexico for his part in training and dispatching Castro's expedition. He spent twenty-three days on the key at Boca de Iglesias awaiting an opportunity to slip back into Mexico without being caught. Finally, entry was made at Tuxpan, the same place from which

Castro had sailed. De la Torre's *Blue Chip* expedition was caught by the Mexican authorities, most probably, according to De la Torre himself and Bayo, because of the reports furnished to Batista by Marisol Alba, the Mata Hari of the Cuban revolution.

Castro's rebels were hitting the army hard at night and withdrawing before dawn to the safety of cover in the jungles and hills of the Sierra Maestra. The rebels were short of arms and ammunition, and Castro would accept no volunteers unless they brought along their own weapons. Some enthusiasts broke into homes in cities and towns to demand that the owners hand over weapons to them so they could go into the hills to join Castro. One group even took the weapons in the Mexican embassy while the ambassador was at a reception.

Ramon Castro kept funneling supplies to Fidel. He also performed another worth-while service for his brother. It was not easy to obtain needed fuel for jeeps and trucks captured or commandeered by the rebels. The vehicles were duly inventoried, and IOU's were left with the owners to ensure payment at a later date. Ramon Castro had studied engineering at the University of Havana while Fidel was a student there, and now he devised a formula to supply his brother with fuel. He manufactured it by using one and a half gallons of 95-proof alcohol, made from sugar cane, with three-quarters of a gallon of gasoline, half a gallon of kerosene and one camphor ball. A second formula was twenty gallons of 95-proof alcohol with one bottle of castor oil. He sent instructions for drivers to reduce the air in the carburetor pipe, tightening it with a ring, or to close the choke tightly.

"With the carburetor procedure," Ramon's instructions read, "the vehicle runs much better. With the choke procedure it works but misses at times."

Fidel lost Ramon's valuable services for several months. The rebels had decided to avenge a series of killings by Colonel Fermin Cowley in Holguin. Cowley had been marked for death ever since the Christmas Eve holocaust of 1956. He was shot and killed by rebel militia as he was about to leave a store in Holguin after purchasing some parts for his airplane. Things became hot

210

for Ramon and he decided to travel to the United States and Spain. He was going to visit his late father's relatives in Spain.

"I had to get a good conduct certificate from the police," Ramon related, "in order to get a visa at the American embassy. Colonel Lavastida, Batista's police chief, told me he would give me the good conduct certificate if I paid him one hundred dollars. I paid the bribe and got the certificate. When I presented it at the American embassy I told the consular officer that the certificate cost me a one-hundred-dollar bribe. He replied that I would not have needed it because I was well known to the embassy."

Ramon Castro made a pilgrimage to the Shrine of Our Lady of Lourdes, where he prayed for his brother's victory. He vowed that after Fidel's triumph he would make a pilgrimage on foot from his home to Cuba's best-loved shrine, the Shrine of Our Lady of Charity of Cobre, a round trip of 125 miles.

Upon his return to Cuba, Ramon resumed his duties as quartermaster general of the now increasing rebel army, while Fidel devised plans for a nation-wide revolutionary general strike to precede an offensive that would, he hoped, topple Batista.

While all this was going on, the State Department through Ambassador Smith in Havana pressured Batista to restore civil rights as a prelude to the holding of general elections June 1. The failure of the Cienfuegos naval revolt and the apparent continued impotence of Castro to win a decision must have contributed to this policy, which was in total defiance of the wishes and plans of the majority of the Cuban people.

Ambassador Smith received a visit from a prominent Havana businessman, Jose Ferrer, owner of the *Concretera Nacional*. A member of the exclusive Brook Club in New York, Ferrer called on Smith to pay his respects when he noted the ambassador's name on the membership list.

"I had had two lunches with Smith here in Havana," Ferrer reports. "At the second one, some time after the Cienfuegos revolt, he told me that Batista had promised to give full guarantees to the people, restore freedom of the press and hold honest elections. I offered to introduce him to leaders of the Civic Resistance Movement to get the other side of the picture.

211

" 'I don't need any more intelligence,' " Ferrer reports Smith as replying. 'I have 250 or 280 men in the embassy who are constantly informing me.' "

Ferrer left the luncheon in a furious state of mind. He was closely associated with the Civic Resistance Movement and was one of its top men in Havana. His wife, Millie, his brother-in-law Ignacio Mendoza, a mortgage banker, and Mendoza's wife Beba were very active in the movement. Leaders of the 26th of July Movement and the Civic Resistance Movement used Ignacio Mendoza's house on the ocean front in the Miramar residential district for their secret meetings.

"I never heard from Ambassador Smith again and never talked to him again until several months later, at the request of a member of his staff." This later conversation is another story.

Smith succeeded in persuading Batista to restore freedom of the press and issue a call for presidential elections for June 1, but bloodshed increased throughout the island. Civil rights were restored on January 27, 1958, in all provinces except embattled Oriente. The rebels made the most of that opportunity and Castro let his words be heard directly from the Sierra Maestra for the first time.

On the night of February 24, 1958, the sixty-third anniversary of the War Cry of Independence made at the city of Baire in Oriente, the people of Cuba were electrified when over their shortwave radio on the forty-meter band they heard a voice say:

"Aqui Radio Rebelde! Transmitiendo desde la Sierra Maestra en Territorio Libre de Cuba!" [Here, Rebel Radio! Transmitting from the Sierra Maestra in Free Territory of Cuba!]

With only brief interludes for reasons of security when the transmitter had to be moved or remain off the air, the people of Cuba tuned in nightly to Radio Rebelde. Under the censorship their only news source had been Radio Bemba, a Cuban idiomatic expression for the grapevine telegraph. *Bemba* is a colloquialism for "big lips" or "big mouth." Soon Radio Rebelde had the highest rating of any of Cuba's stations, and Batista was jamming its broadcasts, especially in Havana.

The 26th of July Movement had established sixty-two branches of the organization throughout the Americas, including Puerto

212

Rico. The members of those branches, including exiles and resident Cubans, worked actively in the field of propaganda and fund raising. One of those active in Miami was Father Juan Ramon O'Farrill, who had been forced into exile after being beaten by Batista's police in 1956. They ruptured his eardrum. He was accused of having stored arms for rebels in his church.

One of the greatest psychological blows struck by the rebels was their kidnaping of Juan Manuel Fangio, the world championship Argentine racing driver. Fangio was politely snatched from the lobby of the Lincoln Hotel in downtown Havana the day before he was scheduled to drive in the II Gran Premio that had been organized by Batista's brother-in-law, General Roberto Fernandez Miranda, to commemorate the anniversary of the War Cry of Baire. Appeals were made by radio and television to the 26th of July Movement to return Fangio safely. The race went on without Fangio and ended in tragedy on the Malecon when cars skidded into the crowd of spectators and killed several. Fangio was delivered to the Argentine ambassador that night, unharmed, with a letter of regret signed by Faustino Perez, chief of the 26th of July underground in Havana.

Another of their feats was the fire in the clearinghouse of Havana when half a million dollars in checks were burned.

The Civic Resistance Movement had increased its strength in Havana and elsewhere under the organization of Dr. Angel Maria Santos Buch and Dr. Luis Buch of Santiago. Luis Buch co-ordinated activities in Havana with Manuel Ray, engineer in charge of the construction of the Havana-Hilton Hotel.

The Civic Resistance Movement was organized into cells of three sections. There was a propaganda section, a fund-raising section and a supply section. Each cell was comprised of ten persons and each person in a cell was urged to enlist another ten persons to organize another cell. The components of this movement were largely from the middle and upper classes, including businessmen, manufacturers, college professors, teachers, white-collar workers and housewives.

Maria Teresa Taquechel was sent to Havana from Santiago and operated under the code name of "Millie Taurel." With Millie Ferrer, the wife of Jose Ferrer, she would transport Manuel

213

Ray from meeting place to meeting place and from hiding place to hiding place. The office of Ferrer's secretary, Mercedes Sanchez, known as "Cuca," was the message center where those who had to see Ray would arrive and sit in the waiting room with their countersign, a piece of paper protruding from between two fingers. Cuca would acknowledge the password and give the visitor the address where Ray could be located at that particular moment.

Castro's guerrillas came down from the Sierra Maestra regularly now to set fire to trains, disrupt communications between Santiago and Manzanillo, between Santiago and Holguin; and only the extreme eastern end was still free from harassment.

In Havana petitions for writs of habeas corpus were filed before the criminal courts to obtain the release of political prisoners. Other lawyers filed briefs requesting the courts to order that missing persons, like Lieutenant Jose San Roman Toledo, be produced or criminal investigation be initiated and charges filed against those believed responsible for their deaths should they have been killed.

Señora Esther Milanes Datin, a fifty-year-old schoolteacher and Roman Catholic, was arrested. As soon as she entered the police station the captain of the precinct struck her on the ear. Ordered to reveal where some rebel arms were hidden, she professed ignorance. She was then subjected to one of the most horrible tortures ever inflicted on any woman who could survive to tell the tale.

Her story became known quite by accident when the Colombian ambassador found her at the police station where he had gone to obtain the release of a citizen of his country. She was released in the care of a physician shortly afterward and confined to a private hospital for treatment. The physician who treated her, Dr. J. A. Presno Albaran, was so horrified and so disgusted with the abuses committed on his patient that he wrote a letter of denunciation which was published in the newspapers. This was followed by a letter from Señora Milanes in which she requested the United Nations, the Organization of the American States and the Inter American Press Association to take cognizance of the atrocity. Following that she had to go into exile in the United States.

214

Back in the Sierra Maestra Fidel Castro signed a law which he had ordered his Judge Advocate General, Dr. Humberto Sori Marin, to write. It was patterned after the law which the patriots enacted during the War for Independence. The law authorized summary courts-martial and penalties including execution before a firing squad for such crimes as murder, arson, theft and looting committed by any person, especially members of the armed forces or persons at the service of the Batista regime. The law was signed on February 11, 1958.

With terror and counterterror increasing, with the rebels marauding in Oriente and other provinces, another expedition landed on the coast of Las Villas province. It was led by Faure Chomon, Secretary General of the Directorio Revolucionario, who had been in exile in Miami since the attack on the palace, in which he had taken part. With a band of men, Chomon now made his way, with arms and ammunition, into the Sierra de la Trinidad east of Cienfuegos.

One group was already there, that which had formed the nucleus of the Second National Front of Escambray. William Alexander Morgan had joined the band and begun to train those men and also fresh recruits. Morgan was to rise from private to major in that army. Chomon and his men operated in a different sector and completely independent of the Escambray force. The 26th of July had a force of 72 men in the same mountains under Captain Victor Bordon. Hence, there were three unco-ordinated small forces operating in those mountains of Las Villas province.

The hierarchy of the Roman Catholic Church met in Havana the last days of February to review the holocaust that was sweeping over the country. The debates were long and grave as reports were made to Manuel Cardinal Arteaga, Archbishop of Havana, by Monsignor Enrique Perez Serantes, Archbishop of Santiago de Cuba; Monsignor Evelio Diaz Cia, Bishop of Pinar del Rio; Monsignor Carlos Riu Angle, Bishop of Camaguey; Monsignor Eduardo Martinez Dalmau, Bishop of Cienfuegos; Monsignor Alberto Martin Villaverde, Bishop of Matanzas; and Monsignor Alfredo Muller San Martin, Auxiliary Bishop of Havana.

Bishop Martin Villaverde was all for stomping to the presi-

215

dential palace to ask Batista to resign forthwith to stop further bloodshed. The zealous separation of powers of the church and the state prevented any such personal action, but the bishops agreed to issue a carefully worded statement which practically amounted to such a request. The statement was issued on February 28.

"The Cuban Episcopate," it read, "contemplates with profound sorrow the lamentable state to which we have arrived throughout the republic, and in particular in the Oriente region. Hatreds increase, charity diminishes, tears and sorrow penetrate into our homes, the blood of brothers is spilled in our fields and in our cities.

"Burdened with grave responsibilities, before God and men because of our condition as spiritual chiefs of our people, we feel obligated to try through all the means within our reach to see that charity reigns anew and that the sad state of our Fatherland ends.

"Guided by these motives, we exhort all who today carry on war in antagonistic camps to cease the use of violence, and, looking only and exclusively for the common good, to find as soon as possible efficacious solutions that can bring back to our Fatherland the material and moral peace that is so lacking. To that end, we do not doubt that those who truly love Cuba will know how to accredit themselves before God and before history, not refusing any sacrifice in order to achieve the establishment of a government of national unity which might prepare the return of our Fatherland to a peaceful and normal political life.

"The government as well as the other Cubans called upon to decide this important matter can count on our most ardent prayers and, in the measure in which it may fall outside of the ground of partisan politics, with our moral support."

At eight thirty that night I filed a story on the above declaration. This was an interlude when there was no censorship, but at eleven o'clock that night I learned that the Ministry of Communications had a duplicate of my text and there was panic at the palace. I had reported that the Episcopate of the Roman Catholic Church had virtually asked Batista to resign.

Pressure from the palace was applied on every newspaper in

216

Havana not to publish the Episcopate statement. The pressure was so intense that Cristobal Diaz, vice president of the newspapers *El Pais* and *Excelsior* and president of the Cuban Press Bloc, was called at the Hotel Astor in New York from the palace to ask him to telephone Havana editors and request they withhold the story. Diaz made the calls.

I toured the newspaper offices shortly after one o'clock in the morning and made *Diario la Marina* my first call. Carlos Castaneda, a television commentator and writer for *Bohemia,* had informed me that one of the newspapers had reported it was going to wait and see what *Diario la Marina,* considered the semiofficial organ of the Roman Catholic Church, was going to do with the story before its editors would attempt to stick their necks out over and above the government pressure.

When I arrived at *Diario la Marina,* a delegation from the Catholic Youth Labor Movement was waiting to see the news editor. I asked the news editor if it were true that the palace was applying pressure to withhold the publication of the story.

"No," he replied. "What the palace has asked is that we defer its publication until a clarification can be made by the Episcopate."

"Do you think," I asked, "that the Episcopate will meet at one twenty in the morning to furnish a clarification because Batista has asked for it?"

He allowed that such a thing was inconceivable. I assured him that should a decision be made to publish the story, the newspaper could rely on the backing of the Inter American Press Association against any attempted reprisal by Batista.

Just then the impatient men of the Catholic Youth Labor Movement broke out of the anteroom into the editorial office.

"We expect *Diario la Marina* to do its duty and publish the declaration of the Episcopate!" they shouted.

"This newspaper has performed its duty for one hundred and twenty-six years," the news editor replied, "and it will continue to do so."

The intruders departed, talking to one another and to me as I left with them, threatening to picket the newspaper with 500 men if it did not print the story.

217

The situation was the same at almost every newspaper. Manuel Brana was ready to resign as editor of *Excelsior* if he were not allowed to print the story. The pressure produced some results on behalf of Batista. A story which would have ordinarily merited an eight-column banner line on page one was given a two-column headline in some newspapers and a one-column headline in others and played either below the fold or on an inside page. Some papers went to press with the story not included in their provincial editions.

Diario la Marina responded on March 2 with a page-one editorial in which it furnished the clarification that Batista desired, pointing out that what the church meant was that the Cabinet should be reorganized and not that the President quit. The palace worked quickly to subvert the move by the bishops and created a conciliation commission to confer with Batista and with Castro, if possible, to put an end to the civil war. But Castro was calling the signals up in the hills at that time because he felt himself getting stronger and was flexing his rebel muscles.

The Episcopate statement caught him in the midst of a high policy and planning meeting with members of the national directorate of the 26th of July Movement. He missed the services of Armando Hart, who with Javier Pazos had been captured when they left the Sierra and reached the outskirts of Santiago some time earlier. Both were in the Boniato prison in Santiago. Preliminary talks were held in Havana by the conciliation commission, but on March 9 Castro made it known that he would not have any part of such a compromise. He wrote a letter as follows:

> Free Territory of Cuba
> Sierra Maestra, March 9, 1958
> 10:45 A.M.

Mr. News Editor of CMKC
Santiago de Cuba.

"Distinguished newspaperman:

"By means of that worthy and patriotic broadcasting station we wish to declare to the people of Cuba:

"1. That the Cuban Episcopate should define what it understands by 'Government of National Unity.'

218

"2. That the ecclesiastical hierarchy should clarify to the country whether it considers it possible that any dignified and self-respecting Cuban is disposed to sit down in a Council of Ministers presided over by Fulgencio Batista.

"3. That this lack of definition on the part of the Episcopate is enabling the Dictatorship to accomplish a move toward a collaborationist and counterrevolutionary negotiation.

"4. That consequently the 26th of July Movement flatly rejects every contact with the Conciliation Commission.

"5. That the 26th of July Movement is interested only in expounding its thought to the people of Cuba and therefore reiterates its desire to do so before a commission of representatives of the National Press.

"6. That a week having passed since our public challenge to the dictatorship—to which, once again trampling the rights of the Cuban Press, it has failed to reply—we set Tuesday, the eleventh, as the last day for the tyrant to say, without any further delay or play, whether he will or will not permit the transit of newspapermen to territory dominated by our troops.

"7. That upon the termination of this limit the 26th of July Movement will make a definitive pronouncement to the country, launching the final slogans of struggle.

"8. That from this instant the entire people should be alert and put on the alert all their forces.

"9. That after six years of shameful, repugnant and criminal oppression, with intimate rejoicing of fighters who have fulfilled their duty without resting a minute in such a long task, we can announce to the country that because of the victories of our arms and the heroic sacrifice of our unbending and invincible people who have left on the road hundreds of their best sons, the chains are about to be broken; already visible on the horizon is the anxiously awaited dawn which in these hours nothing and no one can prevent.

"10. I beg you very fraternally to furnish this statement to all the newspapers.

FIDEL CASTRO

The radio station broadcast Castro's letter on March 11, and that night Prime Minister Emilio Nunez Portuondo repeatedly assured reporters that civil rights would not be suspended and that press censorship would not be reimposed.

The restoration of civil rights had given the rebels more liberty to renew their sabotage operations throughout the country. They took full advantage of it and set fire to busses, trucks, railroad trains, government depots and warehouses, and did everything possible to harass the government. It was unsafe to ride the busses in Havana because one did not know when rebel terrorists would board and set fire to them. There was fear that bombs would be dropped in some stores in the busy shopping street of Galiano and people remained at home. They also stayed out of motion picture theaters for the same reason. Only the night clubs adjacent to casinos in the large hotels were operating safely and almost to capacity. Some judges in Havana could no longer tolerate the state of terror and force that existed in the country. They sent the following letter to the Chamber of Administration of the Court of Appeals of Havana:

"The undersigned, officers of the judiciary, have the honor to state respectfully as follows:

"The administration of justice in Cuba has never been so mocked, ridiculed and abused as it has been recently. Upon reviewing our hazardous past history, we cannot find any record of two sons of a judge having been killed by a soldier, or the homes of two magistrates having been subjected to machine-gun fire, or the home of another judge having been bombed, or of a magistrate acting as an electoral inspector having been arrested by a member of the armed forces, and his having been kept incommunicado and deprived of food. Nor can we find any record of judicial procedure having been prevented by national police patrol cars, or the traditional institution of habeas corpus mocked and ignored after the criminal division of the Supreme Court ordered prisoners to be freed, prisoners who were later on found shot to death, or after the Court of Appeals of this district had ordered that they be presented before the court under the appeals procedure.

"On the other hand, it is notorious that vices like gambling and prostitution are exploited by those called upon to prosecute them and that the list of deaths and murders among prisoners

220

grows daily, even including young people and women, without the authors of such crimes being discovered, owing to the lack of police co-operation.

"There hardly remains any Court of Appeals where, for lack of proper vigilance, a fire has not broken out or a bomb has not exploded. A few steps from the Supreme Court building a man has been found shot to death, and the police have neither been able to prevent it nor to trace the assassins.

"A judge, appointed as special prosecutor to investigate the facts, is publicly subjected to threats and insults with complete impunity.

"Finally, in the municipalities of Santiago de Cuba, Guantanamo, Palma Soriano, Bayamo, El Cobre, Manzanillo and Niquero, it is a notorious fact that cases of violent death (by gunshot, torture and hanging) are daily events, while the judges are prevented by officers of the armed forces from doing their duty and are deprived of the indispensable means to do it.

"This state of affairs makes the judiciary of the Republic appear as a weak and oppressed body in the eyes of the nation.

"The Chamber of Administration of the Supreme Court, in a resolution dated June 25, 1926, warned all judges that 'every officer represents totally, within the limits of his respective incumbency, the authority of the judiciary, with all of its attributes and also with all of its responsibilities, and that each of them, by virtue of his office, is charged with the defense of the prestige of the courts.'

"In similar circumstances, but not so grave as at present, the Chief Justice of the Supreme Court said that 'from the point of view of national stability, it is indispensable to make an effort to keep inviolate the administration of justice and to maintain the strength and autonomy of the bodies which serve it, as a consequence of which it is unlawful to suppress any effort which may be conducive to the maintenance of the constitutional condition of the courts and that when all the efforts to attain that end have been exhausted, it is neither dignified nor edifying for the judiciary to remain silent.'

"In view whereof, and without trying to make any suggestions that could be interpreted as insubordination, but in the firm belief that the above mentioned resolution imposes upon us the obligation to comply with it insofar as we are concerned, we hereby beg this Chamber of Administration to pass such resolutions as it may deem proper.

"Havana, March 6, 1958.

(Signed) "Alfredo E. Herrera Estrada and Fernando Alvarez Tabio, Presidents of Divisions of the Court of Appeals of Havana; Jorge A. Cowley, Fernandez Saavedra, Pedro Lucas Lozano Urquiola, Manuel Gomez Calvo, Juan Bautista More Benitez, Miguel F. Marquez de la Cerra, Eloy G. Merino Brito, Enrique Hart Ramirez, Jose Montoro Cespedes, Magistrates of the Court of Appeals of Havana; Felipe L. Luaces Sebrango, Juan F. Rodriguez Soriano, Judges of Havana."

At the same time, Dr. Jose Francisco Alabau Trelles had been appointed as magistrate and special judge to investigate four cases of homicide within the jurisdiction of San Jose de las Lajas, a city on the road between Havana and Matanzas, and two cases of murder and other crimes in Havana. Accused in the Havana cases were Lieutenant Colonel Esteban Ventura, who had earned the distinction of being the Himmler of Havana as chief of the Division of Subversive Activities of the police department, and Lieutenant Julio Laurent, head of Naval Intelligence.

Dr. Alabau announced the indictment of Ventura and Laurent for murder and ordered them imprisoned in the La Cabana fortress without bail on March 11. On March 12, without consulting his prime minister, Batista suspended civil rights, reimposed press and radio censorship and removed the indictments of Ventura and Laurent from the civilian courts, turning them over to the military tribunals where they were quashed.

Throughout the intervening periods there were several conspiracies within the armed forces which, because of Batista's rigorous counterespionage system, were always nipped in the bud. The latest one involved some officers from Oriente and Camaguey and some noncommissioned officers from Camp Columbia.

Judge Alabau had to go into hiding and then into exile because his life was in danger for having indicted Ventura and Laurent. As soon as Batista announced the suspension of civil rights on the afternoon of March 12, Ventura appeared at the courthouse with two police sergeants in search of Alabau, with his pistol drawn. In a loud voice for everyone to hear, and spewing forth epithets, he threatened to kill the judge if he set eyes on him.

That afternoon Fidel Castro completed the final draft of another manifesto from the Sierra, this time calling on the people to rise in "total war" against Batista. Perez started back from Castro's headquarters the next morning and en route passed the first Cuban newspapermen to climb the mountain to see Castro. They were Augustin Alles, writer, and Eduardo (Guayo) Hernandez, cameraman. They were on assignment for *Bohemia*.

Other leaders of the 26th of July Movement and the Civic Resistance Movement were active in Havana, trying to apply pressure in all quarters to force Batista to resign. Saboteurs had placed dynamite under power lines and gas mains, ready to blow them when the signal was given to start a general strike. The rebels were prepared to cause much damage in the city but sought to avoid it if possible.

On the night of March 14 Ambassador Smith telephoned Dr. Raul de Velasco, president of the Medical Association and president of the Joint Body of Civic Institutions, and asked him to call at his residence the next day, a Saturday morning.

"Ambassador Smith said he wanted to have a conversation with me," Dr. Velasco relates, "because he understood from his contacts that the Batista government was disposed to furnish all kinds of guarantees for the elections June 1 to be carried out with full liberty and he was certain that that was Batista's thinking. He said that as the civic institutions were a nonpolitical organization, that if we insisted Batista do that he was sure that Batista would accept and even agree to invite international organizations to monitor the elections.

"I told Ambassador Smith that I thought he was wrong and asked him if he did not realize that Batista suspended civil rights because Ventura and Laurent were indicted; that he wanted to remove the indictments from the civil courts and quash them in the military courts; that Ventura had gone to the court himself and threatened to kill the judge; that moreover we did not understand how elections could possibly be held June 1 when we

223

were already in the month of March and there was no time to prepare a democratic electoral process; that anyone who opposes Batista is beaten, tortured and killed and has no rights.

"Smith replied that the elections would not be held June 1 but would be postponed to the month of October or November.

" 'Mr. Ambassador,' I said, 'the Supreme Electoral Tribunal is quoted in the newspaper today as rejecting a petition to postpone the elections.'

" 'I'll bet you ten dollars you are wrong,' Ambassador Smith replied and took a ten-dollar bill from his pocket.

"I told him I would not bet him because my father had taught me that, if I take a bet when I know I am going to win, it is unfair, and when I make a bet on my own volition it is stupidity. Smith then said he would bet me thirty dollars that the elections would be postponed. I suggested he read the newspaper. He sent for a copy, read the story and saw I was right. Then he went into another room to telephone Assistant Secretary of State for Inter American Affairs, Roy R. Rubottom.

"After his phone call to Washington he returned to the room.

" 'I guarantee that the elections will be postponed until October or November,' Smith said, 'and that Batista will ask for international organizations to supervise them.'

" 'Mr. Ambassador,' I said, 'the civic institutions are disposed to accept any solution that is good and that has the support of the revolutionary sectors. The elections will be no problem if this administration delivers the governing power to a completely neutral government.'

" 'What will the strong man of the Sierra Maestra think of that?' Smith asked me and flexed his muscle. I told him I was sure the revolutionaries would accept a government without Batista, a neutral, nonpolitical government.

" 'We have got to prevent chaos,' Smith said. 'I have to defend the life and interests of United States business and the United States subjects here.'

" 'The life and interests of the Cuban subjects are also at stake,' I told him. 'Nobody's life is worth while in Cuba today. There is no way in which you can convince the Cuban people that any offer by Batista will be carried out.'

" 'I would consult with Washington and within twenty-four

hours the United States government could get a guarantee,' Smith said.

"I told Smith that the only solution was for Batista to leave, that there was no solution with Batista in office.

"Smith then changed the course of the conversation and I gathered that this was the main reason why he had summoned me.

" 'I have heard by Radio Bemba,' Smith said, 'that the civic institutions have asked Batista to resign. That would be serious because it would be a final break.'

" 'Mr. Ambassador,' I said, 'the institutions have not yet taken a decision and we are still discussing it.'

"Smith asked me to hold it up at least for forty-eight hours, but I told him I would have to report to the members of the institutions."

Dr. Raul de Velasco left the embassy and summoned a meeting of the heads of the civic institutions in Havana and the representatives of the local committees from the entire country, who were in Havana for the occasion. He gave them a detailed report of his conversation with Smith. They decided to complete the drafting of the document in which they would ask Batista to resign and obtained all the signatures required. The original was signed by each person above the name of the organization over which he or she presided.

The following Monday morning Dr. Raul Fernandez Zeballos, head of the Cuban Council of Evangelical Churches, personally delivered a copy of the document to John Topping, political officer at the American embassy, for delivery to Ambassador Smith. The copy which the civic institutions circulated did not contain the names of the signatories but only their associations. Dr. Fernandez was directed by the signatories to make the delivery of the document to the embassy. The statement read:

"TO THE PEOPLE OF CUBA:

"Once again the Joint Body of Cuban Institutions, comprising religious, fraternal, professional, civic and cultural associations, express their opinion publicly on the possibilities of solving peacefully the grave crisis affecting the nation, this time by demanding from the government the decision which the moment calls for if, in a final and desperate effort, the imminent crumbling of the fundamental institutions of the state is to be avoided.

"This committee has always raised its voice responsibly as a belligerent for peace, and in an anguished appeal stated that a solution of the grave national crisis should be found; and fearful of the risk that an outburst of violence would sink the country in anarchy, announced that the Cuban institutions would do their duty under said emergency.

"The moment has arrived: The government, deaf to all appeals and depending upon force, provoked through its attitude the uprising of young Cuban men and women, who exchanged their textbooks for the weapons of insurrection in a youth movement which by dint of heroisms and sacrifices now dictates its policy to the country and adds to their undertakings the support of all the social classes by sheer force of admiration.

"Through six long years of agony, the forces of repression of the regime have been mobilized against them, acting systematically with unsurpassed cruelty.

"Mainly upon defenseless women and helpless young people the action of the armed forces is concentrated continuously and mercilessly, in a way that has no parallels in the history of civil wars.

"The regime has not wished to know what motivates the Cuban youth, and after violating the juridical order of the state through an act of force while invoking the principles of public order, now announces—together with a new suspension of constitutional protection—a new conscription of 7,000 soldiers to crush all protests in a war of extermination.

"It all will be useless: the number of victims will increase, but the rebel movement will be intensified, because together with the young people, the entire nation is stirring, in plain view and in an underground movement.

"The people, in consternation at the continuous shedding of the blood of their best citizens, fail to understand this fratricidal war, or why the military units supporting the regime fight so earnestly to defend the government repudiated by the people.

"The spectacle which the martyrdom of Cuba presents to the world does not move the sentiments of those who seized the power, which they intend to keep against the will of all.

226

"The anguished appeal of mothers is not listened to, nor the voices of institutions independent of all partisan interests; and the grief-laden words of the venerable Episcopate are answered with twisted double talk to impose in a rough tone an obstinate will of rule.

"Until now, the Joint Committee of Cuban Institutions has proposed formulas of compromise and civilized understanding. Conscious that the nation is faced with the danger of perishing, it now calmly demands that the present regime shall cease to hold power, because it has been incapable of fulfilling the normal functions of government and the highest ends of the state.

"In requesting the termination of the regime and the abdication of those in the executive power and the dissolution of Congress, it has based its determined demands fundamentally on the instinct of social preservation, with the intention of contributing to the re-establishment of peace by removing the only cause which makes civilized understanding impossible.

"This request involves the forming—through elections to be held with full democratic guarantees—of a provisional government, comprising citizens of outstanding prestige, which will function in national unity and be appointed with the assent of all the vital forces of the nation, and enable the restoration of peace to the country by adopting such measures and principles as may be conducive, in a brief period of time, to the decision of the historic destiny of Cuba.

"In order to meet those objectives, the provisional government shall follow a course directed by a minimum program containing the following fundamental guiding principles:

"A. Said government shall respect private property and binds itself to fulfill all bilateral or multilateral agreements emanating from agreements under the United Nations, as well as all undertakings and obligations assumed by the Republic, leaving to the Congress, which shall be duly elected, the power to determine if such obligations comply with the Constitution and the laws.

"B. It shall annul all sentences pronounced by the Court of Urgency of the Republic of Cuba and by the courts-martial held subsequent to March 10, 1952, based on political crimes committed with a view to deposing the regime set up on said date.

"C. The provisional government, insofar as its peculiar nature

227

may permit, will be subject to the Constitution of 1940, which will prevail fundamentally insofar as individual rights are concerned.

"D. The legislative arm will be represented by the government, which shall limit itself to the promulgation of the laws strictly necessary for its normal action in order to implement a return to constitutional regime through elections by the people.

"E. Among the laws that it may pass, preference shall be given to those which tend to the commencing and developing of the electoral process, which will culminate in the designation of the constitutional representatives.

"The Committee of Cuban Institutions believes that this is the only solution which offers Cuba a triumphal escape from chaos at this dramatic juncture. And, conscious of its lack of strength to depose the regime by means of violence, hereby appeals to the entire nation to join in united resistance against the oppression, by exercising the rights granted by the Constitution to free men.

"Havana, March 15, 1958

"FOR THE COMMITTEE OF CUBAN INSTITUTIONS:

"National Confederation of Universities Professionals, National Bar Association, Havana Bar Association, National Association of Architects, National Association of Surveyors and Land Appraisers of Cuba, Association of Public Accountants of Cuba, National Dentists Association, Havana Association of Dentists, National Association of Doctors of Science, Philosophy and Letters, National Association of Doctors of Social Science and Public Law, National Association of Pharmacists, Federation of Associations of Engineers of Cuba, National Association of Civil Engineers of Cuba, National Association of Electrical Engineers, Provincial Association of Civil Engineers of Havana, Association of Electrical Engineers of Havana, National Medical Association, Havana Municipal Medical Association, National Association of Chemists, Agronomists and Sugar Chemists, National Association of Social Workers, Association of Veterinarians of the Province of Havana, Association of Journalists of the Province of Havana, National Association of Private Schools Teachers, National Association of English Professors and Teachers, Association of English Professors and Teachers of Havana, National Association of Industrial Mechanics, Association of Industrial Mechanics of the Municipality of Havana, Federation of Young Men of Cuban Catholic Action, Catholic Group of University Students, Cuban Council of Evangelical Churches, Lions Club District C, Council of Governors of Lions Clubs, Lyceum Lawn Tennis Club, Cultural Society "Nuestro Tiempo," National Group of Juvenile Organizations of Cuba, Supreme Council 33 Degree Masons, National Federation of Cuban Private Schools, "Sol de Cuba" Lodge, "Pureza" Lodge, National Association of Chemical Engineers, Sugar and Industrial Chemists of Cuba, Association of Mechanical Engineers of Cuba, National Association of Veterinarians, and all local committees pertaining to the Committee of Cuban Institutions in all cities and municipalities of the Republic."

Smith ridiculed the above as an anonymous and unofficial statement because it contained no personal signatures.

The police and military intelligence immediately began a search for Dr. Jose Miro Cardona, president of the Havana Bar Association, who was considered one of the masterminds of the drafting of that document. The other signatories had to be careful of their movements or go into hiding. Miro was forced to disguise himself as a priest and take refuge in the Church of the Holy Spirit. There he almost aroused suspicion because he was dressed in a priest's garb but had failed to shave off his mustache.

From his sanctuary he addressed a report to the Board of Directors of the Havana Bar Association which read:

"To the Board of Directors of the Havana Bar Association:

"1. Yesterday I delivered to the assistant president, Dr. Silvio S. Sanabria, a copy of the document entitled 'To the Cuban People,' issued by the Joint Committee of Cuban Institutions, of which this bar association forms part by virtue of repeated resolutions of its Board of Directors. Said board, in turn, granted me a vote of confidence to state publicly, whenever I should see fit, the opinion of the body regarding the institutional crisis existing in the Republic.

"2. Before explaining the reasons leading up to my decision, I wish to report my deep gratitude to the members of the board, which I have always tried to serve successfully. All through the six years of office, in two consecutive terms, which is the highest honor I could aspire to as a lawyer, all important resolutions of the body have been passed unanimously. When I first took office following my illustrious professor, Alberto Blanco, I stated at a plenary meeting of the Supreme Court of Justice that I aspired to 'be able to echo always the unanimous opinions of the board.' It has been so in all the problems that the board has had to confront in these six years in which Cuba has lived in permanent crisis regarding legal standards. In this lapse of time the Havana Bar Association has done its duty thoroughly in every way, whether regarding the defense of the judicial arm of government, or of strictly class interests, or regarding assistance to its members, or in an academical sense. And insofar as concerns the defense of liberty, democracy, the Constitution and the law, as well as the way of judging and resolving the complex problems before the nation, the opinion of the board, sometimes severe in judging facts and attitudes, has always been a juridical expression whenever involving peaceful solutions. I consider myself a faithful interpreter of the thoughts of the board.

"3. The copy of the document that I have delivered to the assistant president for the attention of the honorable board reflects totally the opinion given by the board at the meeting held on the fourth of March last, with regard to the statement made by the venerable Episcopate of Cuba and to the request presented by Dr. Enrique Llanso, honorary president of the National Bar Association, at the meeting held by the executive committee on Saturday the eighth instant, with the vote of the representatives of the local associations: that the obstacle to peace is the continuance of the 10th of March, 1952, regime in power, and its cessation should be urgently demanded by the men of the legal profession.

"4. In an appeal to the executive power and its supporting bodies, the above mentioned document proposes cessation of the present regime and the formation of a transitory provisional government 'comprising citizens of outstanding prestige who, in the function of national unity, to be appointed with the assent of all the vital forces of the country,' to which the revolutionary forces, political parties and factions should give their support, as well as the support and respect of the armed forces of the Republic.

"5. No solution appears to be efficacious at this time other than what has been proposed by the Joint Body of Cuban Institutions in order to stop the tragic harvest of blood existing in the country and to prevent the collapse of the fundamental institutions of the state. The proposed solution is, in our judgment, the only one capable of channeling the rising tide of rebellion of our youth and the only logical one, namely, that a provisional government of national unity can lead the country in the shortest possible time to the political reality of generating a legitimate constitutionality by means of a duly guaranteed electoral process.

"6. The present regime, which in its essence is illegal, cannot invoke constitutional provisions in its favor. To assume command without the consent of the juridical status in force; to annul the constitutional document that impedes the continuation of its existence; to suspend the functions of the Congress elected by the people; to issue certain statutes; to grant legislative power to itself; to call for general elections, suspend them and finally hold them in the absence of any opposition; to alter the results of those elections in order to create an artificial minority; to 'rivet' those results so as to prevent legal appeal against them and to decree an amnesty for electoral crimes; to issue a transitory provision fourteen years after the institution of the Fundamental Code of the Republic, which the people had approved in a sovereign act and formally restored subsequently by decree, are acts typical of a de facto government that intends to cover its substantial illegality by means of legal appearances.

"Subsequent to the electoral event alluded to above, which was ineffective by being unilateral, the government rejected every opportunity to validate its damaged origin by refusing to reach an agreement with the political and revolutionary forces of the country. From that moment on, deaf to all appeals, it has depended on force to impose the principle of authority, forgetting that the source of all just government is to be found in the consent of the people.

"7. Having explained the reasons underlying the proposal of the Joint Committee of Cuban Institutions, all of which are in agreement with those set forth at the meeting of March 4, over which I had the honor to preside, and with the proposal of the executive committee of the National Bar Association, I have now to explain only those which justify the moment in which the statements of the above mentioned committee have been made.

"The gravity of the present situation cannot have escaped the illustrious consideration of my colleagues. The new suspension of the constitutional guarantees of individuals, which implies that the government no longer faces a simple problem of public order; the censorship of the press; the crisis of the judicial arm of the government, whose resolutions are being ignored by intolerable attitudes of rebellion and by the disdain of agents of public authority; the paralysis of all teaching in the schools; the state of siege existing in the province of Oriente, the hateful persecution of all citizens, the stalking of death in our cities and country places, not to mention the offenses against the common right of men and women. These are the circumstances in which the former prime minister of the government and a candidate for the highest position in the land, who aspires to appear as the representative of national concord, has spoken words that offend the juridical conscience of the country and which must be evaluated in all their dramatic dimensions and which I copy as follows:

" '. . . One does not have to be a Greek sage to understand that half-hearted measures are impossible, because at the high point which the insurrectional temperature has reached in our midst only a strong and extremely energetic government can keep order, no matter what rights have to be violated or how sacred these may be.'

"8. After hearing these words, which are the terrifying advance notice of violence and indiscriminate retaliation, we feel that there could be no other opportunity in which to make this inevitable pronouncement against the evil and to avail ourselves of the rights which the Constitution of the Republic grants to free men, whereby resistance to oppression enjoys the category of legal right.

"9. It can be assumed that retaliation will be even stronger against the professional associations, and especially the Bar Association, which from day to day has suffered restrictions on its disciplinary faculties in the matter of dismissals, which has been interfered with in the administration of its social security funds, and which has been systematically disturbed in the exercise of its legal functions by virtue of court orders being ignored and the

232

incarceration of men of law. It is the destiny of our profession to fight dictatorships without any other weapons than those of reason, but 'dangerous dignity is always preferable to a useless life,' as the Apostle of our liberties stated.

"We cannot encourage the spirit of fighting nor give support to bloody fury; but it has become necessary to defend stanchly the fundamental institutions of the state. In the Tenth Inter-American Conference of Lawyers, held in the free country of Argentina in the month of November last, a resolution was unanimously passed by the jurists of this continent, whereby 'all bar associations are charged with the duty to fight against all dictatorships in order to insure a regime of law.'

"Having explained the reasons which determined the statement encompassing the thoughts of the Board of Directors, I reiterate the testimony of my highest consideration.

JOSE MIRO CARDONA, President

In the home of Ignacio Mendoza I had interviewed the top leaders of the Havana underground; they were busy building up their partisans for a big blow to force Batista to resign under pressure. The action by the civic institutions and other groups was part of the plan, but it failed to produce results.

The rebel co-ordination was faulty from a psychological point of view. Almost simultaneous with the issuance of the statement by the civic institutions and before that statement could be publicized abroad and circulated in Cuba through underground channels and Radio Bemba, Faustino Perez returned to Havana with the manifesto which he and Castro had signed in the Sierra Maestra. The trip from the mountain hide-out to another hide-out in the capital took him only three days.

Through the underground contacts I was summoned to an interview with Perez. With him came Luis Buch, Manuel Ray, David Salvador, Dr. Fernandez Zeballos, the head of the Cuban Evangelical Churches—all of whom had been at Ignacio Mendoza's house when I went there—and Carlos Lechuga, a newspaper columnist and television commentator who was hiding out.

The meeting was held in the home of Jose Villares, representative of E. R. Squibb and Son. Perez handed me a copy of the manifesto.

233

CHAPTER 8

The burning of the sugar cane fields had long ceased when the manifesto was issued, but the sabotage of transport and communications was increased. Trains were derailed and burned and passengers had to complete their journeys on foot. Freight cars carrying sugar cane were derailed and burned.

The manifesto was almost the equivalent of a field order to all rebels throughout Cuba, and it contained an unmistakable threat to the members of the armed forces. Castro was announcing the plan for the start of what he described as his "total war" against Batista. The manifesto read:

Free Territory of Cuba
Sierra Maestra, March 12, 1958

"MANIFESTO FROM THE 26TH OF JULY MOVEMENT TO THE PEOPLE:

"On refusing to authorize the Cuban press to visit the field of operations and to find out something about the 26th of July Movement's attitude, Dictator Batista not only has shown moral cowardice and military impotence, but also has spoken the last word regarding the outcome of this struggle.

"In the midst of all the harm being done, he could do an invaluable service to the country at this moment, namely, save the bloodshed that will fully come by putting an end to this contest through his resignation, since he must know that he is irremediably lost.

234

"If it is unjustifiable to govern the country by brute force and sacrifice human lives on the altar of the selfish will to remain in power, as he has been doing for the last six years, it is a thousand times more unjustifiable to sacrifice those lives when the unbreakable will of the nation, as expressed by all its social, political, cultural and religious groups, against which it is impossible to govern, has decreed the immediate and inexorable end of this regime.

"Those of us who know intimately what human values the country is sacrificing in its fight for liberty; who know the lives it costs to take each position and carry out every action; who always remember Frank Pais and Jose Antonio Echevarria as symbols of hundreds of other equally courageous young men who have died on the altar of duty; and we who know how much the country will need them when the moment, which is at hand, actually arrives to do creative work, feel and suffer—courageously and with uncontainable indignation—the monstrosity and futility of the crime that is being committed against Cuba.

"If the right to know the truth is denied to the people, how can one expect the slightest respect for physical security, personal liberty and the right of meeting, organizing and electing its own rulers?

"The fact is that the tyranny could not grant anything without being in danger of disintegrating; the tyranny has no other alternative than to disappear.

"If the rebels have been beaten, if the troops of the regime control the hills and the valleys, if our forces do not join combat and are impossible to locate, if what exist are only small groups engaged in banditry, and if against us there stands a strong, invincible, disciplined and combative army, as the Army Chief of Staff in his cynical reports claims, why were the newspapermen not allowed to come to the Sierra Maestra? If they once ostentatiously sent newspapermen in a plane to see that there was nobody here, why are reporters now not allowed to come even close to the southern zone of Oriente? Why do they not repair that insult, among many others, that they have conferred upon the Cuban press?

"The explanation to all of this lies in the shameful defeats that the dictatorship has suffered, in the military offensive that we have quickly destroyed, in the unprecedented acts of barbarity that their hounds have committed against the defenseless civil population, in the true and positive fact that their troops have been expelled from the Sierra Maestra and that the 26th of July army is now in full offensive attacks on the north of the province; in that the demoralization and cowardice have reached such extremes in their ranks that women and children are used as a shield to prevent the action of our detachments; and in that the soldiers and officers are coming over to our side in increasing numbers, abandoning the ranks of the crooked and criminal regime that they have been defending.

"The dictatorship did not wish the newspapermen to learn on the spot, in a direct and irrefutable manner, that more than 300 peasants were assassinated during the six months of suspended guarantees and censorship of the press, that in Oro de Guisa alone 53 peasants were immolated in a single day, that the husband and 9 children of an unfortunate woman were killed.

"It did not want them to see hundreds of humble homes, built through sacrifice, reduced to ashes in brutal retaliation, nor the children mutilated by bombing, nor the machine-gunning of defenseless huts. They did not want the false headquarters reports of each combat to be exposed, because they were trying to deceive not only the people but also the army itself. We would have taken the newspapermen to the scenes of the defeats and the crimes of the tyranny; we would have shown them the prisoners we have taken and the soldiers who have come over to our side. If all the truth of Sierra Maestra were to reach the Cuban papers, the regime would fall by the fearful discredit it would suffer in the eyes of members of the armed forces.

"No other reason could exist for refusing to grant permission. In our territory newspapermen can move around freely and report freely what they see; there is no censorship here, all of which means that freedom to give information does not jeopardize military security and that restrictions to the freedom of the press are not justified even in the midst of war.

"We were sure that permission would be refused, because we knew the reasons for it, but we wanted to unmask the dictatorship, as well as its moral ruin and military weakness, in order to show the people of Cuba that they must have faith in our victory, the same faith that our men have acquired while fighting under the most adverse circumstances, the same invincible faith that the followers of just causes have always had, because the important thing, as Marti said, is not the number of weapons one has, but the number of stars on one's forehead. Now we can fight with the strength of right, as well as the strength of number, with the strength of justice as well as the force of arms. The promise we made one day to the nation will soon be a glorious reality.

"The dictatorship has just suspended guarantees again and re-established the hateful censorship. That shows its terrible weakness. It was enough to announce that the chains were about to be broken and the lightninglike speed with which Column 6 was advancing toward the heart of the province of Oriente, to make them take the necessary measures in the midst of an atmosphere of a general strike. The resignations of the ministers are signs that the ship is sinking and that the people are rising.

"Meeting at the camp of Column 1, general headquarters of the rebel forces, the national directors of the 26th of July Movement unanimously adopted the following:

" '1. To consider that, in view of the visible disintegration of the dictatorship, the ripening of the national conscience and of the belligerent participation of all social, political, cultural and religious groups of the country, the struggle against Batista has entered its final stage.

" '2. That the strategy of the final stroke should be based on the general revolutionary strike, to be seconded by military action.

" '3. That our revolutionary actions should be progressively intensified from this moment until they culminate in the strike which will be duly ordered.

" '4. Citizens should be alerted and warned against any false order. Therefore, contacts and communications should be defined and insured.

" '5. The general strike and the armed struggle will continue resolutely if a military junta should try to take over the government. The position of the 26th of July Movement is unshakable on this point.

" '6. To ratify the appointment of Dr. Urrutia as provisional president and to invite him to select freely and in the shortest possible time his team of colleagues, and to determine the steps to be taken by the government when the tyranny falls, all in accordance with the minimum program set forth in the manifesto of the Sierra Maestra and in the letter to the Committee of Liberation.

" '7. The organization and direction of the strike among the workers will be in the hands of the National Labor Front which, in turn, will assume the representation of the proletariat before the Revolutionary Provisional Government.

" '8. The organization and direction of the strike in professional, commercial and industrial circles will be undertaken by the Civic Resistance Movement.

" '9. The organization and direction of the strike among students will be carried out by the National Students Front.

" '10. Military action will be undertaken by the rebel forces, the 26th of July Movement's militia and all revolutionary organizations which back the Movement.

" '11. The underground papers, *Revolucion, Vanguardia Obrera, Sierra Maestra, El Cubano Libre* and *Resistencia,* will keep the people informed and will be received through the channels of the underground movement, so as to prevent false issues.

" '12. To exhort all journalists, radio announcers, workers of the graphic arts and all newspaper, radio and television companies to organize rapidly as was done in Venezuela, in unanimous response to the new censorship, which is the climax of all the arbitrary actions of the regime, and so become the leaders of the people in the final fight for freedom.

" '13. To exhort the students throughout the country to support more firmly than ever the indefinite strike, once it is started, so that the valiant student youth, who have fought so heroically for freedom, will be the vanguard of the general revolutionary strike. No student should return to class until the dictatorship falls.

" '14. As from April 1, for military reasons, all highway or railway traffic throughout the province of Oriente is prohibited. Any vehicle passing through that zone by day or by night may be fired upon.

" '15. As from April 1, the payment of any kind of taxes to the state, provincial and municipal governments in the entire

238

national territory is prohibited. All payments made subsequent to said date to the tax offices of the dictatorship will be declared null and void and will have to be paid again to the new provisional government, aside from the fact that noncompliance with this measure will be considered as an unpatriotic and antirevolutionary act.

" '16. Any person remaining in offices of trust in the executive branch of the government, or in the presidency of government dependencies, subsequent to April 5, will be considered guilty of treason.

" '17. In view of the state of war existing between the people of Cuba and the Batista tyranny, any army, navy or police officer or member of the ranks thereof who shall continue to render service against the oppressed people subsequent to April 5 will lose his right to continue serving in the armed forces. There will be no valid pretext for using arms against the people in the present circumstances. The duty of every enlisted man is to leave the force, rebel against it and join the revolutionary forces. Any such member of the forces will be received in our ranks with his weapon, his rights will be respected and he will be promoted to the immediate rank above, and will be exempt from the obligation to fight against his former colleagues.

" '18. The 26th of July Movement will refuse only the collaboration of those military men who have been directly responsible for inhuman acts or for stealing. The mere fact of having fought against us will not prevent any military man from serving his country at this decisive hour.

" '19. In view of the news that 7,000 men will be enlisted in the army to fight against the revolution, the 26th of July Movement hereby declares that any citizen enlisting in the armed forces subsequent to the date hereof will be subject to court-martial and be judged as a criminal.

" '20. Likewise, any members of the judiciary, magistrates and district attorneys who, subsequent to April 5, wish to protect their right to continue holding office, must resign from their positions, in view of the fact that the absolute lack of guarantees and of respect for legal procedure makes the judicial arm of the government a useless body.

" '21. To inform the country that Column 6 of the rebel forces, under the command of Major Raul Castro Ruz, has left the Sierra Maestra and has invaded the northern part of Oriente; that Column 8, under the command of Major Juan Almeida, has invaded the east of said province; that rebel patrols are moving in all directions through the province and that armed patrol actions will be intensified throughout the national territory.

" '22. As from this instant, the country should consider itself in total war against the tyranny. The weapons in the hands of the army, the navy and the police belong to the people and should be at the service of the people. Nobody has the right to use them against the people and whoever does so should not expect the least consideration. In order to give the leaders of the revolutionary movement time to act, the campaign of extermination against all those who serve the tyranny under arms will not begin before April 5. From that date the war will be relentlessly waged against the military in order to recover those weapons which belong to the nation and not to the dictator. The people will have to annihilate the military wherever they are found as the worst enemies of freedom and happiness.'

"The whole nation is determined to be free or to perish."

FIDEL CASTRO RUZ
Commander in Chief of the Rebel Forces
DR. FAUSTINO PEREZ
Delegate from Headquarters

Again Castro had violated one of the basic principles of warfare: the element of surprise. He was broadcasting to Batista, and to the entire world, his intended Sunday punch. Perez asked me what comment I had to make on the manifesto in my hand, and I observed that it was their war but I could not understand why Castro insisted on furnishing his enemy with intelligence on a silver platter.

"Those dates don't mean anything," Perez replied. "It could happen any time."

Batista had reinforced censorship of outgoing dispatches and there was a tight censorship on telephone calls—at least for me. It was impossible for me to file a story by the regular communications channels because the censors would not clear my copy. Therefore, I had to resort to the telephone. To transmit a single story it was sometimes necessary for me to make anywhere from five to nine calls, including call-backs from the New York or Washington bureau of the *Chicago Tribune*. The censors would not let the operators place any of my calls to Chicago. Harold Hutchings, Vincent Butler and Eleanor Coleman in our New York bureau and Williard Edwards, Robert Young, Joseph Hearst, Laurence Burd, Philip Warden and Lee Forrester in our Washington bureau were no more exasperated than I when they tried to take my copy over the telephone. Not only did the censor's presence on the line weaken the signal, but he would persistently cut us off.

One Sunday night Batista had issued a statement at Camp Columbia. I placed a call and began to dictate: "President Fulgencio Batista . . ." That was as far as I got. The censor cut me off. I was unable to place another call that night or the next day. I complained to a Cuban friend who approached General Francisco Tabernilla. Tabernilla countermanded the order of total silence and I was allowed to call again, but under the same difficult conditions.

With the aid of bell captains, bellboys and the travel agent at my hotel, I found tourists who were returning to the United States and asked them to carry my copy and file it at the Western Union office at International Airport. One day the Civic Resistance Movement had a courier going to Miami, and Millie Ferrer drove by to pick up my copy and send it on its way.

Batista prepared for Castro's blow. He had the congress vote him powers which enabled him to act as total dictator of Cuba under what he considered a phase of legality.

The same judges who had filed a brief earlier in the month with the Chamber of Administration of the Court of Appeals of Havana filed a short brief, referring to that paper, which terminated with these paragraphs:

"From that day the Chamber of Administration of the Supreme Court has been deliberating on what it should do about these grave matters, and has also received a similar brief from judges of the Court of Appeals of Oriente, which is under consideration together with the above mentioned one.

"At this juncture, Resolution-Law Number I of the government, dictated under the Emergency Law, has been issued by which the provisions of the Organic Law of the judiciary are amended and which provides that officers filing petitions of this kind should be subject to dismissal by means of summary proceedings, and that such dismissal from the judiciary would include loss of pension.

"This monstrous juridical provision, which has no precedents in the annals of justice in the American continent, can be applied retroactively."

Batista began to purge the courts under his new powers and "unreliable" judges were summarily dismissed.

Batista also took other measures to prevent the general strike. He issued a decree-law which authorized the firing of any worker who absented himself and loss of all benefits, privileges and severance pay. Similar measures were taken in every field and the Civic Resistance Movement started a panic by saying that Batista would confiscate bank deposits. The result was a three-day run on banks with millions of dollars withdrawn.

Workers were called on by Castro to contribute one day's pay to the revolution fund. The response was overwhelming.

Batista mobilized his counterpropaganda to halt the intensive campaign from the Sierra Maestra and in Havana itself. A Batista transmitter began to operate on the same frequency as Castro's Rebel Radio, imitating the latter and spreading confusion. Phony propaganda leaflets were printed and distributed in the capital.

While the revolutionary general strike tension was increasing and Batista's propaganda counteroffensive was under way, the heads of the United States Military Mission gave a luncheon in honor of General Francisco Tabernilla at Camp Columbia. He had been promoted to general in chief of the army by Batista under a new law which was primarily designed to permit the dictator to assume that post upon the termination of his presidential term in February 1959. Batista saw to it that the Havana newspapers published photographs of the luncheon to exploit the fact that he enjoyed the support of the State Department and the Pentagon.

This was fourteen days after the State Department, on March 14, established an embargo on all arms shipments to Batista. A

242

consignment of 1,950 Garand rifles, ready for embarkation, was held on the docks at New York. The State Department had responded to the pressure of public opinion in the United States and to the fact that Batista's new suspension of civil rights was a retreat from the promise that he had given two months earlier to Ambassador Smith that there would be guarantees for the June 1 elections.

Several high school students of Santiago de Cuba and Pinar del Rio had been killed on the streets of their cities by police, shot down in cold blood. This so aroused parents and students throughout the country that a spontaneous school strike erupted. The strike spread all over the country and Batista was faced with a mounting crisis.

The strike aided the rebel cause, but in Havana some of the private schools remained open and a small number of students went to class, but these schools closed too during Easter Week.

The Civic Resistance Movement and the 26th of July Movement co-ordinated their propaganda for the strike, alerting the people. The following instructions were issued:

"1. A general strike may start at any time from now on. Everyone must be prepared.

"2. Keep enough supplies on hand for several days, such as first aid material, candles, kerosene, oil, etc.

"3. As soon as you get the order to strike, sabotage your work center and leave the place with your fellow workers.

"4. Do not go back to work until the tyrant is deposed.

"5. Do not stay at any place where you can be located by the forces of repression.

"6. Listen to the guidance given over the 26th of July Movement's radio stations, on long wave around 1,000 kc. and short wave on the 40-meter band.

"7. Do not use any bus driven by police or strikebreakers. It is extremely dangerous.

"8. Proprietors of business places which remain open will be considered as collaborators of the dictatorship. Help to close these business places.

"9. Employers who accuse employees or act as informers, or in any way interfere with the strike, shall be considered and tried as collaborators.

"10. If any revolutionary militant asks you for refuge, give it to him. It is the least that you can do for those who are fighting for our freedom.

"11. Block the public streets with junk, garbage cans, bottles, etc.

"12. Assemble Molotov cocktails to bomb official vehicles. Molotov cocktails are prepared as follows: Fill a large bottle with three parts kerosene to one part used motor oil (obtained at filling stations). Seal the bottle and wrap cotton waste tightly around it. Sprinkle gasoline on the waste cotton and light it just before throwing the bottle.

"13. Throw oil and tacks on the streets.

"14. If you are worthy of the uniform of the armed forces you wear, honor it as follows: Desert your post, do not fire upon laborers or participate in the looting of stores. Take the opportunity that is offered to you to vindicate yourself in the eyes of your brothers.

"CUBANS: Freedom depends on you. Let us show America and the world that Cubans know how to depose tyrannies by general strike.

"Liberty or Death"
26TH OF JULY MOVEMENT

The rebel underground in Havana assured me that the general strike would not start until after Easter Week. In the meantime Fidel Castro had gained military strength. He had just received —on March 28—his first large shipment of weapons and ammunition in the long months of waiting, anxiety and hit-and-run skirmishes. A transport plane, chartered in Costa Rica but actually taking off from a field in Mexico, had landed in the Sierra Maestra bringing Pedro Miret and a group of men who had been trained by Colonel Bayo, together with four tons of arms and ammunition.

The plane was damaged when the Cuban pilot, Captain Roberto Verdaguer, whose twin brother was also a flyer, nosed over on landing. The plane was burned by the rebels after the successful unloading of the men and cargo. The Batista regime issued a communiqué several days later in which it claimed that it had

244

shot down a transport plane that had tried to land in the Sierra Maestra and killed its occupants and some rebels, a total of seven. The occupants and cargo were all safe.

Castro felt strong enough to send small columns marching out of the Sierra Maestra toward the environs of Santiago, Bayamo, Palma Soriano, Manzanillo and Guantanamo. Castro's brother Raul was dispatched to northeastern Oriente to establish the *"Frank Pais Second Front"* in the mountain range of the Sierra del Cristal and Sierra de Puriales.

Raul Castro's column began its march on April 1. Its mission was to harass transport en route and disrupt communications. It was a long and arduous march. To safeguard the column rebel militia from Santiago were pressed into action at Puerto Boniato, on the outskirts of Santiago, to battle an army garrison there. One of the leaders of the militia was Enrique A. Lusson, a resident of Santiago, who turned over to his wife the $100,000 of merchandise in his store and left her and their three children in order to join Castro's active fighters. Lusson was awarded the Frank Pais Legion of Honor for extraordinary bravery and heroism in the Puerto Boniato battle and was assigned to and proceeded to join Raul Castro's column of eighty *barbudos,* or bearded men.

The rebels had grown beards because it obviated the need to shave in the mountains. The beards soon became a trademark of the rebel soldiers and the *campesinos* referred to them as *Mau Mau,* an affectionate, rather than a scornful, nickname.

On April 5, Easter Sunday, I contacted the rebel underground high command. This time the rendezvous was in a recently completed apartment house near the Malecon only a block and a half from the Hotel Nacional. For reasons of security my rebel contact drove me to the building by a circuitous route.

Meeting in a doctor's office on the third floor were Luis Buch, Manuel Ray, Carlos Lechuga, Dr. Fernandez Zeballos and, to my surprise, the hotel medico, Dr. Eladio Blanco. The latter had been working so discreetly that I did not learn until that morning that he was one of the active leaders of the Civic Resistance Movement. It was in his office the meeting was being held.

"We promised we would keep you informed," I was told by

245

Luis Buch and Manuel Ray. "We can now tell you that the strike call will be issued soon, possibly within the next few days."

"How about your communications?" I asked. "Are they all right this time? You had none for the strike on August 5."

"Our communications are all set," was the answer. "We will be in contact with all points and other cities."

That afternoon, weapons were secretly distributed to members of the 26th of July Militia. Armbands, sewn by the women of the Civic Resistance Movement, were distributed that night to the militiamen and to the rebel labor leaders and labor cells. The armbands issued to the labor groups differed from those of the militiamen in that they read: *F.O.N./26 de Julio.* The three letters stood for *Frente Obrero Nacional,* the organization which was to replace the CTC. The militiamen and the F.O.N. shock troops were alerted for action.

On April 1 Castro's columns in Oriente province began their harassment of transportation and communications, disrupting highway and railway traffic and cutting telephone and telegraph communications.

The Communists tried to infiltrate into the general strike movement and published and circulated in mimeographed form a spurious manifesto addressed to the workers of Cuba. Paraphrasing some of Castro's phraseology and using paragraphs from the labor manifesto he had issued to complement the March 12 document, the Communists quoted Castro as saying that they had a right to form a part of all strike committees.

Faustino Perez, on the other hand, fresh from his conference with Castro in the Sierra Maestra, issued the following statement, in the name of the national leadership of the 26th of July Movement, to counter the Communist maneuver:

"One of the excuses put forth by totalitarian tyrannies when destroying elementary human rights is that their opponents are Communists. This form of deceit was used by Hitler and other European totalitarian regimes, and it is still being used by hated dictators in this hemisphere in their efforts to win the support of public opinion in the United States. Deceit, plunder and terror have been the basic elements of tyrannical regimes everywhere.

"The present revolutionary movement to remove totalitarian

246

tyranny and restore elementary human rights to the Cuban people is far from being Communist. All classes of our population, including professional, religious and business organizations issued their courageous joint statement, requesting the resignation of the dictator. When the gruesome details of the atrocities committed by the regime began to appear in the newspapers daily, a most drastic censorship was promptly re-established. It would be absurd for the people to participate in an election under such conditions.

"We have mentioned and shall repeat as often as necessary that our leader Fidel Castro will not be part of the provisional government.

"The forces of liberation in the field and in the cities include many capable men, leaders in their professions, business and industries, who are willing to serve in the provisional government which is to take over when the country has been liberated. This government will include very capable men. The provisional government will hold national elections within the shortest possible time. Based on the present tragic experience, we are determined to adopt all the necessary safeguards to protect our democratic processes, destroyed by one of the most cruel and brutal dictators on March 10, 1952, a date which will be perpetuated in our history as a day of infamy.

"The administration of the territory we occupy throughout the province of Oriente is an example of the kind of national administration we intend to establish. Strict enforcement of the law; protection of human rights, life and property; and the administration of the country *for the benefit of all the people*. When our leader challenged the dictator to allow Cuban newspapermen to visit our territory to witness how we are running this part of the country, he refused.

"The mission of the provisional government, although transitory, will be of vital importance. Law and order must be restored in a country ruled by terror during the past six years; looting and violence will not be tolerated; those guilty of crimes against the people will be tried and punished according to law.

"As a sovereign nation, we shall maintain our relations and obligations with all free and democratic governments, and shall create a climate of confidence and security for the investment of national and foreign capital necessary for our industrial development.

"Only the resignation of Batista can prevent the imminent general strike."

In his manifesto to the workers Castro called on the people, men and women, to make a great sacrifice.

"Sacrifice, no matter how great it may be," he said, "is preferable to the alternatives which have been offered us: to choose between sacrificing ourselves or enslaving ourselves." And he went on:

"Tyranny must never again be allowed to establish roots in our country.

"The workers and the people are not called to strike in order to substitute a military junta for Batista. Whoever might comprise the junta would serve only to pacify the nation, to bring passing remedies for our ills, protect the vested interests under shelter of the oppression and betray the ideals of the revolution sooner or later. We do not want false redeemers of the eleventh hour. This time the blood that is spilled will not be in vain. The strike and the armed struggle must proceed resolutely until the tyranny collapses and an entirely civilian democratic government has been constituted.

"The people must be very alert against the ambitious who will be ready to take advantage of the opportunity to seize power, as if the fall of the regime, which they abandon only when there is no other remedy, was their work and not the heroic sacrifice of the nation.

"Those who occupy military commands in the instant that the dictatorship collapses will have to place themselves unconditionally at the orders of the provisional government.

"Every civilian or military official who facilitates the evasion of the dictator or of any of the figures most responsible for the crimes and thefts of the regime will be subject to revolutionary court-martial.

"Those who have cost Cuba so much blood and so much mourning will have to answer for their deeds.

"The support which the revolution desires from the armed forces is not a *coup de état* plotted in confabs foreign to the fight of the people but the rebellion of enlisted men, noncommissioned officers and officers of the army, navy, and the police in the forts and stations—men who, in the midst of the general strike, wish to embrace the cause of the people.

"The military personnel who, when the April 5 deadline has expired, have been unable to make contact with the revolutionary elements, should take advantage of the opportunity to join when the people flock to the street in the midst of the strike.

"The symptoms and reports that reach our zones of operations show that in the barracks there is extraordinary discontent. In the military commands of the regime there exists the impression that the troops may refuse to continue to obey. The revolutionary current is visibly penetrating the ranks of the armed forces.

"Upon issuing this call to the workers and the people in the name of the combatants of the Sierra Maestra, inviting them to the sacrifice that the Fatherland demands in this decisive hour, once again I reiterate my total absence of personal interest and the fact that I have renounced beforehand every post after the triumph. He who has been the first in the fight will gladly be the last in the hour of triumph."

The Civic Resistance Movement had grown in strength, and as the propaganda prepared and circulated under the most difficult circumstances intensified so did the enthusiasm of the people of Havana who had become part of the movement. Each member of the movement was asked to contribute $1.00 a month in dues, for which he or she received a seal. In the month of November only $2,000 was collected. In December the sum had increased to $4,000, and in January to $7,000. But the collections leaped to $20,000 by the end of March.

The propaganda was directed from the law office of Dr. Luis Botifoll on 23rd Street above the sales offices of Pan-American World Airways. Chief of the propaganda section was Dr. Leopoldo Hernandez, a member of Botifoll's firm, and his co-chief was Carlos Prieto, who for years had been a clerk in the office of the Captain of the Port of Havana. Other members of this propaganda bureau included Eliseo Iglesias, an employee of an advertising agency, and Carlos Lama, a lawyer.

Both the 26th of July Movement and the Civic Resistance Movement had been organized into cells as Castro had ordered.

The cells in the Civic Resistance Movement were designated by letters of the alphabet. Hernandez' cell contained 400 persons, of which he knew only twelve. The system of communication was thus secure.

Shortly before the call for the general strike was issued, the propaganda section in Havana was so organized that it included one printing plant, one Multilith machine, two Ditto machines and nine mimeograph machines. To prepare for the strike the section succeeded in publishing three bulletins a week and as many as 65,000 copies of each bulletin.

Castro was receiving reports of this activity from the man he had appointed to replace Frank Pais. He was Captain Rene Ramos Latour, known under the code name of "Daniel," who had his headquarters in Santiago from which he co-ordinated the entire Havana operation. Ramos was killed in battle in the Sierra Maestra some months later and posthumously promoted by Castro to the rank of major, the highest in the rebel army.

Hernandez, Prieto, Iglesias, Lama and Botifoll organized their propaganda operation in May 1957 because many people in Havana refused to support the Castro movement, considering the rebel chief and his group a bunch of irresponsible hotheads. Hernandez and the others set out to try to erase that view and impress on the people that Castro was heading a good cause and was honest and sincere.

At first much of the propaganda was mailed from Florida for security reasons. Hernandez and Botifoll delivered material to Eliseo Riera-Gomez, a Cuban-American resident in Miami. They did not know until Consul Eduardo Hernandez' brief case was stolen that Riera was listed as a contact man for the consulate. Leopold Hernandez was arrested and beaten by Havana police; he was not tortured. In Miami, Riera was beaten with a baseball bat by irate Cubans. He denied all allegations, but a rebel drumhead court in Miami sentenced him to death should he return to Cuba.

Using the emergency powers voted by his virtually rubberstamp congress, Batista enacted decree-laws in which the Code of Social Defense was amended to make it a crime to report or publish anything distasteful to the government. The text of the Law of Public Order, issued after the Moncada attack, was incorporated into the amended code. Other repressive decree-laws were enacted by the cabinet, and Batista turned to Trujillo and the Somoza family in Nicaragua for arms and ammunition to make him invincible against the rebels.

Cuban commercial aircraft were dispatched secretly to fields in the Dominican Republic to fly back cargoes of bomb fuses, detonators, San Cristobal rifles (manufactured at Trujillo's arms plant) and millions of rounds of ammunition. Cuban pilots who were forced to fly those missions rebelled and flew into exile in Miami. Other pilots joined them in Florida when they refused to fly to Nicaragua to pick up cargoes of arms and ammunition. Soon there were thirty-nine pilots in exile.

Among the cargo acquired by Batista was an abundant supply of napalm, the gasoline jelly incendiary bomb, which Castro feared more than anything else—not for himself and his troops but because of the tragedy that would befall the *campesinos,* whose tinderbox *bohios* with their thatch roofs, and even those fortunate enough to have galvanized iron roofs, would melt under the heat. They would lose their homes and perhaps their lives.

The Trujillo movement issued a statement in an attempt to justify the sale of arms to Batista at the height of a civil war and after the U.S. State Department had invoked its embargo.

"Fidel Castro has been supplied by Russian submarines that have landed arms and ammunition on the coast of Oriente for his rebels," the statement said.

The United States Naval Base at Guantanamo Bay, not far from where Castro was fighting, was useless if such a statement were true.

The rebel underground was relying on a vast plan of sabotage to make the general strike effective. According to the plan, half of Havana was to go up in smoke, electric power lines and gas mains were to be damaged and there was to be a series of explosions and fires that would terrorize the populace, forcing everyone to remain away from work and stay indoors.

The security for the strike was so tight that word was not transmitted properly to cell leaders of either the 26th of July or the Civic Resistance Movement. Some cell leaders were not even notified, and heads of certain unions who were to issue orders for walkouts at eleven o'clock were not given the order to strike until fifteen minutes before. All sympathizers of the rebel movement were warned to be on the alert for false orders to strike. Therefore, many were suspicious or confused when the call for the strike was called promptly at eleven o'clock over the CMQ radio network.

The strikes were total in most interior cities, especially Santiago, Camaguey, Cienfuegos, Sagua la Grande (the latter in Las Villas province), Pinar del Rio and other important centers. Rebel raiders blocked traffic on the central highway in Camaguey province. One hundred and fifty youths took over Sagua la Grande and held it for several hours and then fled into the sugar cane fields, only to be bombed and strafed by aircraft and left for dead.

In Havana there was an explosion of a gas main on the Prado near Animas Street which cut off electricity and gas in the section near the Sevilla Biltmore Hotel and the presidential palace. The palace, though, had its own power. Besides, Batista was lunching comfortably in his residence at Camp Columbia, the only chief executive of Latin America who maintained a home in his principal military fortress.

At 11:05 three automobiles came to a halt in front of a gun store in Old Havana. One car cruised around the block. Two youths, submachine guns in hand, entered a grocery store across the street to cover the young men who were waiting for a chance to enter the gun store.

The automobile cruising the block drew the suspicion of two policemen who ordered the car to halt. When the driver disobeyed and sped on, the police fired. The youths in the grocery store opened fire on the policemen, who took refuge in a warehouse two doors away.

The rebels loaded the guns and ammunition on an army truck abandoned near by. Police reinforcements arrived and a gun battle ensued in which three of the raiders covering the getaway were killed. The police were driven back by Molotov cocktails and hand grenades hurled by the raiders.

General Pilar Garcia, who upon promotion by Batista had been transferred from his command at Matanzas to replace General Hernando Hernandez as chief of the Havana police, issued orders to his force that he did not want them to bring in any prisoners. The order was issued over the police radio at two o'clock that afternoon.

I heard terrifying reports over the police radio while in the *Prensa Libre* office.

"No prisoners are to be reported. Only deaths," a voice said. It was the voice of Lieutenant Francisco Becquer, speaking for Pilar Garcia.

Police patrolling in squad cars queried the order.

"We have arrested a suspicious character," one reported. "He is unarmed. Shall we take him prisoner or kill him? Wounded or dead?"

"We don't want wounded or prisoners!"

Another called in: "We have a man who says he is a lawyer. He has a gun in the glove compartment of his car and a permit to carry it."

"Kill him!"

"But he says he is a friend of Santiago Rey!"

"We don't want double talk. Kill him!"

Marcelo Salado, head of the 26th of July *Frente Obrero Nacional,* halted at a gasoline station in the Vedado district. Police spotted him. They shot him down in his tracks.

Batista was turning the tables on Fidel Castro in Havana. He had declared his own total war against the rebels.

Three men, members of Catholic Action, were seated in the room of Juan Fernandez Duque, a twenty-five-year-old teacher at a near-by Roman Catholic school, at 2:30 that afternoon. The others were Luis Morales Mustelier, twenty-seven years old, a government agricultural bank employee who had not long before returned from the University of Michigan which he had attended on a scholarship sponsored by the U.S. State Department, and Ciro Hidalgo Perez, twenty-two years old, a graduate student.

The police were searching the apartment house when they found the trio in the room. They arrested them and took them to the 8th Precinct Police Station not far away. Their shouts of anguish could be heard as they were beaten by their interrogators. They were seen to leave the station under escort an hour later. At five o'clock that afternoon their bullet-riddled, naked bodies were in the Havana morgue.

By dawn the next morning a total of 92 bodies riddled by

bullets had been brought to the morgue. At 4:25 the previous afternoon, eight corpses were reported by the police radio as being delivered to the morgue. Relatives flocked to the morgue to try to find their loved ones, but for twenty-four hours the police did not allow anyone to enter.

There was no general strike in Havana. Some factories closed. Some bus lines stopped or offered only limited service. A few stores tried to close, windows were smashed and people rushed to loot the merchandise. The same practice was followed at a few factories.

Jose Ferrer, who had closed his Concretera Nacional plant on the airport highway during the spontaneous strike of August 5 and spent ten days in jail because of it, did not order his plant to close. He was as confused by the strike call as some of the other members of the Civic Resistance Movement. His wife Millie notified him at ten o'clock in the morning that the strike was called for eleven o'clock. She knew the hour before many of those who were to issue orders to their action groups.

In Havana weapons had been distributed to 2,000 militiamen of the 26th of July Movement, but when the promised holocaust that was to rock Havana failed to occur most did not appear on the streets.

"I expected a Waterloo but what happened was a Dunkirk," Batista remarked to his friends after he reached the palace from Camp Columbia that afternoon. His spy service and the countermeasures which he had taken, together with the failure of the rebels to take over and hold any radio stations, also helped Batista win the first round of the final battle with Castro.

That night American correspondents (the author excluded) were taken on a conducted tour of the jails by Colonel Ventura, dressed in his white silk suit. John Z. Williams, Public Affairs Officer, mistakenly lent the prestige of the American embassy to the purposely staged affair, apparently acting under orders. Political prisoners were brought out of cells by Ventura and questioned about their reasons for opposing Batista. Care was taken to produce prisoners who showed no sign of having been beaten or tortured. Following the tour, Ventura was host to the correspondents at a post-midnight dinner at the Hotel Habana Riv-

254

iera. The caravan sped through the streets of Havana, eight black cars and one man with an immaculate white silk suit.

Other correspondents who flew to Santiago to report on the fighting there were arrested by the army and ordered to return to Havana. Correspondents were admonished by the Batista regime that they could operate only within the perimeter of the capital and could not venture into the interior.

The Batista regime was showing off the jails to correspondents but not the torture chambers. There was an ingenious torture room in one jail. Prisoners were ordered to step on a scale to be weighed. The floor of the scale, a trap door, dropped like an elevator and landed the prisoner in the basement below. The basement was the torture chamber.

The strike that failed underscored the lack of unity among the insurrectional forces.

The rebel movement also had refused to accept the co-operation of Prio's Organizacion Autentico in the general strike, although partisans of that group co-operated in the provinces. In Havana there was neither co-ordination nor co-operation between the OA and the 26th of July Movement although the former had, according to its leaders, offered unconditional support to the Castro forces.

On the night of April 9 the police, carrying submachine guns, and soldiers and sailors occupied newspaper offices in the city. Some of the reporters and composing room personnel had answered the strike call. At newspapers where linotype operators were missing, naval linotypists were moved in to set the type. Employees of the morning papers were not allowed to leave their newspapers unless they carried a pass signed by the editors; if they failed to return to resume their work, the editor was held responsible.

Only a few weeks earlier several editors were threatened with death by Batistianos, with the official blessing of the dictatorship. They were Miguel Angel Quevedo of *Bohemia,* Sergio Carbo, Humberto Medrano and Ulises Carbo of *Prensa Libre.* These threats were publicly denounced by the Inter American Press Association in a statement issued by John T. O'Rourke, editor

255

of the *Washington Daily News,* who was president of the association at that time. (Dr. Alberto Gainza Paz, editor of *La Prensa* of Buenos Aires, Argentina, is the current president of the I.A.P.A.)

Sergio Carbo found it healthy to remain outside of Cuba for a few months. And while neither he, his son, his son-in-law (Medrano) nor Quevedo were attacked, other professionals did not fare so well. Dr. Jorge Cabrera Graupera, a young lawyer, was arrested on April 9. Before the suspension of civil rights he had filed a petition for a writ of habeas corpus on behalf of a political prisoner.

Cabrera was mercilessly tortured. His fingernails were pulled out, he was beaten unmercifully, he was forced to sit on a pan of lighted kerosene until his buttocks were seared. He was on the verge of death. Cristobal Diaz, president of the Press bloc, obtained Cabrera's release but only on condition that Diaz did not take the lawyer to a hospital or allow him to be seen by a doctor. The next day the lawyer died at his home.

On the night of April 14, I interviewed Faustino Perez, the most hunted man in Havana at that time, at Ignacio Mendoza's house. He had a statement prepared on the fiasco of the general strike. Because of its language it might have been written by Castro, but it was not. Here was a rebel movement that had just suffered its worst military and psychological defeat since the civil war began, and Perez, who was thoroughly saturated with the thinking and confidence of Castro in face of adversity, was voicing certainty that the battle was going to be won.

In Castro's mind there was not the slightest doubt that it was going to be won, but thousands, if not millions, of Cubans were disillusioned by the fiasco. Many were killed on April 9 and another strike that had been succesful in the provinces failed in Havana because Havana did not respond.

"Certain tactical factors inspired by our desire to avoid great torrents of blood, so as not to add any more grief to what the people have already suffered in the struggle against the dictatorship," Perez's statement read, "frustrated from the start the mechanism that had been prepared and halted other contributing factors outside of the movement.

256

"The events of Wednesday in Havana once more pointed up the appetite for blood of the dictatorship, its disdain of the truth and its mockery of public opinion. The revolutionary acts carried out by the 26th of July Movement militia were full of the most genuine heroism and guided by the supreme duty to liberate Cuba from a regime of shame and theft. The decision of the 26th of July Movement is an irrevocable interpretation of the wishes of the people, since far from having disappeared, the causes for the struggle have increased.

"The dictatorship is disintegrating. It depends entirely on the gangs of assassins who carry out the jungle law—not attending to the wounded, refusing to take prisoners, only showing corpses. Innumerable persons have been tortured and even young people have been taken from the jails and killed after having been terribly tortured.

"The revolutionary movement stands firmer than ever, its columns intact. Early on Wednesday it paralyzed the life of the nation. Previously, when it issued the order to withdraw funds from the banks, it served as a plebiscite against the regime. One hundred twenty-five million dollars was withdrawn. The banks which suffered most were precisely those which had negotiated funds through spurious government bonds, which the revolution will not honor. The hangmen of the people cannot be nourished and sustained with the clean savings of the people. They will receive their punishment.

"The struggle is reaching its climax. In Oriente, Camaguey and Las Villas are seen the combative power and vigor of the revolution.

"Our armies in the provinces have been reinforced with the loyal elements of the armed forces of the nation, who have come to do their duty of defending the rights of the people with their arms. Others in the cities have joined the underground movement.

"The 26th of July Movement has always fulfilled its promises and, in accord with the announcement in the 12th of March Manifesto issued by the National Headquarters, the total war that has been started will culminate in the defeat of the tyranny.

"'The fight continues firmer and fiercer than ever and is consolidated by the firm unity of the forces which combat the tyranny as well as by the backing of economic, professional, civic, religious and cultural sections of the nation."

For the 26th of July Movement
FAUSTINO PEREZ

Not long afterward Castro summoned Perez to the Sierra Maestra for a personal report and kept him there on his headquarters staff.

Meanwhile, Batista had cut me off from all communication with the outside world. I was not allowed to receive incoming calls and was not allowed to make any. Local means of communication were ordered not to accept any copy from me. After six days of this news blackout, Ambassador Smith obtained permission from Prime Minister Gonzalo Guell for me to call my wife. When I tried to make another call the following day, I was advised that permission had been granted for only a single call. My stories managed to get through despite the censorship.

Batista tried to discredit Castro among the Roman Catholic population of Cuba and the rest of the world. First, he capitalized on the fact that the general strike was called on April 9, the anniversary of the Bogotazo. The fact that the strike was called that day was simple coincidence; the underground leaders in Havana did not realize it was the anniversary of the Colombian uprising until Batista mentioned it to brand Castro as a Communist.

Then the palace ordered that a statement by Monsignor Enrique Perez Serantes, Archbishop of Santiago de Cuba, in which he commented on a blast that damaged the National Sanctuary of Cobre, reported by correspondents in Oriente, should not be published. Instead, the palace sent an entirely different text to the newspapers with orders to publish it.

Monsignor Perez Serantes tried to have the palace distortion clarified but to no avail. He issued a pastoral letter, dated April 16, in which he transcribed his statement and added:

"Absolutely and totally untrue, lacking all foundation of truth, is the statement which some newspapers published in which they quote us as saying: 'It is a barbaric act, perpetrated by anti-Chris-

258

tian hands, in order to offend the religion of the people of Oriente.' Others have said similar and equally false things.

"All who have been close to us know that we are sure that those responsible for the explosion did not in any way think that there would be the slightest damage to the National Sanctuary as a result of an act that was performed for other reasons."

The rebels had blown up a government dynamite warehouse and the impact shattered the shrine but left the Virgin of Our Lady of Charity of Cobre standing unharmed at the altar.

Castro was favored immensely by Batista's awkward attempts to smear him and discredit his activities.

In the United States we accept as honest official statements issued by the White House, by the Pentagon, or by the F.B.I. But in Cuba, under Batista, the government agencies normally fabricated their press releases or statements without regard for integrity. And this fault was to help Castro enormously because his reports were true.

Two correspondents and one photographer of an American magazine interviewed Batista and photographed his day's activities at the palace after the general strike. The presidential press office issued a statement in which it reported the visit. It listed their names and reported that they were American businessmen who had called on Batista to discuss their plans to invest in industries in Cuba. This was to convey the impression to the Cuban people that nothing was happening in the country and that American businessmen would be calling on him without the concurrence of the American embassy.

Embassy officers were sometimes hamstrung by orders from Ambassador Smith forbidding them to associate with members of the opposition. Some found it very hard to understand how the State Department could be properly informed about what was going on in Cuba if its officers could not talk to the members of the opposition who were familiar with rebel plans and activities.

Smith felt he had his own good sources, and that was true as far as Batista was concerned. They were Burke Hedges, playboy son of an American who had built a textile industrial empire in Cuba, and Senator Guillermo Aguilera. Hedges became a naturalized Cuban not long ago, and Batista rewarded him with an

259

ambassadorship to Brazil. Aguilera was chairman of the senate foreign relations committee.

What embassy officers managed to tell their chief at staff conferences to put the picture of the situation into proper perspective apparently made little impression. Some had excellent contacts among members of the Civic Resistance Movement and, contrary to orders, maintained them.

CHAPTER 9

Vice President Richard M. Nixon left Maiquetia airport May 14, 1958, for Puerto Rico on his return home from his trip around South America, which ended with the Caracas incident. The next day I was visited at the Hotel Tamanaco in Caracas by Sergio Rojas, head of the 26th of July Movement in Venezuela, and Dr. Justo Carrillo, an old friend from Havana, who was the leader of the Montecristi group in the ill-fated Barquin conspiracy.

"Do you want to interview Fidel Castro?" Rojas asked after a while. I replied affirmatively.

"Prepare a questionnaire," he suggested, "and I will have it transmitted to the Sierra Maestra. Then we will arrange a night and a time for Fidel to be at Rebel Radio to read his replies to you."

The next day the questionnaire was transmitted to the Sierra Maestra, and a radio appointment was made for the following Sunday night to get the answers from Castro. That Sunday night, however, a military crisis produced the resignation of two civilian members of the junta, and the 26th of July Movement rebel radio in Caracas was instructed to remain off the air.

The direct shortwave conversation with Castro could not be made but Castro's answers to my questions were transmitted to the secret rebel radio link in Caracas. His answers give another insight to his thinking and to his plans:

"Q. You are accused of being a Communist or a Communist sympathizer because you were in Bogota in 1948 for an Anti-Imperialist Student Congress and participated in the events of April 9 in the Colombian capital. Are you or have you ever been a Communist?

"A. I do not see any relation between the premise that you point out and the conclusion that because of it I am classified as a Communist or a Communist sympathizer. I was one of the organizers of this Congress, and it had as one of its essential objectives to fight against dictatorship in America. On April 9 I joined a mob that marched against a police station. They were followers of Jorge Elecier Gaitan, chief of the opposition Liberal Party, assassinated that afternoon for political motives.

"I did what all the Colombian students did: I joined the people. As far as I was able to, I tried everything possible to prevent the fires and disorders that carried that rebellion to failure, but I was no more than a drop of water in the midst of the tempest. I could have died there, as many anonymous fighters fell, and perhaps nobody would have had any more news about my existence. My conduct could not have been more disinterested and altruistic, and I do not regret having acted in that way because it honors me. Is this any reason to suspect me of Communism? "I never have been nor am I a Communist. If I were I would have sufficient courage to proclaim it. I do not recognize anybody as a judge of the world before whom anyone must give an account of his ideas. Each man has a right to think with absolute freedom. I have reiterated often how I think, but I understand that this is a question that every North American newspaperman feels compelled to ask.

"Q. The movement which you head is accused of being a Communist movement. What is the political ideology of this movement?

"A. The only person interested in branding our movement as Communist is Dictator Batista in order to continue obtaining arms from the United States, which country in this manner is staining itself with the blood of the assassinated Cubans and is earning the antipathy and the hostility of one of the peoples of America who most love liberty and human rights.

"That our movement is democratic is demonstrated entirely by

262

its heroic fight against the tyranny. What is shameful is that a government that proclaims itself before the world as the defender of democracy is helping with arms one of the most bloody dictatorships of the world, and worse for the dictator is the fact that even with the help of the United States, of Somoza and of Trujillo he will not be able to defeat us. They would have to exterminate the entire nation in order to overcome a people who fight for rights of democracy that Trujillo, Somoza, Batista and the Department of State cannot understand. The people of the United States should be told how its erroneous policy is carrying it along roads of discredit. Do you need any other explanation of the increasing hostility of all Latin America?

"Q. You are accused of favoring the socialization or nationalization of privately owned industries in Cuba, especially the North American properties. What is your position regarding free enterprise and guarantees for North American capital invested in Cuba?

"A. Never has the 26th of July Movement talked about socializing or nationalizing the industries. This is simply stupid fear of our revolution.

"We have proclaimed from the first day that we fight for the full enforcement of the Constitution of 1940, whose norms establish guarantees, rights and obligations for all the elements that have a part in production. Comprised therein is free enterprise and invested capital as well as many other economic, civic and political rights. Certain interests are very much concerned that an economic right should not be violated, but they are not worried in the least about the violation of all the other rights of the citizens and of the people. Because of this, if a dictator guarantees their investment, they support him without concern that every day dozens of citizens are assassinated.

"Q. The revolutionary movement to overthrow Batista has apparently not triumphed up to now due to the lack of unity of all the forces in belligerence against Batista. Do you favor unity now?

"A. The 26th of July Movement is in itself the immense majority of the people, united under its direction. The apparent causes should not be confused with the real ones. If the last effort did not triumph, it was due to a tactical error in the manner of

263

launching the strike. However, in the military field we obtained resounding victories and we are now stronger.

"About unity, I have always had the same opinion. I consider that unity should not be made abroad but in Cuba; that from the outside a battle like this cannot be directed. Those were the essential reasons for our differences with the junta of Miami. Actually, we hold an extensive territory, dominated totally by our forces. Into it as many persons as want to can penetrate by safe ways. This is demonstrated by the multitude of newsmen who have visited us. We offer it for a meeting of delegates of all the elements who want unity.

"Q. Another of the reasons why it is said that the revolution which you lead has not triumphed is because you have rejected the possibility of a military junta to replace Batista even if it be for a few days until a provisional government takes over the power. Do you still believe that you can overthrow Batista without the help of the army?

"A. It is true that if we had accepted the hypothesis of a military junta, the dictatorship of Batista would already have been defeated. But that is not a revolution. The military also put Batista in power. We do not settle anything with the overthrow now of a dictator if within four or five years another is imposed. The armed forces should subordinate themselves unconditionally to the people. That the people can fight against a dictatorship and its repressive forces we have demonstrated: without resources of any kind we have fought for eighteen long months, and each day we win more ground and we have more force. We accept the collaboration of the military. Many soldiers have passed over to our ranks, many officers have been imprisoned because they conspired with us; actually we maintain contact with many others.

"But we do not renounce our civilian thesis. The dictatorship must be replaced by a provisional government of entirely civilian character that will return the country to normality and hold general elections within a period of no more than one year.

"We who are the majority organization have proclaimed Dr. Manuel Urrutia Lleo, whose reputation as an honest, upright and capable man nobody doubts.

"Personally I do not aspire to any post and I consider that

264

there is sufficient proof that I fight for the good of my people, without any personal or egotistic ambition soiling my conduct. After the revolution we will convert the Movement into a political party, and we will fight with the arms of the Constitution and of the law. Not even then will I be able to aspire to the presidency of the republic because I am only thirty-one years old. He who sacrifices and fights disinterestedly has, then, the right to wish the best for his country."

Arms shipment to Batista had been halted two months before and yet—as can be seen in the interview—Castro was accusing the United States of still supplying arms. This puzzled me somewhat until a few nights later I heard him broadcast from the Sierra Maestra and charge that rockets had been supplied to Batista's air force. The rebel underground was so efficient that it had photographed the loading of rockets aboard Cuban Air Force transport planes on McCalla Field at the Guantanamo Bay naval base. They had also received a copy of the requisition from the Bureau of Ordnance, U.S. Navy Department, which authorized the exchange of live rockets for a dummy cargo which was shipped by mistake.

It made no difference to the Cubans that the delivery of the rockets to Batista's air force was to correct a mistake. Mistake or not, they could counter in rebuttal, their countrymen would be just as dead if those rockets were fired. It was not until Raul Castro ordered the kidnaping of American sailors and marines, together with American and Canadian civilians, at the end of June 1958, that the rocket error hit headlines around the world.

The last ferry trip made by Candido de la Torre to the Cuban shores from Mexico was on April 8 when he successfully landed a cargo of men and arms from the yacht *El Corojo* to reinforce the third front at Pinar del Rio. He went into the mountains with the expeditionaries and received orders from Castro to return to Mexico to transport more arms.

Colonel Orlando Piedra, chief of Batista's detective force, sent eight agents to Mexico City to devise a scheme to kidnap De la Torre and return him to Cuba. On May 30 he was snatched at pistol point by four Mexican officers, two of them from the air force and two from the army. With Cristobal Martinez Zor-

265

rilla, a Mexican listed on the narcotics traffic record books, apparently acting as co-ordinator of the kidnaping, De la Torre was flown in a private plane to the San Julian air base in Pinar del Rio province.

There he was subjected to four days of torture, and his skull was fractured with blows from pistol butts. Fidel Castro was informed of the kidnaping by secret rebel radio and immediately took to the microphone to denounce the Batista government. Rebel sympathizers in Mexico City demanded an investigation by the government. President Adolfo Ruiz Cortines threatened to break diplomatic relations with Batista if De la Torre was not released and returned to Mexico. The prisoner was transferred to the infantry regiment at Pinar del Rio, then to Military Intelligence Headquarters at Camp Columbia. The following day he was delivered to the Mexican embassy, and Ruiz Cortines sent a special plane to the San Julian air base to pick him up and return him to Mexico. He recovered completely from his injuries.

The terror of Batista's police struck everywhere. Omar Fernandez, president of the student government body of the Faculty of Medicine of the University of Havana, was arrested. He was beaten into unconsciousness in the police station and was then taken, almost dead, to the police hospital.

He relates that General Hernando Hernandez, chief of police, and Colonel Esteban Ventura, recently promoted again by Batista, came to his bedside. They yanked off the oxygen mask which the doctor had placed over his face to keep him alive. The doctor arrived just in time to restore it over the threats and protests of Hernandez and Ventura.

The police officers were trying to make Fernandez reveal the whereabouts of other student leaders who were in hiding. He refused to talk. In an interview I had with Fernandez after he reached exile in the United States, he credited Ambassador Smith with saving his life. He told me that he understood the American envoy had sent an officer of the embassy to police headquarters to inquire about his condition and that query alone sufficed to prevent the torturers from finishing him off.

Frequently, lives of political prisoners were saved when Cuban army and navy intelligence and the police learned that the American embassy was aware that they had been arrested. Also publication of their detention in the United States served as a brake on possible plans to kill political prisoners. Members of the Civic Resistance Movement and the 26th of July Movement in Havana and Miami resorted to this tactic, which contributed to the saving of many a life.

The lives of two sisters, Maria and Cristina Giral, employees of Jose Ferrer at the Concretera Nacional, however, could not be saved. Their case, which was widely broadcast by Radio Bemba, added to the determination of many Cuban men and women to fight Batista to the bitter end. The two girls were twenty-five and twenty-one years old, respectively. One was employed as a receptionist in Ferrer's office and the other worked in his accounting department. On the afternoon of Friday, June 13, an attempt was made to kill Senator Santiago Rey, Batista's former minister of interior. Rey escaped but the police went hunting for the frustrated gunmen.

At five o'clock that afternoon the brother of the Giral girls picked them up in front of the office building where they worked. He drove them to Cienfuegos for Father's Day. They reached Cienfuegos that night and remained there until after luncheon on Sunday.

On the Saturday night while the girls were in Cienfuegos, the police conducted a raid on the apartment house in the Vedado district in Havana where they lived. There was a short exchange of gunfire as the police, apparently, were pursuing suspects of the Santiago Rey shooting.

At eight o'clock Sunday night the brother left his two sisters at the doorstep of the apartment house. Jose Ferrer was alarmed when the girls did not report for work that morning. He got in touch with their brother, who assured him that he had left them at the apartment house the previous evening. Both immediately began to search for the two.

At four o'clock in the afternoon they found the bodies, half naked and badly bruised, in the morgue. The eyes of both were blackened and across their breasts were bullet holes. Their blouses had been torn from them and from the waist up their bare bodies were covered with newspapers. The pedal pushers of one were torn near the vagina, which indicated an attempt at rape. Stains of semen were evident to substantiate that theory. It was not unusual for the police to threaten women prisoners with rape.

The theory that they had been victimized by the police was enhanced when the authorities refused to allow an autopsy to be made of other than the parts of the bodies that had been struck by bullets. Moreover, as the news was quickly spread via Radio Bemba of the tragedy of the two sisters, the police issued an official communiqué, signed by Major Wilfredo Alvarez del Real, commander of the Eighth Precinct (which is on the Malecon adjacent to the American embassy chancery), in which it was certified by that officer that the girls had been caught in the cross-fire during the apartment house fighting "on Saturday night as they were going from one apartment to another. They were felled by the gunfire and their wounded bodies were picked up by the police and taken to the nearest dispensary where they died on arrival."

The police added that they had found a substantial quantity of arms and ammunition in the girls' apartment, "including a book by Leon Trotsky." This last bit of information was injected into the communiqué to indicate that the young women might have been Reds.

"The whole story was nothing but a tissue of lies," Jose Ferrer said. "The police apparently were waiting for the girls when they were left at their house by their brother, and they took them away. They were two fine girls, and their only offense was that, like thousands of other women in Havana, they were members of the Civic Resistance Movement. They were devout Roman Catholics and did not have the slightest taint of Communism."

Ferrer was asked by William B. Caldwell of the American embassy to call at the chancery to give them the details of the case of the Giral sisters. John Topping was invited by Caldwell to sit in on the interview. Topping asked Ferrer to please tell the story to Ambassador Smith.

"What do you want us to do, send down the marines?" Smith asked the astounded Ferrer, the latter relates.

"No, I do not," Ferrer replied, "but I hope you realize what is happening here."

"Have you gone to the police to file a complaint?" Smith asked.

"What police?" Ferrer demanded. "The same police who killed the girls?"

"Well, have you gone to the courts to complain?" Smith continued.

"What courts and what judges?" Ferrer asked. "Don't you remember that Judge Alabau had to go into hiding and then into exile after he indicted Ventura and Laurent?"

"Certainly there must be some persons in this government to whom you can talk about this," Smith insisted.

"Mr. Ambassador, who are those persons in the government with whom one can talk? Please name them for me. You won't be able to name five."

Ferrer reports that Smith mentioned the names of Gonzalo Guell, the prime minister and foreign minister; Amadeo Lopez Castro, a minister without portfolio; Raul Menocal, minister of commerce, and Jorge Garcia Montes, minister of education.

"There Smith stopped," Ferrer reports. "He had only been able to name four, and the four were unconditional stooges of Batista."

The tragedy of the Giral sisters was practically forgotten ten days later when Raul Castro ordered the kidnaping of American sailors and marines from the Guantanamo Bay naval base, together with some American civilians and one Canadian sugar-plantation boss. The rebel raiders also took equipment and machinery from the Moa Bay Mining Company, a subsidiary of Freeport Sulphur Company, and from the Nicaro nickel mines, which are operated by the General Services Administration.

The kidnaping of the sailors, marines and civilians was a grave psychological *faux pas* insofar as American public opinion was concerned, but it gave a lift to the rebel sympathizers throughout Cuba. Castro had returned to the front pages all over the world because of the bold stunt ordered by Raul without consulting his brother, who was busy holding off Batista's biggest offensive since the start of the war. This drive had begun a month earlier, as soon as leaders of the Civic Resistance Movement had finished a strategy and policy conference with Fidel, to reorganize and revitalize the shattered and disillusioned underground, especially in Havana.

Raul Castro issued Military Order No. 32 in which he denounced the indiscriminate bombing and strafing of the civilian population in his sector by Batista's air force, lambasted the use of United States bombs for the purpose and had a few caustic words for the United Fruit Company interests in Cuba and elsewhere in Latin America.

He also ordered a rebel detachment to capture a bus load of sailors and marines who were returning after special liberty to the Guantanamo Bay naval base from the city of Guantanamo, twenty-seven miles away. They were due back at the base before midnight of June 28. Instead they were taken captives along a coastal road to the east and into rebel free territory.

The civilians were taken to Calabazas, where they were shown some of the bomb damage and fragments of bombs that had been dropped.

American Consul Park F. Wollam was dispatched immediately from Santiago de Cuba to obtain the release of the captives. As he was driving his jeep, with the American flag prominently displayed, along the rocky rebel road, Batista aircraft strafed him but fortunately none of the .50 caliber bullets hit him.

The rebel underground in Havana and in the United States now released photostats of the Navy Department requisition of May 8 that ordered the delivery of rockets to Batista's air force. The American embassy in Havana and the State Department in Washington, pressed concerning the matter, issued this statement:

"On March 2, 1956, the Government of Cuba inquired of the United States Government through formal channels concerning the purchase of three hundred 5-inch aircraft rockets for the use of the Cuban Army Air Force.

"A firm purchase order was placed by the Government of Cuba on December 4, 1956.

"On May 2, 1957, the final price was established and a firm contract signed.

"Delivery to the Government of Cuba was made on January 11, 1958.

"Upon receiving the shipment the Government of Cuba discovered that the rockets were equipped with 'inert' [nonexplosive] heads. The Government of Cuba had wanted explosive heads and had understood that that was what the shipment contained. The Government of Cuba therefore reopened this contract with the United States Government.

"Readjustment of the contract was made on February 26, 1958, and final delivery of the correct heads was made on May 19, 1958.

"Since there was a stock of the correct heads available at the United States Naval Base at Guantanamo, Cuba, and since this was the U.S. Naval facility most readily available for the Government of Cuba, the U.S. Department of the Navy directed the Naval Base at Guantanamo to effect the exchange.

"This was merely a rectification of a mistake on an order that had been initiated on March 2, 1956. The exchange was made by exchanging rocket heads, not entire rockets. It was accomplished by the Cuban Army Air Force delivering the inert rocket heads to the Guantanamo Naval Base and picking up the explosive heads in two Cuban Army transport aircraft."

Again, the Cubans argued, mistake or no mistake, their people would be just as dead or maimed by those rockets with the newly acquired live heads. Neither Fidel Castro nor many other Cubans, except Batista and his minority of supporters, could reconcile the March embargo on arms shipments with the replacement of the inert rocket heads.

How did the rebel underground obtain copies of the Navy Bureau of Ordnance requisition for these nine tons of rocket heads? On duty in the Office of the Military and Air Attaché of the Cuban embassy in Washington was a secret agent of the 26th of July Movement. He was Sergeant Angel Saavedra, chief clerk of that sensitive office. Photostats of the requisition had been flown into the Sierra Maestra to Castro from Washington via Florida and were distributed to the rebel underground everywhere. That is why, less than two weeks after the requisition was issued and a copy was in the hands of the Cuban military attaché in Washington, Castro made the denunciation in the question-and-answer interview. Saavedra had been a secret agent of the 26th of July Movement, and head of an important cell in Washington since early in 1957.

The civilians who were kidnaped were from the Moa Bay Mining Company, the Nicaro Nickel Company, the United Fruit

Sugar Company and private plantations. When the sailors and marines were snatched, Vice Consul Robert Weicha flew from Santiago de Cuba to the Guantanamo naval base, borrowed a navy jeep and rode into the rugged mountains to try to locate them and to obtain their release.

Raul Castro and his staff, as well as "Deborah," who had joined him as his secretary, did not have as much confidence in Wollam and Weicha as they had in their predecessors, who could speak fluent Spanish; the new consular heads had difficulty with the language. Nevertheless, Raul let a few of the civilians return after they had been taken on conducted tours to inspect bomb damage.

Batista's offensive kept Fidel so occupied at the front that he did not learn of the kidnaping until July 2. Immediately he radioed his brother to release all of the captives forthwith. But Raul, stalling for more time, released only a few at a time. The freed men were evacuated by navy helicopter from Calabazas.

More than twenty American correspondents were at the Guantanamo Bay naval base to report the kidnapings. Batista exercised censorship in Havana over all the telephone calls and all the cable copy that was filed at Fisherman's Point, the All America Cables office at the base. To avoid that censorship, the cable company sent the dispatches via the Balboa cable office in the Panama Canal Zone, from which station the traffic would return on a direct relay through Fisherman's Point to New York. Thus it usually took anywhere from two to six hours or more for a story to reach New York once it was filed.

All telephone calls from the naval base had to go over the land lines of the Cuban Telephone Company through Havana to the United States. The Associated Press photographers had brought wirephoto equipment with them to expedite their pictures to Miami via telephone. When some correspondents complained that their calls were being cut off, I suggested that the problem be presented to Rear Admiral Robert B. Ellis, base commandant, who could then request Ambassador Smith to take up the matter with the Cuban government.

Admiral Ellis telephoned Smith without delay and conveyed the request. The reply came that afternoon: Batista had given orders that all correspondents would be free to make calls except the author. After the Associated Press transmitted a photograph which showed me translating a letter from Raul Castro to the correspondents at the base, with Eugene A. Gilmore, economic counselor of the American embassy leaning over my shoulder, the photographers were barred from making further picture calls out of the base.

Rear Admiral Daniel J. Gallery, commandant of the Tenth Naval District at San Juan, Puerto Rico, who has administrative command of the Guantanamo Bay, flew in from his headquarters to confer with Ellis about the kidnapings, and Admiral Jerauld Wright, commander of the Atlantic Fleet, flew down from Norfolk in a jet fighter.

"Kidnaping is a heinous crime and is punishable by death in the United States," Admiral Wright told the correspondents. He returned by the same jet aircraft after the brief conference with Gallery and Ellis.

Correspondents were reminded that the American embassy had forbidden anyone to use the naval base as a base of operations for journeys into rebel country because of the Cuban government's objections. Those of us who went did so without the knowledge of Admiral Ellis or members of his staff. The first to go was Jay Mallin, string correspondent in Cuba for *Time* and *Life,* the *New York Post* and the *Miami Daily News.* Religiously, almost every week, Mallin had documented for *Time* the atrocities committed by Batista's police, often flying to Miami to file his copy from there.

Most Americans considered the kidnapings abominable. But for the Cubans they were a means of forcing the United States, at long last, to give some recognition to the existence of a civil war: consuls had to parley with Raul Castro and his officers. And Raul continued to ignore Fidel's orders to release the prisoners.

When Raul Castro, with "Deborah," visited me at a base hospital near Mayari Arriba (I had suffered a jeep accident en route to interview him), I asked him why he had ignored the release orders.

"I told Fidel not to send me any serious orders by radio, but to transmit them in writing," he replied with a smile.

When I asked Fidel later about the remark, he retorted: "Yes,

273

that is true, but at that time it took twenty-five days for a courier to reach Raul with a written message."

I asked Raul Castro about his trip to Vienna to attend a Communist Youth Congress and his subsequent journey behind the Iron Curtain when he was a student at the University of Havana.

"The Communists approached me for a contribution so they could send a delegate to the World Youth Congress at Vienna in 1953," he said. "I wanted to travel and thought this an excellent opportunity. I offered to pay my entire fare if they would let me go and they agreed. So I went. At the Congress I had an argument with a Rumanian delegate on the floor, which led the head of that delegation to invite me to visit his country. I also visited Budapest, Hungary, on that tour. I would travel to China if I had the chance because I enjoy it and I want to see the world, but that doesn't mean I am a Communist."

Raul Castro slept in the bed opposite me in the hospital that night. Before he left, I submitted a list of questions to him, which he carefully answered in longhand; he had both questions and answers typed for delivery to me. (After my conversation with him he issued written orders to release the remainder of the captive sailors and marines at once and dispatched a courier to Puriales with the orders. The trip by jeep took thirteen and a half hours.)

"Q. Why did the Frank Pais Second Front Column kidnap the Americans and take some equipment from Moa and Nicaro?

"A. We were obliged to detain the North American citizens:

"1. In order to attract world attention in general and that of the United States in particular to the crime that was being committed against our people with the arms which the government of the United States of North America had supplied to Batista for continental defense. In one of the clauses of the treaty is the express prohibition that said arms would be used in the domestic questions of the respective countries. And in that way those citizens would serve us as international witnesses.

"2. In order to deter the criminal bombardments—with incendiary bombs, rockets and even napalm bombs—which in those moments were being carried out against our forces and above all against the defenseless towns of the *campesinos* without taking

274

into account at all the fact that they were not military objectives.

"3. Some equipment, like tractors and vehicles, of Moa and Nicaro were taken as strict war necessities, and for the construction of strategic roads within our liberated territories. It filled a social function but it also furnished us with greater facility in mobilizing reinforcements between zones. This would be impossible within a territory as immense as that which we occupy from coast to coast in the east of the province if it were not for those strategic roads that represent more arms for us. With greater mobility we can use what we have in different places.

"And if the United States of North America supplies arms to the government of Batista, we believe we have a certain right to make use of equipment from some properties of the North American government, for the benefit of our cause and better operations for the victorious course of the war.

"Notwithstanding, we have already told those companies that we will not again touch their properties; that upon the triumph of our cause we will pay them for the damage caused. Also we have already returned some of the machinery which we did not use, and we will gradually return the rest. Moreover, we have told them that in the belligerent zones of this Frank Pais Second Front, where large interests of the United States of North America are located, as the responsible power, we guarantee their normal operations. Of course, those guarantees go in hand with the word given to us and to the people of Cuba that no more arms will be supplied to Batista, for if they continue destroying and bombing our defenseless people we will also feel freed of our given word.

"Don't think that we are pleased to take measures of this type, but in the face of two evils, we chose the lesser.

"Q. Why did you decide to liberate all the sailors and marines in one day after having ordered their liberation in groups?

"A. It was decided to liberate the sailors and marines in one day after having ordered them freed in small groups while awaiting the arrival of the written order ratifying that given by our General Staff by radio days ago, mainly because of the crisis that has arisen in the Middle East and the need which your government has for them. For it is not our intention to interfere in any of the domestic questions of your country or of any country.

"Q. Certain elements, including President Batista, say you are a Communist. Why does this accusation prevail?

"A. That Batista accuses me of being a Communist is not strange, for it is just the way every Latin-American dictator tries to label his political adversaries. If I were a Communist, I would belong to that party and not to the 26th of July.

"Therefore, I don't care about Batista's opinion of me. What does surprise me is the attention that is given to this matter, when everyone knows he doesn't do anything but repeat stupid accusations like a parrot. I feel that every time he says that, he is pulling the leg of his interviewers with the same childish tale.

"Q. Do you consider Communism as nefarious and as dangerous as the so-called dictatorships of the extreme right?

"A. I consider nefarious every government imposed by force, be it of the right or of the left.

"Q. What is your political philosophy?

"A. I don't like to consider these questions from a personal point of view because I consider myself only another soldier of our cause. But mine, like those of all the members of the 26th of July, are the doctrines of Marti. We consider ourselves followers of his unfinished work. If we cannot conclude it we will nevertheless have fulfilled our historic role, sustaining until the end the standard of his ideological principles. Behind will come new generations, which rising anew will know how to carry it forward another step. Our struggle is not for today nor for tomorrow but for the future.

"Q. What do you forecast for the future of Cuba?

"A. With a people like ours, who in these tragic and terrible moments have given such a great example of civic virtue, bravery and the spirit of sacrifice, it is easy to forecast a future of real hope for the reconquest of their lost freedoms, the conquest of their full sovereignty and a flourishing economy which would bring everything together.

"Finally, referring to our relations with the United States of North America, we sincerely believe that in 'our America'—as Marti called it—it would be more convenient for them [the U.S.A.] to have friends of the heart in an equality of conditions than false friends obligated by circumstances."

276

Together with the order to release the sailors and marines, Raul Castro dispatched a letter to Admiral Ellis which read:

26th of July Revolutionary Army
Frank Pais' Second Front
Northern Zone
Free Territory of Cuba
17 July 1958

Mr. Admiral of the North American
Naval Base of Guantanamo
"Sir:

"Because of the measures adopted by your nation in the face of the latest international events—taking into account the need your army has for each one of your members in these moments—the Military Commands of the 26th of July Revolutionary Army in the 'Frank Pais' Second Front have decided to order the immediate release of all the sailors who still remain in our liberated territories."

Respectfully yours,
LIBERTY OR DEATH
RAUL CASTRO RUZ
Commander-in-Chief,
Frank Pais' Second Front

Raul Castro had more than 1,000 men under arms on that front. The previous April he had left the Sierra Maestra with only eighty men. The bulldozers his troops had taken from Moa and Nicaro were opening roads just as he said they would and they were much more comfortable to traverse after some of the rugged hills my jeep had to negotiate.

Raul Castro honored a request by Consul Wollam to allow the embassy to station a radio operator with a transmitter in those mountains to keep in contact with the naval base and report on the condition and progress of the captives. The presence of the transmitter expedited the ultimate release of all the men.

Because of my accident and the rebel doctor's refusal to let me attempt returning to the naval base by road, Castro requested Wollam and Admiral Ellis to evacuate me by helicopter, which was done the day after all the sailors and marines were returned.

Before our navy helicopter lifted into the air, Captain Enrique A. Lusson, the hero of the Puerto Boniato battle and now sector commander at Calabazas, asked me to act as interpreter for Wollam on a problem. Standing on the porch of the house by the Calabazas landing strip was one of the rebel doctors who had given me a tetanus shot the previous day.

"The doctor reports," Lusson said, "that a rebel soldier who accidentally shot himself last night is in a critical condition and unless we can get him to a hospital with better facilities than we have he is going to die. Would it be possible to evacuate him to the naval base?"

"I am sorry," Wollam replied. "It would be necessary to consult Admiral Ellis and he would have to consult the embassy in Havana and I don't think we could get the authorization from the Cuban government."

Lusson and the other rebel officers accepted the reply stoically, pointing out that they understood it presented a delicate diplomatic problem. The soldier died that night.

Wollam asked Lusson to release the Cuban driver of the naval base bus, whom they had retained in Puriales where the balance of the sailors were freed. The rebels were holding him under suspicion that he was an informer for Senator Masferrer's private army.

"The admiral has said that he [the driver] will live on the base in the future," Wollam assured Lusson, and added: "He has a wife and three children."

"We have wives and children, too," Lusson answered. "As soon as we complete our investigation you can be assured we will release him. He has seen many of our defensive positions and some of our organization but as soon as we think it is safe, we will release him."

He was released shortly afterward and returned by the rebels to the base.

Fighting with the rebels on that front was an American named Charles W. Bartlett, Jr., a sailor from Sevastopol, California. He had jumped ship at the naval base, being a machinist's mate on the U.S.S. *Diamond Head,* and joined Castro. He was twenty years old.

"I was on liberty in the city of Guantanamo when I saw some soldiers, for apparently no reason at all, beat up some civilians," Bartlett said. "I couldn't stomach it and thought it was an injustice. So I decided to join the rebels."

He was returned to the base in October 1958, after his father appealed to Fidel Castro. He was returned home for court-martial.

At the same time outside of Cuba there was other activity in behalf of Castro and the revolution.

After the arrest of her husband, Haydee Santamaria Hart returned to Castro's headquarters in the Sierra Maestra. With the failure of the general strike, Castro's forces in the hills were demoralized but the rebel chief never showed any sign of defeat. He infused confidence and spirit into his troops and assured them that the victory would ultimately be theirs.

Batista made one grave mistake in not being ready to launch a counteroffensive against Castro as soon as the strike fiasco in Havana and, ultimately, in the rest of the country, became a reality. By the time Batista was ready for an offensive, Castro had revived the weakened morale to an admirable height.

Castro ordered Haydee to prepare for a trip to the United States, which she would have to enter secretly to avoid detention by the immigration authorities.

"You are to be the supreme chief of the 26th of July Movement in the United States," Castro told her. "Get me a million dollars in contributions to buy arms and ammunition and we will overthrow Batista. You are to direct the Movement from Miami."

Haydee Santamaria was secretly flown into the United States and went into hiding in a house in Miami Beach. There she pitched into her task of expediting shipments of guns and bullets to Castro, of raising money, of communicating regularly with the Sierra Maestra and of laying the groundwork for the unity of the revolutionary and political opposition groups.

The 26th of July Movement had stepped up its propaganda activities in the United States. Dr. Antonio Buch, the Santiago medico who escaped Batista's troops when Armando Hart and Javier Pazos were captured, was designated propaganda chief and set up his headquarters in the Chamber of Commerce Building in Miami.

279

Fidel Castro had shattered the unity of the opposition political forces of revolution when he rejected the Council of Liberation in December 1957. Now he was ready to agree to the formation of a Civilian Revolutionary Front, which he had originally advocated in the July 12, 1957, manifesto from the Sierra.

"Tony" Varona flew to Caracas to confer with Castro via the secret rebel radio there on the terms of the unity compact. Complete accord was reached and other political and rebel leaders flew from Miami to Caracas to be ready to sign the pact on July 20, the anniversary of the independence of Colombia. Castro hda dictated the text from the pact from *Radio Rebelde* in the Sierra Maestra to the secret rebel radio in Caracas. Delegates from the various groups approved the text as they arrived, and the pact was signed at a ceremony that historic Sunday. It became a manifesto to the people of Cuba, and read:

"Ever since the treacherous coup of March 10, which interrupted the normal democratic process of the nation, the people of Cuba have opposed with much heroism and determination the forces of tyranny. Each and every form of defiance has been used in these six blood-stained years, and all elements of Cuban life have opposed with real patriotism Fulgencio Batista's dictatorship. The people of Cuba, in their struggle to be free, have copiously shed the blood of their best sons, thus demonstrating that their love for freedom is indefatigable.

"Ever since the long-gone days of student parades and demonstrations, when the first martyrs fell, up to the recent battles, such as the one that took place in Santo Domingo, province of Oriente, in which the dictatorship suffered a crushing defeat, leaving on the battlefield its dead and wounded, as well as large amounts of war material, much blood has been spilled and numerous efforts made to free the enslaved Fatherland. Labor strikes, three large military conspiracies and courageous protests by all the country's civic institutions, have abetted the heroic armed attacks at Santiago, Matanzas, Havana, Cienfuegos and Sagua la Grande. In the cities, sabotage, armed aggressions and other forms of revolutionary tactics have tested the indomitable spirit of a generation true to the immortal words of our national anthem which declare: 'to die for my country is to live.'

"Rebellion has extended over the whole nation. In mountainous regions, new battle fronts have been formed, while in the plains guerrilla columns constantly harass the enemy. At present, thousands upon thousands of soldiers, in Batista's greatest offensive to date, have dashed themselves against the courage of rebels who are defending, inch by inch, the free territory at the Sierra Maestra. In this same zone in the province of Oriente, after ferocious battles, Column No. 6, called *Frank Pais,* controls a third of the province. In the plains of Oriente, Column No. 2 is fighting from Manzanillo to Nuevitas in the next province. In the central region of Santa Clara, the Revolutionary Directorate has been bravely fighting at Escambray, and near-by places for several months. Members of the Partido Autentico and the 26th of July Movement have also been battling in this region. At Cienfuegos and Yaguajay, revolutionary guerrillas are stanchly fighting and marauding. Small guerrilla forces operate in Matanzas and Pinar del Rio. In each corner of Cuba, a struggle to the death is taking place between freedom and tyranny, while abroad numerous exiles are making every effort to free the oppressed Fatherland.

"Aware that the co-ordination of human efforts, of war resources, of civic forces, of the political and revolutionary sectors of the opposition, including civilians, the military, workers, students, professionals, the commercial classes and citizens in general, can overthrow the dictatorship if a supreme effort is made, we, the signatories of this document, pledge our united efforts. We hereby reach agreement in favor of a great revolutionary, civic coalition, made up of all elements of Cuban life, and pledge ourselves to give our best and most patriotic efforts, that thus united we may tumble from power the criminal dictatorship of Fulgencio Batista and regain for Cuba the coveted peace and the return to democracy, the two blessings which can lead our people toward the development of their progress, resources and liberties. We are all cognizant of the need to act in concert and our fellow citizens thus require it.

"This union of the Cuban opposition forces is based on three pillars, to wit:

"First: The adoption of a common strategy to defeat the dictatorship by means of armed insurrection, reinforcing, as soon as possible, all the combat fronts and arming the thousands of Cubans willing to fight for freedom. The popular mobilization of all labor, civic, professional and economic forces, culminating in a great general strike on the civilian front; while, on the military front, action will be co-ordinated throughout the country. From this common determination, Cuba will emerge free, and the painful shedding of blood of our best human reserves will come to an end. Victory will be ours in any case, but will be delayed if our activities are not co-ordinated.

"Second: To guide our nation, after the fall of the tyrant, to normality by instituting a brief provisional government that will lead the country to full constitutional and democratic procedures.

"Third: A minimum governmental program that will guarantee the punishment of the guilty ones, the rights of the workers, the fulfillment of international commitments, public order, peace, freedom, as well as the economic, social and political progress of the Cuban people.

"And as we ask the government of the United States of America to cease all military and other types of aid to the dictator, we reaffirm our position in defense of our national sovereignty and the nonmilitary, republican tradition of Cuba.

"To our soldiers we say that the moment has arrived to deny their support to tyranny; that we have faith in them, for we know that there are decent men in the armed forces. If in the past hundreds of officers and enlisted men have paid with their lives, imprisonment, exile or retirement from active duty because of their love for freedom, there must be many others who feel the same way. This is not a war against the armed forces of the Republic but against Batista, the only obstacle to that peace desired and needed by all Cubans, both civil and military. We urge the workers, students, professionals, businessmen, sugar plantation owners, farmers and Cubans of all religions, ideologies and races to join this movement of liberation that will overthrow the infamous tyranny that has soaked our soil with blood, liquidated our best human reserves, ruined our economy, destroyed our republican institutions, and interrupted the constitutional and democratic evolution of our country, thus bringing about a bloody civil war which will come to a triumphant end only with a revolution backed by all citizens.

"The hour has come when the intelligence, patriotism, valor and civic virtues of our men and women—especially those who feel deeply the historic destiny of our nation, its right to be free and to adopt the democratic way of life—will save the oppressed Fatherland. Our future is great because of our history, as well as because of our natural resources and the undeniable capacity of our sons. We exhort all the revolutionary, civic and political forces of our nation to subscribe to this declaration of unity, and, later, as soon as practicable, we will hold a meeting of all and every representative delegate to discuss and approve the bases of our pledge."

Free Territory of Cuba (for Caracas) July 20, 1958

Signed: Fidel Castro, 26th of July Movement; Carlos Prio Socarras, Organizacion Autentico; E. Rodriguez Loeche, Directorio Revolucionario; David Salvador, Orlando Blanco, Pascasio Lineras, Lauro Blanco, Jose M. Aguilera, Angel Cofino, Labor Unity; Manuel A. de Varona, Partido Cubano Revolucionario (A); Lincoln Rodon, Partido Democrata; Jose Puente and Omar Fernandez, Federation of University Students; Captain Gabino Rodriguez Villaverde, ex-army officers; Justo Carrillo Hernandez, Montecristi Group; Angel Maria Santos Buch, Civic Resistance Movement, and Dr. Jose Miro Cardona, Co-ordinating Secretary-General.

There was no doubt of the authenticity of this unity pact and of Castro's adherence to it, for it was he who dictated the final draft, and the 26th of July Movement gave it wide circulation in the rebel underground in Cuba and also in the United States and Latin America. Radio Continente and its Freedom Network in Caracas broadcast the text in full the night of its signing.

Thus the rebellious opposition began to prepare for what they hoped would be the second and final round against Batista. While this agreement was being reached, Batista suddenly withdrew his army guard of approximately one hundred men from the water pumping station near the United States Naval Base at Guantanamo Bay and authorized United States Marines to assume the duty there.

This action produced a wave of indignation in Cuba, as well as a renewal of accusations that our government was intervening

283

in behalf of Batista. The dictator had set a trap for Castro, apparently banking on a direct attack by the rebels against the marines. Such an attack never transpired and the State Department, aware of the explosive potentialities of the maneuver, succeeded in having the marines withdrawn and in compelling Batista to restore the army guard.

The rebels had no intention of sabotaging the water supply: the marines were withdrawn late on a Friday and the Cuban army did not reassume guard duty until Sunday morning and no harm befell the pumping station.

In the midst of all this, Fidel Castro was busy directing the defense of all rebel positions in the Sierra Maestra against the biggest offensive that Batista had ever undertaken against the rebel army. No one can tell the story of this offensive with more accuracy, eloquence and drama than Castro in his own report from the Sierra Maestra on that August night in 1958.

This offensive, beaten back by the rebel army, proved to be the turning point in the civil war. The tide began to ebb for Batista and rise for Castro on every military front and the fighting soon extended to four of the six provinces. Castro was reinforced by airlifts of arms and ammunition from the United States, Mexico and Venezuela, dispatched by the now co-ordinated rebel groups. The planes landed at secret fields prepared in the jungle, to discharge their cargo and take off again.

Among the Castro supporters and active workers there were many who were friendly, appreciative and grateful to Americans who showed them friendship, including members of our diplomatic and consular corps. "When all this is over," Haydee Santamaria Hart told me, "I am going to give a banquet at my house for one American. He is William Patterson, who was Vice Consul in Santiago and is now in Caracas."

In contrast to this attitude toward individuals, there was general distrust of Ambassador Smith and the State Department.

CHAPTER 10

The turning point of the civil war came at this juncture. The announcement of the unity pact of Caracas and the creation of the Civilian Revolutionary Front was a psychological blow to Batista. On the battle fronts in Oriente his mercenary army was being resoundingly defeated by bearded soldiers, many of whom had nothing but shotguns with which to shoot and none of whom received any pay.

While all this was going on, more recruits were being trained at Camp Columbia to be sent to Oriente. Batista was very careful to ensure mention of the fact, in official communiqués, that members of the United States Military Mission and the military attaché of the American embassy were present at the boot training graduation ceremonies of these men.

When Batista's offensive was being mounted and thirteen combat teams were deployed within a five-mile perimeter under the best-trained officers of the regular army, Castro issued a field order to his troops for the defense of their positions and for an eventual counteroffensive.

"We must be conscious," the order read, "of the minimum time that we should resist in an organized manner and of each of the successive phases that will arise. In this moment we must be thinking of the coming weeks. This offensive will be the longest of all. After its failure Batista will be irremediably lost and he knows it, and therefore he will make his maximum effort.

This is a decisive battle being fought precisely on the terrain best known by us.

"We are directing all our efforts toward converting this offensive into a disaster for the dictatorship. We are adopting a series of measures in order to guarantee:

"1. Organized resistance.

"2. To bleed and exhaust the enemy.

"3. The conjunction of elements and arms sufficient to launch a counteroffensive as soon as the enemy begins to weaken.

"The successive defensive phases are prepared one by one. We are sure that we will make the enemy pay a very high price. At this hour it is evident that he is very far behind in his plans, and although we assume that there is going to be a hard fight, because of the efforts that they will make to try to gain ground, we do not know how long their enthusiasm will last. The task is to make our resistance stronger each time, and that will be in the measure that their lines are extended and we withdraw toward the most strategic positions.

"As we estimate that it is possible that at some points they might break through the Sierra Maestra, precise instructions for each case are contained in the annexes attached. The fundamental objectives for these plans are:

"1. To select a basic terrain for headquarters, hospitals, shops, et cetera.

"2. To keep Radio Rebelde, which has become a factor of importance, on the air.

"3. To offer greater resistance to the enemy every time we concentrate and to occupy the most strategic positions in order to launch the counterattack."

Secret orders sent by Castro to the underground in the near-by cities of Oriente produced a wave of heroic rear-guard action to contain troops there so they would be unavailable as reserves. Patrol cars were fired on, bridges and aqueducts were dynamited, branches of the railroad were destroyed and police and soldiers were harassed day and night.

On June 29, while brother Raul was performing his own little kidnaping stunt, Castro's *barbudos* routed the reinforced combat team under command of Lieutenant Colonel Angel Sanchez Mosquera in a three-day battle at Santo Domingo, in which the

286

commander was seriously wounded. Nearly 1,000 troops were defeated by less than a third that number and 443 prisoners were captured.

Batista's ballyhooed offensive was checked by Castro on all sectors of the Sierra Maestra. Facing the *barbudos* in the vicinity of El Naranjal and El Jigue was a combat team under the command of Major Jose Quevedo, whom Castro had known as a law student at the University of Havana. Quevedo's soldiers were running short of supplies and from June 9 to July 11 there were fourteen contacts with rebel troops.

Castro had written a letter to Quevedo on June 9, recalling their student days and insinuating that Quevedo might find it expedient to defect. Quevedo was not to receive that letter for some time because of the difficulty couriers had getting it to him. Castro told him that he entertained no hatred toward the army officers in spite of their loyalty to Batista and said no army with "true *esprit de corps* among their officers would tolerate the abuses and humiliation which they suffer under Batista." The letter was written in very friendly terms and Castro used the familiar *tu* instead of *Usted* throughout.

On July 3 some rations arrived for Quevedo, but by the tenth they had been consumed. On the eleventh Castro's troops surrounded Quevedo's force and opened fire on it. The fighting continued for two days. On the thirteenth Quevedo ordered his best company, the 103rd, to break the encirclement and reach the mouth of the La Plata River so they could be resupplied. He divided the company into three platoons, sending one along a saddle of the mountain, another along the banks of the river—which was the only place the mules could operate—and one on a straight advance; but they could not break the ring. Two of the platoons returned safely to their main-line positions, but the third was decimated by the rebels, with only twelve soldiers returning.

Quevedo wrote a message and sent a courier to the mouth of the La Plata River where the George Four Company under his command was operating. He asked for reinforcements and rations and urged the frigate *Maximo Gomez* to shoot flares to acknowledge the request. The frigate, which was standing to sea off the coast, shot the flares. Quevedo received air support and attacked the rebels, but the latter, with a better field of fire from their heights, beat back the soldiers. When Quevedo called for urgent reinforcements, and was advised he was getting a full company, he warned against sending the company forward intact instead of piecemeal, but his warning was not heeded. The rebels ambushed the reserve company and took all its ammunition and medicines. The remnants straggled back to the reserve command post.

Castro had learned something about psychological warfare. He moved loudspeakers to the front lines and bombarded the Batista troops day and night with calls for surrender. Castro spoke personally and addressed himself to Quevedo, recalling their university days and lamenting the necessity to fight against him. None of the propaganda broadcast from the front lines contained any insults to the troops or their officers.

Quevedo, however, called for more reinforcements and recommended that all uncommitted battalions to the north be rushed into action. Quevedo was notified he was getting one reserve battalion. And again instead of following his recommendation, that battalion was sent just as the ill-fated reserve company had been. And the result was identical: The battalion was ambushed, the rebels capturing much ammunition, medicines and other supplies. Among the ammunition captured were unopened cases of .30 caliber cartridges. The cases were marked: "G. de N. Corinto." It was ammunition originally shipped to the government of Nicaragua at Corinto, which is the Pacific Coast port of that country. Some troops managed to reach Quevedo's lines and he reorganized his positions. But aircraft dropping rations to his troops missed their mark and the rebels got them all, taunting the starving soldiers.

Castro now sent Quevedo a message suggesting they hold a conference. The major agreed to a truce and a meeting with the rebel chief. During the truce the rebels and the regular army soldiers fraternized, embracing one another, and tears streamed down the cheeks of the soldiers as the rebels handed them food, water, cigarettes and cigars. Quevedo assembled his men and explained the situation to them, indicating that he believed it would be to the best interests of Cuba if they defected. He emphasized that the decision was entirely up to them. The men answered that they would follow him.

At nine o'clock on the night of July 20 Quevedo climbed the mountain, escorted by Dr. Charles Wolf Silva, Castro's emissary, on a mule sent down by the rebel chief at the major's request. Castro and Quevedo met on the trail. That night, while the insurrectionist groups were celebrating the signing of the unity pact of the Civilian Revolutionary Front in Caracas, Castro and Quevedo talked under the protection of the jungles of the Sierra Maestra.

Quevedo asked Castro to release all the soldiers after their defection but to hold him and the officers as prisoners of war. Castro's first concern, Quevedo emphasized, was to make certain that the army wounded would be given preferential medical care by his surgeons.

On July 21 the 163 officers and men who were left of the combat team under Quevedo surrendered. Radio Rebelde announced the surrender of Quevedo and his force that night. Batista's general staff hastily denied it.

By August 20 Castro was ready to announce to the people of Cuba and to the world his first major victory over Batista's army. In his usual eloquent language, he displayed the talents of an experienced war correspondent. His report was so long that he had to split it up into two broadcasts on successive nights, but it served to notify the Cuban people, blacked out by censorship, that the 26th of July army could stand off the 30,000 men under Batista's arms, more than a third of whom were in the Oriente Theater of Operations.

"In the first battle in Santo Domingo," Castro began his report of Batista's offensive, "the shortwave equipment used by Company M, of Infantry Battalion 22, comprising a Minipax and a PRT10 with its war codes, was captured by our forces.

"The enemy command did not even realize this detail, but since then in every battle we were completely aware of the tactical arrangements and orders of the enemy.

"The military command's secret code of June 5, which was captured by us on the twenty-ninth of the same month, was not changed until July 25, and the new code fell into our hands on that very day, together with new shortwave equipment, as the result of the destruction of Company P in El Salto. That code was not changed until the last days of the rebel counteroffensive.

"When an enemy unit was left without communication, because their Minipax was out of order, the rebels themselves ordered the enemy aviation over the radio to bomb the army positions. Batista's technique of deceiving the soldiers by not revealing the hardships and the defeats undergone by any other unit, bore the natural fruit that lies, sooner or later, always give.

"The soldiers easily fell into the same errors which had had costly consequences for other soldiers. They fell into similar traps and even into the very same ones other troops had fallen into days before. No unit command ever received the slightest news regarding the experience that other commands had undergone. Thus, the soldiers as well as the officers did not know what was going on around them. Right now, at the end of the offensive, the headquarters of the dictatorship has just issued the most favorable war report that has been heard in Cuba, regarding the death of hundreds of rebels. The mere fact of publishing so many rebel casualties, which of course, are really army casualties, indicates their acknowledgment of the magnitude of the battles being fought.

"Their cynicism has been so great that on the same day we delivered 163 prisoners and wounded from the army to the Red Cross in Sao Grande—minutes of which were duly drawn up and signed by the colonels of the Cuban Red Cross—which make up a total of 422 prisoners returned, Army headquarters issued a report that the rebels were giving themselves up in Manzanillo, Bayamo and other places. The fact of the matter is that during the 76 days of the offensive, the forces of the dictatorship have not taken a single prisoner, nor has there been a single rebel deserter.

"What will the General Staff tell the soldiers when they see a flood of rebel troops over the length and breadth of the island? Does not the General Staff believe that in that moment their soldiers are going to have the most terrible surprise and the bitterest deceptions about their military command? After having led them to defeat, they lied shamelessly to the rest of the armed forces, saying that the enemy has been destroyed, an enemy who may

290

appear at any minute at the unprotected gates of their forts.

"We can very well repeat now, with more reason than ever, what we said four months ago. When the true history of this struggle is written, and every event is compared with the military reports of the regime, the capacity of the tyranny to corrupt and vilify the institutions of the Republic will be understood: to what point the criminal and barbaric forces at the service of evil will go, and to what point the soldiers of the dictatorship can be deceived by their own commanders. After all, what do despots and hangmen of the people care how their words will be belied in the history books? What they care about is to get out of a tight corner and make their inevitable doom lighter.

"I do not believe that the General Staff lies because of shame. The General Staff of the Army of Cuba has demonstrated that it has no shame whatever. The General Staff lies deliberately; it lies to the people and to the army; it lies to avoid demoralization in the ranks because it refuses to acknowledge before the world its military incapacity, its condition of mercenary commanders sold out to the most dishonest cause that could be defended; because it has been unable, in spite of dozens of soldiers and of its immense resources to defeat a handful of men who have rebelled to defend the rights of the people.

"The mercenary rifles of the tyranny were smashed against the rifles of the idealists, who take no pay. All of their military technique, their military academies and their most modern weapons were to no avail. The trouble is that when the militarists do not defend their country but attack it, when they do not defend the people but enslave them, they cease being armed forces and become an armed gang; they cease being military men and become evildoers; they no longer deserve the salary that they tear from the sweat of the people; with dishonor and cowardice they are bleeding the land and even the sun that shines on them.

"Those of us who thought that Major General Eulogio Cantillo was an officer of a different kind from the Ugalde Carrillos, Salas Cnizares, Chavianos, Tabernillas, Cruz Vidals, Pilar Garcias, etc., have been changing our opinion. Whereas at the beginning of the campaign he was discreetly silent in regard to the course of the operations which were going against him, and gave battalion commanders more humane orders about how to treat the civil population (although it was already too late to offset the horrible crimes that had been previously committed) the latest reports from the army are more cynical and untrue than ever and constitute a real prostitution of character and a dishonor for any clean-thinking man.

"The bombarding of defenseless townships of the Sierra Maestra that he has ordered in these days in cruel vengeance or as a result of a miserable panic; the dispossessing of the peasants ordered by means of thousands and thousands of leaflets dropped from the air; the crimes perpetrated by the bloody Morejon in the neighborhood of Bayamo and other places—these are more than sufficient to include Major General Eulogio Cantillo not only among the pusillanimous ones who have looked with indifference on the chain of corpses that his colleagues Chaviano, Ventura, Pilar Garcia and others have spread among the cities and towns of Cuba, but also among the men who have prostituted to the tyranny their honor and their military career.

"Owing to the length of the report and not wanting to tire the listeners, I will continue tomorrow at this same time, so as to explain the present military situation, as well as our attitude toward the army and the armed forces of the Republic, our position toward the possible military coup, the next advance of the rebel army in the rest of the territory and the part that the people will play in the new stage of the struggle."

The next night Castro resumed his personal report to the people of Cuba.

"Our doctors," he continued, "have attended to 117 enemy wounded. Of this total, only two died. All the rest are well and on the way to recovery. This shows with singular eloquence two things: First, the care with which the enemy wounded are treated. Second, the capability and extraordinary merit of our doctors who, completely lacking in medical resources and working in improvised hospitals, have fulfilled their humanitarian task so brilliantly.

"Besides, we did not want to expose those wounded to the inconveniences and sacrifices necessarily imposed by confinement in hospitals built in the heart of the jungles.

"From the beginning we appealed to the Red Cross to take them to hospitals of the armed forces, which in some cases was

292

absolutely necessary to save a badly damaged limb or even life itself, and because there the wounded would have better nourishment and care, and above all the benefit of visits and attentions from their own relatives.

"Four hundred twenty-two prisoners and wounded were returned to the International and Cuban Red Cross, aside from 21 prisoners wounded in the Battle of Arroyones, who were left near by, to be picked up by the army itself. A total of 443 enemy soldiers, noncommissioned officers and officers were allowed to go free during the rebel counteroffensive. All other wounded and prisoners were returned unconditionally.

"It may look illogical that in the midst of war enemy prisoners are given their freedom. That depends on what kind of war it is and the concept guiding that war. In war one must have a policy toward the adversary similar to that which one has toward the civilian population. War is not a simple question of rifles, bullets, guns and planes. Maybe that belief is one of the reasons why the forces of the tyranny have failed. That phrase of Marti that could have been mere poetry: 'What matters is not the quantity of weapons at hand but the number of stars on your forehead,' has become a profound truth for us.

"Ever since we landed from the *Gramma,* we have followed an invariable policy in dealing with the adversary, and that line has been strictly kept, maybe as it has been rarely kept in all history.

"Ever since the first combat at La Plata on January 17, 1957, up to and including the last battle of Las Mercedes in early August, more than 600 members of the armed forces have been captured by us in the Sierra Maestra front alone.

"With the natural pride of those who follow an ethical standard, we can say that without exception the combatants of the rebel army have complied with the law regarding the treatment of prisoners. No prisoner has ever been deprived of his life. No wounded have ever been left unattended. But we can say more: no prisoner has ever been beaten up. And more still: no prisoner has ever been insulted. All officers who have been our prisoners can attest to the fact that none of them has been submitted to questioning, out of respect to their condition as men and military men.

"The victories we have won in arms, without murdering, torturing or even questioning the enemy, show that attacking human dignity can never be justified. This attitude of ours during twenty months of fighting, with more than a hundred combats and battles, speaks for itself regarding the conduct of the rebel army.

"Today, in the midst of evil passions, it will not have the value it will have when the history of the revolution is written. It is not so praiseworthy from a human point of view that we should be following this line now that we are strong, as when we were a handful of men persecuted like wild beasts in the rugged mountains.

"It was then, in those days of the combats at La Plata and Uvero, that knowing how to respect the life of prisoners had a profound moral value. And even then this would only have been a duty of elemental reciprocity, if the forces of the tyranny had cared to respect the lives of their adversaries who fell into their hands. But only torture and death were the sure fate awaiting any rebel or follower of our cause, or of even a simple suspect captured by the enemy.

"There are many cases in which poor miserable peasants were murdered in order to pile up corpses as a justification of the false reports of the General Staff of the tyranny.

"We can state that 600 members of the armed forces who passed through our hands are alive and with their families. On the other hand, the dictatorship can affirm that more than 600 helpless patriots, many of them unconnected with any revolutionary activity, have been murdered by them in these last twenty months of campaigning.

"Killing does not make anybody stronger. Killing has weakened the enemy forces. By not killing we have become strong. Why do we not murder enemy prisoners?

"First, because only cowards and hounds murder an adversary who surrenders.

"Second, because the rebel army cannot follow the same tactics as the tyranny which it is combating.

"Third, because the policy and the propaganda of the dictatorship have essentially been to show up the revolutionaries as the relentless enemies of any man wearing the uniform of the armed forces. By means of deceit and lies, the dictatorship has tried desperately to make the soldiers become an active part of the regime, by making them believe that to fight against the revolution is to fight for their career and their very lives. What the dictatorship would like is not for us to cure the wounded soldiers and respect the lives of our prisoners, but for us to murder them without exception, so that every member of the armed forces would feel bound to fight and give his very last drop of blood.

"Fourth, because if in any war cruelty is stupid, it never is so much so as in a civil war, where the fighters will have to live together someday and the victors will find themselves before the children, wives and mothers of the victims.

"Fifth, because the example that our combatants are giving must be held up as an edifying stimulus for our future generations, as against the shameful and depressing examples given by the murderers and torturers of the dictatorship.

"Sixth, because the seed of brotherhood must be sown from this moment and should prevail in the future life of the country that we are shaping for all and for the good of all. If the fighters respect the life of an adversary who surrenders, tomorrow nobody will feel that he has the right to use vengeance and political crime in times of peace. If there is justice in the Republic, there should not be vengeance.

"Why do we free prisoners?

"First, because in order to keep hundreds of prisoners in the Sierra Maestra, we would have to share with them the supplies, clothes, shoes, cigarettes, etc., that we have collected with great effort, or, on the other hand, keep them in a state of want that would be inhuman and unnecessary.

"Second, because owing to the economic conditions and high rate of unemployment that exist in the country, the dictatorship would never lack men willing to enlist for a salary. Therefore, it would be illogical to think that the dictatorship would be weakened by our withholding prisoners. From our military point of view we are not so much interested in the number of men and weapons that the dictatorship may have, because we have always supposed that they could count on whatever war resources they may wish to have, since the treasury of the Republic is at their disposal. What interests us is the number of weapons and men that we rebels have for carrying out our strategic and tactical plans. Victories in war depend to a minimum on weapons and to a maximum on morale. Once we lay hands on the weapons that a soldier bears, he no longer interests us, because he would scarcely want to fight us when we treat him nobly. To kill a soldier or submit him to the hardships of prison will only serve as an inducement for besieged and conquered troops to resist even when a military resistance is no longer justifiable.

"Third, because a prisoner at liberty is the best means of belying the false propaganda of the tyranny. Hence on July 24 we returned 253 prisoners at Las Vegas. The minutes of the return were signed by J. P. Schoenholzer, International Red Cross delegate from Geneva, Switzerland. On August 10 and 13, 169 prisoners were returned at Sao Grande, and the minutes were signed by Dr. Alberto P. Llanet, colonel of the Cuban Red Cross. There could be no exchange of prisoners because in the entire offensive the forces of the dictatorship took not a single rebel prisoner. In exchange we demanded nothing, because the freeing of the prisoners by us at that time would otherwise have failed to have any political or moral meaning.

"We accepted all the medicines that the International Red Cross sent when we delivered the second group of prisoners, because we interpreted that as a generous and spontaneous gesture on the part of said institution, which compensated partly for the medicines we spent curing the enemy wounded. The medicines from the International Red Cross arrived in an army helicopter.

"What less could they have done after we had saved the lives of so many soldiers? It is a real pity that the General Staff and the spokesmen of the dictatorship should have started talking politics with a simple and unimportant detail, altering the significance of it.

"Our sentiments toward the members of the armed forces have been demonstrated practically, and facts are worth more than words.

"In our dealings with prisoners we have observed one characteristic circumstance always present, namely, deceit. A machinery of lying operates constantly out of the regime's centers of higher authority. We have captured a great quantity of documents, circulars and secret orders which are very revealing. The

296

troops in the field are deceived. They are assured that the rebels consist of dispersed groups, that our morale is low, that we are armed with shotguns, etc., etc. Logically, when the soldier finds himself up against the reality, he receives a severe shock.

"Generally speaking, no soldier or officer knows what has occurred in the Sierra Maestra. For example, in El Uvero a year ago we took 35 prisoners, cured 19 wounded and then let them all go free. The General Staff does its best to bury this fact. They make the soldier believe that if he is taken prisoner, he will be tortured, castrated or killed. In other words: everything that they do at army and police headquarters, everything that they have seen done to the revolutionaries at army and police headquarters.

"Due to the censorship of the press, the soldier is unaware of what is happening in the country. He reads nothing but the circulars issued by the General Staff.

"Toward the end of September 1957, for example, 53 peasants were murdered in a single day at Oro de Guisa. A few days later the General Staff issued a circular reporting that two battalions had gained a splendid victory, killing 53 revolutionaries.

"The wholesale desertion of soldiers is something hard to disguise. On the night of July 24, at Cerro, 31 of 84 soldiers stationed there deserted as one man—not to mention what is taking place in other battalions. We are well informed regarding these details.

"When an armed organization reaches such a state, it is their duty to analyze the causes leading thereto before it is too late.

"The objectivity with which I am speaking to you allows no doubt regarding the sincerity of my words.

"A handful of murderers, without salvation, who have dishonored the institution to which they belong and whose acts are leading them to suicide, cannot possibly desire to reach an agreement with the revolutionaries; but such an agreement is the only salvation left to the military men who are truly worried about the fate of the army and the country.

"The young officers should be alert to prevent a coup from becoming a hasty maneuver, maybe on the part of the tyranny itself, to save the heads of the accomplices most deeply involved.

"Since we are not disposed to yield in the slightest degree in anything affecting the interests of the people, the 26th of July

Movement and the rebel army are willing to discuss a peaceful solution with the army, exclusively on the following bases:

"1. The arrest and delivery of the dictator to the Courts of Justice.

"2. The arrest and delivery to the Courts of Justice of all political leaders who, correspondent with the tyranny, are the originators of the civil war and have enriched themselves with the public moneys.

"3. Arrest and delivery to the Courts of Justice of all military men guilty of tortures and crimes, either in the cities or in the provinces, and those who have enriched themselves by smuggling and gambling, shady businesses and extortion, no matter what the amount may be.

"4. Delivery of the provisional presidency of the Republic to the person designated by all active combatants or groups against the dictatorship, with a view to calling general elections in the shortest possible time.

"5. Reorganization of the armed forces and separation of same from political and partisan activities, so that the armed forces may never again be instruments of any caudillo or political parties, but will limit their mission to defending the sovereignty of the country, the Constitution, the laws and the rights of the citizens, in such manner that confraternity and mutual respect be established among the civilian and the military, without one fearing the other, as is fitting to the true ideal of social peace and justice.

"The Republic demands better and more honorable politicians, and also demands better and more honorable military men. Unless these conditions are strictly complied with, no one should hold the illusion that war can end, because we would rather die than abandon the goal for which our people have been fighting for six long years and have been yearning for for half a century.

"Nobody has more right than we to demand something for the good of the country, because nobody has given up personal ambition as we have from the very beginning.

"We are waiting for the answer while continuing the fight.

"The rebel columns have advanced in all directions toward the rest of the national territory, and nobody can stop them. If a leader falls, another will replace him. If a man dies, another will

298

take his place. The people of Cuba should prepare to help our combatants. Any town or zone of the island could, in the next few weeks or the next few months, become a battlefield. The civil population must be ready to suffer courageously the privations of war.

"The integrity of the population of the Sierra Maestra, where even children help our troops and who have suffered twenty months of ceaseless campaigning, should be emulated in exemplary fashion by the rest of the Cubans, so that the Fatherland may be truly free, cost what it may, and the promise of the Titan be fulfilled, when he said that the revolution would continue on the march so long as a single injustice needed to be redressed.

"There is a revolution because there is a tyranny. There is a revolution because there is injustice. There is and there will be a revolution as long as there is a shadow of a threat against our rights and our freedom."

With such conclusive evidence that there was a full-fledged civil war raging in Cuba, as was contained in Castro's report, not many Cubans could understand why the United States Military Missions were still training Batista's forces. The Civilian Revolutionary Front could not understand it, either, and directed Jose Miro Cardona to write a letter to President Eisenhower on the subject. This he did as follows:

Miami, Florida
August 26, 1958

The President,
The White House,
Washington, D. C.

"My dear Mr. President:

"The representatives of the political parties, the United Labor Organization, and the Federation of University Students, all of which make up the Cuban Civilian Revolutionary Front, have agreed to send you this message to express our solidarity and congratulations for the concepts of democratic reaffirmation which you uttered upon the inauguration of the new free government of Colombia and the presentation of credentials by the new ambassador from Venezuela.

299

"Your words, Mr. President, were precisely what our continent expected from the leader of a nation that crushed, in Europe, the threatening power of some doctrines which, since they denied freedom, ignored and destroyed one by one all of man's fundamental liberties. All the peoples of America proved, during the Second World War, that they would never submit to any form of slavery.

"However, we still have in our continent strong vestiges of those totalitarian conceptions in the form of military dictatorships, which differ from Nazism and Fascism only in that those systems had at least a doctrinaire content, mistaken and anti-human, whereas American dictators act only because of their uncontrollable love for gold and power.

"Our own country, Cuba, now suffers the prevalence of one of those tyrants, the most cruel and ferocious our America has known. Coming to power by a military coup in 1952, he remains in power only because of the backing of the armed forces turned into a political army; and he jails, tortures, kills or exiles all who demand the right to be free and to live in their own Fatherland without fear. That is, Mr. President, the dramatic case of our unfortunate Cuba, which is today experiencing many external difficulties to achieve its own liberation, as was the case with Colombia, Venezuela, Argentina and other sister republics.

"Those difficulties which are of a domestic nature are being overcome by the spirit of heroism and sacrifice of all Cubans of good will, among whom the love for democracy and freedom runs very deep. But our people must, likewise, face other difficulties attributed to outside factors. For example, the twenty-one American republics have obligated themselves, in international pacts, to respect the dignity of the individual; to guarantee human rights, which are considered essential for hemispheric solidarity, and also to respect the sovereignty of each state.

"The dictatorial regime under which Cuba suffers has systematically failed to carry out the obligations set forth in the Charter of the Organization of American States, which are the foundation on which rests the association of nations in that inter-American entity. And yet the O.A.S. has not taken one single step to demand strict compliance with the said duties of states.

Such a conduct attributes to the strength of the existing dictatorships and stimulates the establishment of others on American soil.

"Finally, Mr. President, allow me to refer to another difficulty which concerns more directly the United States of America. On August 28, 1951, an agreement was signed between the governments of the United States and Cuba, by virtue of which three American Missions were sent to our country: Army, Navy, and Air Force. Article 5 of the said agreement stipulates that the said Missions would be withdrawn at any time, and the agreement canceled, whenever one of the two countries became involved in domestic or foreign hostilities.

"It is well known, and both your government and the Cuban government have so recognized it, that our country has been involved in a bloody civil war for almost two years. Nevertheless, the corresponding Departments maintain those Missions in Cuba, which produces deep resentment, since their maintenance, contrary to the spirit and the letter of the agreement, is proof of the moral and material backing offered by the government of the United States of America to the dictatorial regime in Cuba. The North American Missions (Army, Navy and Air Force) are under the direct orders of the Chief of Staff of the Cuban army, by the terms of the agreement, and it is obvious that they train and support the armed forces of the dictatorship to kill Cubans and to fight against those who struggle to liberate the Fatherland.

"An order from you, Sir, based on Article 5 of the said agreement, would straightway correct that situation. Such an order, furthermore, would implement the beautiful democratic concepts proclaimed by you recently.

"This petition is being made not only by the Civilian Revolutionary Front but also by the people of Cuba, who detest tyranny and believe in democracy; and it is being sanctioned by all who love freedom above all material blessings.

"To maintain the said Missions in Cuba is, moreover, a form of intervention in our internal affairs, not to mention the fact that they favor the forces of evil now oppressing our nation. It is they which have let loose the terrible civil war which is destroying our economic resources and our spiritual values. We know that this tragic process will end with the victory of the people over tyranny; but we are cognizant of the fact that, without the feeling of complacency on the part of other democratic governments, the struggle would be shorter and the sacrifices in lives and brotherly human blood would be smaller.

"Mr. President, call for the withdrawal of the Military Missions, and your words to the new democratic president of Colombia and the ambassador of a free Venezuela will acquire new meaning, for they will then become deeds, as contrasted with mere words devoid of any force, effect, or significance."

Respectfully yours,
J. MIRO CARDONA
Secretary-General Co-ordinator

It is doubtful that President Eisenhower ever was apprised of that letter. It might have been recorded in the White House log as having been received and then bucked to the State Department "for appropriate action and reply."

Six hundred miles from Havana in the safety of his headquarters in the Sierra Maestra, Castro summoned majors Ernesto Guevara and Camilo Cienfuegos on August 21. In their presence he signed a general order, which was to seal Batista's fate.

"Major Ernesto Guevara," the order read, "is given the mission to lead a rebel column from the Sierra Maestra to the province of Las Villas and operate in said territory in accordance with the strategic plan of the rebel army.

"Column No. 8 is given this objective and will carry the name of Ciro Redondo in homage to the heroic rebel captain killed in action and posthumously promoted to major.

"Column No. 8, Ciro Redondo, will depart Las Mercedes between August 24 and August 30. Major Ernesto Guevara is appointed commander of all rebel units of the 26th of July Revolutionary Movement that operate in the province of Las Villas, in both the rural and the urban zones, and is granted powers to collect the tax contributions that our military dispositions establish, make payment of war expenses, apply the penal code and agrarian laws of the rebel army in the territory where his forces operate, co-ordinate operations, plans, administrative dispositions and military organization with other revolutionary forces that operate in the province, which should be invited to integrate into one army corps in order to vertebrate and unify the revolution: to organize local combat units and to appoint officers of the rebel army up to the grade of major of column."

The order then went on to outline the strategic objective, which was incessant attack against the enemy in the central part of Cuba, intercepting and paralyzing the movement of troops between Havana and Oriente. Guevara leaned over a map with Castro, and the rebel chief put his finger on a point north of Manzanillo.

"Your ammunition will be delivered there," Castro said. "You will have to wait there until it arrives in a DC-3 transport that will come from a secret base abroad. Is everything clear?"

Guevara nodded. Castro briefed him and Cienfuegos again on the invasion route about which they had talked so many times. It was to be the route followed by the insurrectionists during the War of Independence, and it was the plan that Castro had decided on when he studied that war while in the Isle of Pines military prison. Guevara handpicked the 150 battle-tested men who were going to accompany him. Their physical condition was an essential factor in their selection. Major Camilo Cienfuegos handpicked the men who would comprise Column No. 2, Antonio Maceo, that would accompany Guevara. They lost no time in getting started.

Cienfuegos, for a time in exile in San Francisco, California, was now a seasoned field commander who in his spare hours in the Sierra Maestra read books on political economy. Guevara had become the most efficient of Castro's field commanders, as forecast by Colonel Bayo. He had proved to be an organizer, administrator and excellent leader. He had established industries in the Sierra Maestra, among them a shoe factory, a uniform factory, a knapsack factory, ordnance plants, bakeries and butcher shops; he had built up hospitals. These not only helped to supply and serve the rebels but gave remunerative work to the natives. Castro himself had supervised the establishment of schools.

The Argentine medico who had reached Guatemala in 1954 and found to his liking, as he has said, "the experiment of the government of Arbenz," who had tried to get work there but refused to join the Communist Party to do so and obtained a job as laborer with the United Fruit Company, who finally volunteered to serve in a hospital in Guatemala City just before the downfall of Arbenz, had been entrusted by Castro with one of the most important—and most difficult—missions of the civil war. Because of his sympathy for Arbenz, Guevara's political ideology was challenged by Cubans who wanted to see their country liberated but wanted no obligation to Communism or to Communists in the task. Nobody, though, questioned Guevara's proved military ability.

On August 27 Guevara ordered his troops to camp in the vicinity of Plurial de Jibacoa in the northern zone of Manzanillo. A hurricane was brewing in the Caribbean and the backlash of the storm was beginning to strike the island. A drenching rain fell on the rebel troops and their vehicles.

At five thirty in the afternoon of the twenty-eighth, the DC-3 was observed on the horizon and contact was made by the rebel radio. Guevara ordered his troops to remove the leaves from the field that would be used as a landing strip. The plane circled the field, then came in to land in pools of water. Just before it came to a halt at the end of the field one of the wings struck a tree. The rebel jeeps raced down the field. The door opened and out came Raul Chibas, returning to the Sierra Maestra from his exile in the United States.

"Have the munitions arrived?" Guevara asked.

"Yes, the full load," Chibas answered. Guevara gave Chibas and the pilot a guide and an escort and sent them into the mountains to rejoin Castro while the troops feverishly raced against time to complete the unloading operation. Cases of 30.06 ammunition were unloaded but before they could finish the job Batista aircraft appeared and strafed them. Station wagons that had been loaded with ammunition sped off in different directions, and the troops dispersed and dropped to the ground. But the damaged rebel plane could not take off and it was set afire.

Guevara took the ammunition that he needed and left the rest stored in a hiding place to be picked up by a detail that Castro would send. Guevara and Cienfuegos resumed their march across the sugar cane fields to the vicinity of Guaimaro on the Oriente-Las Villas border.

The invading troops had to ford rivers swollen by the torrential rains that the Caribbean hurricanes were pouring onto Cuba and they had to keep their weapons out of the water. On September 7 they forded the Jobabo at night under a deluge of rain and entered Camaguey province. Most of the troops were now suffering from swollen feet and athlete's foot. They commandeered some trucks in the vicinity of Santa Cruz del Sur on the southern Camaguey coast but fell into an ambush and Guevara ordered them to occupy defensive positions.

"Place a bazooka behind that algarroba tree!" Guevara ordered and it was promptly done while the rebels opened fire against the enemy in a near-by house. The firing continued, and the rebels pressed a counterattack. The army lost four dead and some prisoners were taken. Rebel Captain Marcos Borrero was killed and two rebel officers were wounded. Aircraft appeared and bombed and strafed the rebels. Later it was learned their position had been revealed by an unfriendly Cubana airline pilot who spotted them as he flew on his regular run in the provinces.

Camilo Cienfuegos' troops had had similar experiences and several times his column was dispersed, but by the seventeenth he had been able to regroup all his men after some had operated as guerrillas until they could rejoin him.

On September 20, bivouacked on the San Nicolas farm, the invading rebels heard this announcement over the radio:

"An official army communiqué reports: General Francisco Tabernilla, chief of the Joint Staff, declared in a press conference that the forces of Regiment No. 2, Agramonte, had surprised a party of bandits in Laguna de Guano, Province of Camaguey, killing one hundred, dispersing the rest who in their flight left arms, equipment and important documents and Communist propaganda. Other groups are surrendering to the authorities. These rascals and rustlers are fleeing from the Sierra Maestra, trying to escape their imminent destruction and were commanded by the well-known Communist international agent, Che Guevara."

The rebels looked at each other and began to joke about the ridiculous statement.

"Well, well," one exclaimed, "we now know that we are all dead and buried."

"Old imbecile!" another ejaculated, referring to Tabernilla.

The broadcast had given the morale of the men a lift, and

Guevara ordered them to break camp immediately and resume their march. They followed the shore line as closely as possible and it didn't take them long to reach the Rio San Pedro. But the army reported their position to a coastal patrol vessel that was offshore, and they had to flee from that place as .50 caliber fire fell on them.

Having expended their rations they lived for two days on hearts of palm, which they cut from the coconut trees. Without guides they entered the swamps and began to pick their way across a railroad right of way. To the rear, at Santa Cruz del Sur, Captain Jaime Vega had run into trouble.

Castro was incensed over what had happened to Vega and to his men, and he gave this report over the rebel radio, which left no doubt that once victory was achieved the "war criminals" would be executed:

"A company of Column 8, commanded by Captain Jaime Vega, suffered a serious setback in the zone of operations in the province of Camaguey. We have not published any information regarding what happened more than two weeks ago, awaiting results of the investigation ordered.

"Any war unit can suffer a tactical misfortune, because the course does not necessarily have to be an uninterrupted chain of victories against an enemy that has always had superior weapons and resources and which, nevertheless, has always borne the worst part of this conflict.

"We consider it our duty in the command of our army, to announce any setback that any of our forces in action suffers, because according to our moral and military standards we consider it wrong to conceal from the people or the combatants any reverses we may suffer.

"The misfortunes should be published, because valuable lessons can be learned from them and we can thus prevent the errors committed by one unit from being repeated by others, and carelessness on the part of one revolutionary officer being repeated by other officers.

"In war, human shortcomings will not be overcome by concealing them or by deceiving soldiers, but by making them known, always alerting commanders and demanding new and redoubled efforts in the planning and execution of the movements and actions.

"But in this case the action was characterized by subsequent facts that the people should know, mainly because they affect very seriously the fate of the armed forces of the nation and if they continue happening, could have very grave consequences for their future.

"We have repeatedly proclaimed that we are not in war against the armed forces, only against the tyranny. But the unheard-of barbarities of certain officers and members of the army responsible therefor could reach a degree in which a military man in active service today could find it hard to justify his freedom from guilt for what has been happening and prove that only the unlimited ambitions of an unscrupulous dictator, plus the treason of a few officers of the 10th of March movement, led the army to assume the unconstitutional, undemocratic and undignified role it is now playing. The facts to which we refer are as follows:

"Not observing the tactical measures of security contained in his instructions, which should always be followed in enemy-controlled territory, Captain Jaime Vega was advancing in trucks on the night of the twenty-seventh of September on a railroad embankment leading from Central Francisco to Central Macareno, in the south of Camaguey province.

"Company 97 of the enemy forces, lying in ambush along the embankment, opened fire on the column by surprise at two o'clock in the morning of the twenty-eighth, with heavy machine-gun support. The heavy enemy fire against the vehicles caused eighteen dead, and eleven wounded prisoners could not be recovered because of the darkness and the superior position of the machine-gun emplacements.

"The wounded rebel prisoners were taken to the hospital at Macareno, where they were attended by the resident doctor and two other doctors from Santa Cruz del Sur, sent for by Lieutenant Suarez, in charge of Company 97.

"On the following day Colonel Leopoldo Perez Coujil arrived by plane, and shortly after Lieutenant Suarez Suquet, Major Domingo Pineyro and his body guard, Sergeant Lorenzo Otano, arrived by car.

"Colonel Perez Coujil distributed a gift of $1,000 in cash among the soldiers. Thereupon, the first thing he did was to strike one of the wounded prisoners in the face, and, after questioning them, instructed Lieutenant Colonel Suarez Suquet to kill all of the wounded. Suarez Suquet appointed Major Pineyro to feign a rebel attack in the course of transferring the wounded to Santa Cruz del Sur.

"They prepared trucks with mattresses, on which the wounded were placed, and after going a few miles, the soldiers started to shoot, while Major Pineyro shouted: 'The rebels are attacking us.' Whereupon Sergeant Otano threw two hand grenades at the trucks carrying the wounded who, thinking they were really being attacked by their rebel colleagues, shouted 'Don't shoot, companions; we are wounded.'

"Sergeant Otano leaped forward, climbed the trucks and, machine gun in hand, finished off the wounded, who were already half dead. Some lost arms and legs, others were badly mutilated, some decapitated; inside the trucks there was nothing but a mass of human blood and flesh.

"From then on, Sergeant Otano was known by his fellow soldiers as the Butcher.

"Then they placed the corpses in a truck, carried them to Santa Cruz del Sur, opened a huge ditch and buried them.

"The narration of these deeds is enough to make the most indifferent person indignant. But no Cuban can feel the facts so much as the rebel doctors who cared for more than one hundred wounded enemy prisoners when the offensive against the Sierra Maestra commenced, or our combatants who carried those wounded on their shoulders and on stretchers from the battlefields to the hospitals many miles away. It is possible that among those murdered rebel wounded, there could be found some who in the battle of Jigue had carried enemy wounded from the points of action to the place where they received first aid, after having climbed almost inaccessible terrain.

"Those wounded who had been murdered in Camaguey had witnessed with their own eyes how 422 soldiers of the tyranny had marched in the Sierra Maestra and were delivered to the International and Cuban Red Cross, and shared with them their medicines, their tobacco and their food.

"The lack of reciprocity could not be more repugnant or more cowardly. And this is not an isolated case on the part of an officer or a given group of troops, but a general custom of the entire army, to a nauseating degree.

"They murdered prisoners when we attacked Moncada; they murdered prisoners when we landed from the *Gramma;* they murdered prisoners when the presidential palace was attacked; they murdered prisoners when Calixto Sanchez landed; they murdered prisoners at the Cienfuegos revolt. But on all of those occasions the army could still have hopes of remaining in power: it was strong, it had not suffered substantial defeats and it could still believe that its crimes could go unpunished by virtue of the helplessness of an unarmed people. What happened in Camaguey is doubly absurd and double cause for indignation. First, because the return of hundreds of soldiers safe and sound by the rebels to the Red Cross is still fresh in the memory of the citizens; and second, because the soldiers of the tyranny are losing the war and have been beaten in several battles, giving up more and more territory every day and are retreating everywhere.

"They are losing the war and yet murder the few prisoners they take, in spite of being an army now vanquished.

"Through that same territory in Camaguey, Column Nos. 2 and 8, under the command of majors Camilo Cienfuegos and Ernesto Guevara, marched victoriously without being stopped by the heavy forces that the dictatorship threw against them. The vanguard has now invaded more than thirty-five miles of territory in Las Villas province.

"What military or political sense can there be in that treacherous attack against the rebel wounded, except inflicting another stain of blood on the armed forces, which will be remembered frequently in history as an unwashable stain on the uniform of an infamous and dishonored army, that can never more be called the army of the Republic?

This deed will be denounced before the International Red Cross and we will demand that their delegates be sent to investigate what has happened; an open letter will be addressed to the armed forces notifying them of the responsibility they are putting upon themselves.

"Besides holding several soldiers as prisoners, we also have a lieutenant colonel who, paradoxically, is wounded and is being attended in one of our hospitals, and a major and two captains.

"The conduct of Colonel Leopoldo Perez Coujil, Lieutenant Colonel Suarez Suquet, Major Triana and the other miserable murderers constitutes an act of infinite cowardice and a total lack of consideration for their colleagues in arms who are being held prisoner by us, without any other guarantee for their lives than our attitude of calm serenity in the face of this kind of vandalism, the sense of humanity and justice which accompanies us in this war we are waging, the ideals which inspire us and our true concept of what honor is.

"Let not those responsible for these acts think that they can escape even if at the last minute the army should rebel against them, because one of our most inflexible conditions is that even if any military coup be carried out, the war criminals and all militarymen and politicians who have enriched themselves with the blood and sweat of the people must surrender, beginning with Batista and ending with the last torturer. Otherwise, they will have to continue fighting the war until their total destruction, because they cannot stop this revolution at all either by the shameful farce that is being prepared for November 3, or any military coup which may be carried out without fulfilling the conditions of the 26th of July Movement, or by means of any prior agreement.

"Those who have sown winds will reap whirlwinds.

"There is no longer any doubt that the decadent and demoralized forces of the tyranny cannot stop the victorious advance of the people. To do that they would first have to vanquish each one of the columns that are already operating successfully in four provinces, and then take the Sierra Maestra up to the very last trench at the top of Turquino Peak, which will be defended by the very last rebel soldier.

"Batista's army has demonstrated to the full extent that this it cannot do.

"An extensive report has been received at general headquarters, to the effect that invading Column No. 2, Antonio Maceo, after having crossed Camaguey province successfully, has entered Las Villas territory. That report contains a detailed account of an extraordinary military achievement and will soon be read by Radio Rebelde so as to give the people an opportunity of knowing about one of the most thrilling episodes of the contemporary history of our country."

While the people of Cuba heard the above report over Radio Rebelde and rebroadcast by Radio Continente from Caracas, Guevara and his men found themselves surrounded by 1,100 troops of the Agramonte Regiment in the swamp they had entered to avoid detection. They were in the water up to their necks, holding their weapons over their heads. But nothing happened because in the still of the night the soldiers appeared to be more frightened than the rebels, who had not eaten or slept for three days. Aircraft bombed and strafed the vicinity regularly but always managed to miss them. The column continued its march through swamps, into open fields, back into swamps again —and by now Camilo Cienfuegos' column had rejoined Guevara— with the troops hardly able to drag their feet any more.

Guevara returned to his chores as medico and examined the feet of the men, joking: "That is nothing; when we get to Havana we will be walking on rugs."

On October 6, exactly sixty-three years to the day since General Maximo Gomez, a Dominican, and General Antonio Maceo, a Cuban, crossed the trail from Jucaro to Ciego de Avila, Major Ernesto Guevara, an Argentine, and Major Camilo Cienfuegos, a Cuban, at the end of a different kind of liberation march, covered the same route.

Three officers of the 26th of July Army in Las Villas were waiting for them the next morning at the border of that province to take the entire invading force to the Sierra del Escambray. When the invading troops reached Las Villas they knelt and kissed the ground.

There Guevara held conferences with Captain Victor Bordon of the 26th of July Movement, Majors Rolando Cubela and Faure Chomon of the Directorio Revolucionario and Major Eloy Gutierrez Menoyo of the *Segundo Frente Nacional del Escambray*. He completed another phase of the mission given to him by Castro. He obtained an agreement on the co-ordination of the three forces for the offensive that was planned to capture the entire province.

311

The safe arrival of the invading columns in Las Villas was reported over Radio Rebelde; and *Diario las Americas,* a Spanish language daily of Miami which is delivered on the desk of every State Department officer dealing with inter-American affairs, published the documents of Guevara's agreement with the other two rebel groups. The Directorio had 1,000 men. The Second Front force numbered nearly 5,000.

As soon as the news spread that the invading columns had reached Las Villas, hundreds of volunteers offered to join the rebel army. Those who could be supplied with weapons, or who brought their own, were taken in. The others were trained as recruits, pending the arrival of guns or their capture from the army.

It was not until October 13, when the civil war had gained momentum, that the State Department replied to Dr. Miro's letter of August 26 to President Eisenhower about the military missions. The department exercised particular care to preserve the necessities of diplomatic protocol, avoiding reference to the Civilian Revolutionary Front or to Miro's title in it. The letter read:

October 13, 1958

"Dear Dr. Miro:

"Your letter of August 26, 1958, addressed to the President, regarding the political situation in Cuba and the presence there of the United States Military Missions, was referred to the Department of State for reply.

"We have noted your comments regarding the remarks made by President Eisenhower, on the occasion of the presentation of Letters of Credence by the new Venezuelan Ambassador to the United States, to the effect that the United States believes firmly in the democratic elective process and the choice by the people, through free and fair elections, of democratic governments responsive to them. At the same time, the United States does follow a strict policy of nonintervention in the domestic affairs of our sister American republics, including Cuba.

"With respect to the request in your letter that the United States Military Missions to Cuba be withdrawn, I should like to point out that these missions were established in 1950 and 1951 during the presidency of Dr. Carlos Prio Socarras, and have continued to this date, operating within the terms of an approved contract agreed to by the governments of the United States and Cuba. In your letter you refer to Article 5 of the mission agreements and state that this article 'stipulates that the said missions would be withdrawn at any time, and the agreement canceled, whenever one of the two countries became involved in domestic or foreign hostilities.' The actual wording of that article reads that the agreements are 'subject to cancellation' (i.e., *may* be canceled) under conditions such as you describe so that withdrawal is permissive rather than mandatory as indicated in your letter.

"The Mission agreements were negotiated in conformity with discussions which had taken place between the two governments on hemispheric military co-operation. The United States Government believes that its missions in Cuba are serving the purpose for which they were established. Governments and administrations change from time to time in both Cuba and the United States but hemispheric defense needs present a constant problem the solution of which calls for a co-operative program carried out on a steady, long-range basis."

Sincerely yours,

For the Secretary of State:

William A. Wieland

Director,

Office of Caribbean and Mexican Affairs

That reply could be summed up as follows: governments may come and governments may go but our Military Missions are not going to be withdrawn come hell or high water. That was a stubborn and mistaken decision by the State Department and the Pentagon. The implication that Prio was to blame for the existence of the missions was a childish and absurd weasel. The generation that was fighting Batista was going to rule Cuba and we were festering sores in their hearts, building up resentments in their minds and fanning the enmity of their relatives and the entire Cuban people by insisting on the continued training of an army by our mission—an army headed for inevitable defeat.

313

Miro replied to Weiland on October 28 and pointed out that he gathered his letter precluded a right of appeal. He countered, in part, with the following:

"Your letter contains arguments that imply an evident error of judgment regarding Cuba, the function of the Military Mission and the future relations between the two nations."

Agreeing with the legal interpretation given by the State Department regarding the permissive right rather than the obligation to withdraw the missions in the event of civil war, Miro added: "By not using that permission power when the civil war is a notorious and lamentable fact in Cuba—admitted by the United States—implies the assumption of a tremendous historic responsibility that will have to have disagreeable repercussions in the relations with those who in the not too distant future will assume the power in Cuba. It is obvious that the fighters of today, rulers of tomorrow, and the people themselves cannot fathom that, invoking the hemisphere defense potential, the North American army trains the soldiers of Batista—who took office ignoring constitutional precepts—who kill Cubans who fight to restore the principles of democracy. This fact is creating a profound resentment in the present generation of Cuba that should be avoided.

"We fought together for independence and we have been together in two wars for democracy; but those ties that appeared indestructible are suffering from a mistaken foreign policy.

"In 1947 the United States ordered the members of its Military Mission in Paraguay to withdraw to their homes in order not to intervene in the internal affairs of that nation. [A revolution had erupted that flowered into a civil war.] In Cuba not only are the soldiers of the dictatorship trained but the Chiefs of Mission grant decorations to officers of an illegitimate government that has shattered the principles of civilized co-existence."

Miro concluded that there could be no honest elections under Batista and that the "insurrectional forces who now dominate almost all of the national territory will continue fighting until they overthrow Batista in order to give birth to a provisional government which, guaranteeing the rights of all, convenes an election that will allow the citizens freely to decide the destiny of the nation rather than succumb to a regime of force, of death, of peculation and of prostitution that reigns in Cuba."

The lobbyists for the Civilian Revolutionary Front, Ernesto Betancourt for the 26th of July Movement, and Carlos Piad, for the Autentico Party, made regular pilgrimages to the State Department to inquire when the missions would be withdrawn. Special delegations also called on Wieland and other officers and met no success. The State Department and the Pentagon undoubtedly appraised the impact of the withdrawal of the missions correctly: this measure would have expedited the fall of Batista, for he exploited the presence of the missions, despite the proviso to withdraw them in the event of civil war in Cuba, as direct support by the United States for him, notwithstanding the fact he could no longer obtain export licenses for arms and ammunition and resorted to rebel tactics to smuggle them out of various ports and airports.

The Inter American Press Association held its annual convention in Buenos Aires, and Jorge Quintana, one of the editors of *Bohema,* reported on the censorship in Cuba and threats against editors. He emphasized (showing photographs which I made available to him) that one of the main reasons for the censorship was to conceal the atrocities committed by the repressive forces.

This forthright attitude brought threats and reprisals. Batista's military, naval and police repression chiefs threatened to kill Quintana if he returned to Cuba. As a result he had to remain in the United States and Puerto Rico until Batista fled.

Castro was strong enough now to prepare for his final offensive that was destined to produce victory. Plane load after plane load of arms and ammunition was reaching him from the United States, Mexico and Venezuela. He had studied the campaigns of the War of Independence in minute detail and had planned to duplicate the march westward toward the eventual collapse of Havana.

On October 10, the ninetieth anniversary of the Cry of Yara in 1868 for independence from Spain, Castro issued two important rebel laws. One was a comprehensive law for agrarian reform, which it will be recalled he had spoken about at his trial for the Moncada attack. The other was Law No. 2, which ordered everyone to remain away from the polls on November 3, the date which Batista had set for presidential elections. Batista's handpicked candidate was Dr. Andres Rivero Aguero, fifty-three, who was going to win come hell or high water. Opposing him was Carlos Marquez Sterling, former President Grau and Alberto Salas Amaro. Batista financed the campaigns of opposition candidates to ensure their going to the polls.

Castro's no-election law, also signed by Judge Advocate General Humberto Sori Marin, showed not only his determination to keep the voters away from the polls but to punish those who insisted on being candidates. His language was now becoming more defiant than ever, for he was on the road to victory and he was certain of it. The law read:

"Whereas the tyranny prepares a new and raw electoral farce for the third of November, totally behind the back of the interests of the people in the midst of the pool of blood into which the Republic has been converted in full civil war—in which the military forces retreat before the victorious push of the rebel troops—without finding formulas capable of masking the elections such as even the technical re-establishment of individual guarantees and of freedom of the press; against a citizenry, in sum, that is persecuted, in mourning and determined to recapture their liberties and rights through the definite end of the usurper regime of thieves, traitors and assassins who have converted the Fatherland into the feudal estate of their infinite ambitions.

"Whereas the participation in the election farce constitutes an act of betrayal of the interests of the Fatherland and the revolution and is classified as opportunism on the part of those who think only of their bastard personal conveniences and work in the shadows at the expense of the Republic when they serve the plans of the tyranny while the best of our people offer their lives on the battlefield.

"Whereas it is necessary for the last time to alert the Cubans who have not yet understood the profound question that is being debated in Cuba and who, insensible to the tragedy that surrounds them, have enlisted in the company of actors of the comedy which the tyranny prepares November 3 by stubbornly lending their names as candidates for posts they never will hold.

"Therefore, in use of the powers that are found invested in this command, the following Law No. 2 is dictated about the electoral farce:

"I. Everyone who takes part in the electoral farce the third day

316

of November of 1958, as a candidate to any elective post, without prejudice to the criminal responsibility in which he may incur, will be barred for a period of thirty years from the date of this law from holding a public or elective post or one by appointment by the state, the province or the municipality.

II. The period having expired in which a candidate cannot resign so that his name does not appear on the ballot, he will show his nonparticipation in the electoral farce by absenting himself from the country and previously presenting himself in the free territory of Cuba, or, in any case by reporting his resignation to the foreign press or through the broadcast means of the rebel army by the thirtieth of October.

"III. Any political agent who dedicates himself to the corrupt system of collecting voting cards will be tried by a summary court-martial and executed on the spot.

"IV. The candidate to any elective post who may be captured in the zone of operations of the free territory will be tried and condemned to a penalty that may fluctuate, in accordance with the greater or lesser degree of responsibility, from ten years to the death sentence.

"V. In the urban zones the death sentence may be executed against the guilty either by the rebel troops or by the militia who operate in the towns and cities."

Florence Pritchett Smith organized a gala Cuban ball at the Waldorf-Astoria Hotel in New York to raise funds for a scholarship for a Cuban dress designer. This fun-making at the height of the civil war further antagonized an already irate people. Requests by Smith for contributions to the scholarship circulated on stationery of the Cuban-American Institute already had brought protests from Cuban members in Havana. The publicity given to the ball—which Batista made certain was carried in censored newspapers and over the radio—did not serve to improve the state of mind of the Cubans toward Smith.

At the same time the secret agent of the 26th of July Movement in the Cuban embassy in Washington obtained a letter written by his chief to the General Staff in Havana. It was dated October 13 and was signed by Colonel Jose D. Ferrer Guerra, military and air attaché. Sergeant Saavedra, the secret agent, made available to Ernesto Betancourt of the 26th of July Movement a photostat of the original letter, and he promptly dispatched it from Washington to Castro in the Sierra Maestra.

Guerra reported to the director of operations of the Cuban army that he had had a conversation with a four-star general and a two-star general of the United States Armed Forces "and both hold important posts in American military establishments in relation with Latin America, which makes their opinions of interest."

He went on to report that one of the generals told him that the 26th of July Movement had tried to stage a demonstration during a World Series game so all televiewers could see them but "the police had dispersed them before they could get on camera."

He then reviewed the generals' criticism of the arms embargo which they called "stupid and prejudicial to both Cuban and American interests" because it allowed Batista to buy Sea Fury aircraft from England. (Castro had already ordered a boycott against all British products in Cuba and against the Shell Petroleum Company because of this sale of seventeen planes to Batista.)

Ferrer Guerra reported one of the generals as saying that Assistant Secretary of State for Latin-American Affairs Roy R. Rubottom had weakened on the arms embargo because he was "afraid of criticism in Congress by persons like Congressman Porter and Senator Morse." Then Ferrer made a statement which was to have subsequent influence on Castro.

"He also said," Ferrer continued referring to one of the generals, "that Ambassador Smith, after his unfortunate trip to Santiago de Cuba, now is a valuable co-operator with the American Armed Forces in his fight with the Department of State to defend the sale of arms to Cuba.

"One of the general officers also stated," Ferrer went on, "that he felt very proud of the fine way the air force of the Cuban army was working." He then added that the same officer said that "when exiled revolutionary elements here asked him to use his influence to withdraw the American Missions in Cuba he answered that 'while Cuba has a friendly government recognized by the United States he will do all in his power to continue the Missions.'

318

"Then conversation," Ferrer reported, "passed to the subject of Cuba, and one general said that although he only know slightly the Honorable Señor Presidente of the Republic of Cuba, he felt admiration for him due to the progress of Cuba in recent years. Comparing the progress of Cuba with the much ballyhooed progress of Puerto Rico, he said that Cuba had progressed very much more in recent years, that in Puerto Rico only isolated improvements were noted. He said that in his opinion the revolutions should be made with votes and not bullets and guns, and that no group has the right to harm a country as the Cuban revolutionaries are doing, trying to discredit Cuba abroad."

There was little wonder that Castro would react most unfavorably to such a letter, especially when certain events that were to follow invited him to suspect a conspiracy to arouse American public opinion so that the arms embargo would be lifted.

CHAPTER 11

Two events in quick succession brought an exchange of recriminatory statements between the State Department and Fidel Castro before the end of October. The first involved nine employees of the Texaco Refinery, two Americans and seven Cubans, who were captured when they discovered a rebel ambush on the outskirts of Santiago de Cuba. The rebels and their captives notified the refinery manager, and letters written by the Texaco employees were delivered to their families. The letters reported that they were well and would be released as soon as their freedom would no longer jeopardize the rebel position.

Lincoln White, State Department spokesman, issued a statement in Washington in which he declared that our government "was fed up with the kidnaping of Americans by the Cuban rebels."

Another incident occurred at Nicaro, when Batista withdrew his troops and the rebels moved in. After the rebels were inside the city, Cuban troops were ordered back and the rebels withdrew to avoid harming the populace. It was reported that American civilians in Nicaro had been held by natives there as hostages against bombardment by Batista's air force. The Navy sent the transport *Kleinschmidt* from Guantanamo Bay to evacuate the civilians; the aircraft carrier *Franklin D. Roosevelt,* which was maneuvering off the naval base, was ordered to stand by in case its helicopters were needed for evacuation.

Another statement by Lincoln White irritated Castro into

320

broadcasting a blistering blast over Radio Rebelde on the night of October 26:

"A communiqué received from the 'Frank Pais' second front reports the possibility that the Nicaro zone, where the United States government has a nickel plant, is being converted into a battlefield.

"Three days ago and without any military reason therefor, the dictatorship surprisingly withdrew the troops that had been stationed there.

"Following the usual tactics, the rebel forces immediately took the territory abandoned by the enemy, offering the employees and officers of the company full guarantees to continue operating.

"Today the rebel command intercepted an order from Colonel Ugalde Carrillo, ordering forces to land again at Nicaro, which will naturally cause an armed conflict. This all forms part of a maneuver on Batista's part, in complicity with Ambassador Earl E. T. Smith and other high officers of the United States Department of State, to provoke the intervention of the United States in the Cuban civil war.

"In its despair, the dictatorship is trying to precipitate a grave incident between the rebels and the United States. The first attempt took place early in July, when the General Staff of the dictatorship, in agreement with Mr. Smith, withdrew their troops from the Yateritas waterworks, which supplies the United States Naval Base at Caimanera with water, and requested the U.S. authorities there to send soldiers to protect the waterworks.

"Batista and Mr. Smith were trying to cause a fight between the United States marines and the rebels, but a great campaign to influence public opinion in the entire continent, plus the responsible attitude of the rebel forces in the face of that self-evident provocation and the efforts on the part of the Civilian Revolutionary Front achieved a diplomatic solution of the matter.

"The United States marines were withdrawn without any incident.

"An unimportant incident took place by pure chance a few days ago which encouraged the intrigue between the American embassy and the Batista dictatorship against the sovereignty of the country.

321

"Two Americans and seven Cubans working at the Texaco plant fell into an ambush prepared by Cuban patriots who were expecting the advance of enemy forces. For strict reasons of security for said employees, as well as for our own forces, the people traveling in the vehicle were detained by us and taken to a safer place. This was done not because they were Americans or Cubans, but simply because when an ambush is discovered by civilians and when the latter do not immediately inform the forces of the tyranny and thus prevent their falling into the ambush, the dictatorship always acts against them. If, on the other hand, the civilians reveal our position, it could be surrounded by superior enemy forces and attacked. It is for this reason that in these cases civilians are held in some safe place, for reasons of security, as much for us as for them, and for as long as the operation may last.

"This act cannot be classified as a kidnaping. Nobody intended to prevent those employees from going to their work. Nothing was demanded from them in exchange for their freedom, and they were treated with every consideration. This was simply what happened and they were freed as soon as the commander of the column withdrew our forces from the road.

"However, Lincoln White, spokesman for the United States Department of State, taking advantage immediately of this incident and seeking the smallest pretext to interfere in the internal affairs of Cuba, made insulting statements against the Cuban patriots, which are equivalent to an open threat against the integrity of our territory and the sovereignty of our people.

"Batista's dictatorship has assassinated more than one United States citizen and has repeatedly attacked and even murdered newspapermen from other countries. Nevertheless, the Department of State has kept silent regarding those deeds, by hiding them from the public opinion of the United States. Why, then, should this simple incident make Lincoln White launch a serious threat and accusations against the 26th of July Movement?

"The town of Nicaro was evacuated by the forces of the dictatorship and, three days later, when the patriots took it over, the dictatorship ordered its troops to land there again. They are now trying to make that place the scene of a battle; the United States government's nickel plants are there, and by causing material damages to the plants, a pretext can be found for sending United States troops to our national territory. It is a plan similar to the one involving the Yateritas waterworks.

"It is the lowest kind of betrayal that the government can commit against its own country.

"We hereby denounce these acts to United States and Latin-American public opinion.

"Why did the forces of the dictatorship give up the nickel plants when they were not being attacked by rebels? Why was a new landing of troops ordered there? What is the connection between these deeds and the aggressive statement made by Lincoln White?

"The rebel command has never felt any hostility toward the United States. When a group of United States citizens were held in the north of the province of Oriente, so that they could see and prove the effects of the bombings of the peasant population—which had been carried out with bombs and planes of United States origin—this command, upon hearing of the matter, immediately ordered that those citizens should be handed over to the authorities of their country, because we considered that they should not suffer as a result of the errors of their government.

"When I gave that order, a United States newspaperman, who was with us in the Sierra Maestra, immediately sent the message to the wire services.

"The latest incident concerning the two United States citizens was purely a matter of chance and arose as a result of the events we have set forth. The fact that seven Cubans were with them and were held at the same time is proof that a question of nationality was not involved.

"If Lincoln White classifies as a transgression of civilized standards the retention of two of his compatriots, who were treated decently and freed as soon as the danger for them and for our soldiers had passed, how would he classify the death of so many helpless Cuban civilians murdered by the bombs and planes that the United States government sold to the dictator Batista?

"Cuban citizens, Mr. White, are human beings just like United States citizens; but a United States citizen has never died by bombs from Cuban planes. You cannot accuse Cuban patriots of these acts, but we can accuse you and your government.

323

"The war that our country is now suffering causes losses and inconveniences, not only to the citizens of your country, but to the residents of Cuba as well. But this war is not to be blamed on the Cubans, who want to recover our democratic system and our liberties, but on the tyranny that has been oppressing our country for six long years, the tyranny which has been supported by United States ambassadors.

"Our conduct is open to the public light. There is no censorship of the press in the territory liberated by our forces. American newspapermen have visited us countless times, and they may go on doing so as many times as they want, in order to report our activities, freely and wholly, to their own people. . . .

"It is proper to point out that Cuba is a free and sovereign country and that we wish to maintain the most friendly relations with the United States. We do not wish any conflict between Cuba and the United States that cannot be solved by the use of reason and the exercise of the right of peoples.

"But if the United States Department of State continues to become involved in the intrigues of Mr. Smith and Batista and if it makes the unjustifiable mistake of committing an act of aggression against our sovereignty, it can be sure that we will know how to defend ourselves with dignity. There are duties to one's country that cannot be left unfulfilled, cost what they may.

"The words and threats in your recent statements do not honor a great and powerful country like the United States. Threats are useful when used against cowardly and submissive people, but they never will be of any use against men who are willing to die in the defense of their country."

It was only natural, in view of the photostat of the letter from Colonel Ferrer, the Cuban military and air attaché in Washington—which the secret agent of the 26th of July Movement sent on—that Castro would consider the succession of psychological blows apparently aimed at him by the State Department a result of conniving.

The State Department was quick to deny Castor's accusations that it was intervening in the Cuban civil war. Lincoln White said that his blunt statement was designed "as a part of a general policy to protect the lives of American citizens." He added: "We have carefully avoided any such intervention, and there is certainly no intention on our part to alter this policy."

The Cubans had a different definition of intervention, especially regarding the continuation of the Military Missions. The Batista regime, on the other hand, voiced its protest through a public relations representative in Washington that "United States diplomats working in Cuba have on many occasions negotiated directly with rebel elements. This direct dealing is not only an insult to the Batista government but contrary to all the accepted practices and usages in modern diplomacy."

Back in the Sierra Maestra, Major Quevedo was still a prisoner, as were captains Carlos Manuel Duran and Victoriano Gomez. On October 27 the three asked to join the 26th of July forces and offered to return clandestinely to the cities to undertake conspiratorial work among their old comrades in the regular army.

"I think that you are more useful here than if you returned to take part in conspiracies," Castro said. "We need you here to try to win over and save army units that are fighting decently. Moreover, with your experience you can help us to plan the final campaign."

Castro assigned the trio to his planning staff. This job did not prevent Quevedo from writing letters to friends in the army attempting to persuade those officers to conspire and defect, which he did with Castro's consent and help.

A secret 26th of July Movement cell had been organized among the pilots of the Cubana Airline. Captain Leslie Nobregas, thirty-two years old, was the head of the cell. He had taken his pilot training at the Embry-Riddle Flying School in Miami and had been with Cubana for six years. The Cubana pilot underground carried most of the rebel secret correspondence for personal delivery to Santiago, Camaguey, Holguin and Miami.

Castro was anxious to attempt to bomb the Moncada fortress. To accomplish this, the rebels needed planes capable of performing the operation in a certain way. Word was sent to Nobregas to co-ordinate the hijacking of certain planes to be flown to the rebel field which Raul Castro had prepared at Mayari Arriba, which had a 3,400-foot runway.

325

Captain Francisco Valliciergo, another Cubana pilot, was instructed to contact the 26th of July Movement in Santiago. The underground chief there told him Castro wanted two planes, and Nobregas took him to see the national co-ordinator of the 26th of July Movement, operating under the code name of "Eloy," in Havana. Eloy approved the plans.

When a Cubana DC-3 landed at Moa in Oriente on a regularly scheduled flight there were three passengers, two men and a girl, waiting to board. When the plane was in flight, the girl went to the lavatory and removed a gun she had strapped around her leg. With gun in hand one of the men then entered the cockpit. The plane was flown to the Mayari Arriba strip, where flights of guns, ammunition and mail had been ferried regularly from Florida.

Orders were sent by Raul Castro to bring him another plane. This time it was more difficult because of the investigation following the first hijacking. The chief of the 26th of July group in Havana, who used the code name of "Machaco," assigned three men and three women to the job.

They boarded Flight 482 at the Camaguey airport. The girls had pistols taped to their legs, but this time the pistols were not needed. For the pilot, Captain Armando Piedra, Cuban skindiving champion, was a rebel sympathizer.

From Camaguey the plane flew to Manzanillo, a regularly scheduled stop. Flight 482 continued its schedule and reached Cayo Mambi on the Atlantic Coast of Oriente. The hijackers went into action, and Piedra turned the plane westward to land at Mayari Arriba. The steward on this flight was a son of Major General Eulogio Cantillo, commander of Moncada.

As soon as it was safe, Castro released the crew members and passengers and delivered them to the Red Cross. The two DC-3's were readied for loads of improvised bombs made from acetelyne tanks. The tanks, filled with explosive, were to be kicked out of the door when the planes reached their targets.

Over in Miami one Cuban-American, Edmundo Ponce de Leon, a resident of that city, and five young Cuban exiles decided they would try to hijack a Cubana Viscount and join Castro's forces. On the afternoon of November 1 they boarded the Viscount in Miami as it took off for Havana via Varadero.

Ponce de Leon and the others forced the pilot to change course eastward near Varadero to head for Oriente. The plane crashed into the sea that night, killing fourteen of its twenty passengers and crew. This was a terrible tragedy and an absolutely unnecessary one, but it was not ordered by Castro or by anyone connected with him—although official announcements issued by our embassy in Havana created this impression.

"That group of irresponsible boys acted on their own," Nobregas said. "They had absolutely no contact with any revolutionary leader. The only persons in Miami who had authority to approve such a plan were Haydee Santamaria Hart and Jose Llanusa, both of whom would have consulted us about it. I would, naturally, have vetoed the plan because the Viscount must land at 120 knots and cannot land at an unlighted airport like Mayari Arriba."

Castro ordered all transport halted from November 1 through November 6 to harass Batista's election plans. Cubana did not fly to embattled Oriente.

In Washington Batista's ambassador Nicolas Arroyo, whose confirmation for the post had been confirmed in the senate by only four votes, scored a diplomatic coup. On the night of October 30 Secretary of State and Mrs. John Foster Dulles were Arroyo's guests at dinner at the Cuban embassy. Batista had a field day with this story, and Havana newspapers headlined it on page one: DULLES TOASTS BATISTA. *Diario la Marina* published a full page of pictures of the dinner in its rotogravure section on November 2, the day before the elections.

Many people were extremely bitter about Mr. Dulles' action at this crucial moment for their country. Even if the occasion was in commemoration of Theodore Roosevelt, as reported, the Cubans did not think it fitting.

The publicity given to the affair made even more Cubans determined to remain away from the polls. As Castro had forecast, the elections were a farce. At least 75 per cent of the people of Havana stayed away from the polling places although voting was mandatory. The percentage was higher in the provinces, and Santiago reported 98 per cent abstention.

The newspaper *Prensa Libre* defiantly appeared on the streets without an election story, and with a two-column picture on the front page of a guerrilla carrying a rifle. The next day the censor was fired.

The Supreme Electoral Tribunal began to furnish election returns after the polls closed. As expected they showed a wide lead for Rivero Aguero.

The General Staff of the army began to supply figures, reportedly received from military commanders throughout the country. These returns leaped far ahead of the tribunal figures. By midnight the army returns had announced a decision in favor of Batista's candidate.

Many people who mistakenly thought that Batista might swing the election victory to Marquez Sterling—to feign a semblance of desire for compromise—were shocked and stunned by the brazen announcement of the count. The ballot boxes had been stuffed by army officers before the elections. The only results that would be recognized were those announced by army headquarters. The rebels obtained dozens of voting identity cards made out in different names but with the same photograph on each card. These had been given in quantity to government ward heelers for use on behalf of Rivero Aguero. Even those who had entertained a faint hope for change without total warfare discarded that fantasy and were convinced that Castro was right: the people of Cuba did not vote on election day. Others had voted for them.

The contributions to Castro's treasury poured in from hitherto reluctant citizens of means. The Castro army had been collecting taxes in the free territory, and Raul Chibas, who had secretly left the United States, was in the Sierra Maestra as its tax collector. Some American firms in the area ignored the demands as the U.S. embassy recommended.

Dr. Manuel Urrutia once again flew from New York to Venezuela, a trip he had made many times in the year past. But this was to be his last journey. From Venezuela he flew to Oriente province in a plane loaded with arms and 1,000,000 rounds of ammunition for Castro's army.

Juan Nuiry and Omar Fernandez, the student leaders in exile, flew from Florida to the Sierra Maestra to join Castro; they became captains in the rebel army. That flight was one of

328

many secret missions flown by Cuban and American pilots.

The day after the elections the government pressured *Prensa Libre,* under threat of closure, to publish at least the bare returns furnished by the electoral tribunal. This the newspaper did. Pressure on *Bohemia* was even greater; police under Colonel Esteban Ventura, wearing his white silk suit as usual, invaded the plant, stopped the presses and closed operations. He stationed policemen at the plant. I was a witness to it.

Editor Quevedo, who was in New York to receive the Maria Moors Cabot Award at Columbia University, was telephoned a report by Managing Editor Lino Novas Calvo. Quevedo's instructions were to stand firm, not submitting to government pressure to print anything about the elections, and let the plant be closed. Quevedo said he would publish an election article and photograph provided he could comment on its fraudulence. Quevedo's firm stand won out, and the police were withdrawn. Closing down *Bohemia* at that moment would have been Batista's best gift to Castro because of the magazine's prestige, not only in Cuba, but in the United States and Latin America.

On November 5 Millie Ferrer and Beba Mendoza drove me to a house in the La Vibora district where I was to interview Manuel Ray, head of the Civic Resistance Movement in Havana. Ray was still eluding Batista's hunters, and under the code name of Campa was directing the subversive activities of thousands of members of the revived cells of his organization.

What Ray told me was not for publication at that time and was not, in fact, to be repeated to anyone. He said that a military conspiracy was under way. It could erupt any time after November 15 and Batista would surely fall by the night of December 31. There would be no general strike before the final blow against Batista, he added, but there would undoubtedly be one to ensure total victory.

Fidel Castro had long planned his final offensive against Batista and he was now ready to start it. It was November 7, only four days after the elections. Castro closed his headquarters at La Plata, the third highest peak of the Sierra Maestra, and marched on foot, at the head of a column of 220 armed men and 100 unarmed recruits, to the northwest toward Bueycito, the site of copper mines more than a thousand years old. He arrived there on November 17, with his column intact.

Castro had planned a surprise attack at Bueycito but the mistress of an army lieutenant had warned her sweetheart that the *barbudos* were on their way. The garrison commander asked sector headquarters at Bayamo for reinforcements for the expected attack. Bayamo replied that no reinforcements could be sent, and the garrison commander ordered a withdrawal, covered only by ineffective rearguard action.

Trucks and jeeps were available for the rebels at Bueycito. Castro ordered the column to advance eastward across the fields toward Guisa, about twenty-five miles away. He rode in a jeep with the faithful and indispensable Celia Sanchez and his personal bodyguard, including Ignacio Perez, one of the four sons of Crescencio Perez who were fighting with his army.

Castro's plan was to bypass Bayamo—where Batista had 2,000 troops, tanks and artillery—continue northward to the central highway, and then move eastward toward Santiago in a pincer movement. On one flank was the column of Major Huber Matos with 245 *barbudos* and on the other was Major Juan Almeida with 350 *barbudos*. They would be called on to support his column during the battles at Guisa and Maffo. His brother Raul was moving west at the head of the Frank Pais Second Front column, now more than 2,000 strong with an additional 1,000 trained but unarmed troops ready to go into action as soon as more guns were captured from the enemy.

Castro ordered an old bridge over the Monte Oscuro Creek to be destroyed to protect the rearguard in the encirclement of Guisa, which was his next operation. His order was to blow up one section of the bridge and mine the rest. This was necessary to prevent tank reinforcements for Batista's forces from crossing the creek. Castro sent out his patrols in what was to be the first of eleven days of decisive action. During this period five battles were to be fought by inspired *barbudos* of the rebel army, fighting for a cause, against 1,800 troops who were defending a dictator with no cause except the lust for power and personal enrichment. The attacks were co-ordinated with Major Juan Almeida, who commanded a newly formed third front in the hills to the north.

One Sherman tank attempted to rumble along the road and Castro ordered Major Hubert Matos to plant a dynamite mine in in its path. The vehicle turned a somersault before it shook itself into immobility. Matos was an expert in destroying tanks in that manner.

"I set a trap for a rat," Castro ejaculated when the tank was doing its flip-up, "and they sent me an elephant!"

Batista's troops withdrew after suffering 200 dead and wounded and losing 21 men as prisoners to Castro, whose troops withstood assaults by Sherman tanks, artillery, aviation and nine companies of reserves.

With Guisa in his hands, Castro proceeded across the fields to Charco Redondo, where he ordered Radio Rebelde to set up headquarters along with the press and propaganda section, in which Carlos Franqui was assisting Major Luis Orlando Rodriguez, the newspaper editor turned soldier.

While the fighting was going on Batista's counterintelligence discovered a plot widespread among the dictator's army officers. This plot had no connection whatsoever with the 26th of July Movement. More than 100 army officers were arrested and Major General Martin Diaz Tamayo was retired as a result of it.

Although Urrutia had been in the Sierra Maestra for some time, it was not until nearly the middle of December that he and Castro met. They had never met each other personally before then. The meeting took place at Rinconada near Charco Redonda, and the two men conferred about future victory. Urrutia then returned to his place of safety near Santiago while Castro resumed his direction of the war.

Castro moved his troops onto the central highway and took Jiguani and Baire and then moved eastward toward Maffo, where again Batista's army used artillery and aviation to try to destroy the rebels. Castro personally commanded this operation. The rebels continued their march, with Major Francisco Cabrera taking near-by Contramaestre.

On the eastern sector, Raul Castro's troops had captured Sagua de Tanamo near Cayo Mambi, and Batista retaliated by ordering his air force to bomb the city. The rebels had withdrawn to protect the civilian population after the capture of the city. Sagua de Tanamo was reduced by Batista's air force with devastating bombing like that of Hiroshima, but, unlike Hiroshima, the side that was devastated was not going to offer to surrender—this was a different kind of war.

Raul Castro moved his columns closer toward Santiago and cut highway and telephone communications. Town after town and city after city fell. Batista's air force continued its attacks against each captured village and even some that were not in rebel hands. Refugees began to pour into Santiago, taxing the supplies of the provincial capital to such an extent that Monsignor Perez Serantes smuggled out a letter to Cuban friends in Miami via Puerto Rico, imploring them to send clothing and food to help the destitute. Wives of Cuban exiles solicited contributions and clothing to ship to Santiago aboard one of the secret flights.

On the invasion front Che Guevara moved his column through the sugar cane fields westward toward the city of Sancti Spiritus, situated on the main highway and railroad link to and from Havana. Camilo Cienfuegos moved his column toward Yaguajay on the northern highway and railway branches.

It was during this period that Castro's former teacher, Father Armando Llorente, responded to an invitation from his pupil to visit him in the Sierra Maestra. The priest made the journey to Oriente at the height of the campaign to take Guisa, Jiguani, Baire and other cities.

"It was an unforgettable experience," he reports. "I was able to appreciate firsthand the hardships and vicissitudes of that group of Cubans who were determined to liberate us or die. It was a war of the spirit against matter. The day I arrived in the Sierra a message was sent to Fidel, who was on an inspection trip of several of his sectors and many miles away. He sent back a note to tell me that he would arrive at seven o'clock. One minute before seven that night he arrived on foot, apologizing that his jeep had broken down and he had to hike the rest of the way. . . . With his men he acted as a counselor and he guided them in a paternal voice."

On December 13 Senator Allen J. Ellender of Louisiana drew some caustic criticism from the *Times* of Havana, which is published by Clarence W. Moore and edited by Milt Guss. It came as a result of Henry Goethals' report of the lawmaker's press conference at the American embassy the previous day. Goethals, grandson of the general of Panama Canal fame, had this to say:

"Maybe that's how it is in the great game of U.S. politics, but there were times yesterday when Senator Allen J. Ellender didn't know what he was talking about. Or at least, that's what he said.

"Asked if he thought Cuba was in a state of civil war, he answered ingenuously:

" 'I don't know of any. Has there been any fighting?'

"The civil war query was prompted by Ellender's remark that U.S. ban on arms shipments to the Cuban government was 'most curious' in light of similar arms shipments by several U.S. allies, including Britain, France, Belgium and Italy.

" 'Of course, I don't know much about it,' Ellender said in opening his discussion on the arms question, 'but if a nation requires weapons to maintain internal security, I personally cannot understand why they cannot be shipped. But if there were a raging civil war going on, my answer to this question would be an emphatic *no*.'

"He added that his understanding of Cuba's trouble was that 'bandits are burning sugar plantations' and that the government was in need of weapons to maintain internal peace.

"He added: 'People on the Washington level evidently feel that the shipment of weapons to the Cuban government under the circumstances might be picked up by Russia for propaganda purposes. But I do not think this is valid. It would be a tragedy for Cuba if civil war were to take place here. The poor people would be the ones to suffer. And Cuba is too prosperous and too wonderful a little island for such a thing to happen. I am hopeful that nothing will occur.' "

There was much more which led the *Times* of Havana to say in its editorial: "Spokesman for Whom?"

"The *Times* will be in the front line to defend the 'rugged individual.' Too few of them in the world these days. And we consider Senator Ellender one. Real rugged example of an individual who says and does what he thinks. So cheers for Senator Ellender.

"Up to a point. The senator speaks for the senator, but we haven't read anywhere that he speaks for the United States. We sincerely hope he doesn't, and we accept our own decision that

333

he does not. But the trial of memories that he leaves behind him will long outlive his brief visit. And Cubans will certainly consider him an official spokesman. How would they imagine that a press conference would be held in the U.S. embassy for a senator unless he spoke with a certain authority. On this basis, scallions for the senator who fails to measure the importance of his own remarks when placed in a position of responsibility beyond his own depth. Come back for a nice trip some day, Senator, but just for fun and not as a self-appointed spokesman."

Moore, who had rejected every offer of subsidy from the Batista regime, expected reprisals from the government after that editorial, but apparently neither the censor nor the officials of the regime understood his sarcasm.

Guevara's main objective was Santa Clara, the provincial capital which in the 1953 census had a population of 77,398. He planned to take the city in a co-ordinated attack by the Directorio and Escambray Front troops and with Camilo Cienfuegos' column moving down from the north.

Castro's main objective was Santiago de Cuba. He planned a co-ordinated attack by the Frank Pais Second Front force under his brother Raul, along with columns commanded by Juan Almeida, Hubert Matos, Rene de los Santos, Efigenia Almejeiras and Jaime Vega, all now majors. And marching with Almeida's column was his judge advocate, Melba Hernandez, veteran of the Moncada attack.

The offensive was on and there was to be no stopping it. The rebels now had radio communications from Pinar del Rio in the extreme west to Baracoa in the extreme east, almost on the tip of the Windward Passage. With the columns in Oriente and Las Villas marched women commandos, armed with shotguns and pistols, organized and trained to fight as a separate unit or with the men, all by now battle-tested.

Rebels in Pinar del Rio were harassing and containing Batista's army as they operated from hide-outs in the Sierra de los Organos. Armed militia were active in Matanzas and the province of Havana, raiding army posts or police stations.

For several months the reprisals of the Batista repressive forces took a large toll of political prisoners. For every bomb that was exploded, two prisoners were removed from jail and summarily shot. One night in Marianao, a borough of Havana, the bodies of 98 political prisoners were scattered through the streets, riddled with bullets. Each had been taken from his cell in reprisal for a raid on a police station.

"Every night we prayed that the underground would not toss any more bombs," several political prisoners told me, "because we feared we would be the next."

There was one equally tragic case of a father who was friendly with a police officer. One day the father asked the officer to arrest his wayward son to teach the boy a lesson not to stay out too late at night. The police officer obliged and put the youth in a cell; the boy was to be held only a few hours and then sent home. A few bombs were exploded that night, and the youth was among the prisoners taken from cells and summarily shot.

While Castro was advancing toward Santiago in the east, Guevara and Cienfuegos were advancing in Las Villas. December 20 was D-day for the offensive there. Cienfuegos launched his assault on Yaguajay in the north. He bivouacked at the Narcisa sugar plantation on December 22, only a mile and a half from the city; he had sent Captain Pinares with the advance guard to the outskirts the previous day to push back the outpost line. The slow advance of Cienfuegos' column began as the Batista troops put up a strong fight. The regular army occupied a redoubt in the Hotel Plaza which Cienfuegos took upon himself to reduce after house-to-house fighting. A battle for possession of the electric plant lasted two hours, after which Cienfuegos went on to capture the Cawy bottling plant and the police station. By that time Cienfuegos was ready to encircle the garrison which had holed up in the fort.

To the south Guevara moved on to Sancti Spiritis, which was important as a railroad junction; also the central highway ran through the city, which was in almost the exact geographical center of the island. His patrols reached the outskirts of the city on the morning of December 24.

Almost at the same time Castro's troops advanced toward Palma Soriano, which for a long time had been the command post of the Oriente Theater of Operations and was one of the larger cities of the province. On December 23 they began their attack.

Castro had promised his brother Ramon that he would have Christmas supper at his house at Marcane in northern Oriente. Ramon had been saving a twenty-four-pound *guanojo*—turkey— in his freezer for a year and a half for this occasion. He had vowed that he would not eat it without Fidel. Brother Raul was also invited but could not make it. Fidel arrived after ten o'clock at night on Christmas Eve with members of his staff, Celia Sanchez and his personal bodyguard.

Ramon's wife and children were there and so were Fidel's mother and sisters. As soon as the dinner was over—and Fidel ate his usual enormous meal—the rebel chief left with Ramon, bearded too, to continue the war.

Guevara's troops entered Sancti Spiritus on Christmas Eve. There were no Christmas trees in the city and hardly anywhere in Cuba, except in some official buildings, at armed forces posts and in some homes of Batista officials and supporters. None was in evidence in Havana.

Batista's ironclad radio censorship was broken by the fall of Sancti Spiritus. Suddenly the people of Cuba were electrified by a voice that rang through the airwaves with: "This is Radio Sancti Spiritus in the free territory of Cuba!" And the 26th of July rebel march and the Cuban national anthem were played over and over again between announcements and news. The first big breakthrough had occurred. People in Havana, though, could not hear Radio Sancti Spiritus because local stations jammed its wave length. But the people in the provinces were able to tune it in, as did the thousands of exiles in Miami and Tampa.

The island of Cuba had been cut in two, for rebels had taken Sancti Spiritus and were threatening the highway and railroad to the east of Yaguajay and other sugar plantation railroads to the south. The country's economic lifeline—sugar—was in real danger now. Unless the war ended soon there would be no 1959 crop.

The planters had presented the problem to Batista the previous week, and he had assured them that by January 10 he would have resolved the situation by routing Castro.

Guevara advanced toward Santa Clara, sixty-five miles to the northeast. His troops fanned out and captured in quick order Cabaiguan, Fomento, Placetas, Cruces, Manicaragua and other towns and cities. Batista pressed his air force into action, and 500-pound bombs purchased from England were dropped on Cruces to take the pressure off the encirclement of Santa Clara.

On the Oriente front, Castro's troops entered Palma Soriano on Christmas Day and began three days of house-to-house fighting until the garrison was surrounded.

At a palace meeting of his high command Batista announced an extreme measure. He recalled General Jose Euleterio Pedraza to active duty, designating Colonel Joaquin R. Casillas Lumpuy as commander of Las Villas to replace General Alberto del Rio Chaviano. Pedraza had been a dreaded police chief of Havana; in April 1958 he had shot down a father and two sons in an apartment house in the capital after their arrest in alleged reprisal for the murder of his son on a highway in Las Villas province.

While Cienfuegos was busy trying to capture Yaguajay he sent some patrols into the province of Matanzas to the west to harass transport and prevent reinforcements from arriving via the northern roads.

The rebel radio network was now heard all over the short-wave dial. The capture of Sancti Spiritus and other cities made both short-wave and long-wave transmitters available. The Second National Front of Escambray forces had moved out of the hills toward Cienfuegos while others of its columns moved northward toward La Esperanza, Cruces, Ranchuelo.

The rebel radios were operating around the clock and transmitting intelligence, operational messages, news and warnings to the populace that Batista's aircraft would bomb and strafe the captured cities.

On the afternoon of December 26 a lieutenant of Batista's air force flew an armed B-26 into Miami International Airport instead of carrying out his bombing mission. The morale of Batista's armed forces was collapsing. And it was evident when I arrived in Havana that night that Castro had almost destroyed their will to fight. This was indicated at Yaguajay where naval units stood offshore ready to land reinforcements to relieve the besieged garrison. Cienfuegos ordered cut the approaches from the beaches at Carbo, El Jucaro and Estrada Real, as well as the highway and railroad to Mayajigua and Caibarien. His troops were ordered to fire in the direction of the naval vessels.

"The beaches are hostile to us," the naval commander signaled naval operations. "It is impossible to attempt to land."

Cienfuegos sent two emissaries to parley with the naval officers. His message was a virtual ultimatum: "Surrender or fight or stand off the coast!"

The naval units turned and stood out to sea, their guns silenced. Another battle had been won.

In the shops of the Narcisa sugar mill rebel armorers and mill workers converted a D-8 Caterpillar tractor into a tank in a round-the-clock operation. They welded on thick plates of steel, equipped it with two .30 caliber machine guns and devised a flame thrower with 500 pounds of pressure and metal nozzles that gave it a range of 1,200 feet. The tank was christened *Dragon I*.

The garrison at the Yaguajay fort was under the command of Captain Abon Li, a Chinese Cuban. A railroad line ran through the patio of the fort. Two sugar cane cars of the Central Victoria were loaded with dynamite and rolled down the tracks. The cars crashed through to shatter the walls and demolish the roof. Notwithstanding this, Captain Li and his troops replied with heavy machine-gun fire and bazooka fire. Batista's air force gave them support, strafing and bombing the rebels, but the rebels fired back at the planes and drove off the pilots.

In Las Villas the rebel radios were talking to each other and to the people of Cuba: "Hello, Placetas. Hello, Placetas. Radio Rebelde de Sancti Spiritus calling," and on and on as the announcers reported every incident of the now fast-moving war and filled their intermissions with the spirited rebel march. Nineteen of the thirty-one municipalities of Las Villas had already fallen into rebel hands. Radio Caibarien joined the freedom network.

In Oriente, Castro received a visitor on December 28 at eight o'clock in the morning. He arrived by Cuban army helicopter.

He was Major General Eulogio Cantillo, commander of the Moncada fortress. He had requested the interview four days earlier, and Castro had replied through Father Guzman, a priest with the rebels, that he would meet him at a time and place to be designated.

By that time, Castro's offensive had captured 750 weapons in Oriente alone, where he had 12,000 soldiers surrounded by his columns. All main roads in Las Villas had been cut, and the island was cut in half.

Raul Chibas, now a major, Celia Sanchez and Major Quevedo were present during the interview with Cantillo. They were joined by Raul Castro and Vilma Espin. The rebel chieftain, flushed with the enthusiasm of the approaching victory, explained to Cantillo the causes of the revolution and the plans for the future. Cantillo told Castro that Batista was willing to quit if the structure of the army was left untouched. Castro replied he would not accept such a condition. He added that he was definitely opposed to letting Batista get away, but that was perhaps beyond his control.

Cantillo agreed to engineer a coup against Batista. At Castro's insistence it was planned for the Moncada fortress in Santiago. Cantillo assured him that at three o'clock on the afternoon of December 31 the Moncada garrison would defect without firing a shot; the garrison at Bayamo was to rise at the same time. Cantillo wanted to return to Havana to talk to some of his army friends there. Though the rebel chief advised him to go to Santiago instead, Cantillo took off at noon in the helicopter and went on to Havana.

In Las Villas Guevara tightened the ring around Santa Clara while Cienfuegos led the assault on the fort at Yaguajay. The people of Santa Clara had risen like a fifth column when the rebels entered the city. Pedraza, who had become director of operations of the General Staff, dispatched an armored train to Santa Clara, loaded with a million dollars' worth of arms and ammunition and armored vehicles purchased from England. The engineer officer assigned to command the train and its 400 troops, Colonel Florentino Rosell, boarded his yacht at the Biltmore Yacht Club in Havana and sailed to exile in Florida.

Colonel Casillas had taken command of Santa Clara and organized its defenses. Capiro Hill on the approaches to the city, which furnished a dominating field of fire, was surrounded by trenches. The city's natural defenses were reinforced there by two .50 caliber machine guns and one 20 millimeter anti-aircraft gun. The police check point on the central highway east of the city was strengthened by an infantry company, while the troops of the 31st squadron were strategically deployed to the south. In the Leoncio Vidal fort of the 3rd Tactical Regiment there were almost 2,000 troops.

Army troops were also deployed in the towers of the Buen Viaje Church, the Nuestra Senora Church, on top and at windows of the eleven-story Gran Hotel, on the roof of the provincial palace and on its balconies, on roofs of police stations, the prison and other buildings and residences.

From his command post near the University of Santa Clara, Guevara gave the order to attack at five o'clock on the morning of December 29. The rebels converged on the positions at Capiro Hill and the District Public Works Building. The armored train, with 17 cars, arms, ammunition, rations for a two-month campaign, electric kitchens, uniforms and engineers and technicians, was on its way with 400 officers and men who had little or no will to fight.

The rebel patrols infiltrated into the city, to cut intersections of the central highway and hold the La Cruz bridge. Major Rolando Cubela, commanding the Directorio troops, applied pressure against the garrison of the 31st squadron. Guevara's troops blocked the railroad with trailers, gasoline trucks and other obstacles. The armored train halted far from its destination. The rebels opened fire against it, tossing hundreds of Molotov cocktails, which burst into flames against the steel plates while the bullets beat a tattoo against them. The regular soldiers fired machine-gun bursts in desperation through the slits of the plates, and the engineer tried to back the train. It was too late— commandos had already torn up the track and the train was derailed.

A white handkerchief appeared at the end of a rifle barrel that emerged from one of the slits. The men were ready to surrender. Some 400 officers and men were escorted to the captured Public Works Building.

The guns captured were distributed among natives of Santa Clara who had been clamoring for them. The fifth column in the city went into action. Automobiles were driven out of garages by their owners and overturned in the streets to serve as roadblocks and prevent tanks from operating. Men, women and children tossed Molotov cocktails at passing armored vehicles. The two and a half months of preparation by the fifth column for this offensive had served in good stead.

Rebels infiltrated along the streets, from house to house and corner to corner, driving back the defenders. Fighter aircraft and medium bombers flew over the city to bomb and strafe though the pilots could not tell the regular army troops on rooftops from rebels. Sea Fury fighters were used, together with Thunderbolts and B-26's.

Monsignor Perez Serantes in Santiago issued an appeal for a halt to further bloodshed as Batista's bombers devastated more cities and towns already captured by the rebels.

On December 30 Cantillo sent word to Castro that some difficulty had arisen and it would be necessary to postpone the planned coup until January 6.

On December 31 at three o'clock in the afternoon, when Moncada did not defect, Castro issued orders to his commanders to march to Santiago and attack that city on January 3. The attack plan had been thoroughly discussed with them at a meeting at his command post on December 17. Another conference was unnecessary.

That same day, the last day of 1958, Cienfuegos obtained the surrender of Captain Li and the rest of his men at Yaguajay, and Guevara, with Cubela, who had been wounded, was advancing inside Santa Clara. Captain Li came out of the fort with his men, holding their hands in the air, and Cienfuegos ordered them detained until further notice.

"This victory has an extraordinary moral significance," Cienfuegos remarked. "Those army troops were the same who burned down homes and murdered *campesinos* in the Sierra Maestra under the command of Lieutenant Colonel Sanchez Mosquera. We had a debt to collect and now we have accomplished it."

Cienfuegos then turned his attention in the direction of Santa Clara to assist Guevara. In Santa Clara, Guevara, through the

341

Red Cross, asked Casillas for a truce to evacuate the wounded to a safe place.

"There will be no truce!" Casillas replied. "I demand the surrender of the rebels."

Though Batista's army was crumbling everywhere, Casillas, his own forces under rout except for the garrison of the regiment where he had his headquarters, was arrogantly demanding the rebel surrender! The rebels countered with an all-out attack against the remainder of the 31st squadron, the police station, the Gran Hotel, the courthouse and the Los Caballitos army post, driving the defenders from them. Except for the fort there were only mopping-up operations left in the city.

In Oriente, Castro's columns moved on closer to Santiago in force, taking Maffo after a heavy battle, San Luis, El Cristo, Dos Bocas and El Caney. Raul Castro's men had already captured Guantanamo, the native city, which had long since been cut off from supplies from Santiago. Batista's troops had withdrawn from the water-pumping station at the Guantanamo Bay naval base, and the rebels were guarding it. The rebel captain there warned his men not to turn off the water as had been done earlier in the month because of confused orders. Rebel patrols, infiltrating with their customary abandon into Santiago, would withdraw after a quick survey of the situation.

That night a wire service reported that Batista's army was driving the rebels from Santa Clara eastward and was administering a crushing defeat to the *barbudos*.

And that night Fulgencio Batista was preparing to flee Cuba.

Batista held a conference in his quarters at Camp Columbia after he had arrived from Kuquine, and wrote the following resignation in his own hand:

"In the city of Havana the first day of January of 1959, meeting in the private office of the President of the Republic in the Military City, the signers of this act certify the statements of the Honorable Señor Presidente of the Republic General Fulgencio Batista y Zaldivar, who spontaneously states:

"That in the early morning of this day the high military chiefs who have at their command the highest posts notified him of the impossibility of re-establishing order, considering the situation that confronts the country as grave; and requested (I quote): 'appealing to your patriotism and to your love of the people that you resign your office.' He stated that the high representatives of the church, of the sugar industry and of the national businesses had addressed him in similar manner:

"Taking into account the loss of lives, the material damage to property and the evident harm that was being done to the economy of the Republic, and imploring God to illuminate the Cubans so they can live in concord and in peace, he resigns his powers as President of the Republic, delivering them to the constitutional substitute. He begs the people to keep order and not to become victims of tumultuous passions which would be unfortunate for the Cuban family. In a like manner he urges all members of the armed forces and the police agents to obey and co-operate with the new government and with the chiefs of the armed bodies, of which Major General Eulogio Cantillo y Porras has taken charge."

Batista signed that with his initials "FBZ," and below was the signature of Anselmo Alliegro, president of the senate, who appended this note: "Constitutional substitute because the constitutional vice president has resigned on being elected mayor." There were also other signatures such as General Francisco Tabernilla, General Pedraza, General Rodriguez Avila and Senior Justice Carlos Manuel Piedra of the Supreme Court, the "constitutional" successor.

Batista left his quarters for the air base at the northeastern end of Camp Columbia. Transport aircraft were waiting. At the gangway was General Cantillo. Dozens of would-be fugitives, officers of the army, navy, air force and police and politicians were gathered at the Air Force Headquarters building.

Batista climbed the gangway and turned to give some last-minute instructions to Cantillo.

"Cantillo," he said, "you know what I have told you you have to do. Call the persons I have mentioned, Drs. Ricardo Nunez Portuondo, Raul de Cardenas and Gustavo Cuervo Rubio, and tell them what my plans are."

"Very well, General," Cantillo responded.

"Try to have these people help you," Batista continued. "They are representative of great zones of opinion and their collaboration is necessary in these moments."

343

"I think so, too, General," Cantillo said.

"All right, Cantillo, don't forget my instructions," were Batista's final words. "On you depends the success of the negotiations from now on."

Batista turned to the crowd below. "Salud! Salud!" he exclaimed and entered the DC-4 aircraft. It was 2:10 A.M. when the plane taxied away from the ramp to the runway to take off for the Dominican Republic.

Events followed in quick succession. Cantillo tried to withhold the news of Batista's flight, but it was news that could not be withheld. Since 9:30 P.M. that night I had been receiving reports from different contacts that Batista was preparing to flee, reports that were most difficult to confirm at the time. They persisted, however, and at two o'clock Jose Ferrer telephoned me to say that he had just received a call telling him Batista had fled. Half an hour earlier, with Clay Gowran of the *Chicago Tribune,* I had left Ferrer's house, and had just fallen asleep. The task now was to obtain confirmation. It came an hour and a half later when Miguel Angel Quevedo called to report that Batista's press secretary, Enrique Pizzi de Porras, had told him he had seen Batista board the plane and leave.

Cantillo met at Camp Columbia with Pedra and the men mentioned by Batista. They had been chosen by Batista the previous year to comprise the Conciliation Commission that Castro had rejected.

Before dawn the following general order by Cantillo was read to the officers at Camp Columbia:

"A great responsibility falls on my shoulders and all you worthy officers, that of saving the country and ending this fratricidal war that has cost so many lives.

"The President of the Republic, not wanting to spill any more blood, has resigned, the senior justice of the Supreme Court, Dr. Carlos M. Piedra, being designated President of the Republic.

"The President has embarked. The chief of the joint staff, the chief of the navy and the chief of the national police have also embarked. The president of the senate and the Vice President of the Republic as well as high officers of the armed forces have resigned.

344

"We have assumed the command of the armed forces and have designated Colonel Daniel G. Martinez Mora as Chief of Operations."

Cantillo sent word that he would receive the members of the Cuban Press Bloc and the Cuban Radio and Television Broadcasters at nine o'clock at his headquarters for an important conference and announcement. But some radio and television stations tired of waiting for the official announcement and broke the news of Batista's flight. Miguel Angel Quevedo of *Bohemia* and Sergio Carbo of *Prensa Libre* refused to go to Columbia. Newspapers prepared extras to report the news, although New Year's Day was normally a press holiday.

Castro spent New Year's Eve in the home of Ramon Ruiz, chief engineer of the Central America, a sugar mill near Palma Soriano, and was having breakfast there shortly before nine o'clock the next morning when he was told the news of Batista's flight.

Castro fingered his beard and then exploded, "This is a cowardly betrayal! A betrayal! They are trying to prevent the triumph of the Revolution!"

He rose from the table, went to the door and called out for his men to hear. "I am going to leave for Santiago now! We have to take Santiago right away. Find Rene de los Santos! Call Calixto Garcia! I want the captains of Santiago here at once! We have to attack Santiago without delay! If they are so ingenuous as to think that they will paralyze the Revolution with a *coup d'état,* we will show them they are wrong!"

One of the men in the room, his dentist, who was also ordnance officer of his headquarters, spoke up: "Pardon me, Commander, but I think you should wait, at least for fifteen minutes." Castro ignored him and continued to summon officers and issue orders. His troops had captured a Sherman tank with its 75-millimeter gun at Maffo. He planned to use that now.

"The tank—tell Pedro Miret to move it from Maffo to Santiago immediately! Huber Matos' troops are to prepare to attack Moncada with artillery. All the troops who are in Palma Soriano and Contramaestre are to occupy positions in El Cobre."

Meanwhile in Santa Clara at that hour, while Castro was busy in Oriente writing his final directive to his troops and to the people, army medicos requested the Red Cross to arrange a meeting with Guevara for them. When they were received, they told Guevara they were offering the surrender of the regiment and the air force detachment without the knowledge of Colonel Casillas Lumpuy.

Guevara accompanied them to the fort to talk with Casillas. "Colonel, I come to ask you to surrender to avoid any more bloodshed," the Argentine said.

"Major, while I have one bullet left, I will not surrender," Casillas replied. "Moreover, I am going to turn Santa Clara into dust, and I will throw you out of the city, cost what it may. With the arms I have you will not be able to beat me."

"Colonel, you have the weapons, but you don't have anybody to fire them," Guevara said with a wry smile. Guevara had hit the mark.

"This interview is ended," Casillas said. "You may come here again whenever you like."

"No, Colonel," Guevara said, "it is you who will have to surrender now." And he nodded his head toward Casillas' officers and men. The surrender followed later, but Casillas fled in civilian clothes and was captured by a patrol of Major Victor Bordon's column in the Central Washington mill. He was to be one of many officers who were tried by rebel summary courts, convicted and executed for murders of unarmed civilians.

At the Central America sugar mill, Castro affixed his signature to the directive and personally broadcast it over Radio Rebelde. In a vibrant voice he said:

"Instructions of the General Headquarters to all commanders of the rebel army and to the people:

"Whatever the news from the capital may be, our troops should not cease fire at any time.

"Our forces should continue their operations against the enemy on all battlefronts.

"Parleys should be granted only to those garrisons that wish to surrender.

"Apparently, there has been a *coup d'état* in the capital. The conditions in which that coup was produced are not known by the rebel army.

346

"The people should be very alert and attend only to the instructions of our general headquarters.

"The dictatorship has collapsed as a consequence of the crushing defeats suffered in the last weeks, but that does not mean to say that the Revolution has already triumphed.

"Military operations will continue unchanged until an express order is received from this headquarters, which will be issued only when the military elements who have risen in the capital are placed unconditionally at the orders of the revolutionary command.

"Revolution, *yes!* Military coup, *no!*

"Military coup behind the backs of the people and the Revolution, *no,* because it would only serve to prolong the war!

"Coup d'état so that Batista and the other big guilty ones escape, *no*; because it would only serve to prolong the war!

"Coup d'état in agreement with Batista, *no*; because it would only serve to prolong the war!

"To take the victory away from the people, *no*; because it would only serve to prolong the war until the people obtain total victory!

"After seven years of struggle, the democratic victory of the people has to be absolute, so that never again will there be in our Fatherland another 10th of March.

"Nobody should let himself be confused or deceived!

"To be on the alert is the order!

"The people and very especially the workers of the entire Republic should listen to Radio Rebelde and urgently prepare all centers of work for the general strike. And as soon as the order is received they should start it if it should be necessary to stop any attempt of a counterrevolutionary coup.

"The people and the rebel army must be more united and more firm than ever in order not to let the victory that has cost so much blood be snatched from them!"

Castro had made his decisions: unconditional surrender of the Batista armed forces and a general strike to ensure it.

In Havana the 26th of July and Civic Resistance Movement undergrounds, caught unawares by the sudden flight of Batista, had to emerge into the open in order to organize the general strike and mobilize the militia to preserve order in the capital. Manuel Ray had returned from the Sierra Maestra with instructions from Castro for the last push in the capital to topple Batista. It took some hours to establish a command post in the CMQ building, opposite the Havana-Hilton Hotel, and general headquarters in the Sports Palace.

Castro made a second broadcast over Radio Rebelde. It was an appeal to the people not to take justice into their own hands and to preserve order. He promised them that every "war criminal" would be arrested, tried and punished. He reiterated the need to preserve order and avoid acts of personal vengeance.

There was a good reason for this appeal. After Dictator Gerardo Machado fled in 1933, Havana and other cities of Cuba were shaken by anarchy and chaos for three weeks. Hundreds of persons were gunned down on the streets in vengeance killings, among them dozens of innocent men. The period of anarchy and chaos gave rise to a clamor at that time for a strong man to put an end to the disorders—and that man happened to be Batista.

Before Castro's broadcast appeal there had been several vengeance killings, especially in the provinces. They came to an immediate halt, and all suspected torturers, assassins and informers were arrested and imprisoned pending trial. Most of them were regular army, navy and air force officers, noncommissioned officers and enlisted men, police officers, policemen and some civilians.

Other civilians who were not in the above category, but who had had some close association with the Batista regime since 1952 were also arrested. Among them was Joaquin Martinez Saenz, president of the Banco Nacional, and Ernesto de la Fe, who had been minister of propaganda in 1952-1954. It was while De la Fe occupied that post that Mario Kuchilan, *Prensa Libre* columnist, was arrested and almost tortured to death, then left on a seldom-traveled road outside of Havana. Lately, De la Fe had held the post of secretary general of a Latin-American anti-Communist organization. De la Fe reported that he was arrested by the Communists and taken to La Cabana.

The city of Cienfuegos had been under siege by the rebels of the Second National Front of Escambray for weeks. That force had also encircled 500 Batista troops who had holed up in the tuberculosis sanitorium on the hilltop of Tope de Collante in the Escambray Mountains and had finally forced their surrender. The effective encirclement had prevented those troops from being committed as reserves in the battle for Santa Clara.

At dawn on New Year's Day Major William Alexander Morgan, after prior arrangements had been made with officers inside, entered the Cayo Loco Naval Station at Cienfuegos and took command of the entire city.

As they usually do in such circumstances, events moved rapidly in the capital.

At eleven o'clock Cantillo escorted Justice Piedra to the presidential palace where the other justices of the Supreme Court were supposed to administer his oath of office. At noon Piedra began, with Cantillo as a smiling witness beside his desk, to sign presidential decrees appointing ministers, but he had not yet taken the oath of office.

At two o'clock a committee of the diplomatic corps, led by Ambassador Smith and comprising Monsignor Luis Centoz, the Apostolic Delegate, and the Brazilian, Spanish and Chilean ambassadors, called at the presidential palace. They conferred with Cantillo and left. The justices of the Supreme Court had refused to go to the palace to administer the oath to Piedra. As one justice explained to me, they would not administer the oath because the flight of Batista was a result of a triumphant revolution led by Fidel Castro and the state of war which prevailed in the country obviated any so-called constitutional succession.

That morning Ambassador Smith had issued a statement that Batista had left of his own free will and expressed the hope that peace would now be restored to Cuba. Later, when vandals were on the loose throughout Havana, he issued another statement advising Americans to remain indoors to avoid the possibility of injury.

Vandalism broke out on the streets of Havana almost at the same time that joyous crowds began to parade in their automobiles or on foot, carrying large Cuban flags. Enormous flags waved from balconies of homes and from church towers. The equipment of several hotel gambling casinos was smashed; slot machines were taken and their contents removed. Parking meters

349

were demolished. Store windows were smashed as looters commenced their field day. The police fired on the crowds, and downtown Havana became a virtual battlefield.

Newspaper offices and printing plants owned by Batista or his friends, particularly Masferrer's *Tiempo en Cuba,* were wrecked. The 26th of July Movement took over the plant of the newspaper *Alerta,* which was owned by Batista's minister of communications, Ramon Vasconcelos.

The Communist Party took over the political offices of Alberto Salas Amaro above the press wireless office in the Parque Central and hung out a banner indicating their location.

Newspaper extras were published that morning and afternoon but by rebel order no regular papers were to be published for three days. Radio and television stations were allowed to operate. *Revolucion,* the official organ of the 26th of July Movement, emerged from the *Alerta* presses—the only paper allowed to be published and circulated in Havana. The only person who could authorize the appearance of the newspapers was Fidel Castro.

In the Isle of Pines prison, a vest-pocket transistor radio smuggled into Cell Block 4 brought the news of Batista's flight to 400 political prisoners. Colonels Barquin and Borbonnet and Armando Hart, of the 26th of July Movement, tried futilely to persuade the prison commander to release them.

When majors Carlos Carrillo and Montero Duque arrived from Havana to confer with Barquin and escort him to Camp Columbia to assume command of the army, Barquin demanded the release of all army, navy and air force officers and all political prisoners, in accordance with an agreement with the 26th of July Movement. He wanted Armando Hart, Quintin Pino Machado and Mario Hidalgo to accompany him. He also wanted the military command of the Isle of Pines delivered to Lieutenant Fernandez Alvarez and the governorship to Jesus Montane.

"I have come to receive orders, not to give them," Major Carrillo told Barquin.

All the prisoners were released and the troops were assembled. Barquin handed the command of the island to Alvarez. The transport plane in which the two majors had arrived—without approval from their superiors—returned to Camp Columbia with Barquin, Borbonnet, Hart, Pino and Hidalgo still in prison garb.

350

In Oriente, Castro had issued an ultimatum that he was marching on Santiago and would attack at 7:00 P.M. unless Moncada surrendered. A letter from Colonel Jose Rego Rubido, regimental commander at Moncada, was on its way to Castro offering to deliver the fort to him without firing a shot. Castro's columns hastened their advance into Santiago.

The prisoners alighted from the transport at the same ramp from which Batista had left hours before and sped in waiting automobiles toward the headquarters of the 1st Infantry Division. Barquin ordered Borbonnet to take command of that division, with two junior officers who had been liberated at the same time, and sent Major Varela to La Cabana to take command there. Lieutenant Villafana was ordered to take command of the air force.

They walked to the General Staff Headquarters in the darkness across the parade ground, where tanks had been deployed. In the office of the chief of the Joint Staff, Barquin told Cantillo that he had taken the infantry division, the air force and La Cabana fortress, and was himself taking command of the armed forces to end the civil war and deliver the presidency to Urrutia. Cantillo was escorted to his quarters under house arrest.

Barquin asked the rebel commanders to proceed immediately to Havana for a conference, but Fidel Castro would have none of that. Radio appeal on radio appeal was sent out by Barquin to Castro for a short-wave conversation with him, but Castro ignored him completely.

Shortly before one o'clock on the morning of January 2, Castro's triumphant columns of bearded warriors and feminine commandos rode into Santiago and entered the Moncada fortress where Colonel Rego Rubido was waiting. The man who as a rebel on July 26, 1953, tried to storm Moncada with a frontal attack now entered that fortress as a liberator.

The cheering, frenetic populace of embattled Santiago de Cuba, overjoyed that their five and a half years of struggle against Batista had ended in victory, swarmed into the streets to welcome the bearded warrior. The last census showed Santiago with 163,237 inhabitants, and every man, woman and child who could possibly do so ran out to catch a glimpse of Castro and his troops, those legendary but long invisible heroes.

Castro addressed the throng in the plaza. Flanked by Urrutia and by Monsignor Perez Serantes, he began to speak at 1:30 A.M. He designated Urrutia as provisional president—Urrutia's election had been ratified months earlier by the Civilian Revolutionary Front—and declared that, as a tribute to its heroic stand against Batista, Santiago de Cuba would be the provisional capital of the Republic. Urrutia would set up his government there without delay, Castro added. Urrutia then spoke and announced that he had asked Castro to become delegate of the armed forces to the President of the Republic, in other words, commander in chief of the armed forces, directly subordinate to the chief executive. Castro then announced he had appointed Colonel Rego Rubido as chief of staff of the army, knowing that he did not intend to keep him in that post for long. Archbishop Perez Serantes, addressing the crowd, praised Castro and his men for their triumph and prayed for everlasting peace in Cuba.

Castro spent part of January 2 in Santiago and then decided to start a historic overland journey to Havana. He left his brother Raul in Santiago to consolidate the military victory there, designating him military commander of Oriente. His brother Ramon accompanied him as quartermaster, attending to every detail of feeding and supplying the 1,500 men in the victory cavalcade.

Castro had reasons for his triumphal march by highway to Havana. It gave the rebel troops time to consolidate their hold on the military fortresses in the capital. The announcement of the appointment of Colonel Rego Rubido as chief of staff of the army served to assuage many regular army officers all over the country. En route to Havana Castro could personally make certain that the rebel position was fully consolidated in each province, that every fort was in the hands of one of his trusted officers. Also he could address the defeated troops, receive a firsthand report of the situation in each city and town he visited and—this cannot be discounted in the least—receive the personal satisfaction and the stimulation of the hero's welcome accorded to him at every place.

Castro ordered Camilo Cienfuegos and Che Guevara to march on Havana and take Camp Columbia and La Cabana, respectively. The Directorio Revolutionario, led by Faure Chomon and

352

Rolando Cubela, also started from Las Villas, with the objective—one which was not co-ordinated with Castro's—of taking the presidential palace. Troops of the Second National Front of Escambray marched in to assume any mission that might be assigned to them.

When the 26th of July militia appeared on the streets of Havana late in the afternoon of the first and promptly restored order by routing the vandals, the people gained much confidence in the Movement's ability to bring and maintain such order. As soon as the well-trained Castro *barbudos* arrived, there was a notable improvement in public manners, because of their courteous, respectful and sober treatment of civilians and tourists. There was little drunkenness and no braggadocio. Though taverns and liquor stores were closed, those who really wanted liquor managed to get it.

The unconditional surrender demanded by Castro had been accomplished with a minimum of difficulties, but there was still one obstacle to overcome. The Directorio Revolucionario had taken 500 rifles and five machine guns and some ammunition from the ordnance depot at the San Antonio de los Banos air base. It had occupied the presidential palace and had tanks and armored cars deployed on the university campus.

It was in such circumstances that I obtained the first post-victory interview with Fidel in Holguin on the night of January 3, thanks to W. D. Maxwell, editor of the *Chicago Tribune,* who authorized and chartered the plane. John H. Thompson, military editor of the *Tribune,* obtained the aircraft for me in Miami and flew on to Havana to cover the story with Clay Gowran while I went in search of Castro. I found him at Holguin. As we landed there in the Piper Apache, we were greeted by hundreds of *barbudos,* who surrounded our plane smiling and waving.

Castro was at the technological school on the extreme western end of the city. It was the only area that had any electricity; because of the war most of Holguin had been deprived of power for three weeks. Castro was in conference with some of his commanders in the principal's office. It was after eight thirty when I got a chance to interview him. He was surrounded by his commanders, some of whom I had met previously in the hills of Oriente. And, of course, there was Celia Sanchez, silent, attentive, ready to spring into action should he need her fine hand to write his orders.

The bearded officers and soldiers hung on Castro's every word as we reviewed the past, present and some of the future. Every one of his utterances was apparently both gospel and law to them. I bombarded him with questions, some of them very pointed, especially as to whether he harbored any resentment against the United States. In those first hours of victory he was magnanimous and replied that at such a time one should not talk about resentments.

"Look here," he said, referring to my questions about Cuba's relations with the United States, "if I have had to be very cautious about my statements in the past, from now on I am going to have to be even more careful."

Castro's words rang with the unmistakable sincerity and conviction of a man who knew in which direction he was traveling and was determined that no obstacle would prevent him from reaching his destination. He had proved that for almost six successive years.

Castro set himself a grueling schedule. He loved receiving the acclaim of people who were grateful for his leadership on their road to freedom.

At the airport at Holguin was a captured British helicopter. Castro's eyes sparkled and his face broke into a smile like that of a child who has just received a toy that he had always wanted. "There is a helicopter out there," he said, pointing toward the airport, "worth five hundred thousand dollars to me. I won't exchange that for anything or for anybody. It's mine now! It's mine!"

The rebel who had had to climb up and down the steep, jagged slopes of the Sierra Maestra for two years now could leapfrog over all terrain obstacles in a 'copter that he had captured from an army that had surrendered to him.

I pointed out to Castro that newspapers had not appeared in Havana since Thursday afternoon and it was now Saturday night; I suggested that he might want to rectify the obvious discrimination that favored the radio and television stations, which had been allowed to keep on operating. I volunteered to carry back to Havana written authorization from him for the newspapers to resume publication; I would deliver it to the Propaganda Section of the 26th of July Movement for appropriate action.

Castro asked for a pad of paper, which Celia Sanchez furnished, while I handed him my ball-point pen. He wrote the following:

"Because of the fact that the written press constitutes a public service of extraordinary value in guiding the people and keeping them duly informed of happenings, and it being evident, moreover, that the press, as well as the radio and television, is closely collaborating with the Revolutionary Movement, we notify the graphic arts workers, the newspaper guild and all distributors that, beginning tomorrow Sunday at twelve noon, we consider it convenient to the revolutionary service that they facilitate the publication of all the organs of the written press as has been done from the start with radio and television and other public services.

"As for the other sectors of labor, as soon as this General Headquarters receives reports from Major Camilo Cienfuegos that all commands of the air, sea and land have been put unconditionally under his control, as has been ordered, I will communicate with the labor leaders so that they may give the order to end the strike, because then the triumph of the Revolution and the first obedience to the civil power of the Republic will be totally assured."

Castro signed it, reread it and was about to hand it to me when Celia Sanchez said, "Don't you want me to letter it?" Castro handed it to her. She copied it in perfect block letters, then returned her finished product for him to read and sign. I carried it to Havana and delivered it to the Propaganda Section of the 26th of July Movement at rebel command headquarters at four o'clock on Sunday morning.

If there was, in Castro's words, any implication that the press should be kept under wraps, it was dispelled when Major Cienfuegos released the order just at noon that same day with the following statement—which he signed as commander in chief of the forces of land, sea and air of the province of Havana:

"It constitutes for me an extraordinary honor that through me our commander in chief has released all the necessary facilities for Cuban journalism and the workers of this sector to return to their labors of reporting and guiding public opinion in the country, that the same may freely exercise their profession, ending once and for all the odious and humiliating censorship to which the press was subjected during the bloody dictatorship crushed by the triumph of the rebel arms."

Castro's romantic designation of Santiago de Cuba as provisional capital of the Republic was not destined to last long. All the facilities for national administration were in Havana, and the presidential palace was the symbol of government. The occupation of the palace by the Directorio Revolucionario—and the refusal of that force to evacuate and turn it over to troops commanded by Che Guevara—created a tense situation, further complicated by the fact that the Directorio had supplied itself with arms and ammunition from the San Antonio de los Banos air base after victory.

Urrutia flew by presidential plane from Santiago to Camaguey on the morning of January 5 to confer with Castro. They met inside the aircraft to confer privately and then were joined by Guevara, who flew in from Havana. Guevara gave a firsthand report of the military situation. It was decided that Urrutia would continue to Havana to assume the seat of government there and that the Directorio should be persuaded to surrender the palace to him. Along with Castro's instructions, the Argentine medico turned military tactician consented to carry back to Havana a story which I had written for delivery to the press wireless.

While at Camaguey, Castro issued orders to his provincial commanders to begin summary courts-martial and try alleged "war criminals," officers, noncommissioned officers, privates, policemen and civilians accused of having killed unarmed civilians or torturing and killing members of the rebel forces. In accordance with the rebel law issued by Castro on February 11, 1958, he ordered those convicted to be executed by firing squads.

There was no constitution in force in Cuba at the time Castro issued that order. There was a revolutionary government that was trying to gain control of the presidential palace, which was in the hands of another rebel force that had co-operated in the attack on Santa Clara and other cities in Las Villas.

Urrutia had selected two more officers from Castro's staff as ministers. They were Luis Orlando Rodriguez, for interior, and Dr. Humberto Sori Marin, for the ministry of agriculture. Sori

Marin was author of a proposed agrarian reform law. Faustino Perez had already been appointed to a new ministry for the recovery of property illegally acquired, and Dr. Julio Martinez Paez had been named minister of public health.

Urrutia designated Prime Minister Jose Miro Cardona and Foreign Minister Roberto Agramonte to parley with the leaders of the Directorio about evacuation of the palace. They agreed to do so upon Urrutia's arrival there. Accompanying Urrutia as his minister of the presidency (equivalent to the post now held by General Wilton B. Persons at the White House) was Luis Buch. Also with him as his minister of public works was Manuel Ray, alias Campa.

It was not until after Castro's victory that the tragedy that befell four students of the Catholic University of Villanueva became known in all its horrible details. The victims were Jose Ignacio Marti Santa Cruz, twenty-one years old; Ramon Perez Lima, twenty-two; Javier Calvo Formoso, twenty-one, and Julian Martinez Inclan, twenty. The four were members of the Catholic University Group directed by Father Llorente.

They had left Havana at eleven o'clock at night on December 26 for Pinar del Rio, after informing Father Llorente that they planned to make contact with members of the underground there to ascertain how they could help from the capital by shipping needed medicines, clothing and foodstuffs. The students were unarmed and made the trip in two automobiles. They were scheduled to return to Havana on December 31 to see the New Year in with their families. There was no concern felt until they failed to appear.

The first clew as to their fate came from a bar in Bahia Honda where a soldier nicknamed "Piel de Canela" boasted that he had helped to arrest four young men en route to Pinar del Rio from Havana. He said they had been taken to the Laz Pozas army post.

Father Llorente set out in a jeep for Pinar del Rio. He located Piel de Canela to learn more of what had happened. Late one night, the soldier said, he heard what sounded like bees buzzing in the cell where the four young men were and investigated. They were on their knees praying the Rosary in soft voices, their bodies trembling from the beatings and tortures they had suffered.

At three o'clock in the morning of the twenty-eighth, they

were taken by Lieutenant Dupairon to Guajaibon about fifteen miles to the west, where they were tortured again. At five o'clock in the morning, they were hanged. Father Llorente went in search of the bodies and found them in a common grave under four feet of earth.

"Believe me," Father Llorente explained, "it was not only finding the bodies of those four dear boys that filled us with sorrow and astonishment. It was the number of corpses that we discovered as we searched. There were thirty, fifty, eighty, all victims of the inhuman cruelty that was carried out in that zone of Pinar del Rio without the least sentiment of charity."

The remains of the four young men were brought back to Havana for burial. An outdoor funeral Mass was held at which Monsignor Luis Centoz, Apostolic Delegate to Cuba, officiated. The four victims of the last hours of Batista's rule are now known as the Martyrs of Guajaibon.

The people of Cuba were shocked by the reports of more and more mass graves being discovered from one end of the island to the other. One man was more indignant than anyone else. He was Fidel Castro and he was determined that, whatever the consequences, those who had done the killing would pay.

CHAPTER 12

Castro made use of the helicopter on his cross-country victory march. This enabled him to dispatch his escorts and staff members ahead by highway while he spent more time in cities and towns. It also enabled him to bypass detours caused by bridges that had been destroyed or damaged by his troops.

In each city where he halted, no matter what time of the day or the night it was, he delivered a speech and explained the purpose of the revolution and his plans for the future. He talked like a Robin Hood and he never stopped until he had exhausted every point of argument to impress upon the people that everything he had done in the past, and all that he planned to do, was for their benefit and that of Cuba.

In Matanzas, for example, he began to speak at ten o'clock and finished at one-thirty in the morning. Then he held a press conference and after that he was interviewed in the provincial palace by Ed Sullivan, who had flown down from New York especially so he could present Castro on his Sunday night television show. It was ten minutes after two when he began; twenty minutes later he was handed a note that Che Guevara had arrived from Havana to confer with him.

Within hours Castro was to enter Havana, but there was little or no rest for him. Captain Enrique Jimenez, a Dominican exile who had been wounded in the stomach during the Maffo battle and, now recovered, was on Castro's staff, tried without success to end the succession of appointments. Castro just could not, or would not, say no to anyone who wanted to talk to him.

Fidel was driven to Varadero, where he slept two hours; early the next morning he proceeded to Cardenas to pay his respects to the parents of his friend, Jose Antonio Echevarria, who was killed the day of the palace attack. The mother of the student leader was waiting for Castro in the foyer of her home. As he entered solemnly, she burst into tears and hugged him close, and he put his arms around her and comforted her. It was an emotional scene that brought tears to the eyes of witnesses, all close friends of the family. That was his last act before he resumed his ride into Havana.

The road from Matanzas to Havana was filled with people who clamored for a glimpse of Castro. Many were disappointed. He hedgehopped with the helicopter to make up his schedule, for he was expected in Havana at three o'clock. He landed at a point south of El Cotorro, where the large Hatuey Brewery of the Bacardi Company is located. His victory column—with their captured Sherman tanks on trailers, with trucks full of triumphant, sleepless, bearded rebel troops, with busses filled with more such troops, with accompanying tank trucks—was stalled in a traffic jam. Castro boarded a jeep to proceed like a broken-field runner evading tacklers as he made his way through the jam.

Castro was scheduled to have luncheon at the brewery where members of the Bacardi family—the firm that manufactures the rum—were waiting for him. There was a banner across the brewery fence painted and placed there by workers, welcoming Castro and thanking him for their liberation. All along the route to Havana there were banners which read: GRACIAS, FIDEL! (Thank You, Fidel!) Camilo Cienfuegos was already devouring his luncheon at the brewery, having come from Havana to accompany Castro into the capital. There was to be no luncheon for Castro that day, for as the brewery siren with steady, deafening blasts heralded the approach of the liberator, an officer-messenger

360

reached him to report that his son, Fidelito, was waiting for him at a gasoline station north of the brewery.

"Let's go!" Castro ordered, and the jeep sped by the brewery as Cienfuegos and other officers ran out to catch up with him.

"It is the most marvelous thing that I have ever seen or expected to see in my life," Joaquin E. Bacardi, technical director and vice president of Bacardi and Company, told me. "Cuba is now free and I hope it will remain so for many years."

Jose M. Bosch, president and general manager of the Bacardi Company and one of the first and earliest supporters of Castro, had returned from his exile in Mexico, ready to help to reconstruct a Cuba torn by civil war.

Just in front of the gasoline station the willing and eager hands of rebel officers lifted Fidelito into the jeep, and father and son were locked in an embrace. Castro beamed with joy as he continued his triumphal ride with Fidelito beside him, but it was impossible to make any progress through El Cotorro. The entire populace was on the streets, and men, women and children—especially the women and children—wanted to touch him, to shake his hand, to kiss him. The jeep could not move. I was seated on the hood of his second escort car, and as the people would see me they would shout: "There is the American newspaperman!" With broad, friendly smiles, they would wave and make the "V for victory" sign that Winston Churchill, one of the best customers of Cuban cigar manufacturers, had popularized during World War II.

The helicopter circled overhead as the Castro caravan tried to crawl past a church. A priest was in the church tower with two men. A large Cuban flag flew from the tower. Castro signaled the helicopter pilot to descend in a near-by field, and the jeep detoured into a side street. Castro boarded the helicopter with his son and flew to a field in a southern suburb of Havana, where he was met by another rebel jeep and escort and sped toward the capital. Thousands of persons were pouring into the heart of the city from all outlying districts. They came in trucks, in busses, in their own automobiles and on foot. They carried placards, banners, Cuban flags and 26th of July banners. They sang and they cheered and they shouted in choruses.

"Viva Fidel! Viva Fidel! Viva Fidel Castro, our liberator!"

The rest of the rebel army and the unsung heroes and heroines were not forgotten either. There were banners which read:

WELCOME, HEROES OF OUR LIBERTY!
HOMAGE TO THOSE WHO FOUGHT AND DIED FOR OUR FREEDOM!

Delegations from the Partido Socialista Popular (the Communist Party) also were on hand with their placards identifying their affiliation. The Organizacion Autentico decorated lampposts and telegraph posts along the victory route with their placards of welcome and praise for Castro.

Castro's original plan had been to proceed directly to Camp Columbia, invite the public inside and address the nation from there. But this was changed so that he could first call on Urrutia at the palace. Urrutia waited for him at the Plaza of Luyano, and Castro rode with the President the remainder of the distance to the palace while the sirens of the factories and the electric plant screeched the news of his passing.

As Castro entered the palace, the women there—some of them wives of cabinet ministers—shed tears of emotion and joy. Castro addressed the nation from the balcony of the palace. It was a short speech, for he had yet to traverse the entire westward route to Camp Columbia. He announced he would make that march on foot and actually started to do so, but his security officers won out. He climbed aboard a Sherman tank on the Malecon and rode in triumph up 23rd Street where thousands had been waiting for hours to see him.

"I must see him! I've got to see him!" one almost hysterical woman said to me, tears flowing from her eyes. "He has saved us! He has liberated us from a monster and from gangsters and assassins!"

That was not the isolated opinion of a lady filled with emotion at the arrival of Castro. It was a general opinion that thousands of Cubans volunteered without the asking. In all my years of reporting in Latin America never had I seen a similar tribute to one man.

Castro rode into Camp Columbia as a conquering hero, and

the ten-mile journey from the palace took four hours. Bearded John H. Thompson, noted war correspondent of the *Chicago Tribune*, who was in Paris when it was liberated in World War II, compared the welcome accorded to Castro with that historic event. And Thompson's beard both startled and pleased the Cubans.

—— The public had been invited by Castro to join him at Camp Columbia, and they swarmed into that hitherto impenetrable fortress by the thousands, jamming the parade ground. Waiting for him on the speakers' stand were, among others, Prio and Tony Varona. White doves were released from cages and three of them flew directly to the speakers' stand. One rested on Castro's shoulder for the several hours that he talked.

There he was in the most glorious hour of his life. A man who in December 1956, at the age of thirty, had been holed up in the Sierra Maestra with only twelve men; who in April 1958 had only 200 riflemen in his rebel army; who for two months, from June to August of that year, held off fourteen battalions of trained infantry with only 300 troops and then, having augmented his armament to 806 weapons—including bazookas, mortars and machine guns—by capturing them from the enemy, counterattacked and drove the enemy from the foothills of the Sierra Maestra; who had directed the organization of an underground sabotage and propaganda such as Cuba never had witnessed; whose columns invaded the provinces of Camaguey and Las Villas and then with rebel groups and columns in other provinces swarmed over the countryside and defeated a standing army of 30,000 men; who forced out a tyrant during whose tenure civil rights were suspended for 779 days, a tyrant with extraordinary powers, including the law of the jungle by which he could authorize the murder of any opponent of the regime, employed during part of that period; and who demanded and obtained the unconditional surrender of the enemy's armed forces—this man was now the undisputed military chieftain of the land. He was the hero of Cuba and had captured the enthusiastic imagination of the entire Western Hemisphere.

That enthusiasm was to diminish in many places as soon as the executions of the "war criminals" began. The speed with which Castro began to mete out rebel justice shocked almost everyone except the people of Cuba. Castro had been telling them for months that the torturers and killers and the informers, who were responsible for the deaths of those they denounced, would be executed as quickly as possible after victory. He had issued the rebel law of February 11, 1958, precisely to provide for that action.

As Castro proceeded overland from Santiago de Cuba on his triumphal ride, he heard the clamor of mothers, fathers, sisters and other relatives for the promised "revolutionary justice" and speedy trials of those officers, noncommissioned officers and civilians who had torn their sons or brothers or other kin from their arms inside their homes, only to leave their mutilated, bullet-riddled or hanging bodies to be found the next day or a few days later in the woods or the fields and even on the streets of their cities and towns. He assured them that he would expedite the justice which he had promised and at Camaguey issued the appropriate orders to all commands.

Bohemia was preparing its "Edition of Liberty," a record-breaking 1,000,000 copies with a painting of Castro on the cover and a caption which read: "Honor and Glory to the National Hero." In it was an article entitled: "Disgrace for North America. Ambassador Smith: Servant of the Despot." There were two photographs especially selected by Editor Quevedo accompanied by descriptive captions. The caption for a picture of Smith laughing read:

"Always laughing out loud over the drama of Cuba, Ambassador Earl E. T. Smith lent valuable services to the dictatorship, disfiguring the realities of the tragedy in order to disorient the State Department. Smith laughed and partied while all of Cuba was drowned in blood and in horror. Now that we are in hours of victory, he should go and never return."

The other picture showed Smith, who is an excellent shot, on the skeet range holding a rifle.

On Saturday, January 10, Smith, who had apparently learned of the *Bohemia* article, cabled his resignation to the State Department and urged that President Eisenhower accept it before nightfall. Smith's wish was granted, and the White House announced his resignation late that afternoon. *Bohemia* appeared on the streets of Havana the next Monday.

There was still no constitution in force and the rebels knew no other form of justice but that of the kangaroo courts which they hurriedly organized from among their men and women officers. The first summary courts-martial were held in the same courthouse at Santiago de Cuba where the Moncada attackers were tried, and the trials were open to the public. Seventy-one officers, soldiers, police and members of Senator Rolando Masferrer's private army were tried and sentenced to death. The rebels dug a trench in a field outside the city and the condemned faced the firing squad in pairs, with the exception of one officer whose execution was delayed to enable a television cameraman to film it. The condemned officer gave the order to fire and his body fell into the trench where the other seventy had fallen. A bulldozer pushed the dirt into it and left an identifying mound. Castro authorized that the film be made available to a television network in the United States. The film was given to CBS without charge, and it was the film scoop of the day. The last officer to be executed admitted in court that he had killed eighteen young men. Those were not deaths in combat. They occurred in jail or in the fields.

The reaction to the executions produced a storm of criticism from Canada to Argentina. The Argentine congress even appealed for a halt. Castro read about the criticism in the United States press and the statements by several senators and congressmen.

"If it is public trials they want," he told me, "I'll give them one like they never saw before! I am going to order the trial of Major Jesus Sosa Blanco to be held in the Parque Central!"

Castro had become the emotional and spiritual hero of Cuba. He was revered, idolized and admired. Wherever he went crowds followed. Men, women and children begged for a glimpse of him. They wanted to see him, to touch him.

He had suddenly emerged from the guerrilla territory of the Sierra Maestra, where the only opportunity he had to talk to the public was through a microphone of Radio Rebelde hidden in a cave, to the plazas and public buildings of the cities. He had acquired both a national and international audience, and each was eagerly attentive to his every word.

Castro made the most of it at the time, but perhaps not the best. His mingling with the public stimulated and invigorated him. It was like that old professional politician, former President Harry S. Truman, out on the hustings again, lashing at the opposition and his critics with a biting tongue.

Castro could not understand the avalanche of criticism that had rolled off the presses against him because of the executions. He firmly believed he was in the right. Each accused, he pointed out, was being tried and was allowed to receive the minister of his faith before his execution.

"Batista never gave any of the people a trial; he just had them killed, and there were no protests or criticism like this," Castro would say. "These men are murderers, assassins. We are not executing innocent people or political opponents. We are executing murderers, and they deserve to be shot."

It was inevitable that Castro would react violently to the criticism from the United States. He undoubtedly felt, and somewhat mistakenly, that the State Department was behind the "campaign" against him and the revolution. Castro's speeches those days were full of fire and brimstone and his target was the United States. He repeatedly criticized the fact that United States Military Missions had trained Batista's army, navy and air force and that our government had equipped Batista with tanks, guns, planes and bombs with which Cubans were killed. The facts were true, but the manner of presentation by Castro in a tone interpreted by the Cuban people as one of righteous indignation lent itself to kindle flames of anti-American resentment.

Castro also mistakenly thought that he needed to employ such tactics to keep the Cuban people united behind his policy. He had apparently underestimated the irrefutable fact that the Cuban people were solidly behind him. He had forgotten that he was no longer a guerrilla warrior and did not realize that he had acquired the stature of a world-wide celebrity.

Although Castro could not conceal his indignation, on formal occasions the United States was no longer a target of his remarks.

Just after he had read in a United States national magazine an implied threat that "intervention is not a thing of the past," he left his suite in the Havana-Hilton to keep an appointment. Fidel has a habit of thinking out loud, and as he walked through the lobby, his group surrounding him as usual, he exploded with indignation: "If there should be intervention, 200,000 Gringos will be killed." The story hit the headlines around the world.

Castro tried to explain the remark at a luncheon at the Rotary Club, where President Urrutia and the Rotarians waited from one o'clock until almost four o'clock for him to appear; before the television cameras and radio microphones he admitted that he had not been misquoted. However, he was quick to add, he had not intended it as a threat, nor had he intended, he said, to be insolent. He repeated that every Cuban would bear arms to repel any intervention, and in that he was telling no more than the bald truth. Armed intervention is to the Latin American what a matador's cape is to a bull.

Castro's blistering declaration was aimed not only at critics abroad but also at people at home. At a luncheon given for him by the Lions Club, he spoke for three hours before the television cameras, most of the time answering questions. At one point he said:

"This afternoon you give me this luncheon here at the Lions Club. Here you also gave luncheons to those who enriched themselves through malfeasance during the dictatorship. You received them with open arms and you gave luncheons to them, too, when you knew who they were and what they did."

Castro did not spare his audiences when he felt they deserved his criticism. He commented: "Who knows how many Batistianos have shaken my hand in the last few days!"

The country was as one in acclaiming Castro. How often in the history of Latin America has a man of thirty-two so captivated a people as has Castro? The euphoria seemed unanimous and nonpartisan. And Castro enjoyed every minute of it. So much so that he worked virtually around the clock so that nobody would be deprived of an opportunity to talk to him. He had been so accustomed in the Sierra Maestra to sleep in the daytime and fight at night that it was most difficult for him to readjust himself to the usual schedule. Therefore, he seldom retired before six o'clock in the morning and only infrequently slept more than three hours.

Castro moved into a suite in the Havana-Hilton Hotel, where several hundred *barbudos* were already billeted. *Barbudos* were also billeted in other hotels. There were no facilities at army posts for them at the time, as the troops of Batista's army were still occupying barracks and quarters. The *barbudos* behaved very well, the management reported.

Castro's voracious appetite is well known but while at the Havana-Hilton, when he could break away from the hundreds of people who wished to see him, he would venture into the kitchen to pick and taste food. An average noonday meal for Castro might—when he is somewhat relaxed—consist of caviar on crackers, cold cuts, asparagus soup, *arroz con pollo* (chicken with rice), chow mein, caramel custard, fruit and then coffee. His favorite beverages are Coca-Cola and the "Malta" of the Hatuey Brewery. Brandy is the only liquor he drinks and then only when he has to talk a lot. He drinks plenty of the strong black Cuban coffee and enjoys chilled French pastry. Celia Sanchez sees that he has multivitamins to build up his resistance.

"Why don't you get more sleep?" I asked him one day as it became apparent he was going to be bedded by influenza. "Sleep is a necessary medicine."

"My medicine is the people," he answered. "I thrive on seeing and talking to the people."

Even his self-prescribed medicine failed to save him from a high fever and a day and a half in bed with influenza. His powers of recovery are remarkable; against the doctor's orders, he left his bed to resume his heavy schedule of activities.

The cabinet duplicated Castro's schedule and worked virtually around the clock. The ministers would meet at night and continue their sessions until dawn.

Julio Lobo, the sugar baron of Cuba who owns fourteen of the country's plantations and mills, compared Castro's fete after the rout of Batista with Francisco Pizarro's conquest of Peru.

When I mentioned this to Castro, he displayed another of his traits with this retort: "Yes, but there was one difference. Pizarro started out with twelve men but returned for more."

368

Castro, however, did not have to return for more. He had the manpower to draw from. Now, when he found himself cornered by public opinion around the world because of the executions, he decided to counterattack. He invited newspapermen from the United States and Latin America to Cuba on an all-expenses-paid junket to witness the trials and to meet with him at a press conference. He ordered the trial of Sosa Blanco to be held, not in the Parque Central as he had planned, but in the five-million-dollar Sports Palace on the Rancho Boyeros highway, where 17,000 people could be spectators.

Castro visited Pinar del Rio to complete his island-wide victory tour. In the capital of the westernmost province the 40,000 inhabitants crowded the streets from noon to wait for him. They had expected him at three o'clock in the afternoon, but at cities and towns enroute the people clamored for him to speak to them and he obliged. He reached the speaker's stand at Pinar del Rio at midnight, began to talk and finished at two o'clock in the morning.

Castro called for a rally on January 21 to support his stand on the summary courts-martial and executions. The CTC declared a holiday to allow the people to attend the rally.

"We will show them that public opinion is behind us and that we are doing the right thing!" Castro said. "There will be one million people at the presidential palace that day."

There were nearly one million. There was no check-off by the labor unions to compel the workers to be present, as Peron required in Argentina or as Batista had done. The workers marched voluntarily. There were at least 500,000 persons in front of the palace and thousands more in the plaza and adjacent streets.

Castro got his mandate from the people to proceed with the executions. He also warned Cuba that if his enemies killed him there were other leaders, some more radical, to replace him. He said he would recommend that in that circumstance his brother Raul be designated deputy chief of the 26th of July Movement to replace him. "Not because he is my brother—we are against nepotism—but because he has the personal qualifications of a leader." Raul Castro is considered by many to be more radical than his brother Fidel.

Castro had some critical words for American companies, especially the Cuban Telephone Company, and spoke in passing about relations with the United States. That night at a reception for the diplomatic corps, the American chargé d'affaires, Daniel M. Braddock, was introduced to Castro. Braddock looked up at the rebel chieftain through his glasses, stuck his chin out and said: "I don't know whether your speech this afternoon was intended to be critical of us but I would like you to know that my government wishes to have the best of relations with you and with the Cuban government. We are sincere about it and we want to be able to help in any way." Castro replied that he was glad to hear so.

Castro's press conference for "Operation Truth" broke all world records. It lasted five hours, and Castro answered every question that was put to him, employing both Spanish and English. His English is good but heavily accented. His Spanish is eloquent.

Castro emerged from the press conference with high esteem, but the performance that followed in the Sports Palace, which enabled Sosa Blanco to say that he felt as if he had been in the Coliseum when the Christians were tossed to the lions, shocked many sympathetic Cubans who watched the trial on their television sets. It will be recalled that in one of his reports from the Sierra Maestra Castro had mentioned the crimes committed by Sosa Blanco. To try to prove to public opinion throughout the world that Sosa Blanco was a criminal, Castro ordered witnesses brought to Havana from Oriente to testify. The witnesses, all from mountain villages, often had to be prompted by the prosecution and by the court. There was no doubt that Sosa Blanco would be convicted, but the reaction against the procedures was so great that Castro ordered a new trial after the defense counsel, Captain Aristides da Costa—who had become famous overnight because of his brilliant performance in behalf of the accused—appealed.

Castro was invited to Venezuela by Rear-Admiral Wolfgang Larrazabal, who had been president of the junta and was the defeated presidential candidate, but he was reluctant to accept. The Venezuelans wanted him there on January 23, the first anniversary of their overthrow of Dictator Marcos Perez Jimenez. At the moment the summary revolutionary court-martial announced its conviction of Sosa Blanco, Castro left for Caracas and did not return in time for his brother Raul's wedding at Santiago de Cuba on January 26. Raul Castro and Vilma Espin were married in a civil ceremony at the Rancho Club, as the bride does not profess any religion.

Two events gave a semblance of revolutionary legality to the executions. The Fifth Criminal Chamber of the Supreme Court, reorganized by the government, denied a petition for a writ of habeas corpus in behalf of a prisoner held at the La Cabana fortress with this unanimous opinion:

"There is a state of war in Cuba that is a product of a triumphant revolution. The revolution is the source of law. The revolution therefore has the right to detain the prisoner."

The first week in February the cabinet, exercising legislative functions, enacted the Fundamental Law to replace the Constitution of 1940, and the following article was written into it:

"Article 25—There will be no death penalty. Excepted are the cases of the members of the armed forces, of the repressive corps of the tyranny, of the auxiliary groups organized by it, of the armed groups privately organized to defend it and of the informers for crimes committed in pro of the installation or defense of the tyranny overthrown December 31, 1958. Also excepted are persons guilty of treason or of subversion of the institutional order or of espionage in favor of the enemy in time of war against a foreign nation."

The Fundamental Law retained the paragraph in Article 40 which Castro used to justify his right to rebel against Batista.

Sosa Blanco was given his new trial. Major Humberto Sori Marin, president of the court, announced the revocation of the sentence; all previous testimony would stand on the record. New and conclusive evidence was introduced at the trial held in the Superior War Tribunal at Liberty City, Castro's new name for Camp Columbia. The proceedings were not televised but were broadcast over the radio and photographers were allowed in the courtroom. Sosa Blanco was convicted, another appeal was quickly rejected and he was executed a few hours later.

"I forgive you, and I hope you will forgive me, too," he said to the firing squad just before he fell.

Castro might have had absolutely no trouble at all with world opinion about the executions if during the first three days the rebel troops had mowed down a thousand suspected torturers, killers and informers without summary courts-martial, without appeals, without the right of comfort from the ministers of their faith. Then, perhaps, such a deed might have been considered as an expected reaction in the hours of immediate victory. But if that had been done, then many innocent men might have been included, as well as those who would receive jail terms and obtain their liberty whenever a general amnesty would be decreed. Castro thought he was being scrupulous by ordering trials even in drumhead courts.

"There were three events in my life," he said, "where I acted selflessly and in good faith and yet was the victim of wrong interpretation of my action. The first was in the frustrated invasion of the Dominican Republic in 1947, the next was the Bogotazo and the third is the executions."

He explained: "I criticized American reaction to our war crimes trials and the failure of Americans to understand the reasons for the executions because what do Americans know about tyrants? What do Americans know about censorship, about a tyrant's atrocities, except in the novels and movies? If you want to know about tyranny go to Santo Domingo—it is appalling."

Castro argued that he had a better case in his war-crimes trial stand than the Allied Powers had at Nuremberg. His position is that he enacted his war-crimes trial law before his war ended, whereas the Allied Powers acted to do so after the war.

He appeared twice on the "Meet the Press" program of station CMQ and explained his plans and hopes for Cuba. He broke a record by keeping all of Cuba awake from 10:45 P.M. to 2:30 A.M. on one of those programs.

When Batista fled, the 26th of July Movement underground had to recover quickly from its surprise and mobilize its militia and labor sections to go into action. But not the Communists. They emerged from within the labor unions with speed and efficiency, for some of their labor leaders had been playing the game with Batista all along. The 26th of July labor chieftains, who were going to become the real leaders, were wearing beards and were with Castro in Oriente.

372

The revolution against Batista was made to order for the Communists after the April 9 general strike fiasco in Havana. The Communists knew by then that Castro enjoyed nation-wide support and they jumped on the bandwagon. They ordered their partisans to enlist in the rebel army and, as Raul Castro said in a speech, "Nobody was asked what his religion was or what his creed might be or what was the color of his skin."

They tried to obtain recognition from the Civilian Revolutionary Front and acceptance as a part of it and were unanimously rejected. They sent one of their leaders, Carlos Rafael Rodriguez, to the Sierra Maestra to await the arrival of the members of that front to meet with Castro, as was stipulated in the last paragraph of the unity pact signed at Caracas. The meeting was never held, but Rodriguez remained in the Sierra Maestra from the end of July until victory.

Castro has repeatedly and categorically stated: "I am not a Communist." Raul Castro has said that if he were a Communist he would belong to that party and not to the 26th of July Movement. There are those who entertain misgivings about one of Castro's most trusted men, Che Guevara, because Communists claim they have found in the Argentine medico a friend, because of some officers under his command and because he made public statements in the early days of victory that were derogatory to the FBI and advocated the burning of all security files. In those files were the names of Cubans accused of being Communists, although many may not have been. Other Cubans fear infiltration of Communists in the officers' corps and ranks of the new rebel army.

General Alberto Bayo (promoted after the Cuban revolution by the Spanish government in exile, together with other of his compatriots) discounts all such misgivings. He asserts that he had not found any Communists among the men he trained for Castro, and that includes Guevara. Bayo points out that the political ideology he encountered is leftist but not Communist. Guevara could be described as a leftist, not anti-Communist.

The Communists would like to capture Fidel Castro but he has shown that nobody will be able to capture him. They won't be able to capture him because the people of Cuba will not stomach Communism and because they recall that the Communists made their greatest gains under Batista. Two leaders of the Communist Party were ministers without portfolio in Batista's government from 1940 to 1944; other leaders enjoyed safe conducts from him in recent years.

The people of Cuba know that dictatorships are the breeding ground of Communism and that while the Communists profess to be champions of democracy their overlords in the Kremlin order the massacre of the freedom fighters in Hungary and elsewhere.

The Fundamental Law reduced the eligibility age for candidates for the presidency from thirty-five to thirty. This will allow Castro to be a candidate in the elections which are scheduled approximately for January 1961. The same law also granted native-born citizenship to Guevara, for he is the only one who comes under this subsection of Article 12:

". . . the foreigners who shall have served in the fight against the tyranny overthrown December 31, 1958, in the ranks of the rebel army during two or more years, and who shall have held the rank of major during one year at least, provided they fulfill those conditions in the manner in which the Law disposes."

Other foreigners who do not fulfill the above requirements but were officers in the rebel army at any time are granted naturalized citizenship. Guevara is thus eligible to hold any office in the land.

The anomalous situation of the existence of two governments, one in the palace and the other in the Havana-Hilton where Castro lived, had to be cleared up. Castro was making policy pronouncements which conflicted with decisions, or contemplated action, of the government. The government had banned all gambling; and Castro announced he favored restoring it for the four large hotels and the two large Cuban night clubs. The government was opposed to the granting of safe conducts to Batistianos who had taken refuge in embassies, and Castro thought they should be given.

As people crowded around him to petition for prompt action on behalf of their problems, Castro told them: "I am not the government. I am not God! I cannot resolve all problems. They will be resolved but it takes time."

On the evening of February 12 Castro visited President Urrutia, who was abed in his palace apartment with chicken pox, and they had a long talk. The next morning Dr. Jose Miro Cardona submitted his resignation along with those of the entire cabinet, including that of Luis Buch.

Miro Cardona had resigned January 17, but his resignation had not been accepted; this time it was definite. Referring to the post of prime minister, Miro wrote: "The Fundamental Law profiles more neatly the characteristics of the semi-parliamentary regime than is provided for in the Constitution of 1940 when it grants to the post the powers of a true chief of government which, in my judgment, corresponds to those assumed by Dr. Fidel Castro, who, because of his historic hierarchy, is the chief of the Revolution."

That night Castro returned to the palace to confer with Urrutia, accepted the post as recommended by Miro, met with the cabinet, outlined a twenty-point program and then retired to plan for his swearing-in ceremony on February 16.

The Fidel Castro of 1947 displayed the fire and the spirit that was to make him the inspirational leader of Cuba a decade later. And just as in the month of February 1959, the Fidel Castro of 1947 considered himself a revolutionary and conveyed an impression that he knew where he wanted to go but always managed to contradict himself en route. His contradictions, it will have been noted, in no way conflicted with his ultimate goals. His program for Cuba in 1959 differed hardly at all from that which he had dreamed of in 1947 and in 1953 at Moncada.

Continually, Castro had denied any desire for high office or power in the provisional government. He reiterated his denial in statement after statement and in speech after speech over Radio Rebelde while in the Sierra Maestra. Yet, as leader of the 26th of July Movement, he was steadily acquiring power and prestige, which he never tried to abuse, and in the end circumstances resulting from his dramatic victory forced him to become Premier.

Castro's twenty-point program included agrarian reform, protective tariffs, industrialization to furnish 200,000 jobs the first year and another 200,000 in the second year, a low-cost housing program, salary increases, the reduction of salaries of ministers, a solution to the casino problem, reduction of rents, reduction of public service rates, a new metropolitan area for the capital, creation of the merchant marine and support of the Gran Colombian Fleet, promotion of a national motion-picture industry, creation of an undersecretary of state for Latin-American affairs, end of all war crimes trials in fifteen days, a campaign to consume national products, a campaign against traffic accidents, a campaign to buy bonds of the Savings and Housing Institute and a World Fair for Cuba.

Castro does not expect all this to be accomplished overnight although he would like to hope it could be. The ministers' salaries were cut to $500 a month at his first cabinet meeting and their monthly personal expenses were reduced. The gambling casinos were allowed to reopen but minus the slot machines, which have been impounded by the ministry of interior. The agrarian reform is under way, and Castro distributed government-owned land to peasants in Oriente and Pinar del Rio, the latter consisting of tobacco farms. *Bohemia* sponsored a popular subscription campaign to help finance the agrarian reform program, and Castro contributed his February salary to it. Electricity rates were reduced by the cabinet in the provinces, and a reduction of telephone rates for the entire country and of electricity rates for Havana was being considered by the cabinet as this was written. The cabinet voted to begin to pay the troops of the rebel army as of February 1.

Many questions have been asked about Castro, and here are some of those questions with my answers:

Q. Is Castro a sincere idealist or an opportunist?

A. He is a sincere idealist who never overlooks an opportunity. His goals are political, moral and social revolution and election to the presidency by popular suffrage. Political in the sense that he hopes by the measures of punishment taken that never again will anyone—once it is restored—attempt to destroy constitutional government in Cuba. Moral because he hopes to end all graft and corruption. Many of the contradictions between his pronouncements and his actions are the rather unavoidable conflict between the generalities of an idealist (which operate in a simple and untroubled atmosphere of abstraction), and a revolutionary movement inspired by dedication and enthusiasm to ideals which suddenly finds itself catapulted into the vortex of the most complete collapse of an enemy armed force in contemporary Latin-American history.

Q. How can Castro justify the execution of officers of Batista's

376

army, who were only following instructions? Isn't this the first time that a successful revolutionist has executed the losers in Latin America?

A. We return to the Nuremberg trial defense arguments again to answer the first part of that question. Some of the army officers may have been following instructions, others killed to try to ingratiate themselves with Batista and others killed because they were homicidal maniacs. This is not the first time that a successful revolutionist has executed the losers in Latin America. A more recent example is that of Argentina in June 1956 when 42 army officers who led a Peronist counter-revolution were summarily executed by firing squads. It will be recalled that there were no bleeding hearts then.

However, revolutionary justice is always one-sided and the Cuba of Castro was no exception. He had urged people not to take justice into their own hands when Batista fled. He had assured them that each "war criminal" would be tried by rebel courts. This was done, but in some cases the people overran the courtrooms, often driven by a lust and a clamor for blood that was equivalent to the taking of justice into their own hands. A criterion was established that if the "war criminals" were convicted the rebel judge was honest and fair. If the accused were acquitted the court must have been in error. One such notable case was the trial of 22 pilots and 22 ground crew members who were acquitted by a rebel court presided over by Captain Felix Pena, a hero of the fighting in Oriente. The flyers had been charged with genocide because they had bombed cities and towns in that province. It will be recalled that Castro had protested that he was denied a fair trial after the Moncada attack. Historians will very likely make a most critical study and analysis of the procedures employed in those trials.

Q. Is there a technical reason (age or otherwise) why Castro is not now President of the Republic?

A. The age factor has been overcome by the Fundamental Law. The technical reason is Castro himself. As he says, elections now would be unfair because he would be swept into office. He does not want the presidency except through popular suffrage (although there are those who would like to push him into it for reasons of adulation and personal gain); and he hopes to organize the 26th of July Movement into a strong political party.

"Elections now would reflect interest on my part," Castro says. "We would be the overwhelming majority party at this stage. It is in the best interests of the nation, therefore, if elections are held when the political parties are fully developed and their programs are clearly defined."

Q. Is Castro strong enough to see the revolution through to a creative end?

A. Yes. He has already undertaken some of the creative projects for the welfare of the people. He is impatient to accomplish his objectives as quickly as possible, but he realizes that there must be sound planning, preparation and financing of each. There might be impetuous action in some cases, and in others he might be pushed too quickly toward an objective and stumble on the way, but his powers of recuperation are great.

Q. Is Castro unfriendly to the United States?

A. No. He has said: "We want to be friends of the United States, but we are a sovereign nation. We have historically been victims of odorous interventions of the United States in our country. There always was in the early years a movement for annexation current in the United States. We have nothing against the United States, and we do not wish to see our sugar quota jeopardized in any way because that is our economic life blood."

With regard to the U. S. Military Missions, Castro said: "That mission was training the soldiers that we fought against for two years. Do you think we could accept training from such a mission?"

Castro has also said that if there had not been United States intervention in the War of Independence the Cubans would have won their independence anyway. That is undoubtedly true, but he overlooks the facts that it would have taken much longer and that it was the United States fleet that bottled up the Spanish vessels of war in the bay at Santiago de Cuba while Admiral Dewey contained the remainder of the fleet in the Philippines. American lives and blood were selflessly and gallantly spilled on the battlefields of Cuba and at San Juan Hill so that the citizens of the island could enjoy the freedoms which Fidel Castro led them to reconquer. If the diplomatic and political aftermath was a

378

mistaken policy, that was ultimately rectified when the Platt Amendment, which had allowed our government to intervene in Cuba, was abolished in 1934.

There are diplomatic and military lessons to learn from the recent civil war in Cuba. A policy of winning governments and losing people must definitely be discarded if we are going to win and maintain the sincere friendship of the people of Latin America. We are looked upon as the champions of freedom, freedom of the people, by the people and for the people, and our message in that regard should be transmitted to the peoples of the Americas.

The retention of the Military Missions in Cuba was a serious mistake, compounded by the fact that there was a proviso in the agreement that permitted their immediate withdrawal in the event of a civil war. Yet it was stated that their continued presence "was necessary for hemisphere defense." In February 1959 the Missions were withdrawn at the request of the Cuban government because Castro felt that officers who trained an army he had defeated could not teach him anything about warfare in his country.

The Central Intelligence Agency, I understand, reported the steady and inevitable collapse of the Batista regime and the indignation over the retention of the Military Missions. Did the other government agencies who were responsible for co-ordinating policy regarding Cuba make adequate and sensible use of this evaluated intelligence? If not, why not?

And there were other members of the embassy staff in Havana who did not spend all their after-office time at useless cooky-pushing cocktail parties but had their ears to the ground and developed friendships with the man in the street, the student and the rebel. Earl Williamson was one and he is now in Washington, and so was Ignacio Carranza, now on duty in Guatemala. The Cuban people are grateful for their understanding and objective approach to their problems, and their discreet inquiries which helped save the lives of political prisoners.

No ambassador should be sent to any post unless he can speak the language of the country. A new look in relations with Cuba began with the arrival of Ambassador Philip W. Bonsal in

Havana. He has a long Cuban background, for his late father, Stephen Bonsal, was a correspondent in the War for Independence.

Q. Will U.S. companies in Cuba be persecuted or nationalized?

A. Not if they have not been involved in any dealings that included unethical business practices that favored the henchmen of the Batista administration. Castro has said that foreign firms will be required to leave all of their profits in Cuba. Lands owned by some U.S. firms might be subdivided in the agrarian reform program with prior indemnification by the government.

An economic lesson that American corporations should learn from the Cuban revolution is that some American businessmen cause resentment against the United States by praising dictators in print and in public speeches. They express their delight to do business with the dictators and, at times, seem to condone the absence of civil rights. This type of American presents to the Latin American the most reprehensible feature of our export economy. Only by assuming a most correct attitude—and by not fawning over the dictator or offering to agree to the payment of bribes or be a party to shady deals and the "promise of a bite"— will the American businessman be able to convince our Latin neighbors that he is not performing a disservice to the principles for which we stand before the free world. Otherwise, he invites unfortunate and inevitable reprisals against himself and his corporation and stimulates resentment against our country and our government.

Q. Will Fidel Castro become a dictator?

A. Not if he can help it, although the existence of a revolutionary *de facto* government without the checks and balances of representative, elected government, including a congress and a senate, lends itself to dictatorial measures. As Prime Minister, Castro enjoys powers similar to those of General Charles De-Gaulle before the Fourth Republic. There are those who would like to encourage him to become a dictator. He did not fight the five-year war against Batista to don the cloak of a tyrant, for he well knows that many of the same people who fought so hard with him in the Sierra Maestra and in the cities, towns and villages in the underground, would be the first to turn on him and demand that he go. He is a fervent fan of public opinion surveys and has reiterated that as soon as his support drops to fifty percent or lower he will step out of the picture.

"Do you think the best army in the world can defend a dictatorship in Cuba if it is opposed by the people?" Castro asks.

Dr. Jose Miro Cardona, now out of the cabinet and back at his law practice, says emphatically that Castro will never become a dictator.

"He is an advocate of the doctrine of Jose Marti," Miro says. "That is the doctrine of democracy, freedom, love of fellow man, welfare of the people and Cuban nationalism. He will never become a dictator."

Rufo Lopez Fresquet, minister of treasury, who was one of the most active leaders in the Civic Resistance Movement in Havana, emits an emphatic "No!" when asked if he thinks Castro will ever become a dictator.

Castro has a deep reverence for civilian, representative, constitutional government. Yet he became exasperated with the political parties and even his own Ortodoxo Party when they vacillated in the fight against Batista. He became impatient with the civic institutions when they failed to elect a provisional president, as he had advocated in the manifesto of the Sierra. He repudiated the Council of Liberation because they wanted a voice in the selection of a coalition cabinet in Miami in December 1957 and announced that he had chosen Dr. Manuel Urrutia to be provisional president on the fall of Batista. He agreed to, and led the list of signatories of, the Civilian Revolutionary Front on July 20, 1958. He said in his interview with me in Holguin that he had to be more careful than ever about his future statements and then blew that caution to the four winds after criticism began to rankle him.

Those were all actions of a guerrilla, of a man who fought all night, was hunted by a dictator's army and air force, and on whose shoulders was the responsibility for the direction of the vast organization that was fighting in one way or another throughout the country and abroad.

He had not yet divested himself entirely of the guerrilla's methods and this can be attributed to the pressure of his responsibilities and work and the lack of sufficient sleep which increases his tensions. Under such conditions he is swayed by impulsive decisions which require rectification because when the problems were originally presented to him all the facts were not made available. But he does possess the qualities of willingness to rectify when he might make mistakes as a result of those impulses.

He has yet to organize his working and sleeping hours so that he can operate more efficiently from an office instead of from the improvised headquarters at his residence at Sierra Cojimar. He said he plans to effect such a reorganization whereby he will work from noon until midnight and clear up some work at home in the mornings.

He was offered $25,000 for his beard by an industrialist but said he won't sell.

"We will not shave until the revolution is a reality," he said. "If the soldiers of the tyranny could not cut off our beards and mustaches, neither will they be shaved by the intriguers of the Fatherland."

Now he is no longer a guerrilla, and he has the enormous responsibility of winning the peace. As the euphoria that followed victory begins to wear off and people examine the deeds of the revolutionary government with a more critical eye, there is bound to be more outspoken criticism. One danger lies in the possibility that those who wish to force Castro into excesses might try to inflame him against any criticism, even though that criticism might be intended as constructive. Critics then might be smeared as making "anti-Cuban and anti-patriotic" statements; fear and intimidation, weapons of dictators, their adulators and of the Communists, would then replace the subsidies which most of the press had enjoyed under Batista and which the revolutionary government abolished in the third decree it issued.

In his defense of the Moncada attack Castro outlined five basic laws that he intended to enact for the welfare of the people of Cuba, and those are incorporated in his program of government. He has never varied from them just as he has not varied from his desire to see Latin America rid of dictators, especially Trujillo. He has lent the moral support of revolutionary Cuba to exiles from the Dominican Republic, Haiti and Nicaragua. The air waves of the Caribbean are filled nightly with psychological warfare broadcasts against those three countries by exiles in Havana. Castro has offered to grant recognition to any insurrectionist group that gets a foothold in the hills of any of those countries, though his domestic problems and diplomatic complications might prevent him from furnishing active armed aid to those expeditionaries.

On the other hand, Trujillo and the Somozas can be expected to take every countermeasure within their capabilities to try to frustrate the planned revolutions. The same is true of Duvalier in Haiti. As Castro himself has often forecast, his victory has sounded the death knell for dictators in Latin America. Can a man who is so imbued with such a missionary zeal to see others free degenerate into a dictator himself?

On August 21, 1958, he said from the Sierra Maestra:

"There is a revolution because there is tyranny. There is a revolution because there is injustice. There is and there will be a revolution as long as there is a shadow of a threat against our rights and our freedom."

If he succeeds in ensuring the consolidation and preservation of those cherished rights to freedom for which millions of Cubans rallied to his cause; if he succeeds in translating into reality and practices the tolerance, justice and the respect for the Constitution and the law which he advocated in his brilliant defense after the Moncada attack and reiterated during his exile in Mexico and throughout the epic of the Sierra Maestra, then history surely will absolve him.

Havana, March 7, 1959

ACKNOWLEDGMENTS

It is impossible to record the names of all the people to whom I am indebted for having been able to accomplish the task of writing this book in twenty days. Many of them appear as characters in the story, and to them I am most grateful. Howard W. Sams, Chairman of the Board, The Bobbs-Merrill Company, Inc., is the man who made this book possible, directed its production and provided me with most helpful stimulation as the writing progressed. W. D. Maxwell, editor, the *Chicago Tribune,* approved the request from Bobbs-Merrill, made through S. I. Neiman of Chicago, for me to write this book. To those gentlemen go my sincere thanks for their confidence.

Mention must be made of Dr. Fidel Castro, who furnished not only valuable information but also the frontispiece letter; Major Raul Castro and his wife Vilma Espin, whom I interviewed in the hills of Oriente as well as in Santiago de Cuba; Ramon Castro; Captain Jesus Yanes Pelletier, aide-de-camp to Fidel Castro; Faustino Perez; Manuel Ray; Haydee Santamaria Hart; Armando Hart; Justo Carrillo; Felipe Pazos; Jorge Quintana; Rufo Lopez Fresquet; Drs. Luis and Hector; Drs. Antonio and Angel Maria Santos Buch; Señor and Señora Jose Ferrer; Señor and Señora Ignacio Mendoza; Dr. Raul de Velasco; Manuel Antonio de Varona; Drs. Luis Botifoll, Leopoldo Hernandez and Carlos M. Rubiera; Carlos Castaneda; General Alberto Bayo; Jesus Montane and his wife Melba Hernandez; Candido de la Torre; Angel Ogawa; Ronald C. Levy; Humberto Medrano; and Ulises Carbo.

Special mention must be made of Dr. Miguel Angel Quevedo, editor and publisher of *Bohemia,* who placed at my disposal his files and all but one of the photographs that appear in this book; and Enrique Delahoza, editor of the "En Cuba" section of that magazine.

I cannot close without expressing my gratitude for his invaluable help to Harrison Platt, editor, Trade Department, The Bobbs-Merrill Company, Inc., who flew to Havana to expedite the editing of the manuscript.

J. D.

384

INDEX

387

Tizol, Ernesto, 30, 43, 50-51, 92, 94
Topping, John, 173, 225, 268
Torriente, Cosme de la, 92, 122
Trigo, Julio, 35
Troque, Eloy, 138 f.

Urrutia Lleo, Manuel, 164, 191, 206, 328, 331, 351 f., 356 f., 362, 367, 374 f., 381

Valdes, Andres, 78
Valdes, Ramiro, 62
Valliciergo, Francisco, 326
Varona, Manuel Antonio de, 120, 178 f., 188, 207, 280, 363
Vasconcelos, Ramon, 96, 350
Vasquez, Gerardo, 124
Vega, Jaime, 306 f., 334
Velasco Guzman, Raul de, 183, 187, 223 ff.

Velez, Pedro, 78
Ventura, Esteban, 222 f., 254, 266, 269, 329
Verdaguer, Roberto, 244
Villares, Jose, 233

Weicha, Robert, 272
Westbrook, Joe, 158
White, Lincoln, 320, 322 ff.
Wieland, William A., 313 ff.
Williams, John Z., 254
Williamson, Earl, 379
Wolfe Silva, Charles, 289
Wollam, Park F., 270, 271, 277 f.
Wright, Jerauld, 273

Yanes Pelletier, Jesus, 40, 49

Zendegui, Guillermode, 118

389

ERRATA AND ADDENDA

In order to meet the great interest in Fidel Castro at the earliest moment this book has been produced with such rapidity that these additions and corrections could not be included in their proper places in the book.

P. 8, l. 5: *for* Aguero's *read* Rivero's
P. 10, l. 29: *for* two thirty *read* one thirty
P. 13, l. 13: *for* 1950 *read* 1948 *and for* mid-term *read* general
P. 38, l. 18: *for* three *read* two
P. 40, ll. 22-25: *delete sentence beginning* Lieutenant Yanes . . .
P. 41, l. 11: *for* Thse *read* These
P. 43, l. 35: *for* Alcade *read* Alcalde
P. 50, l. 34 and P. 61, l. 22: *for* Tassende *read* Tasende
P. 51, l. 38: *for* prosecutors *read* attorneys
P. 77, l. 24: *for* Songa *read* Songo
P. 85, l. 24: *for first* they *read* most of them
P. 90, l. 18: *for* one *read* ones
P. 100, l. 9: *delete* must have
P. 162, insert following l. 25: At this time the Urgency Court at Santiago de Cuba sentenced the survivors of the *Gramma* expedition, who had been arrested in the cities of Oriente, to imprisonment. There was one dissenting opinion. It was that of Judge Manuel Urrutia. He declared that the *Gramma* expedition was perfectly justified under the Constitution of 1940 because the objective was an insurrection against a man who had violated the Constitution. This decision made Urrutia popular in rebel circles and especially with Castro.